PENGUIN BOOKS

# ENGLISH FOOD

Jane Grigson was brought up in the north-east of England, where there is a strong tradition of good eating, but it was not until many years later, when she began to spend three months of each year in France, that she became really interested in food. *Charcuterie and French Pork Cookery* was the result, exploring the wonderful range of cooked meat products on sale in even the smallest market towns. This book has also been translated into French, a singular honour for an English cookery writer.

After taking an English degree at Cambridge in 1949, Jane Grigson worked in art galleries and publishers' offices, and then as a translator. In 1966 she shared the John Florio prize (with Father Kenelm Foster) for her translation of Beccaria's *Of Crime and Punishment*. It was in 1968 that Jane Grigson began her long association with the *Observer Magazine*, for whom she wrote right up until her untimely death in 1990; *Good Things* and *Food with the Famous* are both based on these highly successful series. In 1973, *Fish Cookery* was published by the Wine and Food Society, followed by *The Mushroom Feast* (1975), a collection of recipes for cultivated, woodland, field and dried mushrooms. She received both the Glenfiddich Writer of the Year Award and the André Simon Memorial Fund Book Award for her *Vegetable Book* (1978) and for her *Fruit Book* (1982), and was voted Cookery Writer of the Year in 1977 for *English Food*. A compilation of her best recipes, *The Enjoyment of Food*, was published in 1992 with an introduction by her daughter, the cookery writer Sophie Grigson. Most of Jane Grigson's books are published in Penguin.

Jane Grigson died in March 1990. In her obituary for the *Independent*, Alan Davidson wrote that 'Jane Grigson left to the English-speaking world a legacy of fine writing on food and cookery for which no exact parallel exists . . . She won to herself this wide audience because she was above all a friendly writer . . . the most companionable presence in the kitchen; often catching the imagination with a deftly chosen fragment of history or poetry, but never failing to explain the "why" as well as the "how" of cookery'. Jane Grigson was married to the poet and critic, the late Geoffrey Grigson.

Sophie Grigson was born in 1959, the daughter of Jane and Geoffrey Grigson. She has contributed to many magazines and newspapers, including the *Evening Standard*, the *Independent*, and the *Sunday Times Magazine*. Her first book, *Food for Friends*, was published in 1987, since when she has written many cookery books, including *Sophie's Table* (1990), *Sophie Grigson's Ingredients Book* (1991) and *Eat Your Greens*, which accompanied her television series of the same name. Her latest television series, which has an accompanying book, is about herbs.

# ENGLISH FOOD

## Jane Grigson

With a Foreword by Sophie Grigson

PENGUIN BOOKS

PENGUIN BOOKS

Published by the Penguin Group
Penguin Books Ltd, 80 Strand, London WC2R 0RL, England
Penguin Putnam Inc., 375 Hudson Street, New York, New York 10014, USA
Penguin Books Australia Ltd, 250 Camberwell Road, Camberwell, Victoria 3124, Australia
Penguin Books Canada Ltd, 10 Alcorn Avenue, Toronto, Ontario, Canada M4V 3B2
Penguin Books India (P) Ltd, 11 Community Centre, Panchsheel Park, New Delhi – 110 017, India
Penguin Books (NZ) Ltd, Cnr Rosedale and Airborne Roads, Albany, Auckland, New Zealand
Penguin Books (South Africa) (Pty) Ltd, 24 Sturdee Avenue, Rosebank 2196, South Africa

Penguin Books Ltd, Registered Offices: 80 Strand, London WC2R 0RL, England

www.penguin.com

First published 1974
This edition first published by Ebury Press, an imprint of Random Century, 1992
Published in Penguin Books 1993
9



The illustrations that appear in this book are by:
Clare Leighton (p. 347 from The Sumach Press edition of *The Four Hedges*, 1991, and *The Farmer's Year*, 1992); Eric Ravilious 9pp, iii, vii, viii, ix, 1, 24, 43, 77, 125, 127, 245, 297, and 346); and Gillian Zeiner (pp. 17, 179, 210, 237)

Printed and bound in Great Britain by
Mackays of Chatham plc, Chatham, Kent



British Library Cataloguing in Publication Data
A CIP catalogue record for this book is available from the British Library

ISBN 0–14–027324–7

*For Geoffrey and Sophie*
*and for my parents in whose house*
*I first learnt about*
*good English food*

29 February 1788: We gave the company for dinner some fish and oyster sauce, a nice piece of boiled beef, a fine neck of pork roasted and apple sauce, some hashed turkey, mutton steaks, salad, etc., a wild duck roasted, fried rabbits, a plum pudding and some tartlets. Dessert, some olives, nuts, almonds and raisins and apples. The whole company were pleased with their dinner, etc. Considering we had not above three hours' notice of their coming we did very well in that short time. All of us were rather hurried on the occasion.

REV. JAMES WOODFORDE

# CONTENTS

## Acknowledgements

THANKS ARE DUE to the following people for the recipes and information they have provided: Elizabeth Bolgar; D. M. Dickson; Julia Drysdale and the Game Conservancy; Sandy Grigson; Bobby Freeman; Ann Irving; Winifred McQuiggen; Joyce Molyneux; Peggy Murray; Evelyn Wilcock; Breian Lloyd-Davies; the late Michael Smith; George Willacy; Malcolm Young; H. Horton of the Manchester Library of Social Sciences; Mary Norwak; Tony Jones of the National Federation of Women's Institutes, and the many secretaries of county branches who sent me their publications; Guy Mouilleron, chef-proprietor of Ma Cuisine, Walton Street, London; Mrs Sleightholme and *Woman* magazine; Janet Smith of the Liverpool Record Office, Pamela Harlech; Mrs C. L. Roope; Mary Hatchwell; Fiona Andrews; the late Sheila Hutchins, who helped me find the source of several recipes. Thanks, too, to Marjorie White, who helped with the cooking and with suggestions, and who kept the household going through a long and difficult winter, and to my daughter, Sophie, who also helped with the cooking and with much vigorous criticism. I am also grateful to the copyright holders of those recipes I have quoted from published sources, and due acknowledgements will be found in the text.

# FOREWORD

SHORTLY BEFORE HER 60TH BIRTHDAY, my mother decided that as from official retirement age, she was only going to work on things that really interested her. No more duty jobs or public appearances because she felt she ought to. She had paid her dues and her 'retirement' was to be able to concentrate purely on writing for her own pleasure. One project, long cherished, that she could now make time for was a second revision of her book *English Food*, published first in 1974 and revised once in 1979.

In the unfairly short two years of her 'retirement', Jane never stopped working – there was always so much that did interest her – even between the grim sessions of chemotherapy that failed to halt her cancer. The new *English Food* took shape, and in the last few months before her death she threw herself into the work, aware, perhaps, that time was not on her side. She almost completed it, leaving only the final chapter, 'Stuffings, Sauces & Preserves' untouched.

Almost twenty years after it was first written, *English Food* remains the outstanding book on the subject. Of course, it was written by a marvellous writer. All of Jane's books are a delight to read and to linger over before (and after) heading, volume in hand, for the kitchen. Her recipes always work, too. Something that cannot be said of all cookery writers, sadly. Second-hand copies of her books are comparatively rare. Dog-eared and much loved, they stay on readers' shelves until they fall to pieces and have to be replaced with a new copy.

There's more to it than that, though. Unlike so many other writers, Jane did not view traditional food through the rose-tinted glasses of nostalgia. The debasement of a 'domestic tradition that was once our glory' angered her, but she never romanticised the past, or rejected modern improvements on time-honoured recipes. It tickled her no end, for instance, that the winner of the 'Great Yorkshire Pudding Contest' was a Chinese man from Hong Kong and that his winning recipe was somewhat unorthodox.

She was chauvinistic about English food, but only in the most intelligent and unblinkered sense of the word. With clear-sighted determination she ploughed her way through layers of fossilised myth, to find the original honesty that has characterised the best English cooking. Why deny the French or Italian origins of a dish, or ignore it altogether, when it has become an established part of the English repertoire? The development of a national culinary repertoire reflects the development of the nation itself. Jane's interest in the history of cookery and of individual recipes was the focus of her wider curiosity about the world around her.

All too often books on English food come to a sudden halt either at the beginning of or mid-way through this century. But the history of good English food did not end cataclysmically with the outbreak of the Second World War. It continues, and with her last revisions to *English Food* Jane acknowledges the influence of established ethnic communities, bringing in recipes such as the Three-Gourd Garnish for chicken or fish to sit alongside the more obviously 'English' dishes.

In her 1979 introduction to the book Jane wrote pessimistically about the future of British food, lashing out against the impoverishment of mass commercialisation. By the time she came to revise *English Food* in the late '80s', she wrote again with cautious optimism. Gradually, throughout the decade, small producers providing high quality foods with traditional values had begun to re-establish themselves. That they were able to do so is thanks largely to Jane, and the like-minded food writers who followed her pioneering lead.

SOPHIE GRIGSON
*April 1992*

# INTRODUCTION

THE ENGLISH ARE A VERY ADAPTIVE PEOPLE. English cooking – both historically and in the mouth – is a great deal more varied and delectable than our masochistic temper in this matter allows. There's an extra special confusion nowadays in talking of good and bad national cooking. The plain fact is that much commercial cooking is bad, or mediocre in any country – it's easy enough to get a thoroughly disappointing meal even in France where there exists an almost sacred devotion to kitchen and table. The food we get publicly in England isn't so often bad English cooking as a pretentious and inferior imitation of French cooking or Italian cooking.

It is also true that a good many things in our marketing system now fight against simple and delicate food. Tomatoes have no taste. The finest flavoured potatoes are not available in shops. Vegetables and fruits are seldom fresh. Milk comes out of Friesians. Cheeses are subdivided and imprisoned in plastic wrapping. 'Farm fresh' means eggs which are no more than ten, fourteen or twenty days old. Words such as 'fresh' and 'home-made' have been borrowed by commerce to tell lies.

In spite of all this the English cook has a wonderful inheritance if she cares to make use of it. It's a question of picking and choosing, and that exactly is what I have done for this book. My aim has been to put in obvious dishes on a basis of quality; even more I have tried to show how many surprises there are. I have also included a number of Welsh dishes because I like them, and because they are linked closely with much English food, while retaining a rustic elegance which we have tended to lose.

No cookery belongs exclusively to its country, or its region. Cooks borrow – and always have borrowed – and adapt through the centuries. Though the scale in either case isn't exactly the same, this is true, for example, of French cooking as of English cooking. We have borrowed from France. France borrowed from Italy direct, and by way of Provence. The Romans borrowed from the Greeks, and the Greeks borrowed from the Egyptians and Persians.

What each individual country does do is to give all the elements, borrowed or otherwise, something of a national character. The history of cooking is in some ways like the history of language, though perhaps it's harder to unravel, or like the history of folk music. The first mention of a dish, the first known recipe for it, can seldom be taken as a record of its first appearance. As far as origins go, there's seldom much point in supposing that a dish belongs to Yorkshire or Devonshire, or Shropshire because it's survived in those places and may bear their names. What goes for counties goes for countries. Who's to say whether *Pain Perdu* or Poor Knights of Windsor is really English or French; both in France and England it was a dish of the medieval court. Did the English call it payn pur-dew out of the kind of snobbery we can still recognize, or because they took it from France? And if they took it from France, where did the French take it from? It's a marvellous way of using up stale bread, especially good bread, and who's to say that earlier still the Romans, or the Greeks before the Romans, didn't see the point of frying up bread and serving it with something sweet? In England today *Pain Perdu* has been anglicized into a nursery or homely dish, Poor Knights of Windsor. In France with Brioche to hand, or the light *pain de mie, Pain Perdu* remains a select dish gracefully adorned with brandied fruit and dollops of cream under such names as *Croûte aux Abricots*.

There's no avoiding the fact that the best cooking has come down from the top. Or if you don't like the word 'top', from the skilled, employed by those who could pay and had the time to appreciate quality. In England on the whole the food descends less from a courtly tradition than from the manor houses and rectories and homes of well-to-do merchants – latterly from a Jane Austen world. It hands down the impression of the social life of families in which the wives and daughters weren't too grand to go into the kitchen and to keep a close eye on the vegetable garden and dairy. This was the world in which the great amateur horticulturalist Thomas Andrew Knight in his Herefordshire manor house diversified and improved so many fruits and vegetables in the late years of the eighteenth century and the early years of the nineteenth.

One thing to note is that the great English cookery writers from Hannah Glasse to Elizabeth David have most often been women, in contrast to the French tradition of cookery writing by male chefs. Our classical tradition has been domestic, with the domestic virtues of quiet enjoyment and generosity. Whatever happened when the great mass centres developed in the nineteenth century, English cookery books of the eighteenth century to early Victorian times had been written from an understanding of good food and good eating, a concern for quality. Mrs Beeton had her great qualities, and gave many marvellous recipes. But from the first edition of her book in 1859, you can see the anxiety of the new middle class, balanced between wealth and insolvency, and always at pains to keep up appearances. And keeping up appearances remains the *leitmotiv* of much modern food advertising. Showy photographs in what is called 'full' colour and the message, 'Impress your Friends' or 'Impress his Boss', suggest that without taking any trouble or thought at all, marvellous food will fall out of the packet on to the plate. We need to renew and develop the old tradition of Hannah Glasse, Elizabeth Raffald, Maria Rundell and Eliza Acton as far as we can in our changed circumstances. It is no accident, I hope, that these early writers are being reprinted, often in facsimile, and that their dishes appear on the menus of some of our best restaurants as well as in an increasing number of homes.

SINCE FINISHING THE FIRST EDITION of this book in 1974, I have come to understand the weakness of the domestic tradition that was once our glory, and to a certain extent – in some homes – still is.

The weakness is a lack of professionalism, the lack in each of us, of a solid grounding in skill and knowledge about food, where it comes from, how it should be prepared. Somehow we do not manage in shops and restaurants to keep high standards that constantly remind the cook at home of what food can be. You have only to spend a day visiting Fauchon or Le Nôtre in Paris, or some of the supermarkets of German and Italian towns, and then spend the next visiting the groceries of Piccadilly to see what I mean. How often when you go to a restaurant for a meal are you delighted to eat something far better than you can make yourself? To enjoy some aspect of skill that makes you long to get into the kitchen next day, and see if you can come anywhere near it?

The thing is that if you have a solid basis of skill, and can constantly refer to the highest standards, you have a better chance of adapting to the changes of life than if you merely look in magazines and books for new 'recipes'. The English, like the Americans, are always demanding 'recipes'. And cookery writers like myself provide them. I am lucky in working mainly for a paper that allows me enough space to hint at the fact that words such as apple, cheese, bread are meaningless: that for good food one needs to understand that a Cox's Orange Pippin in a pie will give you a quite different result from a Bramley; that for a good cheese sauce Parmesan must be used because English hard cheeses will put too much fat into the sauce before they can achieve the same intensity of flavour; that sliced bread and frozen poultry are not worth buying – ever. I suspect, from my reading, that mass circulation women's magazines are directed by entirely populist points of view – that one should never suggest that one variety of a fruit will give you something better, because half their readers think they cannot afford it. In a country that spends the amount ours does on hard liquor, gambling, ice cream of a worthless kind, sweets, cakes, biscuits, this is nonsense. If people choose to spend it that way, fair enough. But let them not plead poverty as an excuse for bad food. And let people who provide the awful food not shrug off responsibility by saying, 'Well,it's what *they* want.'

This really is *trahison des clercs*. 'Let them have trash' seems a far worse attitude than 'Let them eat brioche.' The latter came from a complete lack of understanding; the former comes from a conniving complicity in lower standards by people who would not accept them for themselves and their families at home. To provide worthless things, or things that are worse than they should be, shows what you think of your fellow human beings. In the past food was often adulterated by unscrupulous purveyors – sand in the sugar, dried hawthorn leaves in the tea, water in the milk – but at least this was recognized as a vicious thing to do. Now our food is adulterated and spoilt in ways that are entirely legal, even encouraged. Have you managed to buy farm butter recently? Or a farmyard chicken that has run free?

And these crimes against good food are encouraged by domestic science teachers who think it is fine to teach pupils to make pies with pastry-mix and ready-prepared pie fillings. When criticized, they answer, 'We have no time; anyway at least they enable us to teach children the "manipulative skills".' What skills? The skill to turn on the tap and mix the mix to a dough? The skill to operate a tin-opener? The skill to read instructions on the packet or tin? The skill to spoon the filling into a dish? The skill to turn on the oven, a foolproof oven, to the correct temperature? Such 'manipulative skills' are usually mastered at home before school begins, or at the latest in the infant school. The development of taste and true knowledge should be the business of secondary school home economics teachers. And if they are not able to do this through bad organization of the curriculum, they should be seeking to change the system, not conniving in it and excusing themselves. I think it is ironic that the countries of Europe where you get the better food are the countries where such a subject is not taught at the usual state secondary school.

In 1974 I finished *English Food* full of hope. In discovering at least something of our tradition for myself, I began to see that we did have a treasury to be exploited, perhaps exploited into a new cookery of our own. This revision of *English Food*, in 1979, has been completed in a spirit of pessimism. It is France with its strong professional basis of skill that has produced a *nouvelle cuisine*. Oh yes, we buy the books, we have taken it to our hearts – for the moment. This means we are debasing it as fast as we can. One top-circulation women's magazine published an article adapting – sinister word – these new ideas for 'family meals'. The adaptation consisted in suggesting the use of tinned peas and carrots; it completely balked the problem of chicken. Yet the whole point of the *nouvelle cuisine*, and especially that branch known as the *cuisine minceur*, is that ingredients must be first of all of the highest quality and freshness. If they are not, many of the dishes taste as dull as any reconstituted dehydrated convenience pack. The absolutely essential lessons of the style are lost. It has been reduced to a lot of new 'recipes' that will dominate nomenclature for a year or two until the next craze hits these shores. Will Michel Guérard's best-selling books mean we can buy really young fresh peas at the greengrocery next summer? Or better-hung beef at the supermarket counter? Or that shoppers will become more resistant? I suspect it will not.

Or am I wrong? Somehow I can never quite suppress a naive optimism; an optimism that is buffeted every time I visit my local shops, but yet refuses quite to lie down even when confronted with perceived realities. Sometimes I hear from people who live in some pocket of good food that has escaped the attentions of commerce in hastening 'that sad process which Max Weber described as "the disenchantment of the world".'

JANE GRIGSON
*January 1979*

# SOUPS

THE BEST ENGLISH SOUPS ARE UNRIVALLED, but one might wish there were more of them. Soup is a primitive dish. Such soups as mulligatawny and oxtail and mutton broth – or the Welsh cawl – are continuing good versions of very old ways of cooking meat, at least as old as the first making of metal pots. All the same, soups are capable of great refinement and delicacy, particularly the fish and vegetable soups. They have the advantage of being easy to make, and variable within quite wide limits. A soup can be a meal, or it can be the introduction to a meal. It can be a comfort in itself, or an appetizer. And in these late days praise for a good home-made soup is out of all proportion to the effort involved – and it doesn't cost much.

Soup, or pottage as it was called, was eaten by everyone in the earlier centuries of our history. If you were poor it consisted of water thickened with oatmeal, rye flour or bread, and flavoured with such vegetables and pulses as fields and gardens might provide. Bones or a scrap of bacon, milk, cream and butter all helped to give extra interest, as did parsley and other herbs. Root vegetables were known as potherbs, even as late as the thirties, when I was a child: you could go to the shop and get a cheap collection of roots for flavouring soups and stews. I notice that this practice has been taken up by supermarkets, though the name has been dropped. Alas the bargain is not such a good one, as the various vegetables have all been washed, prepared and packed in plastic which deprives them of flavour.

The pottage of the rich in pre-Renaissance times, though made in a similar way in great pots, was more varied and finer in its grace notes. Rice that came from the Arabs on boats that brought us spices, almonds and raisins, was used as thickener, as were eggs and a powdered wheat starch known as amidon. Spices flavoured the soups and soup-stews – the borderline between the two was a tenuous one – as did wine. Thicker soups might be coloured by streaking in ripples of saffron and saunders (sandalwood) which gave a red tint against saffron's glowing yellow. By using the white part of leeks and other pale vegetables, with rice and almond milk, cooks produced an elegant white soup which was still being made centuries later for parties and special dinners in the time of Jane Austen and Eliza Acton.

Cooks to the medieval grand family played with sweet-sour effects in a way that seems decidedly exotic today. Lenten and fastday soups might consist of puréed apples and white wine, thickened with rice flour, embellished with currants, chopped dates and slivered almonds: there would be a flavouring of mace, cloves, pepper, cinnamon and ginger, a marbling of saffron and saunders, and finally a decorative scatter of poached, shredded pears. The French may sneer at our taste for sweet and savoury together, but many such recipes came from the French court in the first place, as did some notable soup-stews such as the civet which we still make in both countries: the name comes from the characterizing addition of onion in some form, *cive* in Old French, which is still used for chives, along with *civette* and *ciboulette*. We think of it as a hare dish: in the grand kitchens of fifteenth century cooks it was made with other game, too, or with fish. Tench, an easily caught freshwater fish, was popular for a civet: it was simmered and roasted (in that order), mixed with pepper, saffron, bread and ale, and finally flavoured with onions fried in oil.

It seems to me that cooks in those days were resourceful at many levels of society. A greater variety of herbs and potherbs was grown in gardens than is normal now. In the middle of the sixteenth century, one much travelled writer, Andrew Boorde, complimented them when he remarked that 'Pottage is not so much used in all Christendom as it is used in England'.

Food writers have remarked that we seemed to have lost our taste for vegetables in some mysterious way in the sixteenth century. Certainly the variety grown seems to have declined, but in quantity vegetables played an important part in people's diets especially if they were poor, especially in the years of wheat famine. I suspect, too, that our ways of cooking them lack finesse. Foreign visitors commented on the many little heaps of vegetables swimming in too much butter.

What happened, I think, was that the style of eating changed, at least for the upper and increasingly powerful middle classes, who were affected by some of the new ideas about eating abroad in mainland Europe of the Renaissance (though not affected enough according to one Italian visitor, Giacomo Castelvetro, writing in 1614: see the vegetable chapter). Instead of being the main item of the meal, soups and soup-stews drew further apart, with the stews becoming less liquid and more elegant. Soups were relegated to the opening stage. If you look at a plan for the first course of a dinner party in an eighteenth century cookery book, say Mrs Raffald's *Experienced English Housekeeper*, you will see that the meal was organized very differently from our dinner parties to-day. For each course the table was covered with a large number of different dishes of varying sizes according to the position they occupied (this is known as the French service). At each end there was a large tureen of soup, one thick and one thin. When the guests had drunk a polite bowlful, the tureens were removed and their place was filled with splendid roasts, beef or venison, and a large fish: these were carved and cut up by the host and hostess. To all the other dishes, people helped their neighbours and themselves.

Sitting down to such a spread of food, much of it cooling rapidly, people came to regard soup as little more than an appetizer. And when this old buffet style was superseded by the Russian service in the middle of the nineteenth century, with one dish being served at a course and everybody eating the same thing at the same time – the way we eat to-day – this status was confirmed. Simplicity and high quality became the standards of a good dinner.

In families, something of the old style remained, with stews and thick soups becoming standard winter fare. Not until the last forty years, with the popularity of Elizabeth David's books, have we dared to serve *civets* and *daubes* and *potées* and *garbures* and *cassoulets* at dinner parties. With the popularity of *nouvelle cuisine* cookery, such dishes went out for a while in the seventies, in favour of delicate soups rather in the Japanese style, followed by decorative plates of beautifully cut meat or fish and a few vegetables. This very tricky and last-minute cookery began to readmit the family soup-stews in a refined form and now a return to *cuisine grandmère*, much easier to control and therefore more economic, is in full swing.

A great relief all round. Nothing is more difficult than trying to give visitors at home a *nouvelle cuisine* dinner with plate-service. Everything gets cold, for a start, and the waits between courses become nerve-wracking. After one attempt, most of us gave it up. All the same it was a comfort to me to read James Beard's introduction to his new cookery book in 1981; the section headed *Feel Free*. He talked of the old tyranny of the Russian service, dinner Escoffier style: 'In my youth, a "proper" dinner had to have something light at each end, like consommé to begin and fruit to finish – you could call the menu diamond-shaped, with a big bulge at the main course. . . . Usually it was a roast, with something starchy and several vegetables.' In the next paragraph comes liberation with his blessing . . . 'the main course is whatever you want to star – the nicest thing, perhaps, that you are offering at that meal. For some cooks, it may well be dessert, though not for me . . . This year for my annual celebration of the first shad roe, we had a luscious pair of sautéed roes apiece – with parsley – then very small paillards of veal with a little cucumber salad . . . and wound up with just a taste of fresh strawberry sorbet. A wedge-shaped dinner, then. And why not? It tasted wonderful, and taste is the only rule a cook need acknowledge, in this happy time of freshness and freedom.'

An English cook has to be quite brave to treat a soup or soup-stew as the main course of a meal. Scotch cooks can do it with their cockie-leekie (see page 195) or the Welsh with their cawl (see page 20). Perhaps we have been put off by the tradition of Dickens and the workhouse, and little boys' bones in the cauldron, and manor house ladies with their charitable soups. Nearly every Victorian cookery book has a recipe for beneficent or charitable soup, to be trotted round the parish by mother and unmarried daughters to the deserving poor. The French chef of the Reform Club, the great Alexis Soyer, caused a sensation by nobly going over to Ireland in the potato famine to save Irish souls with his soup (like most other benevolent soups of the time, it was not very nutritious). But soups are a good thing all the same. We have no need to blush for our Palestine soup, pea soup, smoked haddock soup, proper mulligatawny. And English eel soup and oyster soup are superb, so is the old white soup made from almonds – a masterpiece of delicacy.

Meat or poultry stock is not essential for vegetable soups – indeed it can spoil the flavour when you are using particularly good fresh vegetables. However I can recommend making a simple stock from the peelings and detritus of the vegetables you are using, with such additions of onion, herbs and spices as seem appropriate. Fish stock is no trouble to anyone, as it can be produced in half an hour from a couple of pounds of sole, turbot, whiting, cod or salmon bones, head and skin which most fishmongers will give you for nothing or for a few pence (note that fish bones should not be cooked for any longer than 30 minutes – unless you like your fish soup flavoured with glue).

Which leaves us with meat, poultry and game stock. This is simple for microwave or Aga and other solid fuel stove owners: without trouble they can produce excellent stocks and store them in the freezer. If you put meat on the bone into the pot – bone being essential to many good soups – you do not need to prepare a preliminary stock. Most hearty English, indeed most British soups, are of this type – boiling fowl, boiling beef, boiling mutton or lamb cooked gently for hours in water with a few potherbs. A stock pot is a bad idea outside a professional kitchen, where it can be properly looked after, skimmed, reboiled and used quickly (this is not to say that liquor left over from boiling chicken, beef or fish is not a good idea if you happen to have it, but store it in the freezer and never keep it hanging around). A few years ago it was quite the fashion for cookery books to suggest that you keep a stock pot on the go, adding bits and pieces to it day by day, topping it up with water as you removed the contents for soups. This is a sure route to food poisoning and nasty flavours. When you make a stock, strain the liquor from the debris, cool it fast and freeze it in convenient sized containers as rapidly as possible. It is quite a good idea to reduce the strained stock to a strong flavour and freeze it in an ice-cube tray: the cubes can be stored in a plastic bag, ready for use. This is much more satisfactory than recourse to stock cubes.

Stock or soup cubes are, incidentally, nothing new to the English. Before the days of canning, meat was simmered, and the resulting liquid boiled down to a gluey sediment or glaze, which was cut into small lumps and known as portable soup. Explorers, sailors, anyone on the move would carry a little bagful, then heat up a few lumps with water to make an instant soup, that could be improved with any ingredients to hand (a splash of vinegar, for instance, which is a great brightener of flavour). Today's cubes with their monosodium glutamate give a second-rate flavour and sameness, which is to be avoided.

Some of the pleasure of soups consist in such final additions and embellishments as fried cubes of bread, crumbs of crisp bacon, chopped green herbs, an egg custard *royale* cut into little diamonds. Brandy and port make a wonderful difference to meat and game soups, just as a little dry white wine makes all the difference to several of the fish soups. This has been much more of an English practice than you would suppose, going back at least to the court cookery of Chaucer's time. Cream, chopped parsley, egg yolks, grated Parmesan, a knob of butter are all good enrichments for vegetable soups. The Welsh – and Scots – chop leeks and add them to meat soups before they are served. The leek softens slightly in the heat without cooking properly, and so retains an agreeable crispness and a light overtone of onion which is not in the least aggressive.

## Almond Soup (White Soup)

**A** beautifully white soup which goes back to the cookery of the Middle Ages, the courtly cookery of England and France (the French name is *soupe à la reine*). Almonds then played an even larger part in fine dishes than they do today. As well as its flavour, this soup has the advantage of being made from the kind of ingredients that most people have in the house in summer or winter: perhaps this is another reason why it has survived so many centuries, not just in palaces but in the homes of people of moderate prosperity. In the country, it was a favourite soup for winter parties – in *Pride and Prejudice*, Mr Bingley declared his firm intention of giving a ball at Netherfield, 'as soon as Nicholls has made white soup enough, I shall send round my cards.' Eliza Acton remarked when she gave a recipe for Westerfield White Soup, on which the following recipe is based, that she had not varied the original at all, 'as the soup made by it – of which we have often partaken – seemed always much approved by the guests of the hospitable country gentleman from whose family it was derived, and at whose well-arranged table it was very commonly served.'

For 6

*1½ litres (2½ pts) veal or light beef stock (see below)*
*60 g (2 oz) blanched almonds*
*30 g (1 oz) white bread, weighed without crusts*
*1 egg yolk*
*150ml (¼ pt) each double and soured cream or milk*
*Salt, pepper, lemon juice, Cayenne pepper*
*60 g (2 oz) toasted or fried almonds to garnish, or tiny cubes of bread fried in butter*

STOCK
*Small bacon hock or 125 g (4 oz) lean gammon*
*Meaty veal knuckle bone, chopped in three*
*1 onion, quartered*
*1 carrot, quartered*
*4 sticks celery, sliced*
*1 teaspoon lightly crushed peppercorns*
*2 blades of mace*
*1 bay leaf*
*1 tablespoon salt*

FIRST make the stock. Put meaty items into a large pan and cover with at least 2 litres (4 pts) cold water. Bring to the boil and skim, replacing liquid with extra cold water. When clear, add the vegetables, pepper, mace, bay leaf and salt. Keep at a bare simmer for 4 hours. Strain, chill overnight and remove any fat from the jellied stock.

To make the soup, boil the stock down to 1½ litres (2½ pts). Put the almonds and bread into a blender, add some of the stock and liquidize to a smooth paste. Strain into the remaining stock, pushing through as much as you can (a blender does a more efficient job than a processor). Beat the egg yolk with the creams or cream and milk and add to the soup. If possible leave for an hour or two – this will improve and mellow the flavour.Reheat, keeping the soup well below boiling point so as not to curdle the egg. Add salt, pepper, lemon juice and Cayenne pepper to taste and bring out the flavour. Serve garnished with almonds or croûtons (boiled vermicelli or macaroni was once added at the end, but this seems stodgy to our modern tastes).

## Apple Soup

It is interesting that this soup of most unusual ingredients – unusual in combination, that is – tastes very clear and refreshing in a way that seems entirely modern. Yet the recipe comes from Eliza Acton's *Modern Cookery* of 1845. Miss Acton attributed it to Burgundy – perhaps she came across it when she spent a year in France after the Napoleonic wars – but it does not appear in any French collections of Burgundian recipes. In the end I came across the original version, in a reprinted manuscript from the Bodleian Library at Oxford, of the beginning of the fifteenth century. It's called *Apple moys*, or apple mush (from the French *mol*, meaning soft): the apples are cooked and sieved and added to 'good fat broth of beef'. The seasonings were sugar, saffron, and ginger. On fast days, almond 'milk' and olive oil were used instead of beef stock. The rice or pearl barley are also within the fifteenth-century tradition.

For 6

*1½ litres (2½ pts) beef stock*
*350 g (12 oz) good cooking apples, or Cox's*
*½ teaspoon ginger*
*¼ teaspoon pepper plus* either *some boiled rice*, or *90 g (3 oz) pearl barley, soaked, and simmered in a little extra beef stock until cooked*

Bring the beef stock to the boil, and add the apples roughly chopped, core and all. When they are soft, push the soup through a vegetable mill or sieve. Season it with ginger and pepper, adding a little extra if you like. Mix in the rice or pearl barley and serve very hot.

## Indian Soup

A clear but spicy soup with a lively freshness and a mysterious flavour.

For 6

*1¾ litres (3 pts) beef stock*
*2 large onions, sliced*
*1 large cooking apple, sliced, peel and all*
*1 tablespoon desiccated coconut*
*2 teaspoons curry powder*
*Bones from chicken or game carcass*
*2 large egg whites*
*Salt, pepper, Cayenne pepper (optional), lemon juice*
*Scraps of chicken or game picked from carcass*
*3-4 tablespoons boiled basmati rice*

Simmer the first six ingredients in a covered pan for 1 hour. Strain and blot away any fat with kitchen paper. Beat in the egg whites and continue beating over a moderate heat until the liquid is topped by a dirty-looking, greyish colour. Simmer for 5 minutes without beating, then pour off the clear liquid underneath through a cloth-lined strainer. Taste and adjust seasoning, adding Cayenne if you like a hotter effect. Lemon juice enhances the freshness.

Cut the little bits of chicken or game into neat shreds. Add to the soup with the rice and reheat without boiling.

## CHESTNUT AND APPLE SOUP

MANY EUROPEAN CHESTNUT SOUPS are flavoured with bacon,and made on the heavy side. Understandable, when soup had to be the whole meal. This apple and chestnut recipe is more suitable for soup as a first course only.

For 6

*500 g (1 lb) chestnuts in their shells*
*2 litres (3½ pts) light beef stock or water*
*1 stick celery*
*2 large Cox's apples, peeled, cored, sliced*
*60 g (2 oz) butter*
*125 ml (4 oz) single cream*
*Salt, pepper*
*Bread croûtons fried in butter*

NICK the chestnuts from the centre to the pointed top, at right angles to the base. Boil them in water for 10 minutes, then turn the heat off and remove the chestnuts one by one to peel them. To do this, put your left hand into an oven glove to hold the chestnut, then use a small sharp knife to peel off the shell, and then to remove the inner brown skin. If the chestnuts were a good, fat glossy brown to start with, they should be quite easy to deal with. Making a nick from the centre to the pointed end means that the shell peels off much more easily, and the nut in consequence remains more or less intact (though for this recipe, it doesn't matter if the nuts have crumbled into pieces).

Now cook the chestnuts with the stock and celery for about 20 minutes; meanwhile simmer the apple slices in the butter with a good sprinkling of pepper. Liquidize chestnuts, celery and apple with the stock and the buttery apple juices. Taste and correct seasoning. Add the cream. If the soup is too thick for your taste (the thickness will obviously depend on how many chestnuts had to be discarded), dilute it with water. It should not be too heavy in texture, but light, with a faint sharpness from the apples. Serve with croûtons.

## BROAD BEAN SOUP

For 4

*125 g (4 oz) chopped onion*
*60 g (2 oz) butter*
*250 g (9 oz) shelled broad beans*
*½ teaspoon chopped sage, savory or parsley*
*Salt, pepper, sugar*
*4 tablespoons cream*
*Croûtons of fried bread*

SOFTEN the onion in the butter, without browning it. Add the beans together with 1 litre (1¾ pints) of water and bring to the boil. Put in whichever herb you choose, together with salt, pepper and ¼ teaspoon of sugar. When the beans are cooked, remove a tablespoon of them, rinse them under the cold tap and peel off the white skins; set them aside. Sieve or liquidize the soup. Add the skinned beans and reheat. Correct the seasoning and add a little more sugar if necessary. Stir in the cream and serve with croûtons.

## WATERCRESS SOUP

HERE IS MARGARET COSTA'S VERSION of watercress soup, from *Four Seasons Cookery Book*. A good recipe.

For 6

*500 g (1 lb) potatoes, peeled, diced*
*1 onion, sliced*
*1½ litres (2½ pts) chicken stock or water*
*1 small onion*
*1 large or 2 small bunches watercress*
*Butter*
*Salt, grated nutmeg, pepper*
*2-3 tablespoons cream*

COOK the potatoes with the sliced onion in a little water until tender. Put through a sieve or *mouli-légumes*, then mix to a thin, smooth purée with the stock or water. Grate in the onion. Set aside a few of the best leaves of the watercress to garnish the soup. Chop the remaining leaves and the tender part of the stems; stew in butter for 5 minutes, then add to the soup. Season with salt, nutmeg and pepper as you reheat it. Finish with the leaves you set aside and the cream (use butter if you have no cream).

## GREEN PEA SOUP

For 6

*250 g (8 oz) shelled peas*
*1 medium onion, chopped*
*60 g (2 oz) butter*
*2 rashers smoked streaky bacon, chopped*
*1 litre (1¾ pts) chicken or light ham stock*
*Salt, pepper*
*Chopped parsley*

THIS soup can be made in wintertime quite successfully with frozen peas or with dried split green peas which have been soaked (125 g (4 oz) dried peas). In the latter case, the cooking time will have to be prolonged to an hour.

First cook the onion gently in the butter until it begins to soften and turn gold. Add the bacon and fry for another 2 or 3 minutes. Pour in 600ml (1 pt) of the stock, add the peas and simmer until they are cooked. Liquidize and dilute to taste with more stock, add seasoning to taste – if you are using dried peas it is particularly important not to add salt before they are cooked. Reheat, sprinkle with parsley and serve.

THE PECULIARLY English thing about this soup is the flavour of smoked bacon. It belongs to the tradition of boiled salt pork and pease pudding. In the early summer, you could flavour the soup with other vegetables rather than the bacon, and substitute water for the stock. Slice or shred half a large cucumber with its peel, the heart of a Cos lettuce and a small handful of spinach. Stew them in a little butter with three or four sprigs of mint until they are cooked. Liquidize with the cooked peas.

## JUNE PEA SOUP

A SOUP FOR MIDSUMMER when young peas are at their freshest and sweetest.

For 6-8

*1½ kilos (3 lb) young peas*
*175 g (6 oz) spring onions or young, green stemmed onions, chopped*
*1 clove garlic, chopped finely*
*175 g (6 oz) unsalted butter*
*175 ml (6 fl oz) crème fraîche or whipping cream*
*Chopped mint*

SHELL the peas, stopping when you have 600g (1¼ lb). Reserve four or five of the greenest pods. Sweat the onion and garlic in half the butter, in a covered pan, for 5 minutes, without colouring them. Add the peas, the four or five pods and 1½ litres (scant 3 pts) water. When the peas are tender, liquidize and then sieve into the rinsed out pan. Reheat to well under boiling point. Stir in the remaining butter and the cream. Sprinkle with the mint and serve.

IF YOU want to chill this soup, omit the second addition of butter.

## TOMATO SOUP, HOT OR CHILLED

ONE OF THE FINEST OF ALL SOUPS. Its clear-tasting richness will surprise and delight anyone who has only known the canned variety.

For 4 (hot), for 6-8 (chilled)

*90 g (3 oz) chopped carrot*
*60 g (2 oz) chopped onion*
*1 clove garlic, chopped*
*60 g (2 oz) butter*
*500 g (1 lb) skinned tomatoes (or 14oz tin)*
*750ml (1¼ pts) light beef or chicken stock*
*Salt, pepper, sugar*
*Grated nutmeg*
*2 teaspoons tomato concentrate*
*150-300 ml (¼-½ pt) single cream*
*Chopped parsley*

COOK the first three ingredients gently in the butter. Keep the lid on the pan so that they do not brown, and allow about 10 minutes. Halve the tomatoes into the pan (add the juices, too, if you are using a tin). Add the stock. When the carrot is cooked, liquidize or process the soup, then pour it through a sieve, pushing through the debris but leaving the tomato seeds behind. Add seasonings to taste – the tomato concentrate will not be necessary if you are using tomatoes grown out of doors in a really hot summer; neither will the sugar.

If the soup is to be served hot, bring 150ml (¼ pt) of cream to the boil just before the meal starts and add the tomato mixture. Reheat without boiling. If the consistency is too thick, add more stock or water. Sprinkle the parsley on top.

If the soup is to be served cold, allow it to cool down and then chill it in a large basin. Stir in 300ml (½ pt) of the cream. Check the consistency and seasoning – chilled soups need more liquid and more seasoning than hot ones. Chill again, and sprinkle parsley on top just before serving.

## CARROT AND TOMATO SOUP

FOLLOW THE METHOD ABOVE with the following ingredients, to make an excellent soup in summer when carrots and outdoor tomatoes are at their best. Choose carrots that are beyond the tiny early stage.

For 6

*250 g (8 oz) carrots, sliced*
*1 medium onion, chopped*
*60 g (2 oz) butter*
*250 g (8 oz) tomatoes, skinned, chopped*
*1 litre (1¾ pts) beef stock*
*Salt, pepper*
*About 150 ml (¼ pt) whipping or single cream*
*Chopped chives*

THIS soup may be served cold, but most people prefer it hot I think, unless the vegetables are straight from the garden. Cook as briefly as possible for the best results.

## SOYER'S CLEAR VEGETABLE SOUP

ALEXIS SOYER, THE FAMOUS CHEF OF THE REFORM CLUB, wrote several cookery books, including a *Shilling Cookery for the People (1845)*. Here is one of his simple but good recipes – and one that I particularly like. It has clarity of flavour. When you buy the bone, ask the butcher to chop it.

For 6

STOCK
*1 kilo (2 lb) veal knuckle or scrag, chopped as small as possible*
*60 g (2 oz) butter or dripping*
*60 g (2 oz) lean unsmoked bacon, chopped*
*3 teaspoons salt*
*½ teaspoon pepper*
*175 g (6 oz) sliced onion*

SOUP
*250 g (8 oz) diced turnip, Jerusalem artichoke or carrot, or a mixture*
*90 g (3 oz) mixed diced onion, leek and celery*
*60 g (2 oz) butter or dripping*
*2 level teaspoons sugar*
*1-2 tablespoons chopped chives, chervil or parsley*

PUT the stock ingredients into a large heavy pot with 150ml (¼ pt) water. Stand on the heat and when the water boils, stir for about 10 minutes until you get a thick whitish gravy. Add 2½ litres (4½ pts) water. Bring to the boil, skim and simmer for 45 minutes. Skim again, strain and cool. This can be done in advance.

For the soup, put the diced vegetables and the fat into a heavy pan over a low heat. Stir and when the pieces are coated, stir in the sugar and keep stirring until well caramelized but not burnt. Pour in 1¾ litres (3 pts) of the stock and simmer until the vegetables are cooked. Skim if necessary. Add the chopped herbs, simmer a moment or two longer and serve.

## VEGETABLE SOUP

THERE IS NOTHING specifically English, or Scottish, Welsh or Irish for that matter, about this kind of vegetable soup. It is made with variations all over Europe, and the variations can be anything from a recognizable *pesto* from Italy to an individual bouquet of herbs made by any housewife. Two additions I like are lovage – an idea I got from an English friend now living in Denmark – which gives a celery flavour, and grated cheese which my mother always put into her vegetable soups at the end, to bring out the flavour, although she had never been to Italy or eaten in an Italian restaurant.

To give quantity and weight for the ingredients is perhaps foolish; it may prevent someone who has no leeks from making a perfectly delicious soup with spring onions instead.None the less quantities are an indication, so they are given – but do not treat them as unbreakable laws. As Mrs Chao says in *How to Cook and Eat in Chinese*, if you haven't got an egg-beater, use your head.

For 6

*500 g (1 lb) sliced cabbage*
*250 g (½ lb) salt pork, or streaky bacon, or hock bone, green or smoked*
*1½ litres (2½ pts) water or light stock*
*12 lightly crushed peppercorns*
*6 lightly crushed allspice berries*
*2 carrots, coarsely chopped*
*4 potatoes, peeled and cubed*
*2 leeks, sliced, or 1 leek and 1 onion*
*A few leaves of lovage (optional)*
*1-2 tablespoons grated Parmesan or very dry Cheddar or kefalotiri*
*Dillweed (optional)*
*Cream (optional)*
*Salt, pepper, sugar*

SIMMER cabbage with the meat in water or stock for 30 minutes, with the peppercorns and allspice. Then add carrot, potato, leeks or leek and onion and lovage, if used. Simmer another 30 minutes. Remove the piece of meat – you can either keep it for another meal, or serve it separately after the soup, or cut it up and return it to the soup just before serving it.

Put the soup through the *mouli-légumes* (a blender makes too smooth a texture). Reheat, adding extra water if it seems too thick for your taste. Put in the meat if you are not keeping it for a separate meal or course. Add cheese, dillweed and cream to taste, with the salt, pepper and sugar (just a pinch often helps the flavour).

If you put cheese and oat biscuits (page 345) on the table with the soup, or cheese straws, or croûtons, or fingers of cheese-on-toast, you need little more to follow than salad and fruit.

NOTE: I am sorry to have to say that if you want a good smoky flavour from the cured pork, you will do best to buy a piece of *geräuchter bauchspeck* from a delicatessen. Much English cured bacon is too light and synthetic-pink-tasting for a good soup (or a good anything else, come to that). For a lighter flavour, use salt pork.

## CAULIFLOWER AND FENNEL SOUP

A RECIPE FROM ONE OF THE MOST REMOTE HOTELS IN BRITAIN, Scarista House on Harris, run by Alison and Andrew Johnson. Staying there, or reading Alison's book of recipes, *Scarista Style*, one is amazed that anyone ever gets dinner at all in such a remote place. In theory, the menu of any self-respecting restaurant these days should reflect local supplies, bought in daily. That's fine for the Mediterranean or for California, even at a pinch for southern England. But Harris? Cabbage, the inferior Kerr's pink potato, lamb, venison, an irregular supply of fish, eggs from the hens in the yard – that's the real and limited food of the Western Isles. Alison Johnson manages by Datapost and telephone, by weekly deliveries from Glasgow, and by a complex will-it-won't-it-arrive system of collecting boxes of halibut or scallops from the petrol station or the bottom of the drive.

The situation is complicated by the high Johnsonian standards with regard to the production of meat, shellfish and cheese. She will not use meat from an animal that has been given growth-promoters. No shellfish is bought ready-cooked, since the methods are slow and cause suffering. All the cheese is made from unpasteurized milk. No wonder she rarely finds it practical to use other people's recipes: two or three ingredients will invariably be missing or unattainable. On the other hand, the weekly vegetable deliveries from Glasgow stimulate some unusual combinations. Sometimes they don't work. Sometimes, as in this soup, they are a success.

For 6

*1 small cauliflower, sliced*
*Same weight of fennel, sliced, the green leaves chopped*
*1 medium onion, sliced*
*60 g (2 oz) butter*
*Up to 300ml (½ pt) cream*
*juice of 1 lemon*
*Salt*

SWEAT the sliced vegetables in butter until the onion softens. Cover with about 425 ml (¾ pt) water. Simmer for 10 minutes, then liquidize, adding more water if necessary for a thick purée. Add cream, lemon juice and salt to taste, then reheat without boiling. Scatter on the chopped fennel leaves.

## PALESTINE SOUP

JERUSALEM ARTICHOKES HAVE NOTHING to do either with Jerusalem or artichokes. When these delicious, warty tubers were introduced into Europe from Canada early in the seventeenth century, their taste was considered to resemble the unrelated globe artichoke's. In Italy, to avoid confusion, the family name was tacked on: the newcomers were distinguished as *girasole* – sunflower – artichokes. We seem to have corrupted *girasole* to Jerusalem, and from Jerusalem artichokes we naturally made Palestine soup.

The French were more deliberately fanciful. Six Tupinambas from Brazil had been brought to the French court in 1613, and had been a great success, at about the same time as the new vegetable – also from the New World – began to be popular. The name of one bizarre exotic was borrowed for the other – and the French were soon eating *topinambours*, as they still do. Artichokes took so well to Europe that it seemed at one time as if they might provide a basic food for some of the poorer areas. Their flavour, though, was too strong for daily – sometimes thrice-daily – eating; they were soon ousted as a crop by potatoes, and retreated to the kitchen gardens of the middle and upper classes to provide an exquisite winter soup and the occasional purée.

For 6

*500 g (1 lb) large Jerusalem artichokes*
*125 g (4 oz) chopped onion*
*1 clove garlic, crushed (optional)*
*30 g (1 oz) chopped celery*
*125 g (4 oz) butter*
*2 rashers unsmoked bacon, chopped*
*1½ litres (2½ pts) light chicken stock*
*2 tablespoons parsley, chopped*
*60 g (2 oz) double cream*
*Salt, pepper*
*Croûtons*

ARTICHOKES can be peeled raw like potatoes, but as they are so knobbly it is less wasteful to scrub and blanch them in boiling salted water. After 5 minutes, or a little longer, the skins can be removed quite easily (but run the artichokes under the cold tap first). Keep the water they are cooked in, unless it tastes very harsh (it does sometimes when the artichokes are becoming old).

Cook onion, garlic and celery in half the butter until soft. Add the bacon and stir about for a few minutes, then the peeled artichokes and two-thirds of the stock. Simmer until the vegetables are cooked. Liquidize or sieve, adding the remaining stock and some of the original cooking water if the soup needs diluting further. Put the remaining butter together with the parsley and cream into a warm soup tureen. Reheat the soup to just under boiling point, correct the seasoning, and pour it into the tureen. Stir it well as you do this, to mix in the butter, cream and parsley. Serve with the croûtons.

## MARION JONES'S GREEN FISH SOUP

TWO RESTAURATEURS I MUCH ADMIRE are Marion and Robin Jones of the Croque-en-bouche at Malvern. On their own, with a single helper, they serve a five-course dinner that starts with soup, and offers three choices for the fish course and four for the main course. Then come a number of cheeses and a choice of six desserts. Marion is on her own for the cooking. Robin, who runs a notable wine business, copes with drinks and everything else front of house. He also makes the puddings. The general style of the food is French, but this soup was devised by Marion to cope with the exigencies of local fish and vegetable supply. It is most delicious.

For 8

*½ large onion, thinly sliced*
*1 small leek, thinly sliced*
*30 g (1 oz) unsalted butter*
*30 g (1 oz) flour*
*1 litre (1¾ pts) fish stock, flavoured with fennel and nutmeg*
*500 g (1 lb) skinned fillets of haddock, whiting, hake, ling or conger eel, cut up*
*375 g (13 oz) sprouting broccoli or calabrese*
*About 6 tablespoons cream (optional)*

SWEAT onion and leek in the butter without browning them. When they are soft, remove the pan from the heat and stir in the flour with a wooden spoon. Cook gently for a few minutes, stirring. Remove again from the heat and pour in most of the fish stock. Simmer 10 minutes, season and add the fish. Simmer 1 minute, then leave to cool. Blend at top speed, in batches, until smooth.

Meanwhile, peel broccoli or calabrese stalks, cut off some of the flowering heads for a final garnish and chop the rest. Cook the chopped part in just enough lightly salted water to cover. Drain, keeping the liquor, and refresh under the cold tap (this sets the bright colour). Mix with some of the liquor and sieve into the fish soup, blending again if necessary. Dilute to taste with remaining fish stock and broccoli liquor. Check seasoning, garnish with steamed broccoli flowers, and swirl a little cream into each bowl.

## OYSTER OR MUSSEL SOUP

For 6

*2 dozen large oysters, or 1 kilo (2 lb) mussels*
*4 shallots, chopped*
*60 g (2 oz) butter*
*2 tablespoons flour*
*750ml (1¼ pts) veal stock, or light beef stock*
*Salt, pepper, Cayenne pepper, nutmeg*
*150ml (¼ pt) double cream*
*Lemon juice to taste*
*Chopped parsley*

TO open oysters, first scrub them under the cold tap. Then wrap your left hand (if you are right-handed) in a cloth, pick up the first oyster flat side up and curl your fingers over it. With your right hand, push the blade of an oyster knife (or a short stubby knife) between the two shells at the hinge end. Lever it open. With the tip of the knife, free the oyster from the shell and tip it into a sieve, placed over a basin, so that the juices are saved and separated from the oyster itself.

To open mussels, scrub them under the tap, scraping off barnacles, pulling away the dark thready beard. If any remain obstinately open, or if they are

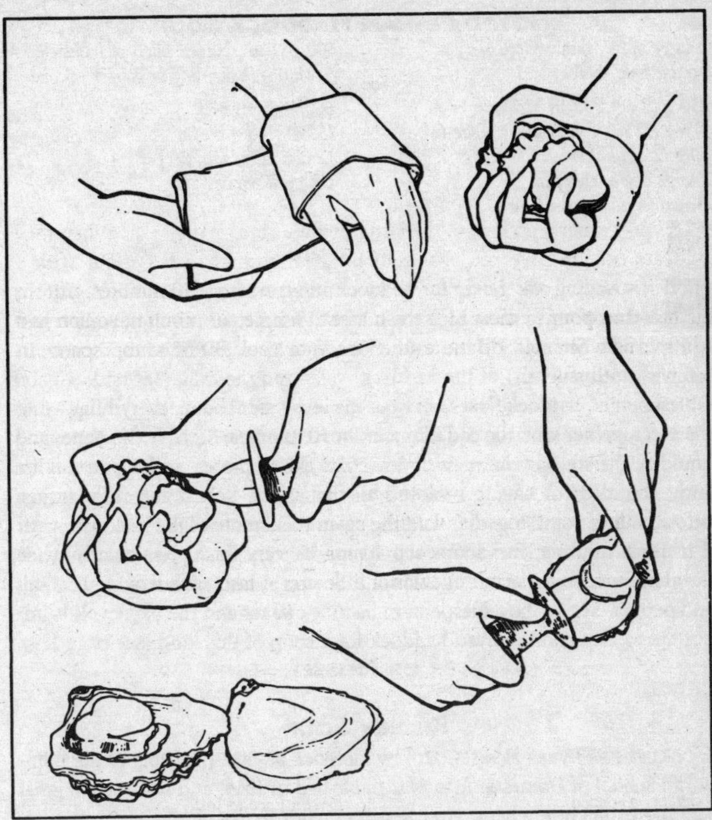

broken, discard them. Put them into a large pan, cover them with the lid and set them over a high heat (no water is usually necessary, but 150ml (¼ pt) can be added if you like). After 5 minutes – shake them from time to time – they will have started to open. Remove them with tongs, discard the shells and put the mussels into a sieve set over a basin. Add the juices from the pan to the juices already in the basin and strain through a muslin cloth.

To make the soup, cook the shallots gently in the butter until they are golden and soft. Stir in flour, moisten with stock and strained shellfish juices. Season with salt, the peppers and nutmeg to taste, and leave to simmer for 20 minutes or so with the lid on the pan. Just before serving, add the shellfish, cream and parsley. Bring up to the boil, pour into a tureen and serve after adding some lemon juice, and checking the seasoning.

## SMOKED FINNAN HADDOCK SOUP

For 4-6

*250 g (8 oz) Finnan haddock*
*375 g (12 oz) cod or other white fish*
*60 g (2 oz) butter*
*1 large onion, chopped*
*Generous tablespoon flour*
*600ml (1 pt) milk*
*150ml (¼ pt) cream*
*Lemon juice, salt, pepper*
*Chopped parsley*

POUR boiling water over the haddock and leave it for 10 minutes. Cut the cod into large cubes. Melt the butter in a large pan, cook the onion in it gently, and when soft add the flour. Cook for a couple of minutes, then moisten with 150ml (¼ pt) of the haddock water and the milk. Set aside a good tablespoon of haddock flakes, and put the rest – skin, bone, everything – into the pan together with the cod. Simmer for 10 minutes. Remove the bones and liquidize the soup – alternatively leave the fish in pieces, so long as you are fairly confident of having removed all the bones. Reheat the soup to just below boiling point, together with the cream, and more of the haddock water if it needs diluting; fish soups should not be very thick, particularly when they have a delicate flavour like this one. Season to taste with lemon juice, salt and pepper. Stir in the tablespoon of haddock flakes and the parsley. It is important to buy good undyed haddock for a soup of this kind (see page 119).

## KIDNEY SOUP

COOKERY FOR EVERY HOUSEHOLD, by Florence B. Jack, principal of the Edinburgh School of Domestic Arts, was published in 1914, and became the great standby in many kitchens. And it still is, with its air of efficient authority. Here is a good recipe for kidney soup from it, a great improvement on earlier versions, with its careful instructions.

For 6

*1 ox kidney*
*45 g (1½ oz) butter or dripping*
*1 onion, sliced*
*2¼ litres (4 pts) beef stock*
*Salt, pepper*
*Bouquet garni*
*6 cloves*
*20 black peppercorns*
*Blade of mace*
*¼ teaspoon celery seed*
*30 g (1 oz) flour*
*1 tablespoon ketchup*
*Lemon or orange juice*
*Sherry (optional)*

CUT the kidney in small pieces, discarding its fat. Brown in the butter or dripping with the onion. Pour in stock and stir well for a few minutes.

Add a little salt. Bring to the boil and skim carefully. Add the bouquet, and the spices tied into a piece of muslin. Cover and simmer only for 3-4 hours until the kidney is tender (this can be done in the oven, on top of the stove or in an electric slow-cooker).

Strain the soup, and, if you can, leave it until next day, so that you can be sure of skimming off all the fat. Rinse the pieces of kidney with a little hot water, and add them to the soup when it is reheated (discard the bouquet and spices). Mix the flour with the ketchup – the kind of ketchup is not specified but mushroom gives a good result, and tomato can be used sparingly – and a little stock from the soup. Add to the soup and cook gently so that it thickens a little. Finally add seasoning, a squeeze of lemon or orange juice and sherry if used. Serve with snippets of toast.

In her notes at the end, Florence Jack also points out that the pieces of kidney may be pounded or sieved (use an electric blender) before being returned to the soup. If you intend to do this, add 1-2 tablespoons of rice or coarse oatmeal when you put in the bouquet and spices. 'A garnish of vegetables cut in fancy shapes is sometimes added to this soup.'

## OXTAIL SOUP

TRY TO AVOID BUYING SMALL, skinny-looking oxtails. They do not take long to cook, it is true, but their flavour is insipid by comparison with an oxtail of decent size.

For 6-8

*1 large oxtail, cut in pieces*
*3 stalks celery, chopped*
*1 onion, stuck with 3 cloves*
*1 carrot, sliced*
*1 small turnip, sliced*
*60 g (2 oz) butter*
*1 teaspoon peppercorns*
*Bouquet garni*
*2¼ litres (4 pts) water*
*Salt, pepper*
*1 heaped tablespoon flour (optional)*
*4-6 tablespoons port wine*

ALWAYS prepare oxtail soup – or oxtail stew, for that matter – the day before it is required. This gives you a chance to skim off the fat completely before finishing the soup; if you do not do this, the flavour is ruined.

Cut surplus fat from the oxtail, then brown it with the vegetables in the butter. Transfer them to a large pan and add the peppercorns, bouquet and water. Season with salt. Bring to the boil and simmer, covered, until the meat is almost dropping off the bones. This can take four hours, or even five.

Strain off the liquor into a bowl. Leave to cool, then place in the refrigerator. Discard the vegetables and bones: keep the meat, dividing it into small pieces that will fit comfortably into a soup spoon, but remove the fat and skin. Season the meat and store it in a separately covered bowl overnight.

Next day, remove the sheet of fat from the liquor. Put the liquor in a pan, with the meat, and bring it to just below boiling point. Taste and adjust seasoning. Consider whether the soup would be improved – or would please the family more – with a modest thickening. If so, mix the flour to a paste with a little of the soup, then pour it back into the pan and simmer for 5 minutes before adding the port.

## CAWL

(pronounced 'Cowl')

CAWL MAY MEAN NO MORE THAN SOUP IN WELSH, but as you can see it is more than an elegant mouthful or two as a prelude to a main course. It is soup on the grand peasant scale from the old days of fireplace cookery, a meal in itself. French *pot-au-feu, potée* and *garbure* and *hochepot* are its close relatives. This kind of dish has no 'correct' version or original recipe. It varies from region to region, according to the local resources, and from house to house within the same village, even from day to day in the same house. We know who invented Chicken Marengo or Peach Melba; we can never know who made the first cawl or *potée*. We cannot even know in which country they were first made. For most people it was a case of putting water into the big iron pot, and as much else as they could find to flavour it and give it substance. The result in Caernarvon was, and is, obviously different from the result in Gascony or Belgium, but the principle was the same. Cockie-Leekie is the same kind of thing, so is Irish stew. They have survived because they were the best versions of these old one-pot dishes; they were so good that even when families became more prosperous, and had separate kitchens and coal and gas stoves, they did not want to lose them.

For 6-8

*Beef dripping or bacon fat*
*1 kilo (2 lb) brisket of beef, or shin or smoked gammon, or half each beef and smoked bacon*
*2 large onions, sliced*
*2 or 3 carrots, parsnips, swede, turnips, cut up (quantities can be varied, according to supply)*
*Salt, pepper*
*2 stalks celery, chopped*
*Bouquet garni*
*500 g (1 lb) potatoes, new when possible*
*Small white cabbage, sliced*
*2-3 leeks, chopped*
*Marigold flowers*

MELT the fat in a heavy pan and brown first the meat, then the onions, carrots, parsnips, swede, turnip. Transfer everything to a large pan or casserole when it is nicely browned. Cover with cold water to within 5cm (2") of the rim of the pan; add a little salt and chopped celery. Bring slowly to the boil, taking off the scum as it rises. Season with bouquet garni, sea salt and freshly ground black pepper. Transfer to a very low heat and leave to simmer for several hours. The friend from whom I had this recipe says that if the heat is gentle enough, the cawl can be left all day or overnight.

Put the potatoes into the pot half an hour before serving (old potatoes should be cut to new potato size), and the cabbage 10 minutes before serving. Chop the leeks finely, but keep them to one side.

To serve, slice the meat and put it into individual bowls with some of the vegetables and some of the soup. Sprinkle the chopped leeks on top – they will be cooked enough by the time the bowls are on the table – and float a marigold flower in each bowl. Ideally the bowls should either be wooden, or flowery Welsh earthenware.

## Mutton and Leek Broth

A magnificent soup, quite one of the best and comparable to any of the more famous European soup-stews. Followed by fruit and cheese, it makes a restoring meal at the end of a long, difficult day.

For 4-6

*125 g (4 oz) pearl barley*
*750 g (1½ lb) scrag end of neck, chopped in slices*
*2¼ litres (4 pts) water*
*150 g (5 oz) diced carrot*
*125 g (4 oz) diced turnip*
*1 small stalk celery, chopped*
*2 leeks, trimmed*
*150 g (5 oz) chopped onion*
*Salt, pepper, sugar, Cayenne pepper*
*Chopped parsley*

Wash and soak the pearl barley for 4 hours. Drain it, and put it into a large pot or pan, depending on whether you will be cooking the soup in the oven or on top of the stove. Remove the largest bits of fat from the meat, and add it to the pot with the water. Bring to the boil and simmer gently for an hour. Add the carrot, turnip, celery, one of the leeks, sliced, and onion, with some salt and pepper. Cook for a further hour – longer if you like (this is a good-tempered soup). Towards the end of cooking time, take out the pieces of lamb; the meat will be dropping off the bones, which can be thrown away. Cut the meat up fairly small, and return it to the pot. Skim off surplus fat. Taste and correct the seasoning, add a pinch of sugar to bring out the flavours and Cayenne to give piquancy; this is a particularly good idea when using lamb, which has less taste than mutton. Finally, chop the remaining leek and put it into the hot soup. Give it a few more bubbles, then sprinkle the parsley on top and serve. The leek will be cooked enough in the heat of the soup, while retaining an agreeable crispness. Wholemeal or granary bread and butter goes well with this kind of broth, or the cheese and oatmeal biscuits on page 345.

Take care to skim off all the fat; in fact it is a good idea to make the soup a day in advance, reheating it and adding the second, chopped leek just before the meal. This gives the fat a chance to rise and solidify on top, which makes it easy to remove.

FOR THE last 10 – 15 minutes of cooking time, add a 15 g (½ oz) packet of dulse if you are able to buy sea vegetables. It adds a delightful freshness of flavour and a beautiful appearance, without being in the least bizarre.

## MULLIGATAWNY SOUP

THE WORD MULLIGATAWNY means pepper water, and it came into English – like most Indian words – in the eighteenth century, from Tamil, *milakutanni* (*milaku* meaning pepper, and *tanni* water).

For 4-6

*1 boiling fowl, or the drumstick and thigh joints of a roasting bird, plus giblets (frozen chickens are no good at all for this recipe)*
*2 onions, sliced*
*90 g (3 oz) butter*
*1½ tablespoons curry powder*
*175-250 g (6-8 oz) moist fresh cheese (e.g. Gervais 'Jockey' brand fresh cheese) or 1 pot yogurt*
*Salt*
*4 cloves*
*Juice of 1 large lemon*
*Boiled rice*

CUT the chicken into pieces, brown the onions in 60 g (2 oz) of butter with the chicken. Stir in the curry powder, fresh cheese or yogurt and some salt, and stew for a little while so that the juices turn to a brownish crust on the bottom of the pan. They should not burn, so this needs watching. Pour in 1¾ litres (3 pints) of water, and leave to cook. Melt the remaining butter in a little pan with the cloves; after a few minutes you will be able to crush them down with a wooden spoon; pour in the lemon juice, mix it all up well and tip into the large pan of soup. Stew for an hour or more depending on the age and toughness of the chicken: the soup is ready when the meat parts easily from the bones, which can then be removed and thrown away. Correct the seasoning, pour into a tureen and serve with a separate bowl of boiled rice. This mulligatawny soup, unlike some of the other recipes, contains no apple, but if you like you can always serve a dish of chopped apple sprinkled with lemon juice to be added to the soup with the rice.

## CURRY POWDER

IF YOU WOULD LIKE TO MAKE A CURRY MIXTURE of your own, instead of using a proprietary brand, mix together:

*4 teaspoons finely chopped onions*
*1 teaspoon ground turmeric*
*1 teaspoon ground chili (chili is very hot)*
*½ teaspoon ground ginger*
*¼ teaspoon finely chopped garlic*
*½ teaspoon roasted and ground coriander seed*
*¼ teaspoon roasted and ground cumin*

## TURKEY AND HAZELNUT SOUP

For 4-6

*1½ litres (2½ pts) turkey stock*
*250 g (8 oz) raw turkey breast, minced*
*1 large egg yolk*
*125 g (4 oz) cream*
*Fresh or dried chervil*
*½ teaspoon paprika*
*Salt, freshly ground black pepper*
*90 g (3 oz) grilled, chopped hazelnuts*
*60 g (2 oz) butter*

BRING the stock to the boil with the turkey breast in it, and simmer for 3 or 4 minutes. Do not allow the turkey to overcook and become rubbery. Liquidize the soup and then sieve it into the rinsed pan.

Whisk the egg and cream together, pour in a ladleful of soup, still whisking, and return the whole thing to the pan. Stir over a moderate heat until the soup thickens slightly, but do not allow it to boil. Add the remaining ingredients away from the heat, adjust the seasonings to your own taste.

TOASTED ALMONDS, or peeled boiled chestnuts, both roughly chopped, can be substituted for hazelnuts. At Christmas time, use cooked turkey if you like – for instance, the thigh, which may still be slightly pink – and simmer it for a few moments only so that it is thoroughly reheated but no more.

## ENGLISH HARE SOUP

A RECIPE FROM ANTONIN CARÊME (1784-1833), the great French chef, who worked for a time for the Prince Regent. He admired several English dishes, including this one, and also gave recipes for sweetbreads on skewers (see page 148), and for cooking sea-kale (page 61).

For 6-8

*1 young hare, jointed, or head and forequarters of a mature animal*
*90 g (3 oz) butter, clarified*
*125 g (4 oz) salt belly of pork or green bacon, diced*
*1 heaped tablespoon flour*
*½ bottle claret or other red wine*
*1 litre (1¾ pts) beef consommé or stock*
*1 large onion stuck with a clove*
*Pinch Cayenne pepper*
*½ teaspoon each mace and black pepper*
*Bouquet garni, with 4 extra sprigs parsley, plus a sprig each of basil, rosemary, marjoram*
*Salt*
*250 g (8 oz) mushrooms, small if possible*

BROWN the hare in the clarified butter, together with the pork or bacon. Stir in flour, then wine and stock. Add all the remaining ingredients, except the mushrooms. Simmer until the hare is cooked, 1½ hours for a young animal, 3 hours for an older one. The flesh should be coming away from the bones. Pour the soup into a clean pan through a sieve. Pick out the hare meat and cut into small, conveniently sized pieces. Also remove the pork or bacon. Discard the remaining debris. Simmer the mushrooms in the soup for 10 minutes, correct the seasoning and put in the hare meat and pork or bacon.

If you are using a cheap red wine, a tablespoon of redcurrant jelly, towards the end of the cooking time, will much improve the flavour. Another alternative is a tablespoon of brown sugar, added gradually to taste.

# CHEESE & EGG DISHES

ENGLISH HARD CHEESES are ideal for cooking, but it is important to use them dry rather than wet, and they are not improved by being purchased in wedges sealed up in plastic. This makes them sweaty and soft and does not improve their flavour. Nor should one put the English hard cheeses into a refrigerator. They are already a specialized form of preserved food. Chilling does not improve the flavour or texture, and they are better bought in small quantities and kept where it is cool and dry. If you do have to keep cheese a long time, wrap it tightly in foil and store it in the bottom of the fridge.

One of the happy developments since I first wrote this book has been the renaissance of cheesemaking in Britain, and in particular the revival of ewe's milk cheeses. In medieval Wiltshire, on the downs, women used to be brought in at the lambing season to milk the ewes and make cheese, and one reason for the Welshness of the Welsh rabbit may be that the Iron and Roman Age Welsh were largely a pastoral people moving about and dependent on flocks and herds. Now we have Beenleigh Blue from Totnes and Humphrey Errington's glorious Lanark Blue from the Border country, and a number of other good white ewe's milk cheeses as well. Although one rarely comes across the exquisite goat's milk cheeses that one can buy in France, there are many creditable examples that are well worth eating and they will, I am sure, get better and better. One soft unpasteurized cheese which excels most of the French Camembert and Brie cheeses, is John Curtis's creamy Bonchester, another Border cheese; if you can buy this one from a cheese-seller who really understands how to store and bring on cheeses before they appear on the counter, invite only your very best friends to share it. John Curtis is one of the founders of the new Specialist Cheesemakers Association, and his standards of purity and quality of milk are such that the results of tests carried out on his farm are exemplary. His production, his example are the great argument against universal pasteurization, as of course is the flavour of his cheeses.

No other country has developed so rich a variety of excellent hard cheeses as England. We may not have anything as piquant as Parmesan or Pecorino (which is, I agree, a pity), nothing quite so useful and sweet as Gruyère or Emmental, but we do have a marvellous choice – Cheddar, Cheshire, Double Gloucester, Caerphilly, Leicestershire, Derby, Lancashire, Wensleydale, Red Windsor, all with their own character to be learnt and exploited by the cook.

Coming from the north, I find it difficult to be impartial. It must be Wensleydale with apple tart, gingerbread or fruit cake. It must be unpasteurized Lancashire, from Mrs Butler for preference, or Cheshire for toasting and making rabbits, or any of the three for a soufflé. If you live in Somerset, and can buy well matured unpasteurized farmhouse Cheddar in perfect condition, which is a little easier to do these days than it was in the seventies when plastic wrappery prevailed, your ideas on the subject of cheese for cooking will be very different.

In fact Cheddar, hard, dry, grated, is the best general-purpose English cheese for cooking. The snag is that, if you want to use it for flavouring, say, for a sauce, you have to use so much more of it than Parmesan, to get the same intensity, that its fattiness can upset the balance of the whole thing. However, a really old, dry piece of farmhouse or Cathedral City Cheddar can give good results, especially when a proportion of Parmesan is used as well. For toasting, which includes the rabbits, the cheese to use is white crumbly Lancashire, with Cheshire as second choice. It is worth experimenting with Stilton, particularly in combination with fruits such as pears, because it retains its individuality in cooking.

My own belief is that for eating there is no better English cheese than a farmhouse Double Gloucester in a properly mature and dry condition. Cheese is one of the last substances with individual variations of taste and quality which is worth shopping around for. On the whole, like strawberries and celery, it is one of the foods which was certainly improved in quality and consistency in the nineteenth century. Even now, cheese does maintain a consistent standard, though it is often sold too young and too bland, in those appalling building blocks that do not taste as good as properly rinded cheese.

In recent years, especially from the middle eighties, thanks to the Rances who used to run Wells Stores, to Randolph Hodgson at Neals Yard Dairy, to James Aldridge at Streatham, good British cheeses are much easier to buy outside London. One might say there is a passion for cheese. Restaurants delight in providing an English cheese board of a most creditable choice and deliciousness. In private houses many more people have cottoned on to the fact that cheese is the finest convenience food of all: a modest selection of four or five cheeses, good bread, and some of the less common varieties of apple that are to be found at farm shops, makes a lunch one can offer to the most exigent guests – and if you start with home-made soup, you have a feast.

What we now have to understand is the rôle of the cheese-seller. By the way he stores and cherishes his stock, the reputation of a cheese will rise – or, sadly, fall. Cheese is a living food and must therefore be treated with understanding and respect for the maker, so that the qualities appropriate to it are at their peak when it is sold.

These days, eggs are in deep trouble. Take care when buying them. It is a scandal that decently boiled or fried or scrambled or poached eggs, mayonnaise and related sauces, classic chocolate mousse, egg-thickened soups should no longer be given to children, elderly people, invalids or pregnant women. This particular elderly person has no intention of giving up these pleasures, but then I know the hens my eggs come from. Only a *British* Minister of Agriculture, Food and Fisheries could accept this situation and issue safety bans in such a calm and unapologetic tone of voice. Then again, to me it is impious that farmers should have been allowed to feed their laying flocks on food recycled from dead, often diseased chicks. It's an incestuous cannibalism for which we are now paying dearly (as we are with the necessary banning of beef offal on account of scrapie or mad cow disease). Many strains of Salmonella have been with us for years: it's this new form of *Salmonella enteritidis* that can be so devastating. True, it may not strike often, but people whose children have been in intensive care, and not restored to their normal healthy vigour for three months, on account of a tainted egg will bear me out. The wicked thing is that with care, with dating, and with the identification of source on the box, the problem could have been dealt with more easily and need never have reached such size. The mixing of eggs from different farms at the packaging station can make a box of them into a form of Russian roulette (and of course it is the mixing of milk from various herds that makes pasteurization of mass-produced cheese essential, leading inevitably to its decline in quality from the old farmhouse style of cheese made from the milk of known herds, feeding on known pastures). When everything is jumbled up, a source of trouble cannot be quickly identified and cut off.

Incidentally, I have concluded from various signs and portents that eggs are now larger than they once were. My husband had one of those old silver steamers which were made for the breakfast tables of 1880 or 1900: inside it had a framework of circles intended to hold four eggs. Yet, when we put four modern eggs of average size into it, the lid wouldn't fit down over them properly. They had never had this trouble when he and his brothers were children. It follows from this that if you happen to be using an old recipe, say for a sponge cake that begins 'Take sixteen eggs', you can reduce the quantity to a dozen (and on top of that you can safely halve all the quantities, eggs included, since the modern family is likely to be much smaller than it was in Mrs Beeton's day). Whether the modern battery egg has improved in flavour is another matter but it is true that eggs remain one of the best buys wherever you are. And of course you can now find them all the year round without difficulty. Even in the town, my childhood seemed to be dominated, in the matter of food, by whether it was the laying season or not: when we went to live in the country for a while during the war, preserving eggs was one of the regular chores. Eggs in isinglass in zinc buckets were to be seen in everyone's cellar or cold larder.

By and large, the best accompaniments of eggs, however you cook them, are sea salt, freshly ground black pepper, good salty butter, cream and good bread – or toast made from good bread, and not from the pre-sliced flannel variety. Egg dishes should be nothing if not a combination of simplicity, purity, flavour and richness. Henry James described what an egg should be when he arrived in Bourg-en-Bresse after a little tour of France when much of the food had been lamentable: "I had an excellent repast – the best repast possible – which consisted simply of boiled eggs and bread and butter. It was the quality of these simple ingredients that made the occasion memorable. The eggs were so good that I am ashamed to say how many of them I consumed. 'La plus belle fille du monde,' as the French proverb says, 'ne peut donner que ce qu'elle a'; and it might seem that an egg which has succeeded in being fresh has done all that can be reasonable expected of it. But there was a bloom of punctuality, so to speak, about these eggs of Bourg, as if it had been the intention of the very hens themselves that they should be promptly served. 'Nous sommes en Bresse, et le beurre n'est pas mauvais,' the landlady said with a sort of dry coquetry, as she placed this article before me. It was the poetry of butter, and I ate a pound or two of it."

Incidentally, if you think of cooking an omelette, do not think you are being exclusively French. The omelette – including cheese omelette – was a regular English dish in the Middle Ages, when it was called a fraysse (or froyse). Cheese has a remarkable affinity with eggs. One good point is that they conveniently cook at about the same rate.

Keep your eye open for other birds' eggs when you go shopping; although there is a basic similarity of flavour between them all there are subtle if slight differences. And of course size can dictate a more delicate or more robust dish.

*Duck:* not for soft boiling since they are laid in messy places sometimes and there could be risk of bacterial contamination. They should be boiled for 15 minutes. Duck eggs are fine for baking: if you remember that the standard hen's egg is about 55 g (2 oz) you can work out the number to substitute by weight.

*Goose:* a rare rich treat, especially when fried in a little butter. An occasional extravagance – 3/6d – in days of rationing after the war for undergraduates at Cambridge was goose egg and chips at a small café near Trinity. I still make it sometimes at home in memory of those feasts, with a tomato salad afterwards. They, too, are good for baking.

*Gull:* a delicacy which is becoming rarer all the time though they can still be found in some smart shops. They are not at all fishy, as you might expect, but have a creaminess from the large yolk.

*Quail:* a new kitchen toy, and a beautiful addition to the table with their shells of pale turquoise splashed with brown, especially if heaped into a little basket. Serve them with mayonnaise, or just plain sea salt, and an interesting brown seedy bread and farm butter. Small boiled – 3 minutes for firm eggs – and peeled quail eggs are a fine embellishment to smoked salmon or sturgeon or halibut. They can also be swaddled in a high quality sausagemeat for miniature Scotch eggs: eat them warm, for preference. Fry a small panful of quail eggs, then cut them into rounds with a petit-four cutter, centring it on the yolks, and put them warm on to identical circles of buttered bread – if you want to be grand, you can cover the bread first with circles of smoked fish, or a sliver of smoked eel, or some salmon caviare (or the real thing if you can afford it).

Quail eggs do not suffer from *Salmonella enteritidis*, so they are safe for children, elderly people and pregnant mothers. Three quail eggs baked in a small ramekin makes an appealing dish for someone who is not feeling well.

## Glamorgan Sausages

There are many recipes for Glamorgan sausages. The ingredients are always the same, but the proportions vary. Sometimes there is twice as much cheese as breadcrumbs. Sometimes the breadcrumbs exceed the cheese by a third. Sometimes onion is used rather than spring onion or leek. The Welsh serve these sausages with potato, but I think this is too much stodge. They are delicious on their own, or with grilled tomato, or a tomato sauce, or a light leek purée and a couple of rashers of crisp bacon, as a supper dish, or first course.

For 4

*150 g (5 oz) grated Caerphilly or Lancashire cheese*
*125 g (4 oz) fresh white breadcrumbs*
*2 tablespoons finely chopped spring onion, or leek*
*3 egg yolks*
*1 heaped tablespoon chopped parsley*
*½ teaspoon thyme*
*1 level teaspoon mustard powder*
*Salt, pepper*
*1 egg white*
*Extra breadcrumbs*
*Lard for frying*

Mix the cheese, breadcrumbs and spring onion, or leek. Whisk the yolks, herbs, mustard and seasoning together – use about 1 teaspoon of salt, and plenty of pepper – and add to the breadcrumbs and cheese to make a coherent mixture. If the breadcrumbs were on the dry side, you may need another yolk or a little water, before everything hangs together as it should. Divide into twelve and roll each piece into a small sausage about 5cm (2″) long. Dip them in egg white, roll in the extra breadcrumbs and fry until golden brown in lard.

If you have a processor, this dish can be made very quickly. Reduce the bread, spring onion or leek and parsley to fine crumbs together. Then add the cheese, with the thyme and mustard powder. Add the egg yolk to bind, season to taste and complete as above.

## Rabbits

Rabbits, not rarebits or rare bits, which are both false etymological refinements. In 1725, Mr J. Byrom recorded in his *Private Journal*. 'I did not eat of the cold beef, but of Welsh rabbit . . . I had a scollop shell and Welsh rabbit.' Mid-eighteenth-century cookery books give Welsh rabbit. Then in 1785 along comes Mr Francis Grose, with his *Classical Dictionary of the Vulgar Tongue*, to smooth away the joke: 'A Welch rabbit, bread and cheese toasted, i.e. a Welch rare bit.' A Glasgow capon, i.e. a red herring, and perhaps Scotch woodcock are other jokes of the same kind. Not very good jokes, you may think, from a time when people were less sensitive about each other's feelings, though in this particular case it seems to have been a joke which the Welsh themselves were happy to share. And whatever the origins of the name, Welsh rabbit was a popular dish in England, already differentiated from Scotch and English rabbits, by the time Hannah Glasse published her *Art of Cookery* in 1747.

The general idea of toasted cheese became especially popular in the nineteenth century; it was often served in special dishes with a lamp or hot water bath below to keep it warm. Toast was served separately (see Lady Shaftesbury's recipe, below).

## WELSH RABBIT

For 2

*125 g (4 oz) grated Lancashire, Cheddar or Double Gloucester cheese*
*3 tablespoons milk or ale*
*30 g (1 oz) butter*
*Pepper, salt*
*1 teaspoon made mustard, or Tewkesbury, or Urchfont mustard*
*2 slices of toasted bread*

PUT the cheese and milk or ale into a small heavy pan. Stir it over a low to moderate heat until the mixture quietly melts to a thick cream. Add the butter, pepper, salt and mustard. Taste, and adjust seasoning (you may, for instance, like more mustard). Put it back over the heat, until it is very hot but below boiling point. Put the two pieces of toast on to a heat-proof serving dish, pour the cheese over them and place under a very hot grill until the cheese bubbles and becomes brown in appetizing-looking splashes. The cheese will overflow the edges of the toast. Serve immediately, with a glass of red wine or ale.

## SCOTCH RABBIT (1747)

'TOAST A PIECE OF BREAD very nicely on both sides, butter it, cut a slice of cheese about as big as the bread, toast it on both sides, and lay it on the bread.'

## ENGLISH RABBIT (1747)

'TOAST A SLICE OF BREAD brown on both sides, then lay it in a place before the fire, pour a glass of red wine over it, and let it soak the wine up; then cut some cheese very thin, and lay it very thick over the bread, and put it in a tin oven before the fire, and it will be toasted and brown'd presently. Serve it away hot.'

USE the grill; and pile the slivers of cheese up to about ½ cm (¼") depth on the wine-soaked bread.

## GLOUCESTERSHIRE CHEESE AND ALE

SLICE SINGLE OR DOUBLE GLOUCESTER CHEESE into thin pieces. Lay them in an ovenproof dish and spread mustard over them in a thin layer – use Tewkesbury mustard (*La Favorite* brand) if you can, or one of the Urchfont mustards from Wiltshire which have the fieriness of English mustard combined with the attractive mustard-seed texture of French *moutarde de Meaux*. Pour in enough ale just to cover the cheese. Put into a moderately hot oven until the cheese is soft and deliciously melted. Meanwhile toast some wholemeal or granary bread, pour over some heated ale, just enough to moisten the toast slightly, and then spoon the cheese mixture on top. Serve with ale.

## LADY SHAFTESBURY'S TOASTED CHEESE

A FEW YEARS AGO I was given the manuscript receipt book kept by Emily Shaftesbury, the wife of the great social reformer, the seventh Earl of Shaftesbury. By the standards of the aristocracy they were poor, always in debt on account of the vast burden of debt inherited from the sixth Earl. The collection is full of good cheap dishes like this one, which came from the wife of Shaftesbury's favourite brother, William. The quantities seem tiny, but this kind of dish should be eaten in small quantities; unless your family and friends have stomachs of iron, toasted cheese can cause indigestion and nightmares.

For 6

*60 g (2 oz) butter, melted*
*175-200 g (6-7 oz) grated Farmhouse Cheddar*
*6 tablespoons cream*
*2 large egg yolks*
*Salt, pepper*

MIX the ingredients thoroughly together, and stir over a low heat until they have dissolved into a thick cream.Keep it under boiling point, but give it time to thicken. Divide between six small pots and brown lightly under the grill. Serve with toast fingers.

## LOCKETS SAVOURY

IN FLORENCE YEARS AGO I learn how delicious cheese is with pears, a combination as popular there as apple tart with cheese in Yorkshire. All kinds of cheese go with pears: Brie, cream cheeses, Gorgonzola, Roquefort and Stilton and some of the new semi-soft English, Scottish, Welsh and Irish cheeses. And so does black pepper; it was quite commonly used to bring out the flavour of fruit in the Middle Ages (and still is in some parts of France, where they make a peppered pear tart – or rather pie). This recipe, though, is a modern one, and was a speciality of Locket's restaurant in London.

For 4

*8 small slices white bread*
*1 large bunch watercress, cleaned and divided into sprigs*
*4 ripe pears (Doyenné du Comice are best)*
*350 g (12 oz) Stilton cheese, sliced*
*Freshly ground black pepper*

TOAST the bread and cut off the crusts. Put the slices into four ovenproof dishes, or one large one. Arrange the watercress evenly on top and cover it with the peeled, cored and thinly sliced pears. Put the Stilton over the pears and slide into a mark 4, 175°C (350°F), oven for 5 to 10 minutes, until the cheese begins to melt and the pears release their aromatic flavours. Grind black pepper on top before serving.

## POTTED CHEESE

THERE ARE MANY RECIPES FOR POTTED CHEESE in English cookery books, from Hannah Glasse onwards. She mixed 3 lb of Cheshire cheese with half a pound of butter, and flavoured it with a quarter-pint of rich Canary wine and half an ounce of powdered mace. 'A slice of this exceeds all the cream cheeses that can be made.'

Other writers have flavoured the cheese with dry or made mustard, with Chili vinegar or Worcester sauce. The proportions of butter to cheese have fluctuated from Hannah Glasse's 8 oz to 3 lb of cheese, to Michael Smith's equal quantities and to an equal quantity of sherry (in *Fine English Cookery*, Faber, 1973). This I find too much, preferring the proportions in *Pottery*, by 'A Potter' (in fact, Cyril Connolly's father), which was published by the Wine and Food Society in 1946, but use Cayenne pepper instead of Chili vinegar. 'A Potter' points out that Stilton or Wensleydale can be used – they must be moistened with port. Gorgonzola or Roquefort or Lanark or Dunsyre Blue should be flavoured with chopped chives and pepper: egg yolk and port or sherry provide the softening element. Now that I serve so much more cheese to show off what our cheesemakers can do, I often have bits and pieces left over. I make the most outrageous mixtures, cutting them up and reducing them to crumbs in the processor, then adding the butter, some Amontillado sherry and plenty of coarsely ground black pepper. A bit of Lanark and Dunsyre, a lot of Single Gloucester and a few cubes of Cheddar, for instance, produce a far more rewarding result than any cook deserves. The thing is to keep tasting, then add alcohol and seasonings accordingly.

*250 g (8 oz) Cheshire cheese, grated*
*90 g (3 oz) unsalted butter, softened*
*About 2 tablespoons port or brown sherry*
*Pinch Cayenne pepper*
*About 60 g (2 oz) walnuts*

MIX cheese and butter to a paste (these days, use the processor, cutting the cheese into rough cubes first). Flavour it with the wine and pepper. Pot and decorate with the walnut halves; or form into a small cheese, turn it in chopped walnuts, then decorate with walnut halves. If the potted cheese is to kept for a while, omit the walnuts and cover with a layer of clarified butter.

## ROLLS FILLED WITH CHEESE AND TOMATO PASTE

WHEN WE WERE GROWING UP, at the end of the War, my mother often made this paste for picnics and expeditions, filling it into the most beautiful and stylishly made bridge rolls that she bought from one of the excellent pastry cooks in the town. These days, such things are difficult to come by: rather poor, spongy and pallid rolls of elephantine size seem to be all that one can buy. You might do better spreading the paste into a split *baguette*, adding greenery, such as lettuce, endive, or watercress. This is not refined eating, but it comes very welcome out-of-doors.

For 6

*6 bridge rolls, about 15cm (6") long*

PASTE
*1 small onion, chopped fine*
*60 g (2 oz) butter*
*3 ripe tomatoes, skinned, chopped*
*1 egg, beaten*
*60 g (2 oz) grated Cheddar cheese*
*Extra breadcrumbs (see recipe)*
*Salt, pepper, sugar*
*1 tablespoon chopped parsley*

SPLIT the bridge rolls, and remove as much crumb as you can without piercing the outside of the rolls. Keep the breadcrumbs for the paste.

To make the paste, cook the onion gently in the butter in a small pan until it begins to soften. Add the tomatoes, which should be the firm and well-flavoured kind. Simmer for 15 minutes or more, uncovered, until the mixture becomes fairly thick. Whisk in the egg, and continue to cook over a low heat so that the paste thickens without boiling. Remove the pan from the stove. Stir in the cheese and breadcrumbs from the rolls – if the paste is rather sloppy, add some extra breadcrumbs. Season with salt and pepper, and a little sugar if the tomatoes were the greenhouse kind. Lastly mix in the parsley.

Fill the rolls generously with this mixture. It makes an excellent picnic dish.

# CHEESE SOUFFLÉ

For 6

SOUFFLÉ
*60 g (2 oz) butter*
*50 g (1½ oz) flour*
*300ml (½ pt) milk or mixed milk and cream*
*4 large egg yolks*
*90 g (3 oz) Cheddar or Lancashire cheese, grated*
*½ teaspoon salt*
*Freshly ground black pepper*
*Good pinch Cayenne pepper*
*5 egg whites*
*1 tablespoon grated Parmesan cheese*

*15 g (½ oz) butter*
*1 tablespoon breadcrumbs from stale bread*
*1 tablespoon grated Parmesan cheese*

FOR a classic soufflé choose a dish of about 1½ litre (2½ pts) capacity – a soufflé dish, a Pyrex dish, or a charlotte mould. If the capacity is less, tie a piece of oiled greaseproof paper or foil firmly round the outside, so that it sticks up about 5 cm (2″). Staple the overlap or tether it with a paperclip. This helps the soufflé to rise dramatically above a too-small dish. It should be removed quickly before the soufflé is served.

Recently I have adopted Alice Waters' method of cooking soufflés – a neat and unashamedly American improvement – by spooning the mixture into a well-greased, shallow gratin dish about 30 cm (12″) long and baking it at a higher temperature for 10-15 minutes, or until the top is nicely browned and puffy, the centre still creamy. I find this much more practical in domestic circumstances. She used crumbled goat cheese and a generous tablespoon of garlic purée as flavouring: the purée is made by baking two heads of garlic, separated into cloves, in olive oil with herbs, thyme especially, then draining off the oil and sieving out the skins and herbs.

Turn the oven to mark 6, 200°C (400°F), and place a baking sheet on the centre shelf.

To make the soufflé, melt the butter in a moderate-sized pan, stir in the flour and cook for a few moments. Keep stirring. Have the milk at boiling point. Remove the flour and butter roux from the heat and tip in the milk all at once. Beat steadily with a small wire whisk until smooth. Still off the heat, add the egg yolks one by one, beating them in thoroughly. Mix in the English cheese and seasonings. Reheat until everything is warmed through, but keep the mixture well below boiling pint.

Whisk egg whites with a pinch of salt until they stand in peaks on the whisk. They should also bear the weight of an egg. Or you can turn the basin upside down – needless to say the whites should not fall out.

Stir a tablespoon of white into the soufflé mixture fairly thoroughly to soften it. Then tip in the rest of the whites, and fold the two mixtures gently together with a spatula or metal spoon. Scrape and lift up the mixture from the bottom of the pan. The whites should lose as little of their lightness as possible, so do not go on too long. A *few* small concentrations of white won't hurt. Add a tablespoon of Parmesan.

Turn the mixture into the buttered soufflé dish. Sprinkle the top with the Parmesan and breadcrumbs mixed together. Place the dish on the heated baking tray in the oven. Shut the door and do not open it for 30 minutes – this will give you a delicious soufflé with a creamy inside.

If everyone is not sitting in their places, as they should be, turn the heat down to mark 1, 140°C (275°F). The soufflé should be all right for another 10 minutes. On the whole, though, it is better to have everyone at table. In a properly trained household, the cry of 'Soufflé!' should have the same effect of assembly as 'Fire!'

## OTHER FLAVOURINGS

### FISH

60 g (2 oz) onion or shallot, chopped and cooked down gently in 60 g (2 oz) butter. Add 250 g (8 oz) cooked, chopped fish, or soft roes, or shellfish. Season with appropriate herbs. Add to soufflé instead of the grated Lancashire or Cheddar cheese.

### SMOKED FISH

200-250 g (7-8 oz) smoked salmon scraps, or any cooked, smoked fish, finely chopped. Use a little cheese to emphasize flavour.

### MEAT

Cook 60 g (2 oz) onion or shallot in 60 g (2 oz) butter, as for fish. Add 200-250 g (7-8 oz) prepared, blanched and minced sweetbreads, or cooked, puréed brains. Or minced cooked poultry, or ham. Plus herbs.

### VEGETABLES

30 g (1 oz) onion and 1 clove garlic cooked in butter, as for fish. Mix with 200-250 g (7-8 oz) cooked, drained vegetables reduced to a purée. Spinach and turnip are very successful. With mushrooms, chop them, and cook them with the onion and garlic once they are soft and golden.

## LITTLE CHEESE SOUFFLÉS

For 8 as a first course
For 4 as a supper or lunch dish

*4 large eggs*
*150 ml (¼ pt) each single and double cream*
*250 g (8 oz) Lancashire cheese, grated*
*Salt, pepper*
*Pinch Cayenne pepper*
*Grated nutmeg to taste*
*2 tablespoons breadcrumbs*

WHISK the eggs thoroughly, then mix in the creams. Set aside two tablespoons of the cheese and add the rest to the eggs and cream. Season with salt and pepper, Cayenne pepper and nutmeg. Grease eight small soufflé dishes or ramekins with a butter paper. Divide the mixture between them, allowing a 1cm (½") space between it and the rim of the dishes as the mixture will rise. Mix the 2 tablespoons of cheese with the breadcrumbs and scatter them over the top. Bake at mark 6, 200°C (400°F), for 20-25 minutes, until the soufflés are well risen and slightly browned. Serve immediately with thin slices of bread baked in the oven until crisp.

## A FRICASSEE OF EGGS

THIS RECIPE COMES STRAIGHT FROM HANNAH GLASSE. All I have added is parsley. In the days before pasteurization, cream rapidly developed a sharp tang, which is why I used a mixture of double and soured cream. Another solution is to use all double cream, plus a final seasoning of lemon juice. The lovely richness of the sauce suggests an idyllic countryside, cows in a pasture with summer flowers, and a steady sound of bees. An interesting thing is that one still finds it on menus in Normandy and the Sarthe, served with trout and other fine fish, or with boiled chicken and rice. Left-over fish – sole, turbot, salmon, John Dory, lemon sole – can be reheated in the sauce and served in puff pastry or shortcrust cases.

For 8 as a first course

*8 large fresh eggs*
*8 large sprigs parsley*
*180 g (6 oz) lightly salted butter*
*150ml (¼ pt) double cream*
*150ml (¼ pt) soured cream*
*Salt, freshly ground black pepper*
*Slices of baked bread, or triangles of toast*

PUT eggs into fast-boiling water for 8 minutes. Run them under the cold tap, and shell and quarter them. Arrange in eight little soufflé dishes or ramekins. Meanwhile chop the parsley leaves. Then melt the butter in a

20 cm (8″) frying pan (do not use an ordinary saucepan, as there must be a large surface for evaporation): when it is melted and gently bubbling, stir in the creams with a wooden spoon. Keep on stirring for a minute or two, until the butter and creams amalgamate and reduce to a thick sauce. Add the parsley, season to taste, and pour over the eggs. Tuck triangles of toast into the dishes, or serve the baked bread on a separate plate. Eat immediately.

## MRS RAFFALD'S BACON AND EGG PIE

APART FROM THE DOUBLE PASTRY CRUST, this is an exact equivalent of the *quiche lorraine*, and the ancestor of our modern bacon and egg pies (which are ruined by the substitution of milk for cream). The double crust makes this pie very suitable for picnics and packed lunches: at more elegant meals, follow the French example and bake it as a flan without the upper crust.

For 4-6

*200-250 g (7-8 oz) smoked streaky bacon*
*4 large eggs*
*300ml (½ pt) crème fraîche or half double, half soured cream*
*Salt, pepper*
*Shortcrust pastry (see note on page 225)*
*Beaten egg to glaze*

PREHEAT the oven to mark 7, 220°C (425°F), and slip a metal baking sheet on to the central shelf to provide a hot base for the pie: this helps to make the pastry less soggy.

Cut up the bacon into pieces. Beat the eggs and cream together and season them with salt and pepper. Use a little more than half the pastry to line a tart tin or shallow pie dish. Put in the bacon, then the egg custard. Cover the pie in the usual way, pressing the edges close together. Brush with beaten egg and bake for 50 minutes, lowering the heat after 15 minutes when the pastry is firm and lightly coloured. This pie is best eaten warm.

## WYAU YNYS MON (ANGLESEY EGGS)

For 4-5

*660-670 g (1¼ lb) potatoes*
*6 medium-sized leeks*
*90 g (3 oz) butter*
*1 tablespoon flour*
*300ml (½ pt) hot milk*
*8 hard-boiled eggs, shelled, quartered*
*60 g (2 oz) plus 2 tablespoons grated Cheddar cheese*
*Salt, pepper*

FIRST scrub and boil the potatoes, then peel them and put them through the vegetable mill. Secondly, trim and clean the leeks. Then chop them roughly and swish them about in a bowl of water to dislodge any remaining grit. Remove them to a colander, then into a saucepan with 30 g (1 oz) butter – the leeks should retain just enough water to enable them to stew gently with the butter, without burning, *so long as the pan is covered tightly*. When the leeks are done, crush them into their cooking juices which should not be abundant. Or liquidize in the blender.

Meanwhile, as the vegetables cook, make the cheese sauce. Melt half the remaining butter in a small pan, stir in the flour, cook for 2 minutes. Tip in the milk, whisking all the time to avoid lumps. Cook for 10 minutes at least – better still 20.

Amalgamate the potato and leeks and beat in the last of the butter; add salt and pepper. The mixture should be light and a beautiful pale green with green flecks. Put it around the edge of an oval gratin dish, or similar ovenproof dish. Put the eggs in the middle.

Add the 60 g (2 oz) of cheese to the sauce, correct the seasoning and pour over the eggs. Scatter the remaining cheese over the top and bake in a hot oven until golden brown – mark 6, 200°C (400°F). Serve on its own as a supper dish; or for lunch with slices of cold ham.

THE SAUCE is improved and lightened by the addition of some grated nutmeg. Anglesey eggs are a homely dish, uplifted by the mixture of leeks with potato, which is delicious.

## OEUFS MOLLETS CHRISTOPHE

OCCASIONALLY WHEN ONE GOES OUT for a meal, some dish appears which is so delicious and so simple that one is angry not to have thought of it oneself. This dish was a speciality of the restaurant at Ramsbury, in Wiltshire, called The Bleeding Horse (it was once an old inn). The 'Christophe' of the title is the original owner of the restaurant, and the inventor of the dish, Christopher Snow.

For 4

*4 large fresh eggs*
*4 small slices smoked salmon*
*4 slices buttered wholemeal bread*
*125 g (4 oz) smoked cod's roe*
*4 generous tablespoons double cream*
*Pepper*

PLUNGE the eggs into fast-boiling water. Leave for 6 minutes precisely (7 if they are extra large). Put under the cold tap, and when they are cool enough to handle, crack them all over gently with a wooden spoon and leave for a couple of hours before peeling. This allows the white to firm up, so that there is less risk of the slightly runny yolk bursting through. Place each egg on a slice of smoked salmon, or wrap it round with the salmon. Cut the bread into circles, and remove a circle of bread from the centre, so that you have four bread rings. Place the eggs and smoked salmon on them and arrange on plates. Beat roe and cream together until very thick, season with pepper to taste. Spoon this sauce over the eggs, and serve with extra wholemeal bread and butter.

## ASPARAGUS AND EGGS

A FAVOURITE DISH FOR PEOPLE who grow their own vegetables, as this simple treatment shows off their fresh flavour well. Purple sprouting broccoli, tiny new peas, artichoke bottoms can all be used instead of asparagus. French recipes often add a flavouring of mustard, chopped herbs such as parsley and chives, and a spoonful of thick cream. A good variation of a recipe that was already popular in France and England in the seventeenth century.

For 4

*250-375 g (8-12 oz) cooked asparagus tips*
*4 slices bread*
*Butter*
*8 eggs*
*Salt, pepper*

COOK the asparagus tips in boiling, salted water (keep the thicker ends of the stalks for soup). Drain them well and put in a warm place. Toast the bread, butter it and lay it on a hot dish. Beat the eggs with salt and pepper. Scramble them with a generous tablespoon of butter, keeping them creamy. Arrange three-quarters of the asparagus on the toast, pour the egg on top and decorate with remaining asparagus.

## ASPARAGUS OMELETTE

For 6

*375 g (12 oz) cooked, trimmed asparagus*
*Butter*
*2 tablespoons grated Gruyère cheese*
*9 eggs*
*Salt, pepper*
*Chopped parsley, chives*

SET aside a few of the best stalks of the asparagus to decorate the dish. Keep the rest warm in the oven – dot them with butter and sprinkle them with cheese, then put a foil covering over them. To make the omelette, beat the eggs vigorously until not a trace of white remains – this should not take long. Add seasoning and a tablespoon of chopped herbs.

Unless you are used to making omelettes, you will find it easier to make three rather than one large one. And if all you have is a 20 cm (8″) omelette pan, then you will have no choice in the matter. Heat the pan, run a small knob of butter over it, then pour in a third of the mixture. Allow it to set firm beneath, and brown a little, before placing a third of the asparagus across the centre – which should still be slightly liquid. Flip the omelette in half, slide on to a serving dish, and make the remaining omelettes as quickly as possible. It follows that the first omelette should be really moist in the middle, as it has to wait around for the next two to be cooked, and it will go on cooking in its own heat.

Put the reserved asparagus around the omelettes and serve immediately.

## MUSHROOM OMELETTE

For 6

*375 g (12 oz) field or cultivated mushrooms*
*1 medium onion, chopped*
*60 g (2 oz) butter*
*Salt, pepper*
*9 eggs*
*Chopped parsley, chives*
*Extra butter*

TRIM any earthy or blemished bits from the wild mushrooms. Rinse them quickly, and slice them. Cook the onion slowly in half the butter in a frying pan – it should soften to a golden colour. Add the mushrooms, and, as their juices begin to flow, turn up the heat, so that by the time they are cooked they are bathed in a small amount of liquid only.

Make the omelette, and fill it with the mushrooms, as in the preceding recipe.

## SEFTONS

THE FRENCH CHEF, EUSTACHE UDE, was a contemporary of Antonin Carême, but unlike him he stayed for many years in England as chef to the Earl of Sefton, an amiable and appreciative boss. This veal custard is simple, delicious and light. It can be served with a light mushroom sauce, if you want to turn it out. I prefer it baked in ramekins so that it need not be cooked too firmly: the custard should shake gently under the top surface when you remove the ramekins from the *bain-marie*. Put them on to individual plates with slices of thin or Melba toast or baked bread.

For 6-8

*600ml (1 pt) veal or other good clear stock*
*6 fresh eggs, beaten*
*Grated rind of 1 lemon*
*Cayenne pepper, salt*
*About ¼ teaspoon ground mace*
*4 tablespoons clarified butter*

BRING stock to the boil and whisk it into the eggs. Add lemon rind and other seasonings to taste, then the butter. Pour into 6-8 ramekins or custard cups. Cover with foil (unless they have lids) and stand on a rack in a deep pan. Pour in boiling water to come about a third of the way up the ramekins. Bring to the boil again and slip into the oven preheated to mark 4, 180°C (350°F), and leave for about 20 minutes, checking after 12 minutes to see how they are progressing.

NOTE: if you want to turn them out, make sure you butter the moulds well before pouring in the mixture. Make a vegetable purée sauce (see page 56), choosing whatever vegetable goes best with the stock you have prepared – say, carrot for veal or beef, leek for chicken, or Ude's own choice of mustard sauce. Pour it round the little Seftons.

## PICKLED EGGS

**A** GREAT ENGLISH PUB DELICACY, at least in Wiltshire, but much better made at home with wine rather than malt vinegar, and quail rather than hen's eggs.

PUT enough eggs to come up to the neck of 2 bottling jars into a pan. Cover with cold water, bring to the boil and boil for two minutes for quail's eggs, 10 minutes for hen's eggs. Tap them and run them under a cold tap and shell them. When cold pack them into the jars, arranging them upright as best you can (hen's eggs, quail's eggs are too small and rounded).

Have ready a spiced vinegar made by simmering a litre (2 pts) wine vinegar with 15 g (½ oz) each peeled, fresh ginger, mustard seeds and white peppercorns, with 3 small red dried chilis, for 5 minutes. Strain and cool. Pour over the eggs to cover them, tuck in the chilis round the edge, close and leave for a fortnight before using with salads or hors d'oeuvre, or for serving with drinks. Do not use a metal cap to close the jar as it will corrode from contact with the vinegar.

This recipe is based on one by Mary Norwak, from the concise and excellent *Preserving Book* (Pan, edited by Caroline Mackinlay and Michael Ricketts); it was published some years ago now – 1978 – but is still invaluable and worth buying if ever you come across a copy in a secondhand bookshop.

# VEGETABLES

THE WORD 'VEGETABLE' only acquired its modern meat-and-two-veg meaning in the eighteenth century. It was first used in print, appropriately, by Arthur Young, the agriculturalist, in 1767, who talked about the 'cultivation of the new-discovered vegetables, and all the modes of raising the old ones.' Before that it meant the plant world generally: I am sure that Marvell was not thinking of W. S. Gilbert's 'attachment à la Plato for a bashful young potato, or a not too French French bean' when he told his coy mistress about his 'vegetable love' that would grow vaster than empires and more slow, but of some glorious tree or flowering climber from the New World. In these earlier times, what we now call vegetables were known as herbs and potherbs. The place where they grew was a herb garden (or a field, of course, for some of the most widely eaten vegetables), a place that was far more useful and less sentimentally romantic than some modern gardeners seem to think.

Etymology may seem a stuffy way to begin a vegetable chapter, but it often encapsulates a reality that is not to be found in, say, cookery books which enshrine a gastronomic Utopia.

In the case of vegetables, it underlines in a general way the personal impression of someone like Gilbert White. In 1778, eleven years after Young's use of the word, he was quite at home with its portmanteau usefulness, the way in which it separated the plants eaten in quantity from plants used as flavouring alone. Every middle-aged person, he wrote, must see how the 'consumption of vegetables' has vastly increased. 'Green-stalls' in cities now support multitudes, gardeners get fortunes. Every decent labourer has his garden 'which is half his support, as well as his delight.' Even farmers provide greens, peas and beans along with bacon for their workpeople. 'Potatoes have prevailed in this little district, by means of premiums, within these 20 years only and are much esteemed by the poor, who would scarce have ventured to taste them in the last reign.' To this increased vegetable diet and to the diminution of salted meat in favour of fresh – as well as to the cleaner habit of wearing linen rather than wool next to the skin – he ascribed the disappearance of leprosy and better health all round.

White went on to comment on the monastic gardens and gardeners of the Middle Ages – a time when the barons 'neglected every pursuit that did not lead to war or tend to the pleasure of the chase'. 'It was not until gentlemen took up the study of horticulture themselves that the knowledge of gardening made such hasty advances.'

Dr John Harvey, to-day's great scholar of garden history, has fleshed out, and qualified, Gilbert White's rather cavalier picture in two remarkable books, which I can recommend to anyone interested in Britain's eating habits. They are *Early Gardening Catalogues* (1972) and *Early Nurserymen* (1974). The titles may seem dusty, but the contents are full of surprise, insight and entertainment. He points out that although there may have been some kind of slump in vegetable gardening in the mix-sixteenth century, about 120 vegetables and herbs were being grown around about 1500. And from that date there was a steady decline in the general repertoire, in spite of new vegetables from the Americas. By 1677 the choice in seed catalogues had been halved, and was down to a third by 1972.

Since Dr Harvey wrote there has been a great widening of choice. Gardeners, at least at a certain level of curiosity and ambition, have returned to the rocket, lovage, orache, garlic, fenugreek, mallows, rue and tansy of the late medieval garden. I notice, too, a return to planting vegetables as well as saladings and herbs in to-day's herbaceous border. One may see multi-coloured cabbages and patty pan squashes fronting the delphiniums, and a diaper of lettuces in a formal bed. It is a style that may seem avant-garde but it goes right back to the square gardens of the fifteenth century as studied by Dr Harvey.

Another authority who has challenged Gilbert White's impressions is Malcolm Thick the agricultural historian. White and other gentleman gardeners of the seventeenth and eighteenth centuries were entranced by the much greater number of vegetable species that they could choose from. Mr Thick maintains that the poor had eaten certain vegetables in far greater quantities than they are given credit for. By the nature of things, the contemporary comments we are familiar with were made by the wealthier classes, by a few livelier spirits who had large gardens of their own, and enough food on their tables generally to demand greater variety. It was the poor choice of different vegetables – and the poor cooking of what there was – that provoked the Italian, Giacomo Castelvetro, to write about the vegetables, herbs and fruit of his native country, in 1614. His manuscript has lately been translated by Gillian Riley and published by Viking and the British Museum of Natural History (1989) in a magnificent illustrated edition, and it gives a fascinating picture of English attitudes to food, attitudes that seem never to have changed from that day to this. Why don't the English grow more asparagus? Why are they so suspicious of the wild mushrooms that grow so abundantly? Why do they never drain their salad leaves properly, and then dress them with far too much vinegar and not enough oil?

His manuscript and Dr Harvey's studies do not contradict the conclusions reached by Mr Thick who has studied market statistics from this earlier period of our history. He concludes that the labouring poor were eating a far greater quantity of vegetables than anyone had thought to mention, and that this was stimulated by the wheat famines of the late sixteenth century which gave a great boost to vegetable sales.

Dutch Protestant refugees from Catholic persecution in the middle of the sixteenth century brought their knowledge of intensive market gardening to England, especially to the areas around Norwich and Sandwich. These immigrations were closely – and suspiciously – monitored. The Dutch were directed to certain places very carefully, where their skill and hard work soon brought them prosperity. In consequence, the 'strangers' multiplied – to our benefit – and when famine struck in the 1590s they were able to ship plenty of root vegetables from Yarmouth to London to supplement the scarceness of bread. Continuing shortages greatly increased the number of market gardens around the capital as well, and around other cities. One landowner and farmer near Shrewsbury describes in a book on kitchen gardens, published in 1599, how by growing four acres of carrots and seven hundred 'tight-headed' cabbages he was able to keep many hundreds of people going during the twenty 'pinch days' before harvest, when the previous year's wheat had run out.

This supplementary nature of vegetables led to recipes for bread which might include parsnip or other root purées in a yeast dough. It is also behind such dishes as beef with carrots for which the Shrewsbury farmer gives a classic recipe of a kind one could follow to-day: he noted that with so many carrots, less beef was eaten (and of course less bread). Malcolm Thick notes that by the early seventeenth century, carrot growing had spread from Norwich to many places in East Anglia, and speculates that this innovation 'may have helped to lay the foundation for turnip growing as cattle fodder a few years after' so making possible the enormous advances in cattle breeding in our eighteenth century.

If, from the agricultural and social historian's point of view, gardening may be defined as 'the ability to produce a large amount of food from a small area of land', in other words market-gardening, from the private gardener's point of view it is the variety and freshness of vegetables that are most interesting. Looking back over the last three centuries, I find it fascinating to note the way that different items go in and out of fashion. Sugar snap peas were much grown in the seventeenth century. Salsify, scorzonera, fennel, celeriac and globe artichokes appeared in all the best vegetable gardens then and through the eighteenth century. Then they seem to have died from the general consciousness – perhaps when towns began to eat up the countryside and the best cooks and the writers of cookery books could not rely on produce from their own garden any longer, but had to buy from markets and shops – to the extent that they are now ranged at the posh or exotic end of the supermarket counter, and appear only in the most upmarket greengrocers and market stalls.

Reading books, letters and journals of the pre-industrial time, one guesses that such post as there was must have rattled with seeds. For the best cauliflowers, wrote John Evelyn, you needed seed from Aleppo. No wonder seedsmen flourished. When Rabelais travelled to Rome, he was charged by his superior, the abbot of Maillezais, to seek out the very best salads and is credited with introducing cos lettuce to France. And travellers ever since, and undoubtedly before, have brought treasures home in this easy form, recollections of lovely meals on the Grand Tour springing to northern life from a paper twist of little brown seeds. We're still at it to-day, hunting down a larger-leafed or purple basil, a tastier variety of tomato, Italian puntarella or a mesclun mixture of salad leaves in the seed shops of France and Italy, though in fact we can probably buy them by post from seed catalogues from firms in this country.

Other, more purposeful and professional travellers went on hazardous journeys expressly for plants and seeds of all kinds, or brought them back like potatoes – as part of the booty of world exploration. As the world opened up, the staff of embassies were charged with sending exotics back to Europe – often there was a passionate amateur plantsman who knew very well what he was about, someone who was seized with the romantic idea of recreating the gardens of the south or of China in our northern climate. I think particularly of the delicious little Chinese artichokes or *crosnes*, as the French call them from the town where they first flourished in Europe. What determination it took to send consignment after consignment back home over the years, until at last in 1882 a very few survived and were grown with success in the garden of the Vice-President of the Societé d'Acclimatation, at Crosne, in Brie country south-west of Paris. Treasured handfuls are still passed from friend to friend in this country, where they have not caught on as widely as in our more appreciative neighbours' gardens.

Once initial discoveries have been made, the whole skill is in cosseting and persuading these seeds or tubers to adapt to our northern weather, in finding the right place, the right microclimate very often. In Britain we have only two native vegetables (three if you include watercress), sea kale and samphire – both of which have been sadly neglected in the recent past until more adventurous chefs and writers have taken them up again. Every other vegetable in our gardens has been developed from imported varieties, from which our plant-breeders and nurserymen have in their turn developed cultivars suitable for our climate and soil. You may see wild carrot and parsnip by the road, wild cabbage on some cliff tops, but cultivated carrots came to us from the Moors, via Spain, Holland and France, along with spinach, and with aubergines which, like John Tradescant's scarlet runners from the New World, were first grown as ornamentals, for their physical rather than gastronomic beauty. The first decent cabbages came to us from Holland.

The great gardening figure of eighteenth-century Britain was Philip Miller, who worked for nearly 50 years from 1722 at the Chelsea Physic Garden. He knew more than anyone else in the world about plants and growing them. He had a good opinion of himself – and why not? – which made his first meeting with the young Swedish botanist Linnaeus decidedly sticky. But he had a big enough mind, or a passionate enough devotion to his calling, to see the point of the Linnaean system of plant nomenclature, and to incorporate it in later editions of his great *Gardeners Dictionary*. He gave Linnaeus all he wanted by way of plants, and more, as did other enthusiasts, and Linnaeus went away with the impression that the English were 'the most generous people on earth'.

To-day there are no more discoveries to be made; all plants are known (though I admit to a hope that somewhere something that has never been eaten outside one small area is waiting to be found). Everything is now concentrated on adaptation and development of known species to produce the cultivated varieties that different parts of the world may require. Alas, rationalization and a narrowing down seem to be the order of the day as far as commercial horticulture is concerned. One is thankful to hear of devotees who collect ancient varieties of vegetable and other seeds, understanding the need – as with animal breeds – for a gene bank. Some pea that has not been grown for 30, 50, 80 or more years may have just the gene that will become valuable in the unpredictable future.

Two problems occupy the most engaged vegetable growers these days, organic cultivation and the adaptation of varieties to the northerly climates of these islands. Following up the latter, I went in 1988 to Harlow Car Gardens on the edge of Harrogate, to see Chris Margrave – as it turned out he had that week been promoted from Trials Officer to Curator. His convoluted path to this distinguished post – Harlow Car is the northern counterpart to the RHS gardens at Wisley – would have interested Gilbert White and Philip Miller. First he studied modern languages and political science, then went on to postgraduate courses for translators and interpreters. To finance himself he worked in the vacations at a garden centre. He had helped his father enthusiastically with the garden as a child, but owing to the usual inadequate careers advice had never thought of horticulture as a career. Peaceful summer afternoons in the plant sheds at the garden centre, half-listening to the cricket commentaries as he worked, made him see sense. He took the diploma course at Kew and paid a visit to Harlow Car – he is a northerner – when their Trials Officer happened to be leaving. Now he is heart and soul devoted to Harlow Car's dual purpose in the matter of vegetables. Firstly, the discovery of suitable varieties, in particular of sweetcorn, tomatoes and beans, in the tricky northern climate with its short season: frosts are likely as late as the first week of June, as early as the end of August, and secondly the education and assistance of amateur gardens. These days, commercial varieties are the concern of the research stations.

To see what hope there is for organically grown vegetables, I went in the same year to see the most highly regarded grower of early and beautiful-looking organic vegetables. One commercial problem is that people have got used to buying perfect unblemished vegetables – and fruit – produced by chemical horticulture: if organic growers are going to compete, their produce needs to be better looking, more regular in shape, brighter in colour than the amateur gardener can manage. And to catch the top prices paid by restaurants, it needs to be early.

Charles Dowding, who grows his vegetables on part of the family farm at Shepton Montague in Somerset, had, like Chris Margrave, a totally different education and training from which he turned away in his mid-twenties back to his childhood interest in the land. His time at Cambridge, though, had taught him to think and he applies his mind to the problems of growing vegetables without chemical herbicides.

One solution has been a system of raised beds, the piling of compost on top of the ground in curved beds that can be reached for cultivation from straw-laid paths on either side. These beds are never walked on, never need to be dug (which means that fresh weed seeds are never being brought up to the surface). After a crop, say, of lettuce, he will sow clover or alfalfa which fixes nitrogen into the soil. As it sprouts, it is covered with polythene which kills it off so that it rots down to fertilize the soil. He will cover beds with a soft plastic covering light enough for the plants to push up as they grow, permeable by the rain, yet thick enough to give protection from the wind. He is a modernist and will take advantage of any new discovery that does not harm the soil. When I asked him about varieties, he replied that he went for the most up-to-date F1 hybrids. In his opinion, flavour comes from the soil, his precious lovingly cherished soil, and the sun which does indeed shine sweetly on the gentle slopes and levels of his land.

Turning away from meat, disgusted by revelations of the manner in which most of our animals are reared, people have lately acquired a new interest in vegetables in Britain. Disappointed, too, by the tastelessness of beautiful-looking carrots and regular 8-or-12-to-the-lb tomatoes, many turn to their gardens for a healthier and more satisfying gastronomy. Even with no more than a balcony or a small backyard and a kitchen windowsill, we are learning the true taste of an out-of-door Marmande tomato and a lusty crop of basil or tarragon or chervil or sorrel. A more lively attitude towards eating generally, means that some of us will go mushroom-hunting in the autumn woods – or will at least buy chanterelles, oyster and other strange mushrooms in the shops – and may even branch out into the pleasure of sea vegetables such as laverbread, or the half dozen different kinds sold in dried form put up by Julian Clokie at Pitkerrie near Tain in Scotland. 15 g/½ oz packs of sugar ware, finger ware, dabberlocks, grockle, summer and autumn dulse and purple nori can all be bought at the best delicatessens. Add them to stews and white meat dishes, to vegetable purées and sauces for their light and lively flavours, as well as for their healthful properties.

In spite of this new turn, we still have a way to go when it comes to eating vegetables as a separate course on their own. A few of the finest vegetables – asparagus, sea kale, globe artichokes – began to come into their own in the middle of the last century when the Russian service was adopted for dinner parties. Before then, such meals included many dishes, served in three buffet courses, everything spread out on the table in a formal arrangement. You ate what was nearest or what you neighbour was polite enough to pass you. Chefs loved the splendour of it all, its lavishness, the display of their wide skills. With the improvements in horticulture and agriculture, though, and increasing urbanization, chefs, and Escoffier in particular, began to see the point of simplicity and quality, the point of serving one dish at a time to everyone at the table. Splendour came from the delicious flavours, thoughtfully juxtaposed in sequence, and from many courses.

It took time to catch on, and the idea of vegetables as a separate course seemed strange to Sir William Hardman in 1863. He was no rustic and insular gentleman, but a wealthy and travelled man, and a generous friend to George Meredith. When he and his wife returned from their summer abroad he invited Meredith to a small dinner party to share the novelties they had brought back with them – 'our continental tour having enlarged our culinary ideas'. Meredith was a natural choice, he and his wife had started writing a cookery book together, under the influence of his gastronomic father-in-law, Thomas Love Peacock, and although the marriage was at an end, Meredith retained his love of good food if not his wife. The novelties were as follows: 'after the soup, a slice of melon. The vegetable separate, and Cabinet pudding iced. A centre of mixed fruits during dinner. Fish knives for the first time.' Melon towards the start of the meal, the new Parisian dish of fruit salad, the iced pudding and the fish knives – up till that time fish had been eaten with a fork and a bit of bread, a habit practised by some old-fashioned folk who regarded fish knives as common for the next hundred years – were all rated a success. Not so the vegetable course, a cauliflower *au gratin*. Unhappily Sir William does not say why – badly cooked? Or perhaps not excitingly enough to be enjoyable on its own? The dish itself was no novelty, it appears as cauliflower dressed with Parmesan in popular cookery books of the 1840s.

Cauliflower is not always easy to cook well. I suspect it may have seemed insipid to people accustomed to a great deal of meat and fish. And the whole idea of vegetables as a separate course remained a hopeless failure in this country until Elizabeth David started writing articles and books in the late 1940s. Her exhortations, combined with the rising cost of meat and a modest sensibility towards the use of grain to fatten cattle when so much of the world's populations is starving, has helped us to appreciate vegetable dishes for their own sake.

Our climate has been against us of course – when I see how easily vegetables grow in the Loire district of France, how good they taste from just that extra little bit of sun, I understand why they play a lesser part in our diets than one might wish. And our over-urbanization at an early date, our early cutting of ties with the country, has led to a lack of knowledge about vegetables. So much so that we are in such a state of ignorance that we tolerate poor quality, even in vegetables that flourish in our climate. Potatoes, for instance. In spite of the splendid diversification in the last 150 years housewives out shopping can buy only a few heavy-cropping varieties with a relatively poor taste. Proper salad potatoes, with a yellow, waxy flesh that holds together, are happily becoming easier to find at the supermarket, but mainly it's back to the garden, or nothing. That's the story of too many vegtables in this country. The contrast between a good seedsman's catalogue and the range at the average local greengrocery is often appalling to contemplate.

I should add that there are a few wild vegetables not at all to be despised – not counting the field mushroom and equally good horse mushroom. Hop shoots from the wild hedgerow plants or the hop garden, cooked in bundles and served with butter like asparagus, young nettles used for purée or soup, comfrey leaves cooked in batter as fritters – these are first rate. Then there is laverbread, a fine vegetable to serve with roast leg of lamb or salmon or lobster, which can be brought in many West Country fishmongers or from market stalls, and in tins in good groceries (it cans well), and the other sea vegetables I have already mentioned. All in all, I would say we have a great future in vegetables if only we are prepared to love and use them, say with the skill of Californian cooks. A revelation of what vegetarian vegetable cookery can be is found in the pages of *Green's Cook Book*, by Deborah Madison and Edward Espé Brown (Bantam Press, 1988). It has something vivid about it, as if the authors were seeing the vegetable world for the first time. I hope it may have a lively influence on English vegetable cooking in the future.

## Asparagus with Melted Butter

THE SEVENTEENTH CENTURY was a great age for improved vegetables in England, a time when knowing gardeners looked to France, and above all to Holland, for better varieties and new kinds. If you look at Dutch still life paintings of the seventeenth century, you will sometimes see bundles of asparagus on dark polished tables, with a tall-stemmed glass, pewter dish and a couple of lemons. The asparagus seems to get larger as the century goes on.

It was this kind that I imagine Sir William Temple introduced to England, and grew at Moor Park, near Farnham in Surrey. One day William of Orange paid him a visit, and was shown round the superb gardens which were laid out in the fashionable Dutch style. The King was kind to Temple's young secretary, Jonathan Swift, and showed him how to cut asparagus with a short rather than a wide stroke of the knife, so that the smaller stalks around remained undamaged for later cutting. The King also set him an example of how to eat asparagus in his fingers, and also to eat it all, so tender was this new strain. When Dean Swift had his own household, he is said to have refused a guest a second helping of asparagus until he had cleared the stalks on his plate – 'King William always ate the stalks'.

The asparagus season in England runs from as early in May as the weather allows until about the end of June. Asparagus is on sale at other times from America, Kenya and Eastern Europe, but you should remember that the sooner asparagus gets from the garden to the pot the better it will taste. In this country we have preferred green asparagus for a long time now, but in other places tastes are different, and asparagus there will be fat, white and very tender for its size. Some people insist on a preference. I am happy to eat fresh asparagus of any kind at any time. You may agree with me that all kinds are good in that short six-week season of the year.

Per person

| | |
|---|---|
| *10 stalks of asparagus* | *30 g (1 oz) melted butter* |
| *Salt, pepper* | *Lemon juice* |

TRIM the asparagus so that the stalks are all the same length (keep the trimmings for soup). Remove the hard outer skin from the stalks with a potato peeler. Tie the asparagus in a bundle with string. Put an inch of boiling water into a pan, with salt and pepper, and stand the asparagus in it so that the delicate heads are steamed. If you do not have a tall asparagus pan, arrange a domed lid of foil over the pan. The asparagus will take between 20 and 40 minutes, depending on its thickness and variety.

You might well copy the French habit of cooking new potatoes with the asparagus, so that they take on extra flavour from the water. The two can be served together with great success, particularly if you are a little short on asparagus.

Flavour the melted butter with salt and pepper, and a squeeze of lemon juice, and serve it in a separate jug. It has also become an English habit to serve asparagus with hollandaise sauce, or with mayonnaise if it is to be eaten cold. Recipes are given on pages 353-4.

## BROAD BEANS IN THEIR PODS

For 4

| | |
|---|---|
| *1 kilo (2 lb) young broad beans, about 7-8 cm (3") long* | *175 g (6 oz) melted butter* |
| *Salt, pepper* | *Lemon juice* |

TOP and tail the broad beans, which should be freshly picked and really young. Boil them in a pan of salted water until they are tender – test them after 15 minutes. Strain off the water, pepper the beans and put them on to a hot serving dish. Sharpen the butter with the lemon juice, heat it to just below boiling point and put it into a separate small jug.

Beans cooked in this way make a good first course. They can be eaten like asparagus, in the fingers, or with knives and forks.

AS BROAD bean pods grow larger, they need to be shelled. Then I would recommend boiling them, until the skins begin to crack, in salted water. Drain them, rinse under the cold tap and then peel off the skins. This is, I know, a chore but it makes all the difference. The broad bean season is so short that it is worth taking trouble.

The beans can then be reheated in a little butter and parsley, in bacon fat with the addition of crumbled, crisp bacon rashers, or with a little butter and a few tablespoons of cream, as an accompaniment to boiled ham or salt pork – don't forget the parsley.

## HAROLD WILSHAW'S BROAD BEAN AND AVOCADO SALAD

WHEN I FIRST STARTED to write about cookery, Harold Wilshaw was the Guardian food correspondent and very good company. He had been a chef in his youth, advised other people on setting up their restaurants and had a particularly good line in vegetable recipes. From him I first had the idea of cooking chicken with Jerusalem artichokes, and he once gave that excellent recipe for Salad Elona (alternating rings of cucumber and halved strawberries, dressed with coarsely ground black pepper, a pinch of sugar and 2-3 tablespoons of dry white wine or white wine vinegar: good with salmon, salmon trout and chicken).

He thought up this particular salad when unexpected guests arrived and there wasn't all that much in the house.He peeled and sliced his one avocado pear and arranged it on a large plate with a good scatter of cooked, skinned broad beans. The dressing was cream sharpened with a little lemon juice, but I tend to use an olive oil vinaigrette. A scatter of chopped parsley, chives or spring onion and green coriander sets the flavour off well.

This dish could be turned into a lunchtime main course, by arranging the salad in a surrounding circle of Cumbrian air-dried ham or Parma ham.

## MANGE TOUT SALAD WITH CHICKEN LIVER AND BACON

AN UNUSUAL VARIATION ON THE WARM SALAD THEME that makes a good first course, or lunchtime dish, for a summer meal.

For 4-6

*375 g (12 oz) mange tout peas, topped and tailed*
*6 tablespoons groundnut, sunflower or hazelnut oil*
*4 tablespoons white wine vinegar*
*6 chicken livers, cubed, stringy parts discarded*
*Salt, pepper*
*6 very thin rashers of streaky bacon, cut into strips*
*Bacon fat or extra oil*
*24 small bread cubes*

COOK mange tout until they are crisply tender in fast-boiling, salted water, without a lid: this helps to keep the colour. Drain and put into a warm bowl. Mix oil and vinegar and pour over the mange tout, turning them. Keep warm, together with 4-6 shallow bowls.

Season the livers with salt and pepper. Cook the strips of bacon in their own fat in a non-stick pan, using a little extra bacon fat or oil if necessary. Remove with a slotted spoon, then fry the bread cubes in the pan. When brown add to the bacon. Finally, cook the liver briefly, again adding extra fat or oil as required. The liver should remain pink at the centre. Put back the bacon and bread to warm through.

To serve, mix the panful of liver mixture into the mange tout and divide between the warm bowls. Eat immediately.

NOTE: a similar salad can be made substituting young broad beans for mange tout peas. After boiling, take the trouble to skin them (see above). Allow at least 2 kilos (4 lbs plus) of unshelled beans.

## CHILLED MANGE TOUT CREAMS

MANGE TOUT PEAS are so easily grown that they have almost become a cliché of modern English eating. And when we don't find them in our gardens, they are imported, especially from Galicia.

For 8

*500 g (1 lb) mange tout peas, topped and tailed*
*2 teaspoons finely chopped spring onion green*
*11 g (0.4 oz) sachet of gelatine*
*Pinch sugar, salt, pepper*
*Lemon juice to taste*
*250 ml (8 fl oz) whipping cream*
*2 egg whites, stiffly beaten*
*Melba toast*

SET aside about 125 g (4 oz) mange tout. Put the rest into a pan with the spring onion. Bring 300ml (½ pt) water to the boil in another pan, pouring most of it on to the peas, but leaving enough to dissolve the gelatine when it has cooled down a little.

Cook the peas until just tender, then liquidize or process the panful. Sieve into a measuring jug – there should be about 425 ml (¾ pt). Stir in the dissolved gelatine while the purée is still warm. Season with sugar, salt, pepper and a little lemon juice to taste, then chill.

When the purée is on the point of setting, with something of the consistency of egg white, whip the cream until very thick but not quite stiff, and fold it in. Then fold in the egg whites. Chill 16 individual oval moulds. Pour in the mixture and leave overnight in the refrigerator, or for several hours.

Cook the reserved mange tout lightly, run under the cold tap and drain. Turn out two creams on to each of eight plates. Put a few mange tout on each plate with the little creams, plus some pieces of Melba toast.

## GREEN PEAS

EVERYONE KNOWS THE ENGLISH STYLE OF COOKING PEAS - with sprigs of mint and a little sugar, then plenty of butter when they are drained. If the peas are tender there is no better way, and no better dish in the early summer – with or without new potatoes, duck, lamb. The very first time I became conscious of the deliciousness of vegetables was during the war. I was about fifteen. The rest of the family was out, and our landlady gave me a blue and white vegetable dish of green peas, just picked from her garden, for lunch. They were so good, such a revelation of what vegetables can be,that I am not ashamed to say that I ate the lot, and can recall their flavour perfectly.

What is less known is that peas can be cooked in their pods, in the same way as the broad beans above. When it comes to eating them, you pick them up in your fingers and chew the tender outer pod away while sucking the peas. The tough white parchment stays behind, to be discarded.

Better still in this line are sugar peas, which have long been a pleasure of English summers (see page 190). And now we have a new variety from America, the Sugar Snap, a mange tout pea that is not flat like a sugar pea, but plump with fully grown peas inside. Somehow the plant-breeders have managed to eliminate the inedible parchment. This pea can be eaten raw; it can be steamed, too, or cooked in various Chinese ways. The only attention it needs is stringing once the pods are mature. At the moment these peas are mainly for gardeners, although some supermarkets are beginning to sell them alongside the flat mange tout peas.

## PEASE PUDDING

IN THE PAST, pease pudding would be tied into a cloth, and cooked in with the boiling meat, usually salt pork or bacon. It is still a most popular dish in the North of England. Any left over can be fried and eaten another day, which makes it a welcome dish in poor households –

*Pease Pudding hot! Pease pudding cold!*
*Pease pudding in the pot*
*Nine days old.*

*500 g (1 lb) dried split peas or whole peas*
*60 g (2 oz) butter*
*1 large egg*
*Salt, pepper*

NOWADAYS many dried vegetables do not need soaking before they are cooked, so much has the quality been improved. If, though, they have been in your storage cupboard for a few months, it is wise to allow three hours' soaking time and to add 1 level teaspoon of bicarbonate of soda to the water if it is at all hard.

To cook the peas, drain them if they have been soaked, then put them into a pan. Cover them with plenty of water and simmer until tender. Split peas will take from 45 to 60 minutes; whole dried peas will need at least 2 hours. Drain off the liquid – keep it for soup – and put the peas through a *mouli-légumes* to make a purée which is not too smooth. Mix in the butter, then the egg and season it well. Put the mixture into a buttered basin and steam for an hour. Turn it out and serve it with boiled salted pork.

## PURÉE OF DRIED PEAS WITH GREEN PEPPERCORNS

THIS VERY ENGLISH PURÉE OF PEAS is much improved by green peppercorns, which are sold fresh in some greengrocery departments, and in tins and jars at good grocers and delicatessen shops. They are the unripe berries from the pepper vine, which are picked green instead of being left longer and then dried to the familiar aromatic and wrinkled blackness. The flavour is quite different, peppery of course, but far more juicy and green-tasting. Peppercorns are an excellent spice, too, for steak, sausages and sausage meat stuffings.

*500 g (1 lb) split, dried green peas*
*1 onion, chopped*
*1 carrot, sliced*
*Bouquet garni*
*Large knob butter*
*About 1 tablespoon green peppercorns*
*Salt, sugar*

SOAK the peas if necessary. Drain and put with enough water to cover them generously into a pan, plus the vegetables and herbs. But *do not add salt*, because it hardens dried vegetables. Bring to the boil and simmer until cooked. Drain off the liquid, put the peas and vegetables through a *mouli-légumes* and mix in the butter. Season with salt to taste, and a little sugar, and the green peppercorns with a little of the juice from the can – if you are not used to them, start by adding a teaspoonful and see how you like the flavour. Very good with duck and pork.

## SORREL WITH EGGS

LATTERLY WE IN ENGLAND have developed a most Athenian characteristic. We are always after some new thing. Which is fine in many ways, but in matters of food often disastrous. We are so busy running after the latest dish, that the good things we've known for centuries are forgotten as quickly as the boring ones. Take sorrel. Most of us have never eaten it, or seen it. Most people with gardens don't grow it. And yet two hundred years ago it was as popular here as it still is in France. No doubt the months-long patch of sorrel, which returns so abundantly every spring, grew near the kitchen door here as it does there, so that even in the rain one could slip out for a handful to liven the soup, or a dish of veal or eggs.

Perhaps it is natural that sorrel should have been valued for its sharpness in the days before lemons were in all the shops; it begins to appear again in March, at a time in the past when stored fruit gave out, the famine time, which the Irish used to call 'the grey blast of spring'. I heard recently about one old woman who lived on Inish Vicillan, a small island of the Blaskets seven or eight miles off the west coast of Kerry, who used to make wild sorrel tarts, sweetened with sugar, a primitive form of the herb tart made with spinach, chard leaves and any greenery you could find, which was popular in the seventeenth and eighteenth centuries (see page 262). Joan Stagles, who is collecting recipes from the Blaskets and who sent me this information, says she was struck by the resourcefulness of the idea, since 'wild sorrel grows plentifully on these islands, whereas fruit of any kind, apart from whinberries and a little rhubarb, was unobtainable except from the mainland, and even there it was scarce and dear.' Mrs Stagles also wondered whether the old lady had picked up the idea in America where she lived for some years, but I think this is unlikely. Perhaps she remembered nibbling wild sorrel leaves as a child, and thought their refreshing acid flavour would go well with sugar in pastry. Her family were the only occupants of the tiny island, and sorrel tarts do not seem to have been made elsewhere in the Blaskets, or in mainland Ireland.

For 6

*250 g (8 oz) sorrel*
*Salt, pepper*
*90 g (3 oz) butter*
*6 eggs*
*12 triangles of fried bread*
*6 wedges of orange*

REMOVE the red stalks from the sorrel. Wash it well and tear away any withered bits. Drain it, and place in a large pan over a moderate heat. Cover, and when the moisture starts to bubble, stir it about until it collapses into a dark purée. Add the seasoning and butter, once the wateriness of the sorrel has evaporated. Keep warm while you deal with the eggs. Plunge them into a pan of boiling water, and cook for precisely 6 minutes (7 if they are extra large). Run them under the tap until you can bear to handle them.

Crack the shells with a spoon and remove them very carefully because the yolks of the eggs should not be hard (if you crack the whites, the yellow parts will run through and mess up the nice appearance). Put the sorrel into a dish, with the eggs on top. The fried bread goes round the edge, and the orange wedges between the eggs.

Spinach can be used in this way, also, and is good, though less interesting. Allow at least twice as much spinach. Or you can use a mixture of the two.

## COMFREY LEAF FRITTERS

COMFREY (*Symphytum officinale*) grows in damp places alongside streams, rivers and ditches. Its large pointed leaves have a soft thick texture and are covered with slightly prickly hairs. They make the most excellent fritters, as Hannah Glasse knew in the eighteenth century. Unfortunately we have lost the habit, but as comfrey is common and costs nothing it is worth reviving in the recipe.

REMOVE the stalks from the leaves, wash and drain the leaves in a colander.

Make the batter from 150 g (5 oz) of flour, a pinch of salt, a tablespoon of oil and about 300ml (½ pt) warm water. Finally fold in the stiffly whisked white of an egg.

Dip the leaves into the batter, and fry them to a light golden brown in clarified butter or oil. They make a most elegant looking dish.

## A WHITE FRICASSEY OF MUSHROOMS

'TAKE A QUART OF FRESH MUSHROOMS, *make them clean, put them into a Sauce-pan, with three Spoonfuls [tablespoonfuls] of Water and three of Milk, and a very little Salt, set them on a quick Fire and let them boil up three Times; then take them off, grate in a little Nutmeg, put in a little beaten Mace, half a Pint of thick Cream, a Piece of butter rolled well in Flour [Beurre Manié], put it all together into the Sauce-pan, and Mushrooms all together, shake the Sauce-pan well all the Time. When it is fine and thick, dish them up; be careful they don't curdle. You may stir the Sauce-pan carefully with a Spoon all the Time.*'

This recipe comes from Hannah Glasse. When using the beurre manié, i.e. a tablespoon of butter mashed with the same of flour – add it to the sauce bit by bit. Do not allow the sauce to boil: it will thicken in 5 minutes or even less. The sauce is unlikely to curdle with modern pasteurized cream.

## MUSHROOMS, OR THE PEARL OF THE FIELDS

IN HIS *Shilling Cookery for the People*, first published in 1854, Alexis Soyer, the great chef of the Reform Club, describes a good method of cooking field mushrooms:

'BEING IN DEVONSHIRE, *at the end of September and walking across the fields before breakfast to a small farmhouse, I found three very fine mushrooms, which I thought would be a treat, but on arriving at the house I found it had no oven, a bad gridiron and a smoky coal fire. Necessity, they say, is the mother of Invention, I immediately applied to our grand and universal mamma, how I should dress my precious mushrooms, when a gentle whisper came to my ear . . .*'

SOYER COOKED THEM ON TOAST, on a stand close up to the fire, with a glass tumbler inverted over them to keep off the taint of the coal smoke. It also kept in all the delicious juices. Here is his method adapted to our happier circumstances.

Wipe the mushrooms, which should be fine large ones, and remove the earthy part of the stalk. Place them, stalks up, on rounds of toast which have been spread with clotted cream. Season them and put a little more cream into the caps. Arrange toast and mushrooms on a baking sheet, and invert one huge or several small Pyrex dishes over them. Leave for half an hour in a fairly hot oven, mark 5-6, 190-200°C (375-400°F).

'THE SIGHT *[Soyer again] when the glass is removed, is most inviting, its whiteness rivals the everlasting snows of Mont Blanc, and the taste is worthy of Lucullus. Vitellius would never have dined without it; Apicius would never have gone to Greece to seek for crawfish; and had he only half the fortune left when he committed suicide, he would have preferred to have left proud Rome and retire to some villa or cottage to enjoy such an enticing dish.*'

I wonder what 'the People' made of such learned flights of culinary fantasy, and hope it didn't put them off the recipe, which is the ideal way of treating our precious field mushrooms.

## MUSHROOMS IN SNUFFBOXES

A GOOD RECIPE for stretching a few small field mushrooms – although it is really a good system rather than a proper recipe.

FOR each person cut a 5 cm (2") slice of bread. Remove the crusts. Score a lid on one side, a good 1cm (½") deep, and about 1cm (½") inside the edge. Fry the slices in butter until crisp and golden brown. Cool slightly, then remove the lids and keep them; remove as much of the centre crumb as you can, without spoiling the boxes. Either reheat when you want to cook the mushrooms, or keep them warm in the oven.

Cook the small mushrooms with a finely chopped onion in butter. Should there be rather a swamp of mushroom liquor, raise the heat to evaporate it to juiciness. Sprinkle with a teaspoon of flour, then add just enough cream to make a binding sauce. Season, and, if you like, add a dash of sherry.

Divide the mixture between the boxes, perch the lids on top and serve.

## LAVERBREAD AND BACON

ALTHOUGH LAVER, BEING SEAWEED, tastes of the sea, it is not fishy or salty as one might expect. The flavour has a hint of oysters (sometimes it is called oyster-green), which goes well with both fish and meat. This sea vegetable is sold washed, boiled to a dark spinach-like purée, and ready to serve. Some people enjoy it spread on slices of thin crisp toast. In cooking it has an important advantage over vegetables of the land – its gelatinous moisture. This helps laverbread, as it is called, to cohere without extra binding ingredients.

Once laverbread was widely eaten in Great Britain – we are, after all, surrounded by sea. Alexis Soyer, the French chef of the Reform Club, was delighted when he discovered this unusual English food in the middle of the last century, and made it a smart society dish for a while. But now it is really a food of the western margins of the British Isles, with only the Welsh exploiting the versatility of *bava lawr*. Soyer would be disgusted. He always deplored the way in which the English turned their backs on the peasant foods of their past.

For 4

*500 g (1 lb) of prepared laverbread*
*Fine oatmeal*
*Bacon fat*

MIX the laverbread with enough oatmeal to make a loose but coherent mixture. Season it and form into little round flat cakes. Fry in bacon fat (with the breakfast bacon, for preference, in a large frying pan) until nicely browned on both sides. These little cakes also go well with a mixed grill which includes bacon, lamb cutlets, sausages and so on.

## LAVERBREAD AS A SAUCE

*250 g (8 oz) laverbread*
*Juice of 1 orange*
*Grated peel of an orange*
*Lemon juice to taste*
*Salt, pepper*

HEAT the laverbread with the orange juice and peel. Season it to taste with a little lemon juice, salt and pepper. Serve with roast lamb – particularly with Welsh roast lamb and new potatoes, and add a few slices of orange to contrast with the deep green of the sauce.

ONE FRIEND, who ran an hotel at Fishguard, used to serve this sauce with lobster. It was a most successful combination.

## MASHED POTATO WITH DULSE

THIS IS A GOOD COMBINATION - the idea came from the novelist Paul Bailey, who is an excellent cook – whether you are serving the potatoes with lamb, beef, chicken or fish.

FOR each 1 kilo (2 lb) potatoes, allow half a packet (7 g/¼ oz) dried dulse. Scrub and boil potatoes without salt, then peel and mash them in the pan. Crumble the dulse as much as you can and fry it – n.b. no soaking – in olive oil. It will turn a deep yellowish green and become crisp. Mix it into the potato, check for seasoning, add a little more oil if it seems a good idea and serve immediately.

MASHED POTATO with dulse can also be mixed with cooked salmon or other good fish, and egg, to make fishcakes.

## SEA-KALE

SEA-KALE IS DELICIOUS; and very English. It is the one vegetable we have developed from a wild species. Along the beaches of Kent, Sussex and Hampshire sand was piled round the young shoots to blanch away their bitterness. Then the shoots were cut and brought to market. 'Very delicate,' John Evelyn wrote in 1699 of this *Crambe maritima*, this wild sea-cabbage which tastes of anything but cabbage. It was soon found to do well in gardens, blanched under old crocks. Two of the master gardeners of the eighteenth century, Philip Miller and William Curtis, worked out the ways of cultivating sea-kale. Carême, the great French chef, who worked for the Prince Regent for a while, commented on the 'sikel' of the London markets which he found very appetising. It is easier to grow than asparagus; and it is as good to eat by itself. Simply tie it in bundles and cook it in boiling salted water or steam until just tender. Drain it well, and serve with melted butter or with hollandaise sauce, in the same way as asparagus.

## Samphire

Samphire or marsh samphire or glasswort (*Salicornia* spp.) has lately come back into fashion, thanks, it must be confessed, to French chefs. It's a plant that grows on low edges of land that are washed by the sea and the only area in Britain where it has been regularly eaten since Adam was a boy, is East Anglia. It can in fact be found in many other places in Britain, but for some reason people either let it go to waste, or gave up eating it. I can't think why, as it is not only freely available but perfectly delicious. On a sunny day, clad in Wellington boots, one can have a happy expedition to find it, and a fine supper on returning home.

The samphire we see around these days at great expense in smart greengroceries (or more cheaply in East Anglian fish shops) is not the same as Shakespeare's samphire that grew so spectacularly on Dover Cliffs:

> *How fearful*
> *And dizzy 'tis, to cast one's eyes so low!*
> *The crows and choughs, that wing the midway air*
> *Show scarce so gross as beetles; half way down*
> *Hangs one that gathers samphire: dreadful trade!*

That was *Crithmum maritimum*, rock samphire, and I would not recommend gathering it on a family expedition, though not all its rocky stations are as fearful as Dover cliffs. It was pickled mainly, and I must confess that I do not like it half as much as the marsh samphire of estuaries and low shores which is to-day's new smart vegetable.

You do not need to go to East Anglia for it. Joyce Molyneux at the Carved Angel in Dartmouth uses local marsh samphire in her dishes. Samphire from the Severn shores is sold as far inland as Marlborough market. In *The Good Food Directory* (Hodder) is listed a shop in Settle where it can be bought. In *British Food Finds*, Henrietta Green mentions two Welsh sources, among others. You may be able to persuade your local fishmonger to stock it in the summer season, but gathering it yourself is the best fun of all. Begin with a visit to your local history museum, if you live in a sea-edged county, and consult the county flora for possible sites. Ursula Bourne, who wrote a book on Portuguese cookery some years ago now, wrote to me about her annual expeditions to gather samphire around Little Wigborough, on the Blackwater estuary. It can be eaten raw and is very good to chew on a hot day.

The name glasswort goes back to the sixteenth century, when 'the ashes of the plant were used in making glass. They provided an impure carbonate of soda for mixing with the same. Foreign glass workers . . . may have taught the English that it was valuable in this way, like other seaside plants and like the kinds of kelp which began to be collected and calcined for the same purpose.

Gerard's names for *Salicornia* included crab grass, frog grass, and the now familiar glasswort'. (Geoffrey Grigson, *The Englishman's Flora*)

*Preparing samphire:*

SAMPHIRE looks like a miniature succulent, with its inch-long sections. Wash it well, removing extraneous greenery, roots and the lower tough part of the stalks. If you have an abundance, just break off the tips about 10 cm (4″) down: this way you have nothing but tenderness and avoid the central threads.

For eating asparagus-style, tie the samphire stalks into bundles and plunge them into a large pan half-full of unsalted, fast-boiling water. It cooks rapidly, 5 minutes plus, rather than the 10 minutes suggested by some books. Keep testing. Serve with melted butter or hollandaise or cream sauces. Nibble the edible part from the tip down, then chew away the tender part from the fibres.

For serving as a garnish or accompanying vegetable to fish or lamb, break off the tender sections only. Put them into a strainer basket or steamer and cook until soft, but still retaining a little crispness. Again don't add salt to the water, samphire is salty enough as you will discover if you chew a little raw (the tips can be used raw or lightly cooked in salads, especially good with shellfish salads).

For freezing – it freezes well – blanch samphire until half-cooked. Cool in iced water and spread on trays. When frozen hard, pack into bags.

For pickling, use the method Mary Norwak quotes in her *East Anglian Recipes – 300 years of housewife's choice* (East Anglia Magazine Publishing). To do this, cook the samphire in water with an eggcupful of vinegar, 'so that the taste of vinegar cooks in it'. Drain, cool and pack into bottling jars. Pour on good quality hot vinegar to cover. When cold, close jars. It can be eaten after a couple days, but will last through the winter.

## STUFFED TOMATOES

For 6

*12 medium-sized tomatoes*
*Herb stuffing, made without any egg (page 348)*
*30 g (1 oz) butter*

SLICE off the tops of the tomatoes, scoop out the insides, and turn the tomatoes upside down on a rack to drain. Meanwhile chop the firm part of the inside (discard juice and pips), and add it to the stuffing. Fill the tomatoes with this mixture. Arrange them in a shallow baking pan or dish which has been well greased with the butter. Replace the tops. Bake for 10-15 minutes. The temperature can be between 180°C (350°F) and 200°C (400°F), mark 4-6, or even higher, so long as the tomatoes are not allowed to burn or collapse: it will depend on what else you are cooking at the same time. Delicious with roast and grilled lamb.

## CELERY WITH CREAM

WILD CELERY IS A COMMON PLANT in many parts of Europe, but it wasn't until the sixteenth century that Italian gardeners had the idea of blanching it to remove the bitter flavour, and make it a good vegetable for the table. It was introduced into England about the middle of the seventeenth century, and soon became a popular salad. This recipe from the middle of the eighteenth century shows how delicious a cooked vegetable celery can be when combined with a rich sauce.

WASH, clean and trim three heads of celery. Cut them into pieces about 8cm (3") long, boil them in salted water until just tender, then pour off the water. Beat 150ml (¼ pt) of cream with 2 egg yolks and seasoning. Add this mixture to the hot celery and stir over a low heat until the sauce thickens without boiling. Serve immediately.

## CUCUMBER RAGOÛT

For 4

*2 cucumbers, sliced, unpeeled*
*2 medium to large onions, sliced*
*Butter*
*8 tablespoons chicken stock*
*3 tablespoons dry white wine*
*Salt, pepper, mace*
*2 rounded teaspoons flour*

BROWN the cucumbers and onions lightly in butter in two separate pans. Drain them and put them together into a saucepan with the stock and wine and seasonings. Cover the saucepan tightly, and simmer the vegetables until they are cooked – about 10 minutes or a little longer. Meanwhile mash the flour to a paste with 2 rounded teaspoons of butter. Add this mixture, bit by bit, to the vegetables so that the juices become a thick sauce which is just enough to bind them together. Correct the seasoning and serve this ragoût either on its own or as an accompaniment to chicken, veal or lamb.

THE WHITE wine gives the cucumbers a light piquancy which is delicious. An exceptionally good and unusual recipe.

## BUTTERED SQUASHES

A RECIPE FOR BUTTERED 'GOURDS, pompions, cucumbers and musk melons', from Robert May's *The Accomplisht Cook* of 1660. Try it with courgettes, custard marrows, or with the Little Gem squashes that some seedsmen are selling these days. Cucumbers are not so successful.

BAKE the squashes in their skins in the oven at mark 5, 190°C (375°F) until tender – the time taken will depend obviously on the size of the squash. Pompions, i.e. pumpkins, could take up to 2 hours. If you are using Little Gem squashes in the autumn, when their skins have hardened, you will do better to boil rather than bake them: the same would apply to courgettes half-grown to marrow size with tough skins (one friend suggest scoring them round the centre so that they can easily be halved for stuffing when cooked).

At the same time put a covered casserole into the oven containing a medium chopped onion and twice its weight in sliced, peeled Cox's Orange Pippin, with a large knob of butter, for each person. When the onion and apple are tender, mash them together with extra butter if necessary, and a seasoning of salt, sugar and pepper. The mixture should not be too salty.

When the squashes are cooked, halve them and scoop out their seeds. Season them lightly and pile the apple and onion stuffing into the centre. Return to the oven for a while, to brown the tops slightly.

Serve small individual squashes on buttered toast. Surround larger squashes with triangles of buttered toast.

NOTE: Robert May also suggests mixing this onion and apple purée with currants and serving it on toast. Scatter the top with a mixture of sugar and cinnamon. This goes well with duck or pork – any meat that you might reasonably serve apple sauce with.

## COURGETTE AND PARSNIP BOATS

A DISH FROM JULIA CHILD, the famous American cookery writer, but I do not apologize for including it, as I hope it may become part of our national repertoire. We have been cooking parsnips for centuries; we have recently developed a passion for courgettes. Who would have thought the two would go so well together?

For 6

*6 courgettes, each about 15cm (6") long*
*Salt, pepper*
*75 g (2½ oz) butter*
*1 kilo (2 lb) parsnips*
*5 tablespoons cream*

TRIM courgette ends, then halve them longways and scoop out the centre seedy part to form boats. Blanch them for 5 minutes in boiling salted water. Do not overcook, or they will collapse. Drain and arrange them on a shallow ovenproof dish. Season and brush them with 2-3 tablespoons of melted butter. Set aside while you deal with the parsnips.

Peel, cut up and boil the parsnips. Reduce them to smoothness in a blender with the rest of the butter and the cream. Check the seasoning, and reheat just before the meal.

Reheat the courgette boats at mark 7, 220°C (425°F), for 5 minutes in the upper part of the oven. Quickly pipe the hot parsnip purée into the boats with a meringue or star tube. Serve at once.

I am no enthusiast for fancy touches. They are so often an alibi in this country for bad food – radish roses dotted over an inedible salad, nasty butter-cream stars on a margarine cake – but in this particular instance the piped purée does look much more attractive than purée put in with a spoon. It's good to be stylish with parsnips, for a change.

## ROAST PARSNIPS

CHOOSE medium-sized parsnips. Peel and cut them into four pieces each. Blanch them in boiling water for 5 minutes.

Put them round or under a joint of roasting beef, so that they become soft and richly brown in the juices and fat of the meat. Allow one medium parsnip for each person (weighing about 180 g (6 oz), if no potatoes are being served.

Alternatively, cook them in a separate pan of beef dripping or oil on a shelf above the beef. They can share a pan with roasting potatoes. This method will make them crisper outside, but one runs the risk that they may become too crusty.

## BUTTERED PARSNIPS

'PARSNIPS NEED BUTTER' should be inscribed in letters of fire in every kitchen. Without butter, or an equivalent fat of quality (which does not mean margarine, but good beef dripping), they can be a depressing vegetable. Cooked this way, they are one of winter's best dishes.

For 4

*750 g (1½ lb) parsnips*
*Salt, pepper*
*90 g (3 oz) butter*
*Chopped parsley*

PEEL the parsnips thinly. Cut off the tops and tails and quarter them into wedges. Remove the inner core if it seems at all woody; divide the wedges into convenient strips. Blanch them for 10 minutes in boiling salted water – they should be almost cooked. Drain them, cut them into smallish pieces and return them to a clean pan with the butter. Shake them from time to time and keep them over a low heat to finish cooking. They should look golden and appetizing and slightly soft, but not mushy or brown. Taste and season them again, this time adding plenty of pepper and the parsley.

## CREAMED PARSNIPS

COMPLETE the recipe above but before adding the parsley, pour in 150ml (¼ pt) of double, or double and single cream. Heat through, and turn into a shallow dish. Serve as a first course, or as a supper dish, with toast or in pastry cases.

## PARSNIP AND SHELLFISH SALAD

COOK the parsnip strips (see above) in salted water. Drain and mix them with an olive oil vinaigrette. Add shelled prawns, or pieces of lobster (or some cold turbot or monkfish) and arrange on a shallow dish. Scatter with chopped parsley and chives.

## PARSNIP AND WATERCRESS SALAD

AN early seventeenth-century salad. Boil and peel some smallish parsnips. Cut them in quarters and dress them while they are still warm with an olive oil and wine vinaigrette. Arrange them round a dish with, or on, lettuce heart leaves, and fill the centre with watercress. Scatter them with toasted pine kernels or almonds or hazelnuts to give an extra crunch – use the appropriate nut oil for the vinaigrette, if you like.

## CARROTS IN 1599

I AM INDEBTED TO MALCOLM THICK for referring me to Richard Gardiner's *Profitable Instructions for the Manuring, Sowing and Planting of Kitchin Gardens*. It was published in 1599, with a second edition in 1603, and is particularly interesting for the picture it gives of how the poor were fed in times of scarcity, and how vegetables were used to supplement the shortage of bread. Mr

Gardiner was a great believer in carrots, and indicates ways of cooking them that we still use. I have modernized his spelling but not his expression.

'It is not unknown to the City of London, and many other towns and cities on the sea coast, what great abundance of carrots are brought by foreign nations to this land, whereby they have received yearly great sums of money and commodities out of this land, and all by carelessness of the people of this realm of England, which do not endeavour themselves for their own profits therein, but that this last dearth and scarcity hath somewhat urged the people to prove many ways for their better relief whereby I hope the benefit of carrot roots are profitable, I will reveal my knowledge herein; and first the use of them amongst the better sort by the cooks.

The cooks will take carrots divided in pieces, and boil them to season their stewed broth, and doth wonderful well therein as daily is known in service to the better sort. Also carrots roots are boiled with powdered [i.e. salted] beef, and eaten therewith: and as some do report, a few carrots do save one quarter of beef in the eating of a whole beef: and to be boiled and eaten with pork, and all other boiled meat of flesh amongst the common sort of people, and amongst the poorer sort also: carrots of red colours are desired of many to make dainty salads, for roast mutton or lamb with vinegar and pepper. Also carrots shred or cut small one or two of them, and boiled in pottage of any kind, doth effectually make those pottage good, for the use of the common sort. Carrots well boiled and buttered is a good dish for hungry or good stomachs. Carrots in necessity and dearth, are eaten of the poor people, after they be well boiled, instead of bread and meat. Many people will eat carrots raw, and do digest well in hungry stomachs: they give good nourishment to all people, and not hurtful to any, whatsoever infirmities they be diseased of, as by experience doth prove by many to be true. Carrots are good to be eaten with salt fish. Therefore sow carrots in your gardens, and humbly praise God for them, as for a singular and great blessing.'

## CARROT AND POTATO CAKE

THIS IS A SIMPLE but unusually delicious thing to serve with poultry, meat or fish. It looks pretty, too, and the ingredients are easily come by. It's from Alison Johnson's *Scarista Style*, like the Cauliflower and Fennel Soup on page 13. Much to be recommended.

For 6

*60 g (2 oz) butter*
*1 medium onion, finely chopped*
*250 g (8 oz) carrots, scraped or peeled, and grated*
*500 g (1 lb) potatoes, scraped or peeled, and thinly sliced*
*½ teaspoon salt*

PREHEAT the oven to mark 4-5, 180-190°C (350-375°F). Choose a 20 cm (8″) sandwich tin or *moule à manquer* about 2-3 cm (generous inch) deep. Cut a circle of greaseproof paper to go on top of the vegetables as they cook.

Using half the butter, grease the tin. Melt the other half and cook the onion in it until it is golden brown. Mix into the carrots, and add the salt. Spread half the carrot over the base of the tin. Cover evenly with the potatoes, and top with a final layer of carrot. Put the paper circle on top and press everything down.

Bake for about 25 minutes, until a knife goes easily through the centre. Remove the tin from the oven, press the contents down again with, for example, a wooden mallet or potato masher. Leave a couple of minutes before turning out on to a hot plate.

## Jerusalem Artichoke and Shellfish Salad

AN IDEAL RECIPE if you can grow the smooth *Fuseau* variety of Jerusalem artichokes: they are available from one or two nurserymen. I have not seen them on sale at the greengroceries in this country, but you may be able to pick out the least knobbly ones for this salad, and buy a few extra so that you can cut neat slices (debris for soup).

For 6

*8 large unknobbly Jerusalem artichokes*
*2 tablespoons lemon juice*
*4 tablespoons hazelnut or sunflower oil*
*1 tablespoon white wine vinegar*
*Salt, pepper*
*6 large cooked Mediterranean prawns, 12 langoustines or 24 pink prawns*
*3 large or 6 smaller scallops, lightly cooked*
*Watercress, lamb's lettuce or oak leaf lettuce*
*2 tablespoons toasted, chopped hazelnuts*
*Chopped coriander, parsley or chives*

SCRUB and cook the artichokes in salted water with the lemon juice. Drain and run under the cold tap. Strip off the skin and any bumpy bits, and trim them so that you can cut neat slices. Put into a dish.

Mix oil, vinegar and seasoning and pour over the warm artichoke slices. Leave them to cool, turning them once or twice.

Remove shells from the edible parts of the prawns or langoustines, leaving heads in place. Cut each scallop in half, then slice into 24 half-circles.

Arrange greenery in a ring in a shallow dish, or make little mounds on individual plates. Arrange artichoke slices and scallop pieces in the centre or on top and scatter with hazelnuts and herbs. Finish off with the prawns or langoustines.

## LEEK AND ONION PUDDING

WE ASSOCIATE LEEKS MAINLY WITH WALES, and have done so since at least the time of Shakespeare. By the middle of the seventeenth century they were out of fashion for all but the poor, though gentry in Wales still ate them.

Nowadays I suspect that leeks are grown with more enthusiasm in the North-East of England and the eastern border country of Scotland than in Wales. Leek competitions, leek festivals, are held in Northumbria; and the best known variety of leek for gardeners is the Musselburgh, so that it was Scottish growers rather than Welsh who improved on the old strains.

Northern leek growers have been busy for a long time. Visitors to the hospital at Sherburn, particularly those who go to admire the beautiful garden in the spring, may be surprised to learn that the lepers who first occupied the place under the protection of the Bishop of Durham were keen leek (and bean) growers. They were provided with a good basic diet by the foundation, but grew their own greens, leeks and broad beans.

This leek pudding was popular in the North-East in my childhood, when filling stomachs as cheaply as possible was the main concern of most women, such was the poverty of the Depression. I think it may still be popular because it tastes so good. You can add 250 g (8 oz) bacon to the leeks, or serve the pudding instead of vegetables with boiled beef or gammon. In the old days these puddings were rolled round the filling, tied in a floured cloth and boiled in water, along with the meat if there was any. Do it this way if you like, but I prefer the crisp outside that comes from steaming the pudding in a basin.

For 6

*Suet crust (see page 243)*
*1 huge onion, chopped*
*Leeks*
*Butter*
*Salt, pepper, teaspoon dried sage*

LINE a 1½ litre (2½ pt) pudding basin with suet crust. Put in a third of the onion, then enough chopped leek to make a good layer, then another third of onion, a layer of leek and a final layer of onion; they should fill the cavity to within 3-4 cm (1½″) of the basin top. Season, add sage and some generous dabs of butter. Cover with pastry and steam in the usual way (see page 244) for about 3 hours.

IF YOU serve this pudding on its own, provide some melted butter by way of sauce.

## LEEK PIE

VARIATIONS OF THIS PIE occur in Cornwall, Wales, Burgundy, Picardy and Flanders. I confess that the onion and the flour are two additions made by a young French friend in Touraine, but they are such a good idea it seems a shame not to take them over from her. However, no one can deny that leeks are a thoroughly English dish – think of the many leek place names indicating the existence of the all-important leek-enclosure (a more sympathetic idea than the Scottish kail – cabbage – yard).

PASTRY
*Puff or shortcrust pastry, see page 225*
*Beaten egg to glaze*

FILLING
*1 onion, sliced*
*90 g (3 oz) butter*
*500 g (1 lb) leeks, trimmed and sliced*
*125 g (4 oz) back bacon rashers*
*125 g (4 oz) clotted or double cream*
*1 heaped teaspoon flour*
*Salt, pepper*

PREPARE the filling in advance, and let it cool. Cook the onion gently in half the butter in a frying pan. When it is soft and golden, add the leeks and the remaining butter. Continue to cook slowly until the leeks are reduced to a soft mass. Take the pan off the heat, add the bacon cut into 1 cm (½″) strips. Mix the flour with the cream and beat the mixture into the leeks so that everything is smoothly amalgamated. Season thoroughly and cool.

Line a 22-23 cm (8″-9″) tart tin, preferably the kind with a removable base, with just over half the pastry. Put in the filling. Brush the rim with a little beaten egg and cover with a pastry lid. Make a hole in the centre for the steam to escape. Decorate in a restrained manner and brush over the top with beaten egg. Put into the oven at mark 7, 220°C (425°F), for about 15 minutes until the pastry is nicely browned, and in the case of puff pastry well risen. Reduce the heat to mark 4, 180°C (350°F), for a further 20-30 minutes.

## LITTLE LEEK TARTS

HERE IS A DELICATE WAY of using a vegetable that always seems rustic and homely. These little tarts can be served as a first course, when you might make them double-crust, or round the joint of roast meat instead of serving separate vegetables.

The main problem with leeks is buying them. On account of all the superfluous greenery, unpackaged leeks seem to be going out of favour. People turn to the trimmed, plastic-wrapped kind – they can see what they are getting for their money, and they are easier to cram into a shopping basket. I think this is a mistake. Earthy, green-topped leeks usually taste better because they have come straight from the field without washing and delay. To be on the safe side, buy 50 per cent more weight than recipes suggest. Any left over can easily be used in soups, sauces, stock-making and so on. On the other hand, if you are slightly short on weight, once you trim the leeks, make it up with chopped onion.

For 6-8

*1 kilo (2 lb) trimmed leeks*
*2 heaped tablespoons butter*
*Salt, pepper*
*2-3 tablespoons cream*
*Puff pastry, see page 225*
*Wensleydale or Cheddar cheese*
*Beaten egg (see recipe)*

HALVE, wash and chop the leeks coarsely. Melt butter in a heavy pan and tip in the leeks. Cover tightly and stew slowly so that the leeks gradually melt to softness. Check after 10-15 minutes and remove the lid if the leeks have given off much liquid. Leave to cook for a further 10-15 minutes, stirring occasionally. The leeks must not stick or colour; they should end up just moist, but in no way wet. By raising the heat and stirring, you can concentrate all the flavour so that nothing has to be drained away.

Season the leeks and liquidize them with just enough cream to make a purée. Roll out the pastry. Cut 24 circles large enough to fit into tart tins. Divide the purée between them. Sprinkle over each one a teaspoon of grated cheese. You can, if you like, roll out the pastry trimmings and cut out lids, or leave them uncovered – this will depend on the rest of the meal and how you intend to serve them. Or you can cover half the tarts.

If you do cover them, brush them over with beaten egg. Bake for 15-20 minutes at mark 7, 220°C (425°F), or until the tarts are lightly browned and puffed up. If possible, serve immediately.

## LEEK, PEA OR ASPARAGUS SAUCE

WE'RE WELL USED TO TOMATO SAUCES. I don't know why we haven't gone further along the road, using other vegetables in the same kind of way. With a blender – better than a processor – you can achieve a smooth emulsion of a sauce-like consistency. Make it on the apparently thick side: it will not taste heavy, and you can smooth out the texture a little more with cream, or butter, or as in the following recipe which includes extra liquid, *beurre manié*:

*375 g (12 oz) prepared, sliced leek, or shelled peas, or sliced, tender asparagus spears*
*150ml (¼ pt) light stock or water*
*About 100 ml (3½ fl oz) soured cream*
*About 3 tablespoons clotted cream or unsalted butter*
*Salt, pepper*

STEW vegetables with stock or water in a covered pan until just cooked. Liquidize to a purée, sieve to remove any fibre or tough bits, and reheat with the cream(s). If using butter, beat in at the last moment. Season to taste.

## TEISEN NIONOD (WELSH ONION CAKE)

For 6

*1 kilo (2 lb) firm potatoes, preferably Desirée or waxy new potatoes*
*500 g (1 lb) onions*
*125-150 g (4-5 oz) butter*
*Pepper and salt*

PEEL or scrape the potatoes, then slice them paper-thin, on a mandolin or the cucumber blade of a grater, into a bowl of cold water. Swish them about well to get rid of the starchy juice, then dry them in a clean tea towel. Peel and slice the onions.

Take a shallow dish or oblong cake tin and grease it with a butter paper (if you intend to turn the cake out at the end, it is a good idea to line the dish or tin with Bakewell paper or foil before greasing it). Put in a layer of potatoes, then a layer of onions and so on, finishing with potatoes. Season the layers and dot them with butter, leaving about 30 g (1 oz) to melt and pour over the top layer. Cover the dish with foil – don't worry if the vegetables mount up above the dish, they subside as they cook. Bake at mark 4, 180°C (350°F), for 1½ hours, removing the foil for the last half-hour so the top can brown. Alternatively bake at mark 6, 200°C (400°F), for an hour. This is a good tempered dish, which will cook at most temperatures convenient to your purposes – just allow more or less time.

When the vegetables are cooked but not too soft, put a serving dish on top of the tin and reverse it quickly. Ease the paper or foil and remove the tin. Flash under the grill for a few minutes to brown the top. There is, on the other hand, no reason why you shouldn't serve the onion cake in its cooking dish like a French gratin. If you decide on this kind of treatment, there is no need to line the dish with paper or foil.

I find the texture of this dish very agreeable, but if you want the French combination of softness underneath and crispness on top, pour in 150ml (¼ pt) of beef stock before cooking starts. Or the same quantity of cream mixed with 6 tablespoons water.

You can also put a joint of lamb on top – Welsh lamb, or one of those tiny gigots of Soay or other primitive breeds – so that its juices soak into the vegetables; if you do this, reduce the butter to 30 g (1 oz), add a little stock, and pour off any surplus fat at the end. For this version, do not be tempted to add cream. A little thyme will enhance the fresh leanness of the lamb.

## PAN HAGGERTY

AN APPETIZING NORTH-EASTERN DISH of potatoes and onion, which should be better known all over the country – and might be if it weren't for the insistently homely nature of north-easterners, who would prefer death to appearing grand in matters of food. The cheese and the pan-frying in beef dripping make it taste quite different from the Welsh *Teisen Nionod*, or a French gratin, though in idea and construction it much resembles them.

For 4

*500 g (1 lb) firm potatoes*
*250 g (8 oz) onions*
*125 g (4 oz) grated Cheddar cheese*
*Beef dripping*
*Salt, pepper*

PREPARE the vegetables as for *Teisen Nionod* (above). Melt about 60 g (2 oz) of dripping in a 20-23 cm (8″-9″) frying pan. Remove it from the heat, and build up the potatoes, onion and cheese in layers, with seasoning, finishing with potato. Put the pan on the heat again and fry the vegetables gently at first, until they begin to cook, then at the end a little faster so that the underneath browns. Invert the pan haggerty on to a plate, put a little more dripping in the pan and slide it back again to brown on the other side. Alternatively leave it in the pan and brown it under the grill.

## GLAZED TURNIPS

*1 kilo (2 lb) young summer turnips*
*60-90 g (2-3 oz) butter*
*1 level tablespoon sugar*
*Freshly ground black pepper*
*Chopped parsley*

PEEL the turnips, which must be young and sweet, not the kind that is only fit for cattle. Cut them into rough cubes of about 1cm (⅓″). Plunge them into a pan of boiling salted water, and leave them to boil for 5 minutes. Try a cube – it should be almost cooked but slightly resistant. If it is still hard, continue the cooking for another 3-5 minutes. This blanching process is very important, and it can be continued for longer if the turnips are beginning to feel their age. The point is that they should not be strong-tasting, neither should they be mushy.

Strain off all the water, and transfer the turnip to a large frying pan in which the butter has been melted. Sprinkle the sugar over them. Cook over a moderate heat, turning the pieces over regularly so that they begin to caramelize slightly to a pale golden brown. Sprinkle with parsley and serve.

Turnips cooked in this way are delicious with roast duck, or baked ham.

## CHESTNUTS AS A VEGETABLE

For 4

*500 g (1 lb) chestnuts*
*1 large onion, chopped*
*1 clove garlic, chopped fine*
*60 g (2 oz) butter*
*60 g (2 oz) bacon, cut into strips (smoked or green, according to taste and the main item of the meal)*
*2 Cox's eating apples, peeled, cored, diced*
*Salt, plenty of black pepper*

PEEL the chestnuts (see page 8), and chop them coarsely into knobbly pieces about 1cm (⅓") long. Cook onion and garlic slowly in the butter in a covered pan, until they are golden and transparent. Stir in the bacon; raise the heat slightly but be careful that the butter does not burn. When the bacon looks transparent, add the diced apple. Fry for a few minutes until the mixture looks and smells savoury and appetizing. Lastly add the chestnuts and cook until they are thoroughly heated through, and the pan juices reduced to a small amount of liquid. Season, particularly with pepper, and serve with chicken, guineafowl, turkey and game – or with pork, salt pork and veal.

THIS MIXTURE can be used to stuff a bird before it is roasted. Or it can serve as a garnish.

If the apple is omitted, it makes a particularly good dish when mixed with boiled brussels sprouts or lightly cooked cabbage. For a first course, or a supper dish, blanch 20-24 cabbage leaves in boiling salted water for 10 minutes. Put a good tablespoon of the above mixture into each leaf; roll the leaves up into little packages, turning the sides in, and place them in a single layer in a large pan. Pour enough light stock or water to come 1½ cm (½") up the pan. Cover and simmer for 30 minutes. Reduce the pan liquid to a few tablespoons and beat in 60 g (2 oz) butter. Pour over the rolls and serve.

# FISH

FISH IS THE GREAT SCANDAL OF ENGLISH EATING, and of English cooking. We live in islands surrounded by a sea that teems with fish. Yet we eat fewer and fewer kinds, and those not always the best, even allowing for different judgements in matters of taste. I suppose this is the fault of commerce – the commercial desire being always to deal in tons of three or four species, rather than in hundred weights of thirty or fifty – but we have connived in its malpractices. After all, commerce is just as important in other European countries, yet the choice of fish available to the private customer is ebullient and high in quality by comparison. If you go to Madrid or to Alsace, both places which are much further from the sea than anywhere in Britain, fish counters sparkle with choice and brilliance. When I go shopping in Tours market, over 120 miles from the wholesale fish market at Nantes, the main counter has a choice of over 100 different kinds of fish, including shellfish, freshwater as well as saltwater fish, smoked and dried fish. And the quality is an education to an English cook.

The truth is that we have a very poorly organized trade, run by people without ambition or desire to improve things. There are of course exceptions, but too few of them. I think of Jack Shiells, of C. Newnes, now retired, at Billingsgate, who was responsible for the importation of fish from the Seychelles, those glorious rainbow creatures of bright turquoise and red and gold, which arrive from a quarter of the way round the globe in better condition than fish from our own seas. And at a reasonable price. Yet how many of them do we see out in the provinces? Such energies as the trade possesses seems to be concentrated solely on the restaurants of the capital, and the few fishmongers who have the intelligence and energy to serve their customers well.

My model fishmonger is, alas, not British but American. George Berkowitz of Boston. He runs a chain of restaurants in the city and its area, about five or six of them, under the name of his company Legal Seafood. Every morning his buyers, ex-fishermen who know about fish from the sharp end, are down at the quay and on the phone to other ports of the New England coast, choosing for that day's menus. What they buy goes to a central commissariat, where it is prepared not just for the restaurant kitchens, but also for the fresh fish counters that are beside the restaurant tills (when you pay for your excellent lunch, you are then naturally tempted to buy your dinner). There, too, they make the accompanying salads and sauces required. The design of the restaurants is delightful, strong in wood, simple but elegant lettering, a comfortable but undaunting ambience that attracts secretaries, mothers out shopping with their babies and toddlers, solicitors, professors from Havard – a classless mix. You cannot book a table, but while you queue you can eat oysters and drink white wine. Then when you get your table and give an order, your dish will arrive the moment it is cooked so that you can eat it at its best, whether or not the rest of the dishes are ready as well. The range of the menu goes from the cheapest to the most expensive, from scrod to shad roe in the spring season or Maine lobster from the vivarium tank. The cooking is simple and direct, to show off the stiff-alive freshness of the fish. I should also add that Mr Berkowitz flies fish in to central America as well, so that restaurants hundreds of miles from the coast can put the morning's catch on their dinner menu the same day.

Mr Berkowitz runs a small company with his sons. He is always looking for new aims, to keep everyone on their toes. I have tried to persuade him to set up in England, but why should he with that vast continent to conquer? The nearest to him, though inevitably on a much smaller scale, is the Loch Fyne Oyster Company, run by John Noble and Andrew Lane at Cairndow in Argyll. They grow oysters in the loch, smoke salmon, cure gravadlax and pickle herring in the Scandinavian style: moreover they make a central point for energetic fishermen and other fish farmers, despatching their wares to restaurants and private customers all over Britain. If I order langoustines, oysters and salmon for a party one morning, it will be delivered by the following midday. An excellent service, but one that I shouldn't need to use at all being only forty odd miles from Bristol fish market: local shops should be able to supply what I need in top quality, but they make no attempt at choice and true freshness. So much of their stock is limp with that grey, veiled look to indicate that it is far from being the top of the catch.

The Loch Fyne Oyster Company opened an excellent small restaurant in Argyll, run on Berkowitz lines, close to the water in 1987. In 1990 another one was opened in Nottingham and a third in 1992 in Eltham. I hope these will be as great a success as the Scottish restaurant, and will stimulate an empire-building zeal in their proprietors. There are far too few restaurants of any kind in this country selling top quality, simple food at reasonable prices. As the architect, Edward Cullinan, remarked in a different context: 'We have enough masterpieces, what we need is a better standard of ordinariness.' The trouble is that the Loch Fyne restaurants cannot be considered as ordinary, when you look around at the rest of the country: my contention is that they should be ordinary, that we should be able to take such quality for granted.

Of course it is not only the freshness I complain about, it is the limited choice. Take squid, for instance. Most of us believe it to be an exclusively Mediterranean pleasure, something you eat on holiday in Greece, Italy or Spain. But squid of excellent quality are fished in our waters.

There are parallel mysteries about our appetite for freshwater fish. We neglect pike, one of the best for firm sweetness. It is the angler's favourite fish, more pike are caught than anything else I believe, yet you never see it on sale: someone told me recently that they are just left on the bank to die (they used to be put back in the water, but their predatory habits have altered this). Perch, wild carp and tench rarely come our way either. Above all, we have taken to a neglect of the eel – except when it's embedded in jelly, which is not the best way of eating so delicate and fine-textured a fish. When I first wrote this book, eels were exported to Holland from Britain – that was why we were deprived of them. Now it seems that their lead levels are so high that they cannot be exported to Europe. Pollution has continued our deprivation. I find this a scandal. If you want to eat the tiny elvers that swim every springtime up the Severn water, you need to go to Spain, where elvers briefly cooked in oil with garlic and chili are on many menus. A lovely dish.

When *English Food* first came out, it seemed that fishmongers would soon be stocking unfamiliar species from the lower depths of the sea to take the place of over-fished sole and herring and cod. There were some experiments, but the strangers have not materialized. I suspect they were not so good to eat nor as beautiful as the newcomers we occasionally see from the Seychelles.

Since the mid-seventies, the great difference in the fish trade has been the produce from farming. In the main salmon, but a certain amount of turbot and miniature Princess scallops, which are young versions of the small Queen scallop. Trout farming was the first to get going, and it was overdone. The gap between farmed and wild was too great. The trout has turned into a mass market fish for an ignorant public: the only tolerable way of eating it is smoked. Farmed salmon can vary widely, and I deplore the English habit of not labelling the production from different farms as I deplore the habit of not labelling chicken with their lifespan and details of diet and rearing. In Norway, for instance, if you want top quality farm salmon – which is almost as good as wild salmon that has been well-caught and well-handled – you go for Mowi fish. They are tagged and numbered and identified. You can rely on them for quality. In Britain where everything is, it seems, ruled by price, you can buy good farm salmon one week and poor farm salmon the next without knowing until you have it on the plate. A lot of it is overcoloured, too. I detest that bright, tinned salmon colour and would welcome the choice of buying paler fish as an alternative.

The trade will, of course, maintain that the British just refuse to pay for decent quality fresh food. They'll put their money into confectionery, bought cakes and biscuits, home improvements, gambling, but not into the diet that dictates their health and vitality. This has an element of truth about it. Nonetheless, good cheese shops flourish, and so do better bakeries, so it cannot be entirely just. I suspect that people are unwilling to pay for greying, limp fish which is all they are offered. The few intelligent fishmongers do not appear to go bankrupt – but of course they do work harder, and use their heads more.

By tradition, the prime English fish – shellfish and smoked fish apart – are still turbot, sole, red mullet, sea trout, salmon, pike, eel, wild trout and herring. Brill, sea bass, grey mullet and John Dory come pretty close for quality. Fresh inshore cod is a revelation after cod on ice from the Arctic. Whiting, too, when small, fresh and pearly, are excellent when they are given the delicate treatment they deserve. I never used to like plaice, until I went to Ireland and discovered just how delicious it can be when fresh from the water: then it is one of the best flat fish, though nothing can ever come up to a good Dover sole.

Smoked and salted fish are another matter, altogether on their own, the supplementary creation of another edible substance as different from the original as salami is from pork. Luckily, we retain these old methods of curing and salting. There are few choicer things to be eaten than undyed kippers and bloaters, the best silvery Finnan haddock or smokies or smoked salmon or smoked eel. We have not been greatly given to salting fish. I do not quite know why. Scandinavian, German and Dutch cooks do such brilliant things with salted herrings – it is incredible that we have never copied them on any scale. We have no festival similar to the Dutch celebration of fresh caught young herrings in the spring: they have been lightly salted on board ship, and are eaten with no further preparation. A most delicious and simple treat. Then there is salt cod which can be the basis of the most piquant and satisfying dishes, as every Portuguese cook knows.

Potting fish in butter (which has been the fat for northern fish as olive oil has been the fat for preserving fish from the Mediterranean) is a practice that goes back to Tudor times, but commercially the potting of fish has lost much of its savour and importance. Whereas potted shrimps were a delicacy before the last war, the modern practice of refrigerating the shrimps before putting them down in butter has been fatal. The only thing to do is pot your own shrimps – or crab or lobster or trout – if you can come by them in a truly fresh state. At least it's not difficult (don't forget the spices, mace in particular, and do use lightly salted Danish butter, as Lancashire shrimp packers have done since the beginning of the century).

The best of the canned fish are traditional imports – brisling from Norway, sardines in – *n.b. olive oil* – oil from Portugal and Brittany, and of course anchovies, which have been a part of English cooking for hundreds of years. Few fish retain more consistent quality than the tiny brisling which go under the brand name of Skippers. They are not a sardine, biologically speaking, but they are smoked and most delicate to eat.

As to shellfish, there have been changes and some improvements since I first wrote this book. Oysters were already being farmed in the mid-seventies, but they are of much better quality now, and much more available than they were then. The finest natives, which Caesar conquered Britain for, are still an expensive luxury. The new farm oyster is a different type, the less sensitive and less subtle oyster, originally from Portugal (*Crassostrea angulata*), or more usually these days from the Pacific (*Crassostrea gigas*). This latter oyster, as its Latin name suggests, is an enormous creature in maturity: the advantage to the farmer is that it can be harvested young when it is roughly the same sort of size as the native or Portuguese oyster, having taken less time to get there. If these oysters are grown in the best estuarine conditions, their quality is very high indeed.

The cheapest shellfish are crabs and mussels, the latter being so inexpensive that they are a luxurious bargain. Crabs are dearer these days than they once were, and so more difficult to buy: unfortunately you rarely see them in their live state, which means that much of the time they are boiled in bulk and overcooked. Visiting Cromer a few years ago, I found this to be the case with the much vaunted local crabs. They lack succulence, verging on the dry. A great disappointment. If ever you get the chance to buy live crabs – especially live spider crabs – and live lobsters, take it. The same applies to prawns and langoustines (i.e. Dublin Bay prawns, *Nephrops norvegicus*, or scampi), though in the latter case I do find that Loch Fyne Oysters can be trusted to cook them properly. Incidentally, never buy made-up scampi dishes – you are not getting the real thing: what manufacturers do is push the fish together into a machine that extrudes them in a long roll and this is chopped off at scampi-like lengths – which does them no good at all.

Scallops are the sweetest of all shellfish, but the best go off to Spain, Paris and top restaurants. If you buy frozen ones, remember you are paying for quite a lot of water. Since visiting the Princess scallop fishery at Ardtoe in the Highlands I have been keeping my eye open for these tiny, sugar-lump-sized delicacies at local fishmongers (without success). We went out into the loch and hauled up the bundles from the line strung out from buoys. Soon knives were flashing and we were being given the tiny scallops to eat all fresh from the sea – what a feast it was!

There is one thing I should say about cooking fish, so that it does not need repeating every recipe. Season fish in advance of cooking, at least half an hour, better still longer. It improves the flavour and firms up the texture in a most striking way. This has been one of my best discoveries in recent years. If the fish is by some rare chance very fresh, it then needs no more than slicing and serving with a dressing of lemon and olive oil, and a light scatter of an appropriate herb, salt and pepper. Mostly, of course, you will need to cook it further.

# SALTWATER FISH

### Herrings in Oatmeal

THE BEST WAY OF EATING large plump herrings (small ones are best cooked without being filleted). If you like, rashers of streaky bacon can be fried first and their fat used for cooking the fish. Bacon, especially smoked bacon, goes well with herring (and with cod and monkfish, even with scallops if the rashers are thin and used with a light hand). Serve the crisp rashers with the fish, plus a few new potatoes.

For 6

*6 herrings*
*90 g (3 oz) fine or medium oatmeal*
*125 g (4 oz) butter*
*Salt, pepper*
*Lemon quarters*

ASK the fishmonger to fillet the herrings from the back, so that they look like uncured kippers when they are opened out, with the thin part in the centre. Season with salt and pepper and leave for a while. Just before cooking, press them, skin side and cut side, into the oatmeal so that they are coated with it. Fry them in the butter until cooked and lightly browned. Serve them with lemon quarters.

## DEVILLED HERRING OR MACKEREL

A PEPPERY MUSTARD TREATMENT brings out the good qualities of such fish as herring and mackerel.

For 6

*6 very fresh herring or mackerel, with soft roes*
*3 level tablespoons Dijon mustard*
*2 teaspoons sunflower or groundnut oil*
*¼ teaspoon Cayenne pepper*
*Salt*
*100 g (3½ oz) fine dry breadcrumbs*
*100 ml (3½ fl oz) melted butter*
*Parsley sprigs*

CLEAN fish, removing the roes carefully and leaving the heads in place. Rinse fish and dry them, slashing them two or three times diagonally on each side. Rinse and dry roes.

Mix mustard, oil, pepper and a little salt. Brush roes with this mixture and restore them to their cavities. Brush the herrings over, too, then roll in the breadcrumbs.

Preheat the grill. Line pan with foil. Lay herrings on rack, sprinkle with melted butter and slide under the heat. Baste from time to time, and turn once. Total cooking time, allowing for basting, will be about 12 minutes. Serve garnished with parsley. Lemon quarters and boiled new potatoes or bread and butter go well with this dish.

## SOUSED HERRINGS

HERRING COOKED THIS WAY MAKES A GOOD COLD DISH, so long as you don't overdo the vinegar. I recommend you follow the Scandinavian practice of serving them with a bowl of cream, beaten with lemon juice, salt and pepper, and flavoured with chives.

For 6

*6 fine herring, beheaded and boned*
*Salt, pepper*
*150ml (¼ pt) best malt vinegar*
*1 level tablespoon pickling spice*
*1 small hot red chili, deseeded and cut in strips*
*3 young bay leaves, halved*
*3 shallots or 1 medium onion, sliced*

PREHEAT the oven to mark 3, 160°C (325°F). When cleaning the herrings, set aside the roes for another dish. Season the cut sides and roll them up, starting with the head end and securing them with cocktail sticks. Tuck them into a deep close-fitting dish. Pour over the vinegar with an equal amount of water. Scatter over the spices and put pieces of bay leaf between the rolled herring, with the shallot or onion. Cover with foil and bake for about 45 minutes, or until the fish are just done (they will cook a little more as they cool down).

If the cooking dish is unsuitable for the table, remove the rolls to a serving dish. Strain over some of the liquid. Pick the more sightly spices and pieces of bay from the sieve and arrange on top and around the herring. Serve on their own, with wholemeal or rye bread and butter, or as part of a salad meal.

## WELSH SUPPER HERRINGS

(Swper Sgadan)

THE COMBINATION of herrings, potato and apple is popular all over northern Europe. When it occurs as a salad, beetroot is often added as well.

*500 g (1 lb) herrings, filleted from the belly*
*1 tablespoon made mustard*
*75 g (2½ oz) butter*
*Salt, pepper*
*750 g (1½ lb) firm potatoes*
*2 cooking apples, peeled, cored, sliced*
*1 large onion, sliced*
*½ teaspoon dried sage*

SPREAD the herring fillets out on a board, and remove the head if the fishmonger has not already done so. Mix the mustard with 30 g (1 oz) of softened butter and spread the cut sides of the herrings with it. Season them and roll them up. Grease a pie dish with 15 g (½ oz) of the remaining butter.

Using a mandolin if possible, slice the potatoes very thinly (the cucumber blade of a grater can also be used). Blanch them for a minute in boiling, salted water, or for 2-3 minutes if the slices have been cut more thickly by hand. Put half of them into the pie dish with seasoning, then half of the apple and half of the onion slices. Put the herring rolls on top and sprinkle them with sage. Finish the layers in reverse order, ending with potato. Pour over boiling water to come about halfway up the dish. Melt the remaining butter and brush the top layer of potatoes, seasoning with salt and pepper. Bake in the oven pre-heated to mark 5, 190°C (375°F) until the potatoes are crusted with golden brown flecks and the herrings are cooked – about half an hour.

## ISLE OF MAN HERRING PIE

A VERY SIMILAR DISH TO THE WELSH SUPPER HERRINGS above was served at the Mheillea or Harvest Home on the Isle of Man. This is what Suzanne Woolley has to say in her book on the island's cookery (see page 113),

*'There was always great rejoicing when the last of the corn was reaped at harvest time, and it was usual for the farmer to provide a supper for all the workers. . . . When the last sheaf of corn was cut it was made into a garland with wild flowers bound with ribbon in the shape of Ceres, the Goddess of the Harvest. This garland, known as "The Maiden", was then carried by one of the women reapers to the highest part of the land amid the cheers of the other workers. A smaller sheaf taken from the "Maiden" and preserved until the following harvest was called "the harvest doll" [what we should call a corn dolly].'*

MRS WOOLLEY remarks that the herrings were normally cooked with potatoes, but that her recipe was found in a late eighteenth-century cookery book. There is of course no reason why some potatoes should not be included as well, on the lines of the previous recipe.

For 6

*Shortcrust pastry, see note on page 225*
*6 fresh herrings*
*½ teaspoon mace*
*Salt, pepper*
*Butter*
*3 large cooking apples*
*2 medium onions, thinly sliced*

ROLL out the pastry and line an ovenproof dish, leaving enough over for a lid. Scale, clean and gut the herring. Cut off heads, fins and tails and bone them: to do this, put the herring on a board, backbone up, spreading out the slit sides of the belly. Press gently along the backbone from neck to tail, until you feel the bone giving. Turn the herring over, and you will find you can pick out the backbone complete with most of the whiskery bones still attached (separate bones can be pulled out). Season the inside of the fish with the mace, salt and pepper.

Spread a layer of softened butter over the pastry in the dish, and place the herrings on top. Peel, core and slice the apples. Arrange them on top of the herrings, with the onion on top of the apple. Dot with more butter and pour on 4 tablespoons of water. Cover with the pastry lid, brushing it over with a little beaten egg or cream so that it will glaze nicely. Bake in a moderate oven, mark 4-5, 180-190°C (350-375°F), for about 40 minutes. Check after 30 minutes, if the herrings were on the small side, by pushing a larding needle or skewer through the central hole of the lid, so that it pierces a herring; you should be able to feel whether the herrings are cooked by the way the needle or skewer goes in.

## SOFT ROE TART

THE SIMPLEST WAY of cooking soft roes is to coat them in flour seasoned with salt and Cayenne pepper, then fry them in a little butter, and serve them, scattered with parsley, either with or on toast. In the heat they curl up most attractively and make a delightful first course or supper dish. On account of their rich creaminess, they also lend themselves to smooth tart fillings very successfully.

For 4

*20-22 cm (8-9") pastry case, baked blind*
*125 g (4 oz) mushrooms, sliced*
*30 g (1 oz) butter*
*250 g (8 oz) soft roes*
*150ml (¼ pt) soured cream*
*2 eggs*
*Salt, pepper, Cayenne pepper, lemon juice*

SPREAD pastry case with the mushrooms which have been lightly cooked in the butter. Pour boiling water over the roes, leave for 2-3 minutes to firm up a little, then drain them. Blend or process with remaining ingredients, seasoning to taste. Pour over mushrooms. Bake 35-40 minutes at mark 5, 190°C (375°F). Serve hot or warm with a tomato salad.

## CREAMED ROE LOAVES

A CHEAP VERSION OF THE RECIPE on page 110, using soft roes.

Hollow out and crisp small rolls as in the recipe for oyster loaves, but fill them with this mixture:

For 8

*325-375 g (10-12 oz) soft roes*
*3 shallots, chopped, or 3 tablespoons onion, chopped*
*60 g (2 oz) butter*
*150ml (¼ pt) each single and double cream, or 150ml (¼ pt) each single cream and milk, plus a level dessertspoon flour*
*Chopped parsley and chives*
*Lemon juice, salt, pepper, Cayenne pepper*

CUT roes into 1 cm (½″) pieces, more or less. Soften shallot or onion in the butter over a low heat in a covered pan. Stir in the flour if used. Moisten with creams, or cream and milk. Cook to a rich, thick sauce. Add roes to poach until they are just cooked. Add herbs, lemon and seasoning to taste. Divide between the rolls and serve very hot.

## SOFT ROE PASTE

*200 g (7 oz) soft herring or mackerel roes*
*125 g (4 oz) softened butter, slightly salted is best*
*1 level tablespoon double cream*
*Salt, Cayenne pepper*
*Lemon Juice*
*Chopped parsley*

TRY to find perfect pairs of roes. The best way of doing this is to buy soft-roed herring or mackerel, and set the roes aside when you cook the fish: they will have a better flavour and consistency than the broken and messy roes which have been flung together on to a separate tray. Season the roes with salt and cook them in 30 g (1 oz) of the butter. Sieve them and while they are still warm – just tepid, not hot – mix in the butter: the roes should not be so hot that the butter turns to oil. Mix in the cream, then season again, adding a pinch of Cayenne and lemon juice to taste and a little chopped parsley. Serve chilled, but not chilled to hardness, with thin toast or baked slices of bread.

## GOOSEBERRY SAUCE FOR MACKEREL

ON MAY 26TH, 1796, Parson Woodforde and his niece, Nancy, had for their dinner 'a couple of maccarel boiled and stewed gooseberries and a leg of mutton roasted'. In other years, they were not so lucky; the gooseberries did not always ripen for the arrival of the first spring mackerel.

*250 g (8 oz) gooseberries*
*30 g (1 oz) butter*
Either *1 egg*
Or: *150ml (¼ pt) béchamel sauce*
Or: *150ml (¼ pt) double cream*

TOP and tail the gooseberries. Melt the butter in a pan, add the gooseberries, cover them and leave them until they are cooked. Mash them down; or sieve them, if you like a very smooth sauce (I prefer it slightly knobbly). Mix in one or other of the remaining ingredients, to soften the sharpness of the gooseberries. Add a little sugar if the gooseberries were very young and green, but the sauce should not be sweet like an apple sauce.

THIS SAUCE is also good with roast duck, pork, goose, lamb, or veal.

## GOOSEBERRY STUFFING FOR MACKEREL

*250 g (8 oz) gooseberries*
*60 g (2 oz) butter*
*4 tablespoons breadcrumbs*
*Salt, pepper*
*Pinch of Cayenne pepper*

TOP and tail the gooseberries and soften them over a low heat with one-quarter of the butter. Mash them roughly; add remaining butter when they are tepid, and mix in the crumbs.

Divide the stuffing between four boned mackerel. Place them in a buttered dish and bake for 30 minutes at mark 5, 190°C (375°F).

## WHITEBAIT

WHITEBAIT are the small fry of herrings and sprats, a great delicacy of the past, but now a dish for everyone since the arrival of frozen food.

ALLOW them to thaw if they are frozen. Then pour a little milk over them, drain them and shake them in a large paper bag with some seasoned flour until they are coated. Shake off any surplus and fry them in deep oil. Two or three minutes is enough time. Never be tempted to cook a large batch all at once – they will stick together in a most unappetizing way. Ideally each tiny fish should be separate from its neighbours, crisp and brown and succulent in the middle.

Put the whitebait on to a serving dish, sprinkle them with Cayenne pepper if you like (for devilled whitebait), and serve with brown bread and butter, and lemon quarters.

WHITEBAIT DINNERS were held first at Dagenham to celebrate the completion of a vast land-draining scheme in Essex. One year Pitt, then Prime Minister, was invited. He came with several members of the government and soon the whitebait dinners became a political celebration at the end of the parliamentary session. After a while Greenwich took over from Dagenham, and became very popular for the dinners. People flocked out of London in the summertime to celebrate the season when whitebait were being caught in shoals in the Thames off Blackwall.

## POACHED TURBOT WITH SHRIMP SAUCE

THE SHRIMP SAUCE served with the turbot is a variation of the notorious 'melted butter' of England, our one sauce according to foreign visitors. It is easy to make badly, if you do not add enough butter; and if you overheat it the butter will turn to oil – should this happen, add a little ice-cold water, then more butter and beat vigorously with a small whisk. Nowadays, this way of thickening and enriching a sauce with butter is very popular with *nouvelle cuisine* chefs in France.

For 6

*1½ kilo (3 lb) chicken turbot*
*Milk*
*Water*
*1 slice of lemon*
*Salt, pepper, butter, parsley*

SAUCE
*300ml (½ pt) cooked shrimps in their shells*
*1 level tablespoon flour*
*175 g (6 oz) butter cut in pieces*
*Powdered mace or nutmeg to taste*
*Pinch Cayenne pepper*
*Salt*

To stop the fish curving out of shape in the pan, cut it along the backbone on the dark, knobbly-skinned side. Put it, dark side down, into a large pan and cover it with half milk, half water. Add the lemon and seasoning. Bring slowly to the boil and simmer for 10 minutes or until the flesh loses its transparency and the fillets can be raised from the bone very slightly. Slide the turbot on to a serving dish – use an old-fashioned one with a separate, pierced strainer, if possible, so that the fish is not swilling about in milky wetness. Rub the skin over with a bit of butter, or a butter paper to give it a silky shine, sprinkle on a little parsley and serve with the following sauce.

Pick the shrimps, putting the shells and so on into a pan. Set the meat to one side. Pour 300ml (½ pt) of water over the debris and simmer it steadily for 10 minutes, then pour it into a measuring jug, through a sieve. Press to extract as much juice as possible. Add water to bring the liquid to 300ml (½ pt). Mix smoothly with the flour and heat gently, adding the butter, bit by bit. Simmer for two or three minutes, then put in the shrimps which were set on one side. Season to taste and serve separately.

THE MILK and water used for poaching the turbot can be simmered with the turbot bones and skin after the meal. This makes a splendid jellied stock for soup next day.

Turbot and other left-over fish can be reheated in butter and cream, and served in small pastry cases. Delicious, if overcooking is avoided.

## HALIBUT WITH ANCHOVIES

JOSEPH CONRAD, THE GREAT NOVELIST, liked good food. And for most of his life, it had to be cheap. Luckily his wife was an ingenious cook. She even published two books of her recipes. Here is a good one for halibut.

For 4

*1 heaped teaspoon anchovy paste or Patum Peperium*
*125 g (4 oz) butter*
*500-750 g (1-1½ lb) halibut steak*
*6 tablespoons white breadcrumbs*
*250 g (8 oz) tomatoes, peeled, chopped*
*Extra knob of butter*
*1 teaspoon Worcester sauce*
*Salt, pepper, sugar*
*6 anchovy fillets, split*

MASH anchovy paste or Patum Peperium with the butter. Spread on both sides of the fish, and place it in a baking pot that has been greased with a butter paper. Sprinkle breadcrumbs over the top. Bake at mark 5, 190°C (375°F), for about 30 minutes until the fish is cooked and the crumbs lightly browned. Meanwhile cook the tomatoes in the extra butter, until they are reduced to about 4 tablespoons of purée. Add the Worcester sauce, and salt, pepper and sugar to taste. When the fish is ready, pour off its juices into the tomato purée, boil it up, adjust the seasonings and pour round the fish. Arrange anchovy fillets on top in a criss-cross, and serve with matchstick potatoes.

## WARM SKATE SALAD WITH SHAUN HILL'S DRESSING

SKATE WAS CERTAINLY A FAVOURITE FISH WITH THE ENGLISH when I was a child. We had it often, poached with caper sauce, or with black butter and capers which was originally a French idea. Another French idea that has caught on more recently is the warm fish salad. The idea is simple, but for success you do need top quality fish and time just before serving (or a second pair of hands). I first had this particular dressing at Gidleigh Park and Shaun Hill, the chef, gave us the recipe. Colin White , who was also there with his wife Gwen, now uses it for warm squid salad. It would be good, too, for sole or red mullet. Cut all these fishes in strips before cooking them; this speeds things up and gives you better control.

For 4

*Mixed greenery, eg 1 handful each rocket, radicchio, frisée*
*4 small skate wings*
*Olive oil, salt, pepper*

SAUCE
*Handful of parsley leaves*
*1 shallot*
*Small clove garlic*
*3 tablespoons well-flavoured fish stock*
*About 6 tablespoons olive oil*
*Salt, pepper, lemon juice*

WASH, trim and dry the greenery. Make a central mound on each of four plates. Next make the sauce: chop parsley, shallot and garlic together. Put into a bowl over a small pan of water, and add stock and oil. Just before serving, set over the heat and warm the sauce to tepid (no more). Season with salt, pepper and lemon juice.

Meanwhile, cook the skate wings in a little oil until the ribs of flesh can be raised in neat pieces from the bones. Season them and distribute on top of the greenery. Spoon a little warm sauce over the fish especially. Serve immediately.

## ELIZA ACTON'S SOLE STEWED IN CREAM

PUT A LARGE CLEANED SOLE into a close-fitting pan, adding just enough boiling water to cover it, and salt. Simmer 2 minutes only. Pour off the liquor and add enough Cornish or double cream to come just over halfway up, with pounded mace, Cayenne and a little salt. As the sole cooks, spoon the cream over it. When it is done, remove it to a serving dish. Flavour the sauce with lemon juice. If you like, mix some cornflour with a little of the fish water, and thicken the sauce further.

Turbot, brill, cod and eel may all be cooked in the same way: allow a little longer initial simmering time for thicker fish. The second stage of cooking in the cream may be carried out in the oven if this is more convenient. Keep basting so that the top of the fish glazes slightly in the heat. This is a lovely, pure-tasting way of cooking first-class fish. Serve a few small potatoes with it, or some poached cucumber dice, finished in a very little butter and parsley.

## CAVEACH OF SOLE

CAVEACH IS AN OLD WORD, deriving from the Spanish *escabeche* – a particular method of pickling fish, by frying it and then covering it with vinegar. In days when fish supplies were even worse than they are now – though with more excuse – it was a handy recipe to know. Now the method is used to make a lively marinated salad for eating within a few hours, or, at the latest, next day. A variety of fish can be treated in the same way, from herring, mackerel, sardines and pilchards to weever and John Dory.

For 6

*8 fillets of sole*
*Salt, pepper, Cayenne pepper*
*200 ml (7 fl oz) olive oil*
*1 medium onion, red if possible, thinly sliced*
*Finely shredded rind of 1 lemon*
*2 small bay leaves, halved*
*3 tablespoons white wine vinegar*
*Coriander, chervil or parsley, finely chopped*

FLATTEN the fillets slightly with a rolling pin and season them. Fry in a little of the olive oil until they are cooked through and very lightly browned.

Quickly cut each fillet into three and put the pieces into a warm shallow serving dish – glazed earthenware, for instance. Scatter with the onion, lemon rind and bay leaves. Mix vinegar with the remaining olive oil and pour over the fish while it is still warm. Add extra seasoning to taste, cover and chill in the refrigerator for at least 3 hours, or until the next day. Scatter with whichever herb you have chosen, and serve with bread and butter.

If you want to turn the caveach into a grander-looking first course, arrange some salad greenery on six plates, drain the fish and arrange it on top with some onion, lemon and bay. Scatter with chopped green herbs.

# FRESHWATER FISH

## SALMON IN ITS OWN JUICES

THIS HAS LONG BEEN A FAVOURITE OF MINE - cooking salmon in foil so that you end up with some juices as well from which to make a sauce. There are two ways of proceeding once you have wrapped the fish, depending on whether or not you have a fish kettle. I should also say that they both work well for any other large fish.

START by scaling and cleaning the fish and trimming off the fins. A good fishmonger will do this for you, but it's not difficult if you have to do it at home. Cut off the head if the salmon is too long for kettle or oven, and wrap it separately.

Cut a large piece of foil, enough to enclose the fish (and a separate piece for the head if necessary). Make two foil straps and lay them across the piece: they make removing the cooked salmon to a dish much easier. Butter the foil and straps if the salmon is to be eaten hot, oil it if it's to be served cold (butter congeals in an unsightly way when it cools). Season the foil and the fish, including the cavity. Wrap to make baggy parcel(s).

*Using the fish kettle:* lay the parcel(s) on the rack and lower it into the kettle. Cover. Cover it with tepid water and lay a dish or board on top to keep it submerged. Put the kettle across two burners and bring it slowly to the boil. For eating cold, allow the water to boil thoroughly for a second, then remove the whole thing and leave to cool down. By the time the fish is tepid it will be perfectly cooked, unwrap it, keeping the juices and lay on a dish, or an oiled piece of hardwood. Skin it if you like, cutting neatly at the head. If the head has been cooked separately put it in place and disguise the join with herbs, or slices of cucumber, or a ruffle of mayonnaise. If you are dextrous, you could raise the two top fillets, remove the bone, and then replace the fillets. Decorate with cucumber 'scales', or leave in its pristine beauty. Some people remove the central brown part, but I think this is far too delicious to discard.

For eating hot, allow the salmon to boil gently for about 5 minutes, and leave off the heat for a quarter of an hour. Then unwrap and serve with the boiled down juices, beaten into an hollandaise sauce.

*Using the oven:* lay the parcel(s) on a baking sheet. For fish up to 2½ kilos (5 lb), bake in a cool oven, mark 2, 150°C (300°F) for 1 hour. For fish over that weight, allow 12 minutes per 500 g (1 lb). Remove from the oven and leave to cool in the foil.

For eating hot, bake in the oven preheated to mark 4, 180°C (350°F) for 50-60 minutes. Remember that time is dictated by the thickness and not the weight of the fish.

## Salmon in Pastry, with a Herb Sauce

This is slightly adapted from an excellent recipe of George Perry-Smith's that often appeared on the menu of his restaurant in Bath, The Hole-in-the-Wall, which for many years in the fifties and sixties was the best restaurant in the country outside London. It was so popular that there were three sittings-for dinner; people sat on the stairs to wait their turn, feasting their eyes on the glorious hors d'oeuvre table which was another great speciality, a blazing still-life of delicious vegetables and fish dishes, many of them made to Elizabeth David's recipes. The style – 'real cooking in a whitewashed room' – drew all the brightest young talents to serve an apprenticeship there and a dynasty of restaurants was the result. This particular dish shows George Perry-Smith's lively pursuit of good but unusual combinations: it was inspired by a medieval recipe which accounts for the brave but entirely successful blend of sweetness with fish.

For 6

*1¼ kilos (2½ lb) tailpiece of salmon*
*125 g (4 oz) butter*
*4 knobs preserved ginger, chopped*
*1 heaped tablespoon raisins*
*1 rounded tablespoon chopped, blanched almonds*
*250 g (8 oz) shortcrust pastry*
*Beaten egg glaze*

SAUCE:
*2 shallots, chopped*
*1 heaped teaspoon chopped parsley*
*1 teaspoon mixed chervil and tarragon*
*60 g (2 oz) butter*
*1 teaspoon flour*
*300ml (½ pt) cream (single, or single and double)*
*Salt, pepper*
*1 teaspoon Dijon mustard*
*2 egg yolks, mixed with 2 tablespoons cream from the cream above*
*Lemon juice*

ASK the fishmonger to skin and bone the salmon into two roughly triangular fillets. Mix the butter, ginger, raisins, and almonds together; use half to sandwich the two pieces of salmon together and put the rest on top. Season the salmon well, and enclose it in the pastry. Cut away any surplus and use it to make a restrained decoration for the top. Slash the pastry two or three times to allow the steam to escape. Brush over with egg glaze and bake for 30-35 minutes at mark 7, 220°C (425°F).

Meanwhile make the sauce. Sweat shallots and herbs in butter until soft. Stir in flour, then cream and seasoning. Cook for 10 minutes. Finally beat in the egg yolk mixture and set over a low heat to thicken without boiling – keep stirring. Sharpen to taste with lemon juice.

Place the salmon in its pastry on a hot dish; serve with the sauce in a separate sauceboat.

## SALMON STEAMED IN SEAWEED WITH DULSE HOLLANDAISE

**A** SLIGHT ADAPTATION OF TWO RECIPES from Karin Perry's admirable *Fish Book* (Chatto, 1989). It's an unusual cookery book, as Mrs Perry travelled all around Britain, listing sources of good lively fish, interviewing people connected with the business and peripheral trades – for instance Julian Clokie who runs a sea vegetable business in Scotland, near Tain – and then giving some of her elegant recipes which are in the modern eclectic style, designed to bring out the virtues of lightness and flavour that were often submerged in old-fashioned English fish cookery.

The recipe was originally intended for halibut, but I have used it several times for salmon with great success and conclude that it would work well with any good whole fish, grey mullet, sea bass, young inshore cod, or even a gigot of monkfish. Obviously you would need to adjust the steaming time accordingly. The last time I saw Jeremy Round, before his tragically early death, we ate salmon cooked this way out in the garden under the medlar tree. With it came purple potatoes that had flourished in our Wiltshire clay soil, and mange tout peas, and of course the hollandaise. It was all a great success, in recollection a bitter-sweet day.

For 4-6

*1¼ kilos (2½ lb) salmon, scaled, cleaned*
*Salt, pepper*
*15 g (½ oz) packet dried fingerware*
*Melted butter*

SAUCE
*200 g (7 oz) unsalted butter, cubed*
*1-2 tablespoons crumbled, dried dulse*
*3 egg yolks*
*Lemon juice, salt, pepper*

SEASON fish inside and out and set aside for at least 30 minutes, in the cold. Pour boiling water generously over the fingerware and leave for 30 minutes to expand, then drain and rinse.

Put two little soufflé ramekins, upside down, into the fish kettle so that the rack will stand above the level of the boiling water. Cut a piece of foil large enough to cover the kettle eventually (you will not be able to use the kettle lid, as the lugs of the rack will rise well above the rim).

Lay half the seaweed on the rack. Brush the fish on one side with melted butter and lay it, butter side down, on the seaweed. Brush the top of the fish with butter and cover it with the remaining seaweed, tucking it round.

Pour boiling water into the kettle to come most of the way up the soufflé dishes. Put on to the stove across two burners, adjusting the heat to maintain a steady boil. Put in the rack, cover with foil and steam for 15 minutes. Test by pulling out one of the dorsal fins to see if the salmon is just about done. Remove the kettle from the stove, put back the foil lid and leave the salmon for 5-10 minutes to complete the cooking. Serve the salmon in its seaweed jacket, then remove it so that you can cut away slices of fish – give everyone a small piece of the seaweed, too. Provide new potatoes and samphire if you can get it, otherwise mange tout or cucumber lightly blanched and finished in butter, along with the sauce.

*To make the sauce:* when you are setting out the ingredients for this dish, put the butter somewhere warm so that it softens. Pour boiling water over the dulse, leave 2 minutes, then tip into a sieve and refresh under the cold tap. Pat dry on kitchen paper.

Beat yolks in a bowl with a tablespoon of water. Stand over a pan of simmering water. Whisk in the butter, bit by bit. When it is all incorporated, add lemon juice, salt, pepper and dulse to taste. Serve immediately.

NOTE: if you are used to making emulsion sauces of this kind, you can do it directly in a heavy pan over a low heat, which is quicker. I am against making hollandaise too soon and having to keep it warm: invariable it curdles in the uncertain circumstances of domesticity. Better to keep your guests waiting and do it at the last moment. You can of course make it a day in advance, cool it quickly and store it under a thin layer of melted butter in the refrigerator: leave the seasoning until you reheat the sauce, stirring it carefully over barely simmering water.

## SALMON FISHCAKES

THE USUAL THING FOR FISHCAKES is about half each of potatoes and fish, with various flavourings such as parsley and anchovy, bound with egg. I have come to prefer this version with rather less potato and a certain amount of thick béchamel sauce: certainly it's a little more trouble, but the result is less dry. Other fish can of course be used, but salmon is supreme for fish cakes. I came across the recipe initially in Partridge's Christmas catalogue of 1988. The shop – a combination of an old-fashioned grocery and a more modern breadth of choice – has been going for about 15 years now, in Sloane Street: it was started by the Shepherd family.

For 8-10 fish cakes

*500 g (1 lb) poached, flaked Scottish salmon*
*60 g (2 oz) butter*
*90 g (3 oz) flour*
*425 ml (¾ pt) milk*
*1 tablespoon chopped fresh dill or parsley*
*1 tablespoon lemon juice*
*Salt, pepper*
*1 egg*
*100-125 g (3½-4 oz) freshly mashed potato*
*About 60 g (2 oz) breadcrumbs*
*Butter and sunflower oil for cooking*

MASH the salmon. Make a thick sauce by melting the butter, stirring in the flour and cooking it gently for a few minutes, and then moistening with the milk. Cool slightly, then add salmon, herbs, lemon juice, salt and pepper to taste. Beat in the egg and the potato. Chill in the refrigerator for 1 hour.

Divide into 8-10 equal portions and form into fish cakes. Roll in the crumbs. They can then be chilled again for a few hours. Fry 3-4 minutes a side in half butter, half oil. Serve with lemon wedges and sprigs of parsley.

## FRIED EEL WITH FRIED PARSLEY

For 4

*1 kilo (2 lb) eel*
*Seasoned flour*
*125 g (4 oz) clarified butter*
*175 g (6 oz) lightly salted butter*
*Juice of 1 lemon*
*1 dozen large sprigs of parsley*
*Corn oil*

ASK the fishmonger to skin the eel, and cut it into 8-10 cm (3-4") pieces. Turn them in seasoned flour and fry gently in the clarified butter, until they are golden brown all over, and the flesh begins to part easily from the bone.

Meanwhile melt the lightly salted butter, season it with the lemon juice and pour it into a small jug. Stand it in some very hot water, until it is needed.

Place the cooked eel on a serving dish, and keep it warm while you fry the parsley. To do this pour an inch of good oil into a saucepan, make it very hot (about 180°C (350°F)) and put in the parsley sprigs a few at a time. They will rapidly darken. Remove them and tuck them round the pieces of eel. They taste deliciously sandy yet crisp, and go very well with the mild eel and its sauce. Fried parsley makes a good edible decoration for fish, and it is a pity it has gone out of fashion.

## JELLIED EEL MOUSSE WITH WATERCRESS SAUCE

AN ELABORATION OF OUR JELLIED EEL by a French chef, Guy Mouilleron, who worked in London at the Café Royal and then Ma Cuisine in Walton Street. He enjoys experimenting with English dishes. He thought of the silver eel, nosing its way through the thready stems of watercress in a stream, and found that the flavours had an affinity. A beautiful-looking dish, with the jellied whiteness of the mousse and the pale green of the sauce, flecked with darker green.

For 6

*2 eels, weighing roughly 1¼ kilos (2½ lb) in all*
*3 egg whites*
*450ml (¾ pt) double cream*
*Salt, pepper, nutmeg*

SAUCE
*1 good bunch watercress*
*150ml (¼ pt) double cream*
*Salt, pepper*

ASK the fishmonger to skin the eels for you, and, if he will, to cut the fillets away from the backbone. When you get home, cut off a generous one-third of the messiest looking parts. Season the rest, and set it aside, while you make a fish mousse. To do this, put the trimmings you cut away into the liquidizer with the egg whites, and reduce to a purée: the best way of doing this is to cut the eel into bits and drop them on to the whirling blades. Use the egg white to lubricate the mixture. Transfer the purée to a bowl set over ice. In another bowl whip the cream until thick but not stiff, then work it slowly into the eel purée. It takes about 10 minutes to work the whole thing into a coherent mass. Season it well.

Take an earthenware or stoneware terrine, respectable enough to appear on the table, and layer into it the eel mousse and the eel fillets. Cut a piece of butter paper to fit the terrine, place it on top, then cover the terrine with a double lid of foil. Either steam the mousse for 1¼ hours; or put it into a pan with boiling water to come halfway up the side, and bake it in a moderate oven until the top is just firm – mark 3-4, 160°-180°C (325°-350°F). Remove the terrine to a cool place. When cold, put it into the refrigerator overnight.

Serve with the following sauce: remove enough leaves from the watercress to make a tablespoon when chopped. Liquidize the rest with the minimum amount of water to reduce the watercress to a murky slush. Push it through a sieve, add the cream and whip until thick. Season and fold in the chopped leaves.

## SEDGEMOOR EEL STEW

MONKS FROM THE ABBEYS of the Somerset marshlands made the landscape of the levels with their draining works – now we have a world of pollarded willows, long strips of meadows between the long canals which are called rhines, a splendid source for eels. This country stew can easily be adapted to other firm freshwater fish, or even to monkfish, weever, John Dory.

For 4-6

*1½-2 kilo (3-4 lb) eel*
*Rough or dry cider*
Either: *1 tablespoon each butter and flour, mashed together*
Or: *150ml (¼ pt) clotted, Jersey or double cream*
*3-4 tablespoons chopped parsley*
*Salt, pepper*
*4-6 slices bread, toasted or fried in butter (optional)*

ASK the fishmonger to skin, clean and cut the eel into neat pieces. Simmer head, skin and flat tail pieces in half water, half cider to cover, allowing 20 minutes.

Arrange the pieces in a single layer in a sauté pan (non-stick or stainless steel). Season lightly, then strain on the eel stock and add extra cider to cover them. Bring to just below boiling point, and keep the liquid at this temperature until the flesh parts company from the bones, given a little assistance.

Remove the pieces to a serving dish, add extra seasoning. Taste the liquor in the pan. *Either* reduce it slightly to concentrate the flavour, and thicken with the *beurre manié* paste, stirring it in in little bits. *Or* reduce the liquor until it tastes quite strongly and add the cream. Last of all, adjust the seasoning, mix in the parsley and pour over the eel. Cut the bread into triangles and tuck it round the dish.

If your family is tender about fish bones, remove the fillets and serve them on the bread, pouring a little sauce over each helping.

## EEL PIE

EEL PIES, often a simple turnover or dish pie of eel seasoned with salt, pepper, and perhaps a little sage, baked in shortcrust or covered with puff pastry, were popular at fairs, like pickled salmon and gingerbread. Dr Kitchiner gives a more elaborate recipe in *The Cook's Oracle* of 1843. He calls it an 'Eel Pie worthy of Eel-Pie Island', where Londoners went to enjoy themselves and fish and picnic by the Thames. A very similar recipe in its ingredients is made by Ann Jarman at the Old Fire Engine House restaurant in Ely. She found the recipe in a local Women's Institute publication – this reminded me that my mother-in-law who came from East Anglia was still using Dr Kitchiner's book in her Cornish kitchen at the beginning of this century. The connection may not therefore be as coincidental as it seems. It's a wonderful recipe, which would be well worth trying with monkfish if you cannot buy eel.

PASTRY
*175 g (6 oz) flour*
*90 g (3 oz) chilled butter (see method)*
*Pinch salt*
*Single or soured cream or iced water to mix*
*Cream or beaten egg to glaze*

FILLING
*750 g (1½ lb) skinned eel*
*The eel trimmings*
*500 ml (18 fl oz) fish or chicken stock*
*4 finely chopped shallots*
*Butter*
*Seasoned flour*
*3 tablespoons medium dry sherry*
*150ml (¼ pt) cream*
*½ teaspoon thyme*
*3 tablespoons chopped parsley*
*Salt, pepper, lemon juice*
*2 hard-boiled eggs, sliced*

FIRST make the pastry. Put flour into a bowl. Using the coarse side of a grater, grate the hard, chilled butter on to the scales until you reach the correct weight. Mix lightly into the flour with the salt, then add enough cream or water to make a soft but coherent dough. Chill for 1 hour.

Cut the eel into 2.5cm (1") pieces. Simmer the trimmings in the stock for 20 minutes.

Soften the shallot in a little butter until soft but not brown and scatter them in the base of a shallow pie dish of a generous 1 litre (2 pt) capacity. Turn the eel pieces in seasoned flour and brown them lightly in the shallot pan, adding a shade more butter if necessary (if you use a non-stick pan, you can keep the quantity of butter down). Place on top of the shallot.

Strain the stock into the pan and deglaze it. Allow to bubble vigorously to reduce it slightly, then add 2 tablespoons sherry and the cream. Bubble for a further 2 minutes. Taste and add herbs and seasoning, with a few drops of lemon juice to bring out the flavour. Pour in the last of the sherry if you like. Pour over the eel. Put the egg slices on top and leave until cold.

Cover the pie with the pastry in the usual way, glazing it with cream brushed from the bottom of the pots, or with egg. Preheat the oven to mark 7, 220°C (425°F) for 15-20 minutes, or until pastry has set and begun to colour. Lower the heat to mark 4, 180°C (350°F) and leave a further 20 minutes. Check occasionally. Serve hot or warm, with young peas or a chicory salad.

## ELVERS IN THE GLOUCESTER STYLE

ELVERS ARE TINY EELS. Although they have taken three years to make the 2,000-mile journey from their birthplace in the Sargasso Sea, they are no more than inch or so long, tiny thread-like creatures of a fragile transparency. One might think they had no strength, to look at them, but formed into long cordons or 'eel-fares' (elver derives from eel-fare) they push powerfully upstream, up the Severn, the Loire, the Gironde and many other rivers of Europe, until they reach the streams where for another five to nine years they will live and grow, before making the dark return journey home as full-grown silver eels.

The elver fisherman sets out in the spring on a dark night to catch the turn of the tide. He carries a bucket for the eels, as well as a scoop net and a couple of forked sticks to hold his lantern. The *Illustrated Guide to the Severn Fishery Collection*, on sale at the Gloucester Folk Museum, says that in normal years several tons of elvers are caught between Sharpness and Tewkesbury on the Severn. It also points out that elvers are the only fish fry which may legally be caught as food.

For 4

*500 g (1 lb) elvers*
*8 rashers fat streaky bacon*
*A little bacon fat or lard*
*2 eggs, beaten*
*Salt, pepper*
*Wine vinegar*

WHEN you go to buy elvers, take along an old pillowcase so that the fishmonger can tip them straight into it.

At home, add a handful of kitchen salt to the elvers and swish them about, still in the pillowcase, in plenty of water. Squeeze them firmly to extract as much water as possible, then repeat the washing process again with some more salt. This gets rid of the sliminess. You may need to rinse them again and pick out tiny twigs, leaves and pieces of grass.

To cook the dish, fry the bacon until crisp in a little bacon fat or lard. Remove it to a serving dish, and turn the elvers into the bacon fat which remains in the pan. Stir them about for a few seconds until they become opaque, then mix in the beaten egg and cook for a few seconds longer. The important thing is not to cook for too long. Taste and add seasoning. Put the elvers on top of the bacon, and sprinkle with a little vinegar. Serve very hot.

## PIKE

THE BEST THING WITH THIS FINE FISH is to fillet it, and get rid of the worst of the bones. Cut off the head, and with a very sharp little knife slit along the belly. Clean it thoroughly, under the tap, but make sure of keeping the roe – the hard roe in particular is delicious as the eggs are large and grainy, caviare-size. With the cut side spread apart, turn the fish back up and press firmly all along the backbone until you feel it give (the same technique as filleting herring). Turn the fish over, and pick out the backbone. Now scrape the two long fillets away from the thick skin; they come away easily because pike is a firm fish like sole. Season the fillets, and cut them into pieces of reasonable size. Put them into a dish, and if you can manage it, sprinkle them with a couple of tablespoons of Madeira and one of brandy – more or less according to the amount of pike, but in that proportion. There should be just enough to make a little juice in the dish. Turn the pieces over occasionally and leave them for several hours.

When you come to cook them, drain the fillets, turn them in flour and fry them in butter with the roe until they are nicely coloured on each side. Serve them with a cream sauce flavoured with the marinade juices, or with a lightly curried velouté. If alcohol is out of the question, serve the pike with a purée of sorrel enriched with a little cream and butter, or with an hollandaise sauce. Tiny boiled new potatoes are a good addition.

## BAKED CARP WITH SOFT ROE STUFFING

THERE IS A WORLD OF DIFFERENCE between carp caught from the river and the muted products of a German or Israeli fish farm. For a start they are different varieties, but the freshness of running water with its weeds and tiny forms of floating life are what make the difference. The first carp I ever cooked came from a French river, the Loire. We wrapped it up, with seasoning and butter and a splash of white wine, in a foil parcel, which was laid on a grill over some smouldering charcoal. After 10 minutes we turned the package over to cook the other side. Then we ate it with lemon juice, bread and butter and glasses of white wine. I have persisted with farm carp, but have never found one which came near the perfection of that river fish.

Another way of cooking carp, a recipe for the kitchen, comes from the early nineteenth century:

For 6

*1½ kilos (3 lb) carp*
*2¼ litres (4 pts) water*
*6 tablespoons vinegar*
*175 g (6 oz) butter*
*Salt, pepper*
*¼ teaspoon each mace, nutmeg, cloves*
*Bouquet garni*
*1 onion*
*2 anchovy fillets (or 1 generous teaspoon anchovy essence)*
*600ml (1 pt) dry white wine*
*1 tablespoon flour*
*Lemon juice*

If you buy a carp, ask the fishmonger to clean and scale the fish, and also to remove the bitter gall sac at the back of the head. When you get it home, wash it in the water and vinegar very thoroughly.

Choose an ovenproof dish into which the carp will fit closely and snugly. Spread two-thirds of the butter over the base, lay the drained carp on top, and add seasonings, spices, herbs, onion and anchovy. Pour on enough dry white wine barely to cover the fish – you may need less than 600ml (1 pt), it depends on the size of the dish. Cover with foil, and put into a fairly hot oven, mark 5-6, 190°-200°C (375°-400°F), until cooked. This will take 30-40 minutes. When the carp is done, put it on to a serving dish and strain the cooking juices into a clean pan. Taste them and correct the seasoning; boil down a little if they seem watery. Mash the remaining butter with the flour, and add it to the barely simmering sauce in little knobs. Keep stirring, and in about 5 minutes the sauce will thicken nicely. Taste and add a little lemon juice to sharpen the flavour. Pour the sauce over the fish and serve.

This method can be applied to any sizeable freshwater fish; or to several small ones – in which case, reduce the cooking time accordingly. The sauce can always be enriched by a spoonful or two of cream, or by a liaison of egg yolk and cream added after the butter-and-flour thickening.

If your carp had a soft roe, use it to make the following stuffing:

*The soft roe, chopped*
*30 g (1 oz) white breadcrumbs*
*Milk*
*1 small onion, chopped*
*30 g (1 oz) butter*
*Heaped tablespoon chopped green herbs*
*1 teaspoon grated lemon rind*
*½ teaspoon anchovy essence*
*Salt, pepper, lemon juice*

Put the roe in a basin. Mix the crumbs with just enough milk to turn them into a soft paste. Cook the onion gently in the butter until soft. Mix together all the ingredients, with the seasoning and lemon juice last of all, to taste. Stuff and sew up the fish.

## Roach

Roach can be a little dull unless they are cooked very quickly after being caught. They are a beautiful fish, with silver to red scales, and reddish eyes and fins. They seem to have caught a sunset light, which goes, unfortunately, when they are scaled.

Here is a simple recipe which makes the most of them. First of all bring 125 g (4 oz) butter to the boil in a little pan. Let it bubble for a moment or two then put it aside to cool, while you scale and clean the fish and season it inside. Strain off the transparent butter through a muslin-lined sieve into a frying pan. Now that the butter has been clarified, it will not burn so easily – very important for the slow cooking of fish.

Turn the roach in seasoned flour. Heat up the butter in the pan, and put in the roach. They should cook gently for about 6 minutes a side. If you keep the heat moderate, they will develop a crisp, golden brown skin, and will not be overcooked. Serve them with quarters of lemon, and brown bread and butter, or boiled new potatoes turned in butter and parsley.

### WATER-SOUCHY

THE CHARM OF THIS SIMPLE FISH STEW lies in the freshness of the fish: it is really an angler's way of preparing a mixed bag for his supper. The longer the fish has been caught the less good the water-souchy will be.

The name comes from the Dutch *waterzootje* and the dish has been popular in England since the seventeenth century. It comes in all kinds of spelling, watersoochy, water-souchy, waterzöoi, but the formula is always the same.

For 6-8

*2½ kilos (5 lb) freshwater fish, preferably perch, but a mixture of eel, perch, carp, and so on, does very well*
*90 g (3 oz) butter*
*2 cleaned chopped leeks*
*2 chopped stalks of celery*
*Bouquet garni*
*2 tablespoons chopped parsley*
*Salt, pepper*
*Water*
*Croûtons of bread fried in butter*

PICK over and clean the fish, removing the skin from eel if you like (it can be a little fatty), and then cut it into chunks. Spread the butter over a large saucepan, add the vegetables, herbs and seasoning, and put the fish on top with more seasoning. Cover with water. Bring to the boil and simmer for 20 minutes until the fish is done, but not overdone. Serve with croûtons.

## SHELLFISH

### HOW TO BOIL CRABS, LOBSTERS, PRAWNS AND SHRIMPS

ALWAYS BOIL SHELLFISH IN SEA WATER if you can, adding extra salt until the brine will keep an egg floating. If tap water is the only kind available, add salt until it, too, will bear an egg.

With crabs and lobsters, the R.S.P.C.A. recommend putting the creatures into the cold water in a large pan, so that they quietly expire without suffering as the water warms up. Cover the pan and weight the lid down. When the water is at boiling point, allow 15 minutes' simmering for the first ½ kilo (1 lb), then 10 minutes for each subsequent ½ kilo. Remove from the water to cool down. With lobsters, some people hold them firmly and plunge their heads into the pan of fast boiling, salted water. This kills them instantly. Another way that is only suitable if you want to cut the lobster up subsequently, is to place a knife across it, just below the head part, then bang it down smartly with a wooden mallet.

If you arrange your shopping so that you pick up crabs and lobster last, just before you go home to cook, ask the fishmonger to kill them for you. When you get back, you can then plunge them directly into boiling water.

With prawns and shrimps, prepare the same brine as for crabs and lobsters. Bring it to the boil over a high heat, and plunge in the prawns or shrimps. By the time the water boils again, the smaller shrimps will probably be done. Larger prawns can take 3 minutes boiling. Always be guided by colour and flavour, i.e. try one. Prawns lose far less flavour if they are put into a large shallow pan with no water at all, covered, and set over a high heat to cook in their own juice. Shake the pan and turn the prawns until they change colour and are cooked. If appropriate to the dish, for instance a risotto, fry the prawns in a little clarified butter or olive oil.

Once the shellfish are cool, they are best served as simply as possible. Mayonnaise and brown bread and butter, with lemon quarters, are by far the best accompaniment.

## POTTED SHRIMPS

THE BEST KNOWN OF LANCASHIRE DELICACIES. Records and recipes go back to the eighteenth century, but it was only in the early thirties, when Young's opened their first London shop in Beauchamp Place, that they became popular outside the area. Under a thick layer of clarified butter the shrimps kept good for a week, a semi-preserved food in small earthenware pots; nowadays they are packed in cartons and stored in freezers.

The shrimps – mainly the brown *Crangon crangon* – are fished by boat, sometimes by horse and cart in water up to 5 feet, along the sand breasts of the channels, in the hard ridgy bottoms that make the trawl bump horribly and the boats vibrate. The shrimps were once boiled on board in salt water with extra salt, in coal-heated boilers. First they were put into the cod end of an old trawl net, then dunked into the boiling water – the colour changes through green to red – and finally put overboard to cool off rapidly in the sea. A rough hard trade, and for the men with the horses and carts sometimes a painful one, if they happened to tread on the poisoned spine of a submerged weever fish.

When the boats returned the women and children – in the days before Factory Inspectors came round – were waiting to pick the shrimps and pot them in spiced butter. It often meant working until three in the morning. At first shrimp-picking was a home industry, but now there are centres for it and people do not have to work all night, as the shrimps are stored in the cold.

Unfortunately this has meant a loss of quality – and so has the addition of frozen shrimps from abroad, as anyone old enough to remember Young's potted shrimps before the war will know.

If you happen to live near the sea and go shrimping, you might try potting your catch. For every 600ml (1 pt) of picked shrimps you need 125 g (4 oz) Lurpak butter, melted with ¼ teaspoon powdered mace, a pinch of Cayenne and some grated nutmeg. Heat the whole thing through, put into small pots and cover with a layer of clarified butter, then foil. Serve with brown bread and butter. Danish butter, incidentally, has always been used in the Lancashire shrimp potting industry.

## ELIZABETH DAVID'S POTTED CRAB

MRS DAVID HAS ADAPTED OLD RECIPES for potted meat and fish, and published them in a pamphlet, *English Potted Meats and Fish Pastes*. This potted crab is particularly successful as a lunch dish; serve a green salad, or purple sprouting broccoli salad afterwards. It is a good recipe, too, for lobster.

*1 kilo (2 lb) crab, boiled*
*Black pepper, mace, nutmeg, Cayenne pepper*
*Lemon juice*
*Salt (see recipe)*
*About 250 g (8 oz) slightly salted or unsalted butter*
*Clarified butter to seal*

PICK all the meat from the crab, being careful to keep the firm and creamy parts separate. Season both with spices and lemon juice – salt may be necessary if you bought the crab ready boiled. There will be about 300-350 g (10-12 oz) meat.

Choose an attractive round stoneware pot, or an oval one. Pack the crab meat into it, in layers. (If you prefer it, use four to six individual pots or soufflé dishes.) Melt the butter and pour it over the crab meat. There should be enough just to cover it – the quantity required will depend on the amount of crab meat you had the patience to pick out of the shell, and on whether you used one or half-a-dozen pots. It is only fair to point out that Danish – especially Lurpak – or French butter gives the best result with potted meat and fish: it is made in a different way from English butter, and has a milder flavour and better consistency for this kind of dish.

Put in a *bain-marie* and bake in the oven preheated to mark 2, 150°C (300°F) for 25-30 minutes. Cool, pour over a layer of clarified butter. When that has set firm in the refrigerator, cover with foil. All potted dishes are, or so it seems to me, better eaten the following day: if covered with a good 1 cm (½″) of clarified butter, they will be safe in the refrigerator for three or four days.

## CRAB TART

IT IS DIFFICULT TO BE PURIST about English cookery, or about any country's cookery for that matter. Once people begin trading and travelling, food begins to change. A preamble like this may well make you suspicious of my intentions. You are right to be suspicious, because the detail that makes all the difference to the deliciousness of this tart I came across in France.

For 6

*1 kg (2 lb) crab, boiled*
*Salt, pepper, Cayenne*
*Shortcrust pastry*
*3 eggs*
*250 ml (8 oz) whipping cream*
*1 tablespoon each grated Parmesan and very dry Cheddar*

REMOVE the crab meat from the shell patiently, discarding the dead men's fingers too. Put it into a bowl and season it.

Line a 22-25 cm (9-10″) tart tin with the pastry. Put in a sheet of foil, weighted down with beans, and bake blind for 10 minutes at mark 7, 220°C (425°F). Meanwhile mix 1 whole egg and 2 egg yolks into the crab, then the cream and the cheeses. Adjust seasoning. Whip the two whites remaining until stiff and fold into the crab mixture. Pour it into the pastry case (remove foil and beans first). Return to the oven. After 5 minutes, lower the heat to mark 5, 190°C (375°F), and leave for a further 30-40 minutes. The mixture will puff up slightly, like a soufflé, and turn golden brown, but the final test is the centre, which should just have lost its liquid wobbliness under the crust. Serve straightaway with brown bread and butter.

NOTE: it's the stiffly beaten egg whites that make the difference. This tart can also be made with other shellfish: I once used a mixture of prawns, scallops and left-over cooked monk-fish with great success.

## ELIZABETH DAVID'S PRAWN PASTE

AN EXTRA GOOD RECIPE from *Spices, Salts and Aromatics in the English Kitchen* (Penguin, 1970). Potted fish and meat, which were so popular in the nine-teenth century, depended on the weary arms of kitchen maids and skivvies. They are becoming popular again now that we exploit electricity instead.

*500 g (1 lb) prawns in their shells, or 250 g (8 oz) peeled prawns*
*6 tablespoons olive oil*
*Juice of 1 lime (or ½ lemon)*
*Cayenne pepper*
*About ½ teaspoon dried basil*
*1 heaped saltspoon coriander seeds*

REMOVE the prawns from their shells and pound them to a paste with the oil and lime or lemon juice (lime adds the better flavour). If you use a blender, more oil will be required. Season with a pinch of Cayenne pepper. Warm the basil in the oven, crumble it and add to the prawn mixture, along with the crushed coriander seeds. Taste and put in a little salt if necessary. Turn into a small pot and store, covered, in the refrigerator for no longer than 36 hours. Eat chilled with thin, hot toast.

## SPICY PRAWNS

IN THE FIRST EDITIONS of *English Food*, there was a recipe for curried prawns. This Moroccan recipe from Claudia Roden's *Book of Middle Eastern Food* is so much better, and so much more to modern English taste, that I now make it often instead and decided to substitute it in the book as well as on my table. The first time I ate it was at a splendid Sunday lunch cooked by Paul Bailey, the novelist, who used to write a restaurant column for the *Telegraph*. Everyone liked it so much that it has become part of his repertoire, along with David Wilson's little pots of chocolate with rosemary (see page 259), and the lovely fruit salad in the same section (see page 282).

For 4

*500 g (1 lb) large, unpeeled and uncooked prawns*
*3 large cloves garlic, crushed and finely chopped*
*About 4 tablespoons olive oil*
*Salt*
*1 teaspoon paprika*
*1 teaspoon ground cumin*
*½ teaspoon ground ginger*
*Good pinch Cayenne pepper*
*Bunch of green coriander, chopped*

AS Mrs Roden says, large prawns are quite easily found, and are cheapest in Chinese supermarkets. Some have skins that are too tough to eat, so peel them. Otherwise simply defrost, then remove heads, limbs and tails, twisting them off so that the black vein comes away at the same time.

Fry the garlic in oil until it begins to waft delicious smells at you, add salt and spices, stirring, then the prawns. Fry quickly, stirring and turning until they are pink. Add coriander and cook a minute longer. Serve immediately with some bread and white wine, or with rice flavoured with saffron, garnished with lightly fried pine kernels and friend onion slices.

NOTE: parsley can be substituted for green coriander, but the dish loses a lot of its magic subtlety.

## SHELLFISH PUFFS

For 6

CHOUX PASTRY
*150ml (¼ pt) water*
*Scant teaspoon sugar*
*75 g (2½ oz) butter*
*125 g (4 oz) strong or plain flour*
*4 eggs*

FILLING
*500 g (1 lb) prawns in their shells*
*or 750 g (1½ lb) lobster, boiled*
*or 750 g-1 kilo (1½-2 lb) crab*
*425 ml (¾ pt) béchamel sauce, fairly thin*
*2 heaped tablespoons Lancashire cheese, grated*
*2 egg yolks*
*2 tablespoons double cream*
*100 g (3 oz) butter*
*125 g (4 oz) mushrooms, chopped*
*1 small clove garlic, chopped*
*Salt, pepper*

MAKE the choux pastry puffs first, a day or two in advance if you like. They can be stored in an airtight tin, and reheated when required. Bring the first three ingredients to the boil in a moderate-sized pan. Remove from the heat and immediately tip in all the flour. Mix with a wooden spatula, then set over the heat again and cook for a few moments, stirring until the dough forms a coherent waxy ball. There will be a floury film over the base of the pan. Cool the mixture, still in the pan, for five minutes, then beat in the eggs one by one (an electric hand beater is a good idea). The paste will turn a sheeny yellow and hold its shape. Pipe in small mounds on to two or three baking trays lined with Bakewell paper, or on to the base of a confectioner's bun tin. Invert metal biscuit tins over the baking trays, or place the lid on the bun tin. Bake for 35 minutes at mark 8, 230°C (450°F), without opening the door. Take the trays or tin from the oven, raise the lids carefully by the side *away from you* (steam can be very painful). If the puffs are not brown enough they can be returned to the oven for a further five minutes. The point of covering the pastry is that it puffs up to a larger, lighter shape when it cooks in its own steam.

To make the filling, first remove whichever shellfish you have chosen from its shell. Put the shells and general debris into a pan, pour on the béchamel sauce and simmer for 15 minutes. Then sieve the whole thing energetically – it is surprising how much flavour there is in the shells which are so often just thrown away. Add the cheese, egg yolks and cream to the sauce, and stir it over a moderate heat until it is very thick (*don't* boil it). Season and beat in half the butter. Cook the mushrooms in the rest of the butter, together with the garlic. Tip them and their juices into the sauce, together with the shellfish meat. Reheat this filling gently, so that the shellfish is warmed through without further cooking. Season again.

Split the puffs and put a good spoonful or more of the shellfish filling inside. Serve immediately, as a first course.

THIS FILLING can also be used for vol-au-vents cases, large or small.

## MUSSEL AND LEEK ROLYPOLY

PEOPLE SOMETIMES SHUDDER at the mention of rolypoly puddings, but they can be light, and, with a piquant filling like the one in this recipe, delicious enough to please the most demanding eater. The original idea was to use oysters – which of course you can do – but I've taken to mussels because they are cheaper and very nearly as good. If you do decide on oysters, just open them and use them as they are, keeping the juice carefully for the sauce which will benefit from cream rather than butter, or a mixture of both.

For 6

CRUST:
*300 g (10 oz) self-raising flour*
*Pinch salt*
*150 g (5 oz) shredded suet*

FILLING
*48 large mussels, scrubbed, beards removed*
*About 90 g (3 oz) finely chopped onion*
*2 leeks, washed, trimmed, thinly sliced*
*2 rashers streaky bacon, derinded, chopped*
*3 tablespoons chopped parsley*
*Salt, pepper*

SAUCE
*125 g (4 oz) chilled, cubed, unsalted butter*
*Chopped parsley*

To make the crust, sift flour and salt into a bowl, add suet and mix to a light, soft dough with very cold water. Roll out to a rectangle barely 1cm (½") thick.

Heat the mussels, in batches, in a shallow covered pan over a very high heat until they open. Take the least time possible. 10 seconds is sometimes enough if the heat is really high, and the mussels are in a single layer. Drain and strain the liquor through muslin into a small pan: shell the mussels and allow them to cool. Discard any mussels that refuse to open.

Mix onion, leek, bacon, parsley and seasoning (very little salt, plenty of pepper). Leaving a clear margin on three sides of the pastry, scatter this mixture over it. Place the mussels evenly on top. Brush pastry rim with water, then roll up from the unrimmed edge. Press the edges lightly together. Wrap the roll in buttered foil, making a closely sealed, baggy parcel to allow room for the crust to rise. It can help to wrap the foil parcel in a cloth; tied at each end with string, it is much easier to handle. Put on a rack in a self-basting roaster, filled with boiling water to about a third of its depth. Boil for 2 hours, replenishing with more boiling water to maintain the level as needed.

Carefully unwrap the parcel, pouring any juices into the pan with mussel liquor. Taste these juices and if they are not too aggressively salty, reduce them a little, while you slip the rolypoly on to a dish and put it into the oven for about 10 minutes to crisp slightly – mark 5, 190°C (375°F), though if you have it on a little higher for some other purpose this will not matter, just keep an eye on things.

To finish the sauce, take the mussel juices off the heat and whisk in enough butter to make a creamy sauce. Add pepper and parsley. Serve separately in a small jug. At this juncture, when tasting the sauce, I always remember Anne Willan telling me to season a sauce slightly more strongly than you think pleasant, because its purpose is to add relish to blander food. In this particular case, this is very true indeed.

## OYSTER LOAVES

THIS IS ONE OF THE BEST OF EIGHTEENTH-CENTURY DISHES. It was taken to America, and became popular in New Orleans in the nineteenth century, where it acquired the endearing name of *la médiatrice*. 'It was the one thing a man felt might effectively stand between his enraged wife and himself when he came home after spending an evening carousing in the saloons of the French Quarter.' He would buy his mediator in the market there, and hurry home with it, all crisp and hot. Now it makes rather an expensive first course for a special meal (though mussels can be used instead); I hope it will become cheaper as oyster farming develops in Britain. Do not, of course, use the fine natives for this (or any other cooked oyster dish). Portuguese or gigas oysters are the thing. When I can buy them, I use part-baked rolls for this dish: otherwise round soft rolls that are not too coloured on top. Once in France I used brioches, which were particularly delicious: their cost was offset by the cheapness there of oysters.

For each person

*1 large or 2 small rolls*
*About 50 g (1½ oz) butter, melted*
*4 oysters*
*pinch Cayenne pepper, or 3 drops Tabasco sauce*
*Salt, black pepper*
*2 tablespoons soured cream*
*2 tablespoons double cream*

CUT a topknot from the rolls, scoop out the crumb, being careful not to pierce the outside, and brush them and the topknots, inside and out, with melted butter. Place in a hot oven, mark 7, 220°C (425°F), for 10 minutes, until crisp and golden. Meanwhile scrub and open oysters, and drain off the liquor. Cook them in the remaining butter until they turn opaque (about 1½ minutes). If you are making this dish for several people, use a 20 cm (8″) frying pan rather than a saucepan for cooking the oysters. Remove oysters from the pan with a perforated spoon, cut them in two or three pieces according to size, and set them aside. To the pan juices, add the strained oyster liquor, seasonings and cream. Boil down steadily to a very thick sauce, stirring constantly with a wooden spoon at first, then with a small wire whisk if the sauce shows a tendency to separate during the last stages of reduction. Correct the seasoning, reheat the oysters in the sauce, keeping it just below the boil, and pour into the rolls. Replace the topknots and serve immediately.

## MICHAEL RYAN'S WARM SCALLOP SALAD

I LEARNED AN EXCELLENT WAY OF COOKING SCALLOPS a year or two ago, from Michael Ryan of Arbutus Lodge in Cork. They ended up lightly done, the fresh flavour unimpaired.

For 4

*8 large scallops*
*150ml (¼ pt) freshly made hollandaise sauce*
*2 tablespoons olive oil*
*1 teaspoon each dry white wine and white wine vinegar*
*Salt, pepper*
*The flat shells of 4 scallops*
*4 small handfuls of mixed salad greens, washed, dried*

SEPARATE the corals from the white meat. Pound and sieve them into the warm hollandaise sauce, stirring well for an even colour. Trim the tough edge bits from the white scallop meat, and slice each piece into five or six even discs. Mix together the oil, wine and vinegar, with seasoning. Brush over the white side of the scallop shells. Arrange 10 or 12 overlapping slices of scallop on each shell. Cover each shell with foil, tucking it under the whole thing for a close seal. Refrigerate until required.

In good time before serving, switch on the grill to maximum. Warm four plates. Arrange the salad greens in a semi-circle on the plates. Warm the sauce carefully, stirring, over barely simmering water and divide between four little pots. Put on the plates and keep just warm.

Remove scallop shells from the refrigerator and unwrap them. Put on to the grill rack and brush them lightly with the oil mixture. Slide under the heat for 90 seconds. The scallop discs will be almost but not quite opaque and warm. Put a shell on each plate and serve.

## STEWED SCALLOPS WITH ORANGE SAUCE

A REALLY DELICIOUS EIGHTEENTH-CENTURY DISH. The flavour of orange, particularly of Seville orange, goes beautifully with fish. If you want to make a richer sauce, beat an egg yolk with 3 tablespoons of double cream and stir into the sauce after adding the flour and butter – stir it over a low heat being careful not to boil it. The recipe can easily be adapted to fillets of sole, whiting, etc.

For 6

*150ml (¼ pt) dry white wine*
*150ml (¼ pt) water*
*1 scant tablespoon white wine vinegar*
*½ teaspoon ground mace*
*2 cloves*
*18 scallops*
*15 g (½ oz) butter*
*1 tablespoon flour*
*Juice of a Seville orange, or the juice of 1 sweet orange plus the juice of ½ a lemon*
*Salt, pepper*

SIMMER the wine, water, vinegar and spices in a covered shallow pan for 5-10 minutes. Add salt and pepper to taste, and more spices if this seems a good idea – their flavour should not be strong but it should hang unmistakably over the dish. Meanwhile slice the scallops in half crossways, then slip them into the simmering liquid and poach them as briefly as possible. They should not be overcooked.

Transfer the scallops to six small plates and keep them warm. Measure the cooking liquor and boil it down to 250 ml (8 fl oz). Mash the butter and flour together and divide into little knobs. See that the liquid is at simmering point, then whisk in the butter and flour knobs to thicken the sauce. Keep it at a moderate heat, without boiling; finally season with the orange juice, or orange and lemon juice, and more salt and pepper if required. Pour over the scallops and serve at once. Laverbread, reheated with orange juice, goes well with this dish, or steamed samphire tips (see page 62).

## SCALLOPS WITH WHITE WINE AND JERUSALEM ARTICHOKES

JOYCE MOLYNEUX, OF THE CARVED ANGEL RESTAURANT in Dartmouth, was George Perry-Smith's star pupil at the Hole in the Wall, in Bath, in its great days. Now she runs the Dartmouth restaurant as chef-proprietor. Her food is a model of the eclectic English style of to-day, based on Elizabeth David, and drawing on ideas from all over Europe to form her own very personal repertoire. Like George Perry-Smith, she held out for a long time against a book, saying that her recipes weren't original enough, but the *Carved Angel*

*Cookery Book* (Collins), written with the help of my daughter, Sophie, was published in 1990. My own feeling is that Joyce Molyneux has caught the best of our times as far as food is concerned. In Christopher Driver's phrase, she has done that difficult thing for an English chef of 'expressing a nationality through a language evolved elsewhere.'

Inevitably, this brings one up against the question of originality. Joyce Molyneux declares that her recipes aren't original – the idea of scallops and Jerusalem artichokes she took from a soup recipe of Margaret Costa's in *Four Seasons Cookery Book* of 1970. Apart from the rare innovating genius, chefs exploit and adapt a tradition. If you have read enough, eaten at enough places, travelled enough, you can spot the source of most seemingly original ideas.

For 4

*8 large scallops*
*about 375 g (12 oz) Jerusalem artichokes*
*60 g (2 oz) butter*
*4 tablespoons dry white wine*
*Salt, pepper, parsley, lemon juice*

REMOVE corals and slice scallops into 16-24 discs, according to their thickness. Peel, trim and cut-up enough artichokes to give you 175 g (6 oz) of 'matchsticks' (use up trimmings in soup).

Cook artichokes gently in butter. When almost tender, add scallop discs and white wine with seasoning. Cook for a minute, add corals and leave for a further 1-2 minutes – avoid overcooking.

Scoop out all the pieces into one hot dish, or four small ones. Reduce liquid if necessary by fast boiling. Check seasoning, adding parsley and lemon to taste. Pour over scallops and serve immediately.

## SCALLOPS WITH CHEESE SAUCE

A DELICIOUS WAY OF COOKING SCALLOPS from the Isle of Man, based on a recipe from Suzanne Woolley's *My Grandmother's Cookery Book, 50 Manx Recipes*. On the island people call scallops 'tanrogan' – this was originally

*'the name given to the scallop shell when it was filled with cod oil to provide a lamp for the fishermen. A rush which quickly soaked up the oil, was used for the wick. Miniature scallops, "queenies", have become increasingly popular in recent years and are exported in great quantities all over the world [alas, for the natives of the British Isles]. They can be stewed in wine or milk, fried in bacon fat, or deep-fried in batter. There are between eight and twelve scallops to the pound, compared with forty to eighty queenies.'*

In this particular recipe, the sauce quantities given by Mrs Woolley are adequate for about eighteen normal-sized scallops – and in these expensive days, that should be enough for a first course for six people. The seas around the Isle of Man are a famous and fruitful fishing ground for scallops.

For 6

*18 scallops*
*150ml (¼ pt) fish stock*
*1 medium onion, quartered*
*1 bay leaf*
*Salt, pepper*

SAUCE
*30 g (1 oz) butter*
*30 g (1 oz) flour*
*Milk*
*60 g (2 oz) well-dried-out Cheddar, grated*
*2-4 tablespoons double cream*

WHEN you buy the scallops, ask the fishmonger to give you six of the deep shells. Scrub them well, and set aside to drain. Also prepare enough mashed potato to pipe a border round the edge of the shells, if this is the kind of thing you like. On the whole I prefer to miss out the potato: if you want a starchy accompaniment, line the shells with puff pastry, bake them blind, and serve the fish in the pastry cases.

Remove the corals from the scallops and set them aside for the moment. Slice the white parts across so that you have thirty-six discs of scallop meat. Put them into a wide pan with the stock, onion, bay leaf and seasonings. Cover the pan and simmer very gently for about 10 minutes until the scallops are just cooked; add the corals after 5 minutes. Strain off the liquor, but keep the scallops warm in the pan over boiling water or in a low oven.

To make the sauce, melt the butter, stir in the flour and cook for 2 minutes. Add the strained scallop cooking liquor, then enough milk to make a moderately thick sauce. Simmer 10 minutes. Correct the seasoning if necessary, stir in half the cheese and the cream.

Divide the scallops between the shells or pastry cases, placing the corals on top. Pour over the sauce. Scatter with the remaining cheese, and brown under the grill.

NOTE: if you have to make advance preparations, the scallops can be cooked earlier in the day, and so can the sauce. Reheat very gently together, before dividing between the shells and browning under the grill.

# CURED FISH

## RED HERRINGS

BEFORE THE DAYS OF REFRIGERATION, red herrings were the food of fast days inland. Their preparation was the great industry of the East Anglian coast from the Middle Ages. One of Shakespeare's contemporaries, Thomas Nashe, even wrote his poetical *Lenten Stuffe* in their honour. Red herrings were thoroughly salted, and then thoroughly smoked, until they became hard and dry and reddish in colour. Although you do not see them in English shops these days, they are still made at Great Yarmouth, and sent out to tropical countries where even the humidity and heat cannot spoil them. Once they were slave food, now they are the food of the poor, a cheap, storable, provider of protein.

If you ever manage to buy some, soak them well in water or milk. Then grill them or toast them in front of the fire, basting them with butter or olive oil. Serve them with scrambled eggs or potatoes mashed with plenty of butter. Or think of them as anchovies, to be used as a relish rather than a main food.

## BLOATERS

THE LIGHT AND SAVOURY BLOATER cure is only three or four hundred years old. It reflects a more organized and comfortable existence, when luxuries like these could be enjoyed by people in moderate circumstances. The best bloaters come and always have come from Great Yarmouth: they should be eaten within 36 hours as the cure of salt and smoke is so light. Of course, with refrigeration they can be stored for longer periods – which is why they are on sale all over the country – but for the best bloaters you must still go to the East Coast and eat them straightaway. Bloaters can be grilled with a bit of butter in their bellies, or reheated in the oven. Or they can be mashed with butter and turned into a paste for eating with hot toast (see page 116), a favourite way with the Victorians. However, bloaters, like kippers, are delicious when eaten uncooked: use them in salads with apple and beetroot and celery, or eat them in the Polish way with cream and chives poured over them, and a few onion rings.

## GRILLED BLOATERS

Per person

*1 or 2 bloaters*
*1 teaspoon melted butter*
*A lemon quarter*

CHOOSE plump, soft-roed bloaters. Ask the fishmonger to chop off the heads and fins. At home, score the fish two or three times on each side. Brush them with butter as you place them on the grill rack. Have the grill well heated. Put the bloaters underneath for 2 minutes. Turn them and give them a further 2 minutes. If the grill was hot enough, they will be crisp and appetizingly brown at the edges; their juices will be sizzling and the rich appetizing smell will ensure that they are eaten immediately. Put the lemon quarter beside them, and serve plenty of unsalted or lightly salted butter to spread on wholemeal bread.

BLOATERS CAN also be baked – though I think that the fierce heat of a grill serves them better. Place them in a buttered dish, dab them with butter and give them 10 minutes in a moderate oven, mark 4-5, 180°-190°C (350°-375°F). Squeeze lemon juice over them before serving with wholemeal bread and butter.

If you want something more elaborate, bone the grilled or baked bloaters as quickly as you can, and serve the hot fillets on buttered toast, or on a creamy ring of scrambled egg.

Another elaboration, with less fiddling at the last moment, is butter flavoured with mustard and chives, or with chopped parsley and lemon juice. This can be made days in advance if you like, but remember to remove it from the refrigerator in time for it to soften to a spreadable consistency. I think that Dijon mustard is the best kind to use.

## BLOATER PASTE

AS A DISH FOR BREAKFAST AND TEA, bloaters have acquired a Dickensian air of fog and domestic stuffiness which is not to their advantage. This is backed up by the name, which has a coarseness quite inappropriate to their delicate piquancy. When Peggotty remarked, in *David Copperfield*, that she was proud to call herself a Yarmouth bloater, she certainly didn't mean that she was a fat, hearty creature, but that she was nicely rounded, and sweet but well-spiced in character, and fit for a discriminating man.

The names goes back to the sixteenth century, and for people in the trade it had a useful accuracy. It meant that these herrings had been treated so lightly with salt and smoke that they were still plump and puffy – bloated, if you like – with moisture, unlike the dry, almost brittle, red herrings. The French use the equivalent word – *bouffis* – for their Boulogne-cured *harengs saurs*: although they are saltier than our bloaters, and sometimes need a brief soaking, they have the same combination of sweetness and gaminess, because they, too, have been cured lightly, with the guts and roes still inside to improve the flavour. The mild spice of these two cures, the rarely achieved balance to mildness and piquancy, makes bloaters and *bouffis* two of the best things to eat in Europe.

POUR boiling water over a couple of bloaters, and leave them for 10 minutes. Drain them, remove the skin and bone and weigh the fillets. While they are still warm, pound them – either by hand, or in a blender, or with an electric beater – with an equal weight of lightly salted butter. Sharpen to taste with lemon juice, season with freshly ground black pepper and a little salt if it seems necessary. Serve with hot toast. If you care to smooth it down in a pot and cover it with a good layer of clarified butter, bloater paste can be stored in the refrigerator for two or three days.

## BLOATER AND POTATO SALAD

THIS DISH GETS RIGHT AWAY from the high-tea image and shows how delicious bloaters can be at the start of a dinner party. The problem here is the potatoes, though happily it is more easily solved now than it was when I first wrote this book. These days some of our better supermarkets sell such waxy varieties as Fir Apple or La Ratte potatoes, and gardeners are more easily able to buy them, too. Desirée is the best of the common varieties for a potato salad.

For 6 as a first course

*3 fine bloaters*
*500 g (1 lb) waxy potatoes*
*1 heaped tablespoon chopped chives*
*Olive oil*
*Lemon juice*
*Salt, pepper, sugar*

THERE is no need to cook bloaters. Strip off the skin and remove the fillets from the bone, having first removed the roes and set them aside for some other dish. Divide into strips, or cut into pieces if the fillets look messy, and lay them in the centre of a dish.

Meanwhile boil the potatoes in their skins. Mix the remaining ingredients to a vinaigrette in the proportions you like – I use 5 tablespoons of oil to about 1½ of lemon juice. Sprinkle a tablespoon over the bloaters. When the potatoes are cooked, removed the skins, cut them into cubes and turn them gently in the remaining vinaigrette. Leave them to cool, then arrange them round the bloaters, and serve well chilled.

GOOD UNDYED kippers can be used instead, but not the mahogany, deep-frozen kind.

## KIPPERS

THE LATEST OF ALL THE HERRING CURES was developed by John Woodger of Seahouses in Northumberland from an old system of curing salmon (kippered salmon, and so kippered herring, and so skippers). Red herrings and bloaters are cured whole, but Woodger adopted the salmon technique of splitting the fish down the back, before salting them briefly and then smoking them over an oak fire like bloaters, again briefly for a light cure. True kippers are not mahogany brown from dye, but a pale silvery golden colour. They can still be bought in Northumberland, from a firm in Craster, and from the Isle of Man where dyeing is forbidden by law, and from one or two small concerns on Loch Fyne. Fishmongers in other parts of the country who smoke their own fish will often produce excellent kippers as well. They are usually grilled, sometimes even fried, which works well enough if they are cooked in pairs with a good knob of butter in the middle, but they should be cooked gently, and turned over still in their sandwich form so that only the skin comes in contact with the pan. This prevents the kippers drying out.

My own preference is for jugged kippers: put them into a deep stoneware jug, pour boiling water over them and leave them for 5 minutes.

Cut in strips and arranged, without cooking, on slices of brown bread and butter, kippers make a delicious first course which works out a good deal cheaper than smoked salmon.

## KIPPER PASTE

*1 pair Craster, Isle of Man or Rothesay undyed kippers*
*Slightly salted butter*
*Salt, Cayenne pepper, mace*
*Lemon juice*
*1 tablespoon double cream (optional)*

ANY kippers can be used for this paste, but it is worth choosing the highest quality undyed kippers because the flavour is so much better. Put them in a deep stoneware jug. Pour boiling water over them, and leave for 10 minutes. Drain them carefully, then remove skin and bones. Weigh the fillets and pound them with an equal weight of butter, while tepid but not hot. Season with salt, spices and lemon juice to taste. If you like a particularly light texture, fold in the cream which should first be whisked. This paste will keep for a week in the refrigerator, under a good layer of clarified butter and a close-fitting lid of foil.

## SMOKED MACKEREL

**A** FAIRLY NEW ENGLISH DELICACY, that has become popular in the last four or five years. Be careful when buying, as sometimes it has been hot-smoked to a pulpy, unpleasant softness: cold-smoked mackerel is much superior in flavour and closer to smoked salmon in texture, but being more difficult to cure, it is much harder to find. Half a mackerel is enough for one person, though obviously this depends on their size and the rest of the meal; but always serve it in small quantity.

HALVE and bone the fish, arranging the pieces, skin side up, on a bed of cress or lettuce. Serve with lemon quarters and brown bread and butter.

A tart gooseberry sauce goes well with hot smoked mackerel: stew about 200 g (6-7 oz) topped and tailed gooseberries with a knob of butter and a tablespoon of sugar. Once the juices run, remove the lid so that any wateriness evaporates quickly. Sieve or put through the *mouli-légumes*. Add to 150ml (¼ pt) whipping cream. Taste and add more sugar if you like, but keep it on the tart side. Grate in enough horseradish, or add a good proprietary brand, to give a hint of earthiness to the flavour.

## SMOKED SPRATS

ONE OF THE CHEAPEST OF LUXURIES. They can be grilled briefly and served with plenty of brown bread and butter and lemon quarters, or they can simply be skinned and served as part of an hors d'oeuvre instead of sardines – some dry white wine makes a good dressing.

## FINNAN HADDOCK

FINNAN HADDOCK IS ALWAYS COOKED (recipes on pages 18, 120). Make sure you buy the proper haddock, and not the unpleasantly dyed 'golden fillet', which is usually whiting. Finnan, which is to say Findon, is the name of a small fishing village near Aberdeen which made a speciality of curing haddocks. The method is now used everywhere in Britain; the results should be silvery and brownish-gold and thoroughly natural in appearance. Smaller haddock and occasionally whiting are beheaded, gutted and left whole and cured in the Arbroath or Eyemouth manner. Sometimes you will see them strung together in pairs in the old-fashioned manner. These 'smokies', as they are called, can be reheated briefly under the grill or in the oven, and eaten with plenty of butter and bread, or used for kedgeree.

## KEDGEREE

KHICHRI IS A HINDI DISH OF RICE AND LENTILS, which can be varied with fish or meat in all kinds of ways. The English in India worked up their own versions, and soon kedgeree became a popular Victorian breakfast dish. The sad thing is that it became institutionalized as a handy way of using up any left-over fish and rice: it came to table stodgy and tasteless. Left-overs can be used to make a good kedgeree, but the cook's hand should be generous with butter and cream, and the proportion of fish to rice should be more or less two parts to three, cooked weight.

Well-flavoured fish like salmon and first-class kippers and bloaters make a delicious kedgeree. So do shellfish such as mussels: use their liquor to cook the rice.

For 4

*A 500 g (1 lb) piece smoked haddock*
*Olive oil*
*1 large onion, chopped*
*175 g (6 oz) long-grain rice*
*1 teaspoon curry paste*
*Butter*
*3 hard-boiled eggs*
*12 or more prawns, body-shell removed, heads left in place*
*Chopped parsley*

POUR boiling water over the haddock and set over a low heat for 10 minutes. It should not boil. Take the haddock from the water, discard the skin and bones, and flake the fish. Meanwhile put a thin layer of olive oil into a pan and brown the onion in it lightly. Stir in the rice, and as it becomes transparent mix in the curry paste. Pour 600ml (1 pt) of the haddock water over the rice, and cook steadily until the rice is tender and the liquid absorbed. Watch the pan, and add more water if necessary. Mix in the flaked haddock pieces and a large bit of butter, so that the kedgeree is moist and juicy. Turn into a hot serving dish. Arrange the egg slices and prawns on top, sprinkle with parsley, and serve with lemon quarters and mango chutney.

## FINNAN HADDOCK AND MUSTARD SAUCE

*3 Finnan haddock, about 1½ kilos (3 lb) in all*
*600ml (1 pt) milk*
*150ml (¼ pt) water*
*1 medium onion, sliced*
*1 carrot, sliced*
*2 cloves*
*¼ bay leaf*
*30 g (1 oz) butter*
*1 rounded tablespoon flour*
*Mustard to taste, ready-mixed English, or Dijon*
*Salt, pepper*

CUT each haddock into two pieces longways. Bring milk, water, onion, carrot, cloves and bay leaf to the boil in a wide shallow pan. Put in the haddock, skin side up, and leave for 10 minutes – the liquid should just simmer. Place the fish on a serving plate, cover with butter papers and keep it warm. Melt the butter in a small pan, stir in the flour and cook for 2 minutes.

Stir in gradually enough of the strained haddock cooking liquor to make a smooth, fairly thin sauce about the consistency of single cream. Raise the heat and allow the sauce to bubble down gently to a thick consistency. This will also increase the flavour. Finally season to taste with the mustard, starting with a teaspoonful and gradually adding more, and then with salt and pepper. (I confess to a preference for Dijon mustard, or the speckled *Moutarde de Meaux*, as they are less ferocious than English mustard and more agreeable in flavour.)

Pour the sauce over the haddock and serve with some boiled potatoes turned in butter and chopped parsley.

## SMOKED EEL

IN THE SEVENTIES, many eels were caught in England, and then sent to Holland for smoking. A strange situation when you think of our passion for smoked salmon. Smoked eel is an even greater delicacy – why wasn't it smoked here? Now, in the nineties, the lead level in eels is so high that they are not safe to eat. They have to be imported into Holland from elsewhere in Europe. A strange situation – in this country we are deprived of more and more of our good things, thanks to pollution of one kind or another. Why aren't we out on the streets with banners waving?

If you do manage to find the rare small smokehouse which prepares eel, buy a 10 cm (4") length per person. Skin it, raise the fillets from the bone, and lay them on buttered wholemeal or rye bread. Provide lemon wedges for people to squeeze a little juice over them.

## SMOKED TROUT

THESE DAYS A COMMONER DELICACY, since smoking is the only way to make the over-produced farm trout edible. Cooked fresh they are dull, occasionally muddy in flavour, and bear no comparison with the wild trout that is such a treat. As well as the usual brown bread and butter and lemon quarters, horseradish cream is often served with it – double cream flavoured with horseradish, lemon juice and a hint of sugar to taste.

## SMOKED SALMON

THE GREATEST OF OUR LUXURIES, when bought from a first-class curer. The variety of cures and qualities is astonishing. Don't imagine that cheap smoked salmon is a bargain – often it will taste very coarse, and the colour will sometimes, not always, be an indication of this. It is much better to buy less and be pleased with the subtlety and fineness of the best product. As a general guide the best smoked salmon comes from Scotland, and it should carry the quality mark of the Scottish Salmon Smokers' Association. I have eaten salmon to match it in Ireland, and there are excellent establishments in London that smoke salmon to their own recipes. One should be prudent, rather than doctrinaire, and once you find a brand that satisfies you, make a note of the name and stick to it.

If you buy a side of smoked salmon, you have the trouble of slicing it (not an easy knack to acquire) but there is the bonus of trimmings that can be used successfully as a flavouring for creams, omelettes and scrambled egg (cut them into small evenly sized slivers and add them to the eggs before they are cooked).

Otherwise eat smoked salmon with brown bread and butter – both of the finest quality – and, if you like, a very little lemon juice. Some people claim that the best way of eating it is wrapped round a spoonful of Russian caviare: I have never been in a position to test this claim, unfortunately, and cannot pretend that it is a normal item of good English eating, but I pass the suggestion on nonetheless.

## BAVAROIS OF SMOKED SALMON

A LOVELY RECIPE OF FRANCO TARUSCHIO'S, which he serves at the Walnut Tree Inn, at Llandewi Skirrid near Abergavenny. It's one of the nicest places to visit in the British Isles.

For 10

*750 g (1½ lb) smoked salmon*
*250 ml (8 fl oz) crème fraîche, or half double, half soured cream*
*½ level teaspoon Cayenne pepper*
*Juice of ½ lemon*
*8 level teaspoons salted red salmon or other roe*

SAUCE
*2 tablespoons finely chopped shallot*
*Olive oil*
*1 kilo (2 lb) tomatoes, skinned, seeded, chopped*
*Salt, pepper*
*1 teaspoon red wine vinegar*
*Chives to garnish*

RINSE out 10 ramekins, small soufflé dishes or cups with cold water. Do not dry them. Line them with strips of smoked salmon, trimming away any excessive overhang (there should be a little, to flip over at the end). Process remaining salmon, with the trimmings, gradually pouring in the cream(s), Cayenne and lemon juice to taste. Fold in the salmon roe and divide between the salmon-lined pots. Bring over the salmon ends, pressing the whole thing together gently with your fingers. Cover with clingfilm and chill until just before serving.

To make the sauce, cook shallot until golden in a little oil. Add tomato and stir-fry until you have a purée. Season with salt, pepper and vinegar, then sieve. Correct the seasoning and cool.

Turn out the bavarois on to 10 plates, and spoon a little sauce round each one. Scatter with chives. Serve with some good wholemeal or rye bread.

## ANCHOVIES

ANCHOVIES UNFORTUNATELY ARE NOT A NORTHERN FISH. Our experience of them has always been of the salted kind. Anchovies were and are an important relish in our food and cookery. They took the place of the Roman *liquamen*, a pungent essence of fermented small fish and fish entrails, in much European cookery of the past. For us it was anchovy essence to give a fillip to Melton Mowbray pork pies, to spike a roasting joint of lamb or beef, or set off the pale flavour of cold poultry in a salmagundi (q.v.), to flavour a fish sauce. My husband remembers nostalgically the delicate, pale pink effect of Lazenby's anchovy essence in his mother's Friday sauces: modern brands cannot apparently compare with it, neither can sauces flavoured with crushed anchovies straight from the can or salt.

I find anchovies useful in meat cookery to liven a beef stew or casseroled pigeons. They dissolve so perfectly that they are unidentifiable, their sharp piquancy blends well into the sauce. Their main role, though, has been as an identifiable relish, to stimulate appetite and thirst in such dishes as the ones following. So popular were they that earlier cookery books are full of tricks for preparing small fish caught in our own waters to simulate anchovies. Hannah Glasse recommends that you layer a peck of sprats with an astonishing mixture of 4 lb of saltpetre, 2¼ lb of salt, two pennyworth of cochineal and 2 oz of sal prunella. After six months they will be ready. 'Observe that your sprats be very fresh, and don't wash nor wipe them, but just take them as they come out of the water'.

That such preparations were not altogether successful, we may judge by the continuing importation of anchovies from Southern Europe, whether canned in oil or packed in salt.

### ANCHOVY MATCHSTICKS

*250 g (8 oz) puff pastry*
*2 hard-boiled eggs*
*1 tablespoon cream*
*2 tins anchovies in oil*
*Salt, pepper*
*Beaten egg to glaze*

ROLL out the pastry and cut it into two equal-sized oblong pieces. Mash the hard-boiled eggs and mix them with the cream; season with salt and pepper. Drain the anchovies of their oil and arrange the fillets evenly on one piece of pastry in two rows – leave a good 3 cm (1½″) between each fillet, and between the two rows. Put a little of the egg mixture on top of each anchovy. Brush the pastry between the anchovies with beaten egg, place the second piece of pastry on top, and press down all round the edge and between the anchovies. Cut between the mounds, so that you have a number of matchsticks. Place them on a Bakewell lined metal tray, brush them with beaten egg and bake them for 15-20 minutes at mark 7-8, 220-230°C (425-450°F). They should be well risen and light, with an appetizing brown top. Eat them straight away if possible, as they lose their charm if they have to be reheated.

## To Make a Nice Whet before Dinner (1769)

THIS PIQUANT DISH OF ELIZABETH RAFFALD'S can be served before a meal, as she suggests, with the drinks, or as a first course, or a supper dish. It is excellent.

FRY some slices of bread, half an inch thick, in butter. Lay an anchovy fillet on each one. Cover thickly with Cheshire cheese, grated and mixed with some chopped parsley. Dribble melted butter over the top and put under a hot grill until brown.

## Canapés à la Crème

A FINE MIXTURE OF HOT, rich, piquant and cold. It was intended as a savoury and the recipe comes from *Savouries à la Mode*, by Mrs de Salis, which was published at the end of the last century, when savouries were very much the thing at the end of dinner. Nowadays when there is no one in the kitchen to help during a meal, most people prefer to serve a cold pudding or fruit – savouries have become the first course instead.

FRY circles of bread in butter, cutting them about 1 cm (½″) thick. Put three anchovy fillets on each slice and place them on a hot dish. Quickly put a spoonful of chilled clotted cream in the centre of each one and serve immediately.

## SCOTCH WOODCOCK

A POPULAR VICTORIAN AND EDWARDIAN SAVOURY, although nowadays we generally prefer such dishes as a first course. The name of the dish – like Welsh rabbit – sounds like an English joke: eggs and anchovies being the poor Scotch substitute for woodcock, the best of game birds. Or did the Scotch think of it themselves? Certainly the Welsh seem to have thought up the name of Welsh rabbit.

For 6

*1 tin anchovies*
*175 g (6 oz) unsalted butter*
*6 thick slices of bread*
*4 large egg yolks*
*300ml (½ pt) whipping or double cream*
*Salt, pepper, Cayenne*
*Chopped parsley*

DRAIN and mash the anchovies with one-third of the butter. Cut rounds from the bread, toast them and spread on the remaining butter while they are still hot. Next spread them with the anchovy paste. Arrange on a serving dish, and keep them warm. To make the 'woodcock', beat the yolks with the cream, add seasoning with a good pinch of Cayenne, and stir over a moderate heat until you have a creamy thick sauce; on no account let it come close to boiling point or it will curdle. Pour over the toast, sprinkle with a little parsley and serve.

SEE ALSO *Halibut with Anchovies*, page 89.

# MEAT, POULTRY & GAME

FOREIGNERS HAVE ALWAYS CONDESCENDED TO ADMIRE the range, quality, quantity and – heretofore – the cheapness of English meat. There have been foreign travellers, especially in the eighteenth and nineteenth centuries, who have considered that our industrial ills came from the fact that good meat was available to the lower orders, making them uppity and demanding and prone to form associations and trade unions – instead of remaining supine on cabbage water.

One should remember that during the eighteenth century the population of Britain doubled, from 8.5 million at the beginning to 16.5 million at the end. This may seem enviably spacious to the overcrowded southerner to-day, but at the time it created problems – and opportunities.

People left the country and crowded into towns. They needed to be fed – a great stimulus to the brighter farmers and landowners of Britain, who went in for Improvement with passion and a capital I. In fact the idea was not new. Along with other aspects of the Enlightenment – the writing of cookery books, for instance – it originated in the seventeenth century. And it was a direct result of the Civil War. One Royalist in exile, Sir Richard Weston, came across a number of Flemish farmers who by growing the right crops in rotation had made their poor land productive. First they sowed flax, then turnips, then oats undersown with clover. Turnips and clover enabled them to keep many more animals through the winter: more animals provided more manure, more manure meant larger crop yields. He was not the first Englishman to know about this – the habit of peasants in the Limousin, Aquitaine and Savoie of growing turnips to feed themselves and their cattle was noted in the *Maison Rustique*, translated by Richard Surflet in 1616 – but he seems to have been the first to study the method and publish his findings in 1650 in a *Discours of Husbandrie used in Brabant and Flanders*, noting the 'huge IMPROVEMENT' it brought.

The great apostle of Improvement was the writer and agriculturalist, Arthur Young (1741-1820). You have only to read in the most superficial way the journals of his travels to catch the excitement and energy of his persuasive powers. Through his efforts, production per acre was doubled in Britain, and land in cultivation increased by 10,000 acres. As a farmer, he was a failure; so, in the end, was his great hero, Robert Bakewell, in the sense that the influence of their ideas was greater by far than their personal success and solvency.

Bakewell (1725-1795) lived at Dishley Grange, in Leicestershire, now trapped in the sprawl of Loughborough. Intent on improving his livestock, he looked around for the most perfectly developed animal of the time. Anyone who is familiar with Stubbs's paintings will know that this was the racehorse – thanks in part to centuries of royal patronage (I forget which Charles it was who said the only living creature he felt comfortable with was the horse, because it treated him as an equal).

Bakewell applied the inbreeding methods that had been so successful with horses to his own longhorn cattle and Leicester sheep. By breeding from animals with the traits he required, he achieved 'two pounds of mutton where there was one before', and at an earlier maturity. At the annual Dishley letting, he hired out and sold pedigree bulls and rams to other farmers. These occasions became a sort of agricultural fair, at which ideas and experiences were exchanged.

The two Colling brothers applied his methods to their local Teesdale shorthorns, raising first the vast and much painted Durham Ox, then the prodigious Comet, the best bull ever. In turn their methods influenced Hugh Watson, of Keillor in Angus, in his pioneer work on the black, polled cattle now known as the Aberdeen-Angus. Breeds do not, of course, remain static, even when the desired standards have been set, though certain salient features will be retained – in the case of the Aberdeen-Angus a blockiness of shape that indicates a high concentration of weight in the prime roasting joints, as well as its black coat, its naturally polled head and its mild character. Moreoever, its meat is marbled discreetly with just the right amount of fat to give it tenderness and flavour.

By the time the Aberdeen-Angus herd book was started – rather late in the day, in 1862 – there was no longer any thought that all our meat could be supplied by British farmers. The population had doubled again, more than half the population lived in towns, and with free trade there was no point in self-sufficiency as far as the mass market was concerned. 'Instead there was a strong motiviation to produce the world's best pedigree livestock. This is why British breeds generally have shaped the western world's farm animals, yet in their native country have given way on many occasions to foreign imports of meat.' The first import of lamb from New Zealand, in the refrigerated hold of the Dunedin, docked in this country in May 1882, the start of a great trade which put lamb within reach of many more people, and demoted it from the top status that it enjoys, for instance, in France. Though, I suppose, the national tendency has always been towards beef, the roast beef of old England.

More widely considered, was this reliance on adequate and cheap imported beef and lamb one of the reasons for the decline in our standards of good eating? To the town-dweller, such meat comes as if by magic from nowhere. We have been long cut off from the experience of food production. We have come to regard it with as little curiosity as if it were boot polish. I remember the situation during the last war, which became a coals-in-the-bath sort of cliché, when children evacuated from the big towns refused to drink milk because it came from those dirty cows rather than from a nice, clean tin. This always raises a laugh, but many people's attitude towards food generally is precisely the same to-day – except that now it has to be wrapped in nice, clean plastic. And the production of food is becoming so sanitized, so sterile, that should we venture abroad, stomach troubles become inevitable. This already happens to American travellers – are we destined to suffer in the same way from our demand for foodless food? Is this over-urbanization the reason why we have not understood the demands we should have been making from the intensive farming of the last 40 years, and now find ourselves landed with quantity rather than quality, with boredom, repugnance and even, it now seems, with an increase in food poisoning and pollution? We have not controlled the farmers, our demands have not balanced their progress, and we have lost out. What butcher these days dares to sell brains, sweetbreads, spinal marrow, for fear of scrapie? We have not understood the impiety of feeding ruminant animals with the rehashed bodies of dead sheep: now we see an almost bibilical judgement, in the matter of offal, and in the matter of eggs and poultry as well, from the appalling practice of feeding battery chickens on the recycled bodies of their dead fellows.

Pigs are another matter. Pigs will eat anything, indeed they were the great scavengers of towns before the era of dustcarts and rubbish collections. And being so convenient and easy to rear, the pig was the ideal animal for cottagers. A side of bacon hanging in the chimney to smoke was every countryman's aim, and its flavour would improve his soups, and yield some kind of a joint for Sunday eating. The high point of cured pork was ham, preferably dry-cured which gave it the chance to mature to a slow perfection. It became a symbol of festive occasions, such as the meal provided for mourners, as H.G. Wells describes in *Mr Polly*: 'The funeral in the rather cold wind had proved wonderfully appetising, and every eye brightened at the sight of the cold collation that was now spread in the front room . . . There were two cold boiled chickens, which Johnson carved with great care and justice, and a nice piece of ham, some brawn, and a steak-and-kidney pie, a large bowl of salad and several sorts of pickles, and afterwards some cold apple tart, jam roll, and a good piece of Stilton cheese, lots of bottled beer, some lemonade for the ladies, and milk for Master Punt: a very bright and satisfying meal.' I recall the rather more robust humour of Lancashire and one of the Eli stories. Eli was very ill, he lay dying upstairs in the bedroom. His wife ran up and said, 'Eli my dear, Eli my darling, is there anything you'd fancy by way of a bite of food?' 'Oh yes,' he said, 'I fancy a slice of that ham I can smell you cooking downstairs.' 'Oh Eli, you can't have that. That ham is for the wake!'

Wonderful hams we have cured, York ham, Suffolk ham, Bradenham ham, and we have made some good brawn and saveloys. Once sausages were the succulent delight of Saturday lunchtime and Sunday breakfast: I remember Palethorpe's Cambridge sausages with nostalgia. In those pre-war days the pork was blended with stale bread from the bakery, and a very good combination that was. Now it is blended with inert rusk, and the particular mildness of a first-class English sausage has gone for ever. When you add to that the sludge of meat recovered mechanically from the pig carcasses, which legally can be included as 'meat content', it is easy to understand why few sausages are worth eating to-day.

It has to be admitted that, as a nation, we have failed to exploit and appreciate the pig to its limits. Going to France in 1961, keeping house there, we were completely puzzled by the charcuteries. Nothing in England had prepared us for them. It was to disentangle this puzzle, to explain its elements to myself, that I first began to write about food. Odd, perhaps, to have built a career on the pig.

Or not so odd. Many skilful citizens do this in mainland Europe. Charcuterie even provided a foreground for that remarkable novel of Zola's *Le Ventre de Paris*. The main villain is a plump, pretty charcutière, Lisa, a charming piglet of a woman in starched white. She was queen of 'a world of good things, things that melted in the mouth, things of great succulence.' She dressed her shop window in a manner that any visitor to France to-day will recognize. In front, pots of rillettes alternated with mustard. Nicely crumbed little cones of jambonneau (boned knuckles of pork) backed them, along with black pudding curled like snakes and andouillettes marshalled in stacked pairs. There were loops of sausages draped from hooks, wonderful pâtés.

It's the separation of skill from butchery, the voluptuous pleasure that we miss. As far back as 1475 in Paris, the cooked meat sellers – known literally as *chaircuitiers* – allied themselves with the pâtissiers, i.e. the pastrycooks, who had the legal right to sell meat pies and pasties. This was a marriage of great potential – the most skilful of the meat trades in partnership with the most skilful of the bakery trades – and it shows in the best charcuteries five centuries later.

We were once known for our pork pies, and other pies as well. Pies, like puddings, were a great English speciality. I suppose that the reason for our modern failure is that our butchery trade was not stiffened by the same legal props and alliances: with the increasing demand for cheap food, cheapness rather than quality, all professional skill has gone. It is amazing to recall that pork pies were once so special that some people even had cases made so that they could be carried safely on long coach and train journeys when they went visiting. A friend of mine used to recall the anticipation with which his family awaited the arrival at Christmas of one particular uncle, who came down, I think from Lincolnshire, with a magnificent pie that fitted exactly into the black leather pie-case. Pork pies became his favourite food for life, and he would mourn over some that I bought for his entertainment, bewailing their slump since pork in the last 40 years has gradually had the succulence bred out of it. So, too, have brawns and chitterlings hit an all-time low and nearly vanished from view: what you do see for sale is turned out with so little subtlety and elegance, it's no wonder they have lost favour.

For black puddings, you need to go north, to Lancashire above all. Lincolnshire still keeps its chine stuffed with parsley, a delicacy much appreciated by Verlaine, who worked in those parts as a schoolmaster; a good stuffed chine can be delicious, but if the herbs are stale it tastes unpleasantly musty.

Bacon was once our passion, but it was a passion that brought down the trade at the end of the nineteenth century. The public preference was for the Wiltshire Cure, bacon cured on the side with the back leg, which we owe to the Harris family of Calne, in Wiltshire (where pigs were fattened on the whey from cheesemaking). 'British pig farmers were unable to supply the quantities of *consistently good meat* [my italics] that were required. The Danes, who were heavily dependent on pig farming for foreign earnings, spotted the opportunity. British pig breeders failed to compete with the scientific approach adopted by the Danish pig industry and lost the market.' Shall we ever get it back? Interestingly, the Danes have only ever produced bacon for export – they do not eat it themselves.

As with beef and lamb, our superiority in animal breeding was not much to our benefit after the last war. Self-sufficiency was the cry. Intensive farming the answer. Inevitably we lost a number of the most interesting breeds that provide the resources for future development.

Take the famous Berkshire pig, that incorporates the plumpness and early maturity introduced in the eighteenth century from Chinese and Neapolitan breeds, the dish-shaped profile rather than the straight nose of the wild boar and the ancient European pigs that ran in the oak forests to fatten on acorns. In 1949 about 200 boars were registered. Thirty years later there were only 16.

Things have got so bad, with beef, lamb and pork, that some people have taken a stand. They want to save what they can, trying to recapture what has nearly been lost forever. Their aim is to discover a new and more rewarding path for the future. These ideas were behind the founding of the Rare Breeds Survival Trust in 1973. After 19 years it now looks like something more than a charming hobby for the well-heeled or cranky middle-classes. One might say the same of its natural ally, the organic farming movement (the bluster of the conventional farming community that has taken such a bad turn over the last 40 years, bad gastronomically if not financially, provides a barometer of its importance). By maintaining and restoring rare breeds we keep a credit account of characteristics that can be drawn on as required in the future. In organic farming, we see salvation for our polluted land and rivers, some limit at least to the damage, and the hope of better health for our children.

My four farmers for the future are Anne Petch of Heal Farm in Devon, with her Middle Whites, Tamworth, Gloucester Old Spot and British Lop pigs, and her lively business in primitive lamb; Richard Wear, flock-master, of Butcombe in Avon who works with Anne Petch; and Richard Young and his sister, who rear Red Lincoln and Black Welsh cattle on a model organic farm near Broadway.

Richard Young is deputy director, and a most estimable example, of the British Organic Farmer. By long family experience, by intelligence and humanity, the Youngs have shown that organic farming works. Every farm should be like their Kite's Nest. Animals have space and liberty – no overstocking, no intensive units, no growth-promoters, but a harmony of arable and livestock farming. There are no long journeys to the slaughterhouse, and one or other of the family goes with the animals to reduce stress to the minimum possible. Then the meat is hung for a fortnight or so. I envy people living within reach of their farm shop and in the local delivery area.

Richard Wear also comes from a farming family, and works with his wife and son. Between them they have about 1,000 sheep on their upland farm to the south of Bristol. They specialize in bringing on primitive breeds, which on account of their small size and remoteness were ignored by the great breeders of the past. To-day the small joints they produce – a gigot weighs no more than 1½ kilos (3 lb) – are practical. Their leanness and the flavour that develops during their slower growth to maturity (6-8 months by contrast to the 11-16 weeks of conventional breeds) are in line with modern ideas on good and healthy eating.

On the Wear farm you may see 20 different kinds of sheep, including such rare breeds as Portland (little tanned noses), Manx Loghtan (the name means mouse-brown), St Kilda (deep brownish black) and White-faced Woodland. The energetic North Ronaldshay sheep that keep a wary distance, and run and jump like deer, have to be kept in separate fields as they have a disruptive effect on other sheep and lead them astray. They are culled from the seaweed-eating feral sheep of Orkney, from the flock that the Rare Breeds Survival Trust safeguards on its island of Linga Holm. They are transported to Avon once a year, in slow stages, and it takes expert stockmanship to bring them on over a six- or eight-month period.

Richard Wear can tell by a glance when a sheep is ready for market, or by simply putting a hand on its back. He explained that with immature sheep you can see where the parts of the body join, even under thick winter wool. When there are no telltale shadows, and the body is a smooth unity, they are right.

His main customer is Anne Petch who can now supply a complete range of top quality meat by mail order. Without such a specialist outlet, Mr Wear could not afford such an interesting flock. For the future, these two enterprising farmers envisage the public spending a rather more sensible proportion of its income on better and healthier food. They also feel that farmers in the west of the country, who have always been more entrepreneurial, more open to change than farmers in, say, East Anglia, will be ready – as they and the Youngs are – to meet the demand.

Anne Petch in particular is a proven and tried warrior. Despairing of most pork on sale, she went into business in 1979. Hard strife for two or three years. Much local antagonism. Regulations brought in to protect the consumer were used against her, a fellow producer, but one with rather more go and intelligence than was comfortable. I can see that this slender blonde girl in her check shirt and jeans must have appeared a frail target to pick off. Her straight and steely intelligence, the warm enthusiasm she has somehow managed to preserve, made their mark and she has prevailed. She is now a much respected member of the National Pig Breeders' Association, as well as a powerful voice on the council of the Rare Breeds Survival Trust.

Poultry and game are, for very different reasons, the mavericks of the meat trade, representing its worst – frozen battery chicken – and its best – woodcock, grouse, perfectly hung pheasant and roe deer. Loss of the sense of taste must be one of the worst features of the British palate. Allied with a new passion for sterility, it could spell the end of any chance of being able to buy good meat, poultry and game (as well, of course, as cheese and eggs). When I once complained about the blandness of the average, mass-sale sausage, I was reminded that for maximum sales it must offend nobody at all. A prime recipe for nullity, since inevitably it will please nobody at all either.

I didn't realize quite how far we had lost flavour in poultry until I visited Tom Bartlett of Folly Farm, near Bourton-on-the-Water. He, too, is a member of the Rare Breeds Survival Trust. Indeed before the Trust was ever thought of he was rescuing breeds of waterfowl and farmyard poultry that were fast disappearing. Birds on sale to-day are mainly hybridized creatures – mongrels of innominate descent – bred for snappy growth and the quick efficient buck. Flavour is the first thing to go because flavour depends on a lifespan double that of many birds on sale. It depends also on exercise, and the freedom to peck around for food. And on hanging, too. I cannot think why English poultry farmers have not brought in something like the French *Label Rouge* system, which weeds out the best birds, presents them well with a label containing much information. First of course the type of bird, *Poulet de Bresse, Poulet de Loué, Poulet Noir des Landes*, and so on. Then the farmer's name and the bird's number. You are also told the bird's age – very important if you are dithering between two birds of the same weight, the one which is older will taste better. Its rearing – *en plein air* – and feeding – mainly cereals – are also detailed. The system, which can be applied to other foods as well, is policed by the State, so there is no chance of internal corruption.

We know and are told too little. Wool is pulled over our eyes to the point of blindness. Take Aylesbury duck. Sounds nice and historical. It was once the preferred breed for its rich, fine deliciousness. Don't be fooled. What you have on your plate has barely an Aylesbury gene in its body. You have to go to somewhere like Folly Farm to buy your own breeding stock if you want to sample the real, right thing. I despair, but then I think of how cheeses have developed in the last 10 years: it's not an impossible dream to envisage the district around Aylesbury alive again with flocks of these excellent birds.

We need to support and encourage small poultry farmers of good will by paying for better birds. What I resent is being entirely reduced to a Mills and Boon choice, no chance to savour the Jane Austens or Mark Twains or Seamus Heaneys, let alone the Shakespeares or Wordsworths of the barnyard world. At Folly Farm you will find a Bodleian of possible future choice. At least you can go home with new-laid eggs, bright white ones, opaque or translucent, green and greyish or duck-egg blue, and occasionally the rare black eggs of the iridescent beetle-green Cayuga duck from America or the azure eggs of the Araucuna hens (a pair first landed in Shetland from a stray Armada ship).

Mr Bartlett's 140 species provide as absorbing a study in their names, histories and habits – and give as deep an insight into human existence – as old roses or fruit and vegetable varieties or cheeses. He saw with sadness that the Standard of the once-popular Silver Appleyard duck had been lost. He set about finding the family of Reginald Appleyard, its distinguished breeder and a great judge of birds, and persuaded the daughter to let him into her attic. There they found a painting – now at Folly Farm – showing exactly how the ducks should look. Tom Bartlett has thus been able to restore the true Standard, and the Standard as well of the Miniature Silver Appleyard, ideal for small gardens. Both kinds are good layers and provide good eating.

After hearing Mr Bartlett talk, I was intrigued to see the proper Toulouse geese and Rouen duck (almost as far removed from to-day's Rouen ducks sold in France as the old Aylesbury is from our birds); their breastbones keel the grass, two fingers' width from the ground. There, too, were the huge Embden geese – originally from Germany – that once kept strangers away from our Wiltshire farmyard, and chickens named for *de Crèvecoeur* (who wrote *Lettres d'un cultivateur américain*, first published in London in 1784), for the Brahmaputra river and for the Malay jungle where the main ancestor of to-day's birds – *Gallus gallus* – was first domesticated 4,000 years ago.

Game animals and birds are man's oldest food as far as meat is concerned. The deer swimming across the river painted on the walls of Lascaux, the bones in every palaeolithic excavation, are evidence of that. The surprising thing is that deer in particular who can become extremely tame and biddable, have never been fully domesticated. Sheep, goats, cattle, dogs have all become part of human society over the best part of 9,000 years. Why were deer ignored by Neolithic farmers, when venison had been the most widely eaten meat in Palaeolithic and Mesolithic times? Bones of red deer have been found in 95 per cent of European sites: in southern parts this means a period of 50,000 years.

The ancient Assyrians kept vast hunting ranges of deer, sport to hand, the prospect always there to gladden the master's eye. The Romans also kept deer in parks, but mainly for food. The same was true of the Normans in England (who also introduced the rabbit) – there were some 2,000 deer parks, run as a source of food like the dovecot and the stewpond or vivarium. Apparently there was a lively trade between parks, and deer were moved about in carts regularly – which suggests that when they are handled and looked after, they become tame enough not to panic.

The reason venison became less important as a meat – note the retention of the French word for deer meat, just as beef remains the word for bull or cow meat with the Anglo-Saxon ox retained for the offal and extremities alone – was the introduction of turnip culture. Turnips were the answer to winter feeding: they made it possible to overwinter cattle and sheep *in large numbers*. The ancient virtue of deer in this respect is their much reduced winter appetite. What people then preferred was fat on the joint, whether of beef or of mutton: once they were assured of year-long plenty, they were able to drop the leaner venison. Flavour, with game of all kinds, and tenderness, depend on hanging, which is an extremely skilful matter of judgement with the different species of bird and creature, less perhaps with venison than with pheasant and wild duck.

This leanness is of course what makes game a desirable meat to us now. Determined efforts are made to increase supply, and bring venison or pheasant to a wider market. Game is naturally lean.

Efforts are being made to promote venison as the meat of the future, and – because it is, in a sense, unnecessary – a meat whose increasing production we should, as consumers, be able to influence. As one deer farmer said, 'Let's get it right this time! We don't want venison to be the battery chicken of AD2000'.

Most of the venison on sale comes from the wild and from parks – and from three or four species of deer. The largest, the Monarch of the Glen, is the red deer: some claim that, at its finest, it comes from the Highlands. Those brought up on J.W. Fortescue's heroic *Story of a Red Deer* will claim that Exmoor stags are finer. Next in size is the fallow deer, the gentle, spotted creature appearing in misty crowds in the distance of great parks. Third and best of all to eat is the roe deer, especially young roe deer, the *chevreuil* of three-star French menus, for its combination of wild flavour, tenderness and convenient size. A fourth species is the small sika or Japanese deer, a fairly recent introduction via Powerscourt in Ireland. Derek Cooper wrote to us in 1983 about the first sika he had ever bought (from Duncan Fraser, the great game expert of Bunchrew, Inverness): it was 'outstandingly good. A great deal of fat on its small and delicious leg so we roasted it just like a leg of lamb. It tasted like a cross between duck and goose with extra subtleties.'

Peering anxiously at dark and unfamiliar cuts in the game butcher's window, one may feel intimidated by the differences between species, indeed between animals. In *Game for All*, Nichola Fletcher – Britain's first deer farmer – says that with game, each individual needs to be assessed separately and hung accordingly. 'Even with farmed game, which starts off by being a more consistent product, huge differences can be obtained by changing the hanging conditions.'

This means you need to find a game butcher you can trust. State your preference, order in advance, or be prepared to be guided towards an alternative. It is all a matter of taste. For instance, I like game to taste of game, in other words to be gamy. I don't want venison stew to taste like *boeuf bourguignonne*. I have found venison bought from supermarkets to be on the tasteless side: one batch was even watery when browned for a stew. It had not been hung for long enough.

You need to be wary, which is why I suggest the need for a good game butcher. As the green-minded will be happy to know, 'the whole point of deer farming is that they are efficient at converting grass [a natural foodstuff, not to mention potatoes, carrots, apples, etc] into lean meat.' There is no danger that deer will ever be – can ever be – 'continuously housed' (a damnably polite way of saying imprisoned in crates or other forms of confinement). The deer farmers are trying to do things properly, to prevent cowboy practices before they ever start. I hope they pull it off, and that the farming of deer will not lead to nullity. Sad if venison ended up as boring as farmed trout or frozen chicken or sausages – all items that within living memory were once delicious to eat. But as one farmer has remarked, when describing the practicalities of farming deer, 'Let's hurry up and try to give cattle, sheep and pigs the privilege of such kid-glove treatment!' Yes, indeed.

For anyone who wants further to study the quality and history of different animal breeds, and gain many insights into the history of our meat-eating habits, may I recommend two books:

*Domesticated Animals from Early Times*, by Juliet Clutton-Brock (Heinemann & British Museum (Natural History), 1981)

*Two Hundred Years of British Farm Livestock*, by Stephen J.G. Hall and Juliet Clutton-Brock (British Museum (Natural History), 1989)

# BEEF & VEAL

## ROAST BEEF WITH YORKSHIRE PUDDING

*2-2½ kilos (4-5lb) joint sirloin with undercut, on the bone or ribs of beef*
*Beef dripping or oil*
*1 onion, sliced*
*Salt, pepper*
*1 teaspoon sugar*
*1 teaspoonful of flour*
*300 ml (½ pt) beef stock*

THESE are the minimum sizes for joints of beef on the bone, as far as successful roasting is concerned. Although boned joints make for easier carving, the flavour is better if the meat is left on the bone. Rub the meat over with salt and pepper, and leave overnight.

Next day, weigh the joint and calculate cooking time – 30 minutes to the kilo (15 to the pound) for rare meat, 30 minutes to the kilo (15 to the pound) plus 20 minutes for well-done meat, at mark 7, 220°C (425°F).

Put enough dripping or oil into the roasting pan to cover the bottom, and put the pan into the preheated oven. After 5 minutes, add the joint which you have placed on a rack or trivet. Forty minutes before the end of cooking time, pour the Yorkshire pudding batter into the pan. It will acquire an extra good flavour from the drippings of the meat.

Cook the onion very slowly meanwhile in a little dripping in a small pan. Mix in the sugar and let it caramelize to a deep mellow brown. Stir in the flour, then add the beef stock. Simmer for at least 20 minutes, and correct the seasoning.

When the meat is cooked, place it on a serving dish, with the Yorkshire pudding cut in pieces around it. Pour off the fat from the roasting pan, and add any meat juices which have not been absorbed by the pudding to the gravy. Strain it into a hot sauceboat.

Serve horseradish sauce, page 351, and roasted parsnips with beef. Other suitable vegetables are carrots, courgettes, glazed onions, roast potatoes.

## BONED ROAST SIRLOIN

WHEN A VERY SPECIAL MEAL IS PLANNED, and you want to be absolutely confident about a joint of beef, it is worth ordering by post a boned rolled sirloin of Aberdeen Angus. Harrods will do this, and so will a first-class provincial butcher such as Charles MacSween and Son, 130 Bruntisfield Place, Edinburgh. For peace of mind, it is worth paying the special delivery charges.

Here is some good advice from Harrods: 'Set your oven as high as it will go' – above mark 10, 260°C (500°F), if possible – 'put in your beef and leave for 15 minutes. Turn the heat down to mark 4, 180°C (350°F), and leave for 30 minutes per kilo (15 minutes per pound).' This gives you rare beef. For a joint of 2½ kilos (5 lb) upwards, reduce the oven temperature to mark 5, 190°C (375°F).

The snag about this method is low Sunday and holiday gas pressures. With such problems, you will do better to stick to the method of the recipe above.

## YORKSHIRE PUDDING

ON ROAST-BEEF SUNDAYS, my mother's father, who had reached heights of power and respectability in the Bank of England, forgot what was due to his position and remembered the ways of the Northumbrian farm at Old Bewick which his family had come from. The roast beef went back to the kitchen after the main course, but the Yorkshire pudding remained to be finished up with sweetened condensed milk. I do not know how my grandmother took this – she prided herself on her elegant desserts – but my mother shared his delight in the crisp and sticky pudding. When she had a home of her own, and a family, she passed his taste on to us, who only remembered him, in spats and spectacles and pin-striped trousers, from old photographs.

Try it. But the pudding should be roasted *above* the beef, and you will have to forgo the meaty juices, at least as part of the pudding. There is, of course, no reason why you shouldn't just make the Yorkshire pudding on its own, as a straightforward second course.

*250 g (8 oz) flour*
*Pinch salt*
*3 eggs*
*Up to 600 ml (1 pt) milk, or half milk/half water*

Mix flour and salt, make a well in the centre and break the egg into it. Add a little milk. Beginning at the centre, stir these ingredients into a batter, gradually pouring in the remainder of the milk, or milk and water, until the batter is of a creamy but pouring consistency (the quantity will depend on the size of eggs).

THIS RECIPE HAS REMAINED UNCHANGED since the eighteenth century. According to Mrs Anne Wilson, again of Leeds, who wrote *Food and Drink in Britain* (Constable, 1973), the first recipe for what we now call Yorkshire pudding comes from *The Whole Duty of Woman*, published in 1737. The frugal intention was to make use of the dripping and juices which fell from joints of meat roasting on a spit (these, in grand houses at any rate, were the semi-official perquisites of the kitchen boy whose job it was to turn the spit: he dipped his fingers into the pan to help him keep going). The interesting thing is that the author instructs us to place the batter under a joint of mutton. Ten years later, Hannah Glasse gives us her recipe, the batter identical with ours today, and she calls it Yorkshire Pudding – she doesn't specify which sorts of meat it should be eaten with, but she does mention that marvellous northern habit of eating it alone with the gravy.

*'Take a quart of milk, four eggs, and a little salt, make it up into a thick batter with flour, like a pancake batter. You must have a good piece of meat at the fire, take a stew-pan and put some dripping in, set it on the fire; when it boils, pour on your pudding; let it bake on the fire till you think it is high enough, then turn a plate upside-down in the dripping pan [i.e. the pan under the joint] that the dripping may not be blacked; set your stew-pan on it under your meat, and let the dripping drop on the pudding, and the heat of the fire come to it, to make it of a fine brown. When your meat is done and sent to table, drain all the fat from your pudding, and set it on the fire again to dry a little; then slide it as dry as you can into a dish, melt some butter, and pour it into a cup, and set it in the middle of the pudding. It is an exceeding good pudding; the gravy of the meat eats well with it.'*

NOTE THAT until Imperial measures were introduced in the nineteenth century, the pint measured 16 fluid ounces as it still does today in America.

## THE PRIZE-WINNING CHINESE YORKSHIRE PUDDING

SEVERAL YEARS AGO, six chefs competed at Leeds in the 'Great Yorkshire Pudding Contest'. To the chagrin of native cooks, the winner was Mr Tin Sung Chan from Hong Kong, who ran the Chopsticks Restaurant. 'His methods were unorthodox,' wrote the *Guardian* reporter, 'his ingredients oddly arranged, but his pudding swelled to the height of a coronation crown and its taste, according to one of the judges, was superb.'

*300 ml (½ pt) milk*
*4 eggs*
*Just under ½ teaspoon salt*
*Dash of pepper*
*½ teaspon* tai luk *sauce*
*250 g (8 oz) plain flour, sifted*

MIX all ingredients except the flour, beating them well together. Let them stand for 15 minutes, then whisk in the flour. Heat a roasting pan and some dripping from the meat in the oven, which should be at mark 8, 230°C (450°F), then pour in the batter and leave for 20 minutes 52.2 seconds.

For years I puzzled over *tai luk* sauce, asking at Chinese groceries without success. Then an enterprising niece found what seems to be the answer: her request for *tai luk* was greeted with much laughter: apparently it means 'mainland', i.e. 'mainland China'. So *tai luk* was a kind of secret-ingredient joke, an amiable joke at the expense of Yorkshire patriotism.

## SHEPHERD'S PIE

'1885. *Pall Mall Gazette*. The Eastbourne board of Guardians have ordered a mincing-machine . . . for the use of aged and toothless paupers in their workhouse.' Originally mincing meant chopping something with a knife. With meat, it helped to make the less noble parts edible without prolonged cooking. Fair enough. But with the first mincing-machines, prison, school and seaside boarding house cooks acquired a new weapon to depress their victims, with watery mince, shepherd's pie with rubbery granules of left-over meat, rissoles capable of being fired from a gun.

If you use fresh meat, trim it free of fat and mince it or chop it yourself at home, if you season the dish well, if you cook and mash the potatoes especially for it, shepherd's pie – or cottage pie, as it's sometimes called – can be well worth eating. Anyone can cook steak. It takes a modest and generous skill to turn cheaper cuts of meat into something good.

For 6

*1 large onion, chopped*
*3 cloves garlic, chopped*
*3 tablespoons oil*
*500 g (1 lb) beef, chuck or shin, minced, or lean lamb*
*1 tablespoon tomato concentrate*
*150 ml (¼ pt) dry white wine*
*300 ml (½ pt) beef stock*
*3 heaped teaspoons of cornflour*
*Salt, freshly ground black pepper*
*1-1½ kilos (2-3 lb) potatoes*
*90 g (3 oz) butter*
*300 ml (½ pt) milk*
*30 g (1 oz) grated cheese, preferably Cheddar*
*1 tablespoon grated Parmesan*

STEW onion and garlic in the oil until soft. Raise heat and add minced meat, stirring it about until it is nicely browned. Mix in tomato, wine and half the stock. Slake cornflour with remaining stock, and pour into the pan. Season well, particularly with the pepper, and simmer for 10 minutes, covered. Pour off any surplus fat.

Meanwhile boil potatoes in their skins, peel them, and mash them with butter and milk.

Put the minced meat into one large or a number of small individual pots, and cover it with the mashed potato. Fork the potato up and sprinkle it with cheese. Bake for 10 minutes at mark 6, 200°C (400°F), then reduce the heat to mark 4, 180°C (350°F), and bake for a further ¾ hour. If more convenient, shepherd's pie can be baked for an even longer time at a lower temperature to suit your convenience. The 10 minutes, though, at a high temperature, is a good idea to start the top browning.

## SHIN OF BEEF STEW

THIS WAS SUBSTANTIALLY THE RECIPE USED in our family nearly a century after Francatelli published it, in his *A Plain Cookery Book for the Working Classes*. The main difference was that the meat was floured before frying, and salt was never added until the end. It was one of our favourite dishes. I remember asking my mother why she bought shin of beef, when other people bought the more expensive – and therefore better, or so I thought – stewing beef. She showed me how the rounded nuggets of meat are patterned with a transparent gelatinous membrane which holds them together, and adds a smooth, jellied texture to the sauce. Nowadays I always buy shin of beef on the bone when I can, and get the butcher to saw it across into slices (like the Milanese *ossi buchi*). This way the sauce is even better, and one has the delicious marrow as well. Or else I buy and cook the meat in one piece, which takes longer of course. The meat is sliced and served on a bed of potatoes and glazed carrots, and sprinkled with parsley. The sauce is reduced by boiling to increase the flavour, and served in a separate sauce boat. It does not look in the least like a stew. I always serve meat and sauce separately, because the older members of the family cannot bear the sight of a stew after their early institutional experiences.

One or two practical suggestions. Stock, or better still stock and red wine, can be substituted for water; the seasonings can be improved by the addition of garlic and a bouquet garni. Always remove the fatty outer skin from the beef, and cook the stew the day before it is needed. Allow it to cool to tepid, then strain off the sauce into a bowl and put it into the ice box of the refrigerator. The fat will rise quickly to the surface – there is always some, however carefully you trim the meat – and can be removed easily. Restore the shin of beef to the sauce, and reheat slowly and simmer for 20-30 minutes before serving.

Garnishes such as olives or mushrooms with glazed onions and triangles of fried bread, enable you to serve the dish a second time without it being too obvious. Extra vegetables can be added at the end.

*2 kilos (4 lb) shin of beef*
*Dripping*
*2-3 tablespoons of flour*
*375 g (12 oz) carrots, sliced*
*375 g (12 oz) onions, sliced*
*Salt, pepper*
*Water*

'FOUR pounds of leg or shin of beef cost about one shilling; cut this into pieces the size of an egg, and fry them of a good brown colour with a little dripping fat, in a good sized saucepan, then shake in a large handful of flour, add carrots and onions cut up in pieces the same as the meat, season with pepper and salt, moisten with water enough to cover in the whole, stir the stew on the fire till it boils, and then set it on the hob to continue boiling very gently for about an hour and a half, and you will then be able to enjoy an excellent dinner.'

## BRAISED BEEF AND CARROTS

A GOOD VERSION OF BRAISED BEEF AND CARROTS that I had from a young Irish friend, Carmel O'Connell, who used to work with that splendid chef, Colin White. She recommended using brisket – I bought a piece of well-hung Aberdeen-Angus – but topside could be substituted, or that muscle that runs down the shoulder blade, sometimes called salmon or feather cut, if you can persuade your butcher to cut it for you. English butchers are loath to do this, preferring to cut across several muscles rather than removing and trimming one nicely shaped piece of meat, but people living in Scotland, or who are lucky enough to have a butcher who understands French cuts, may be able to manage it. If more convenient, the dish can be cooked in a low oven.

For 6-8

*2-2½ kilos (4-5 lb) piece rolled brisket*
*Lard*
*6-8 fine large carrots, peeled*
*Up to 1 litre (1¾ pts) poultry stock, unsalted*
*Generous sprig of thyme*
*Salt, pepper, chopped parsley*

CHOOSE a flameproof pot that holds the meat closely. Brown the beef in a little lard and put it into the pot. Slice carrots thinly, in the processor or on a mandolin. Arrange a quarter of them around the beef. Pour in stock to come 5-7 cm (2-3") up the pot and tuck in the thyme. Bring to the boil and cover. The lid need not fit very tightly, as a certain amount of evaporation is desirable.

Keep the pot at a gentle bubble, checking it every half hour, adding the rest of the carrots in three batches and topping up the liquid level with more stock. After 2 hours it should be cooked, but be prepared to give it a further half hour. The dish will come to no harm if it has to be kept warm for a while, so allow plenty of time.

Transfer the beef to a hot serving dish, and surround with the drained carrots which will be extremely succulent. Season them, sprinkle with parsley and keep warm. Strain liquid into a shallow pan and boil down to concentrate the flavour. Season, pour a little over the beef and carrots, and the rest into a hot sauceboat. Boiled potatoes go well with this dish.

NOTE: the original recipe suggests cooking the dish one day and reheating it the next for an even better flavour. If you do this, chill the pot fast in ice cubes and water, refrigerate overnight and reheat thoroughly.

## BEEFSTEAK STEWED WITH OYSTERS

For 4-5

*750g (1½ lb) beefsteak (see recipe)*
*Salt, pepper*
*18 fine oysters*
*60 g (2 oz) butter*
*300 ml (½ pt) water*
*60 g (2 oz) port*
*15 g (½ oz) butter*
*1 rounded tablespoon flour*
*Triangles of bread fried in butter*

ANY good beefsteak will do for this recipe, from chuck to rump, but you will have to allow for the stewing time accordingly. Trim off fat and gristle and cut it into neat pieces. Season them and put them aside while you open the oysters, into a sieve set over a basin. Leave the oysters to drain, while you brown the meat in the butter. When it is a good colour on both sides, pour in the oyster liquor and the water, which should barely cover the meat. Put a lid on the pan and leave everything to stew until the beef is tender – this will take from 1 hour to 2½ hours, depending on the quality of the steak.

When the meat is ready, pour in the port wine. Mash the butter and flour together, and add it to the sauce gradually in little knobs. You may not need it all to thicken the sauce, which should be kept over a moderate heat just below boiling point. Adjust the seasoning, add the oysters to warm through for a minute or two: they should not cook too long or they will become tough. Put the steak and oysters with the sauce into a dish, tuck the bread round the sides and serve very hot.

## SUSSEX STEWED STEAK

For 6

*1-1¼ kilos (2-2½ lb) slice top rump or chuck steak, trimmed*
*Salt, pepper*
*Flour*
*1 large onion, sliced*
*6 tablespoons stout*
*6 tablespoons port*
*2 tablespoons mushroom ketchup or wine vinegar*

SEASON the meat and rub it all over with the flour. Put it into a shallow ovenproof dish in which it can lie flat. Put the onion on top in an even layer. Pour in the stout, port and ketchup or vinegar. Cover the dish with a tight-fitting lid of foil, and put it into the oven at mark 1, 140°C (275°F), for 3 hours. Serve with mashed potatoes, and some field mushrooms if you can get them.

IF YOU do not have a suitable dish, wrap the whole thing in a double layer of foil, fastening it very securely (it is a good idea to butter the foil first), and place it on a baking tray.

## MARROW-BONES

MARROW-BONES MAKE A FIRST COURSE that is easy to cook, succulent and light to eat. Once they were popular – Queen Victoria had marrow on toast every day for tea, I believe – now they seem to have been filched from us in the interest of our dogs, judging by advertisements.

You will not find marrow-bones in a supermarket. Look instead for an old-fashioned family butcher and be prepared to order them well in advance (you may also have to join a queue of customers who are already in the know). Ask him for one or two nicely cut pieces of marrow-bone per person.

Mix up a little flour and water dough to stick over each end of the bones to hold the marrow in place, then wrap them in cloths or pieces of foil. Stand them upright on a trivet in a pan (fish-kettles are ideal for cooking marrow-bones). Pour in boiling water, almost to cover, bring back to the boil, reduce heat to maintain a steady simmer, cover and leave for 2 hours.

For serving, have ready plenty of dry toast. Unwrap the bones and remove the blobs of paste. Stand them on plates, wrapped in napkins if you want to be really correct, and provide marrow spoons if you have such a thing – the Italians call them tax-collectors, and they are handy for winkling out the marrow. Shellfish scoops will do instead, or even skewers, or a pointed knife, as the marrow will drop out of the bone quite easily. It can then be spread on the toast, salted and eaten.

I reflect that Peking Man burnt bones in the fire and split them to extract the marrow. One of man's earliest experiences of the high pleasures of eating.

NOTE: some butchers, a very few good ones, sell the marrow already extracted from the bones. To cook it, cut it into even lengths and place in a wire basket. Have ready a pan with boiling beef or veal stock or salted water. Plunge in the basket, bring back to simmering point and leave for at most 5 minutes. Drain, cool slightly, then cut across into even discs. Arrange in overlapping rows on fingers of lightly buttered hot toast. Sprinkle with salt, pepper, Cayenne and a few drops of lemon juice. Put into the oven to become very hot. Serve with a light dusting of parsley. Lucky Queen Victoria!

## VEAL ROLLS

ALLOW one large, thin, escalope of veal for each person. Spread it with a thick layer of parsley and lemon stuffing, or herb stuffing (page 348), and roll it up starting with one of the long sides. Tie it with thread in three or four places, then cut it into three or four pieces. Brush each piece with beaten egg, dip it into flour and string it on to a skewer, one skewer for each person. Grill for 20-30 minutes, preferably on a spit, basting them from time to time with melted butter. Serve them with fried mushrooms and lemon quarters.

## VEAL (OR LAMB) CUTLETS

WHEN preparing veal or lamb cutlets from the best end of neck, dip them into beaten egg, then into a mixture of breadcrumbs made piquant with chopped parsley, marjoram, thyme, winter savory and grated lemon peel. Press the breadcrumbs well into the meat, then fry it gently on both sides in clarified butter. When the cutlets are done, transfer them to a serving dish. Sprinkle the pan juices with 2 teaspoons of flour, then stir in about half a pint of veal or lamb or chicken stock to make a sauce. Off the heat, whisk in a good knob of butter, correct the seasoning and sharpen it with lemon juice. Strain into a sauceboat and serve with the cutlets.

Slices of boned veal or lamb loin may be cooked in the same way: they should not be cut too thick – about half an inch is right. The method can also be used for reheating roast veal or lamb which has not been overcooked in the first instance.

Lemon quarters, mushrooms, watercress, a few boiled potatoes, are the right kind of setting for meat cooked in this way. The sauce should be well seasoned, and not too copious or thick.

## MINCED VEAL AND EGG

ALEXIS SOYER, BORN IN FRANCE IN 1809, lived mainly in England, cooking and writing for 'the higher class of epicures . . . and the easy middle class', in particular at the Reform Club, where his splendid kitchens were among the sights of London. He used his fame to help the unfortunate. In the potato famine of 1847 he organized a soup kitchen in Ireland. He revolutionized army catering in the Crimea – there are many middle-aged ex-soldiers today who have cooked on the army stove he invented – while Florence Nightingale was tackling the hospitals. In the 1850s he wrote a *Shilling Cookery for the People* and dedicated it to Lord Shaftesbury.

I wonder if the Earl found Soyer's preface embarrassing. He knew the stinking lives of the poor at first hand, but Soyer bade a lofty farewell to the Reform club and set off to find out how The People lived as if he were going to Africa in search of pygmies.

The resulting book is strange, always fascinating. Classical allusions jostle tales of gin-drinking crones turning ox cheek to burnt sacrifices. Soyer deplored bad drains and cookery in prosperous industrial Yorkshire, and the Irish habit of throwing fish on to potato fields as manure rather than eating it – 'They actually manure the land with gold to reap copper.' He exhorts his readers to codliver and its oil, to wholemeal bread, to curing hams, to using herbs and their own ingenuity. He gives a superb course in good plain cookery, which had its effect on the educated but frugal middle classes rather than on The People who could not for the most part read what he had written for them.

Another point for gratitude, Soyer invented the kitchen timer, that invaluable device that saves many of us from daily disaster.

*60 g (2 oz) chopped onion*
*1 clove garlic, chopped*
*50 g (1½ oz) butter*
*250 g (8 oz) trimmed, minced veal*
*1 rounded teaspoon salt*
*½ teaspoon black pepper*
*Pinch cinnamon*
*Pinch nutmeg*
*1 teaspoon thyme*
*1 heaped teaspoon flour*
*150 ml (¼ pt) milk*
*Lemon juice or wine vinegar*
*4 eggs*
*4 slices bread fried in butter*

SOFTEN onion and garlic in butter, then raise heat and brown lightly. Stir in the mince, and as it turns opaque and begins to brown mix in seasonings and flour. Pour in the milk, then simmer – do not boil – for 20 minutes. Taste occasionally, adding more spice or thyme. Finally sharpen the flavour very slightly with lemon or vinegar. Meanwhile poach the eggs, or boil them 6 minutes and shell them carefully. Serve minced veal in its thick creamy sauce on the bread, topped with the eggs. Follow with a green salad.

## CALF'S BRAINS WITH BLACK BUTTER

For 6-7

*750 g (1½ lb) calf's brains, blanched (see recipe below)*
*Butter*
*1½ tablespoons white wine vinegar*
*1 heaped tablespoon capers*
*1 level tablespoon chopped parsley*
*Salt, pepper*

IF the brains are not in good shape, slice them as neatly as you can. Fry them on both sides until golden brown in a little butter. Place them on a warm serving dish (around, or on, a bed of spinach is a good idea). Keep them hot. In the pan, melt a good large egg of butter – about 100 g (3½ oz) – and when it is sizzling stir in the vinegar and capers. Boil hard for a moment or two to drive off the vinegar fumes (don't put your head over the pan), add parsley and seasoning, quickly pour over the brains and serve.

Triangular croûtons of fried bread can also be tucked round the edge of the dish, or toast. If you blanch the brains well in advance, cook the spinach and fry the croûtons, you can finish off the brains very quickly at the last moment, while spinach and croûtons reheat.

## BRAINS WITH CURRY AND GRAPE SAUCE

For 4

*750 g (1½ lb) brains*
*Salted water*
*Milk*
*30 g (1 oz) butter*
*1 rounded tablespoon flour*
*1 teaspoon curry powder*
*150 ml (¼ pt) hot chicken stock*
*150 ml (¼ pt) double cream*
*250 g (8 oz) grapes, preferably Muscat grapes, peeled and pipped*
*Triangles of fried bread*

RINSE the brains under the cold tap, and remove the fine membrane that holds the blood vessels, easing it out of the convolutions. If this proves difficult, soak the brains in salted water for an hour and try again, rinsing them well.

Put the brains into a pan, cover them with milk and bring them to the boil. Simmer for 5 minutes, until the brains are firm. Strain off the milk, which will be needed for the sauce. Slice the brains, arrange them on a serving dish and keep them warm.

To make the sauce, melt the butter in a small pan, stir in the flour and curry powder and cook for 2 minutes. Add the hot chicken stock gradually, then 150 ml (¼ pt) of the milk the brains were cooked in. Simmer for about 20 minutes, stirring from time to time. Add the cream and correct the seasoning. Last of all, tip in the grapes and any juice, and leave for a few moments to heat in the sauce, which should be the consistency of double cream but not gluey. Extra stock can be added if necessary.

Pour the sauce over the brains and garnish them with triangles of bread fried in butter.

THIS SAUCE goes well with boiled chicken, or with sweetbreads which have been prepared in the usual way and then fried.

## SKUETS

I FIRST CAME ACROSS THIS RECIPE in French, in Carême's *L'art de la cuisine française au dix-neuvième siècle*, which first came out in 1833. He describes it as an

English recipe, and praises it. I imagine he may have come across it in England while he was working for the Prince Regent. The odd thing is that it is not in the most popular cookery books of the eighteenth and early nineteenth century. I came across it eventually in *The Compleat Housewife*, by E. Smith, a reprint from the fifteenth and eighteenth editions, of 1753 and 1773 (the earliest edition now held is the third, of 1729). This early recipe lacks the bread sauce, and the crumbs are pressed into the skuets of meat before they are hung up to roast before the fire. Carême's refinements really make the dish.

For 4

*500 g (1 lb) veal or lamb sweetbreads*
*Salt*
*Light veal or chicken stock*
*2 teaspoons lemon juice or wine vinegar*
*8 thin rashers of smoked streaky bacon*
*16 mushrooms*
*Chopped parsley and thyme*
*Freshly ground pepper*
*Browned breadcrumbs*
*Bread sauce (page 356)*

To prepare sweetbreads, place them in a bowl and cover them with water. Stir in a tablespoon of salt. Leave for an hour or longer if you like. If they are frozen, leave them for several hours. Drain them, rinse them with cold water and place them in a pan. Pour enough stock over them to cover them by about ½ cm (¼″), and add the lemon or vinegar. Bring slowly to the boil, and simmer gently until they lose their raw pinkish white look and turn opaque. This takes a couple of minutes with lamb's sweetbreads; veal sweetbreads, being much larger, can take 20 minutes. Pour off the cooking liquor, which can be used in soups and sauces (some sweetbread recipes use the stock to make the appropriate sauce). Run the sweetbreads under the cold tap and pull off the gristly bits. Go carefully, though; if you pull off too much, sheep's sweetbreads will disintegrate into very small knobs. Put the sweetbreads on a plate, with another plate on top to press them. They can now be left in the refrigerator for later use, or overnight.

To assemble the skuets, cut the sweetbreads into slices or chunks about an inch wide, and divide them into four even rows. Cut the bacon into enough small pieces to go between them, and put them in place. The mushrooms should be fitted in at appropriate intervals. Scatter with chopped parsley and thyme. Now take four skewers and run them through the four lines of sweetbreads and bacon, etc. Brush them over with melted butter and grill them under a medium heat for about 15 minutes.

Serve them on a long dish scattered over with the browned crumbs. The bread sauce should go in a separate bowl.

# LAMB AND MUTTON

FIRST-CLASS LAMB has become a problem in England since the importation of cheap, refrigerated New Zealand lamb made it a meat for the most homely occasions (mutton seems to have disappeared altogether – it needs a very knowledgeable butcher, and lost its reputation during the last war, when butchers were not able to carry on their trade in the proper manner). Nowadays I sometimes conclude that our best lamb all goes to France: certainly it is instructive to visit a butchery there and see how highly lamb is regarded – and what a price it is, and how delicious it is.

However, perseverance and a certain obstinacy should lead you to a butcher who can supply local or at least very good English lamb. And remember these lines when you are making your choice:

*The mountain sheep are sweeter,*
*But the valley sheep are fatter,*
*Therefore we deemed it meeter,*
*To carry off the latter.*

'THE WAR-SONG OF DINAS VAWR' *by T. L. Peacock.*

I choose the sweetness of Welsh mountain lamb from Radnor when possible, but that may be because we live near enough to Wales to make an expedition to Cardiff from time to time. There we buy real Welsh lamb in the covered market, and some laverbread to go with it, before sauntering off, our minds at peace, to contemplate the Impressionist paintings in the gallery. (We find that our best expeditions satisfy both body and soul – something that English restaurant-keepers do not always understand.)

You may prefer to uphold the honour of your district in Scotland, Northumberland or Devon – so long as you have found a knowing family butcher who cares as much for what he sells as what he takes. Londoners may complain that it's no longer possible for them to choose their lot, arguing preferences at dinner like any Forsyte. But people living around Romney Marsh are worse done by. They have to look across at flocks of sheep feeding on the salt marshes, and know that the meat will bypass *their* butchers and be served to tourists in Normandy, Brittany and Paris, as *agneau pré-salé, spécialité de la maison*, price to match.

Mrs Beeton sternly remarked that Wales was the only part of Britain to have the correct conditions for true *pré-salé lamb*. Half a century later, John Meade Falkner described the reclaimed marshes around Chichester (in *The Nebuly Coat*) and said that sheep grazing behind the dykes had as good a flavour as any *pré-salé* mutton the other side of the Channel. Certainly French buyers today share his opinion. Now, one may even wonder about the lamb served on Mont St Michel. Customers sit in high restaurants, looking across the bay at the sheep advancing and retreating, with the tides, over the moss-like verdure. Are there really enough of them to feed all those summer visitors? Surely not!

An elegy for *agnus britannicus*? Not entirely. Since 1974 when I wrote the first version of *English Food*, enterprising farmers led by the Rare Breeds Survival Trust have restored old breeds of sheep. With a little effort, you can now find miniature joints of Soay, Jacob and Ronaldsay lamb from suppliers such as Anne Petch and from the increasing number of organic and Guild butchers. Things are looking up.

## ROAST SADDLE OF LAMB

For 10-12

*1 saddle of lamb with its kidneys 4½-6 kilos (9-12 lb)*
*Salt, pepper, thyme*
*Butter*
*Flour*
*150 ml (¼ pt) port or red wine*
*450 ml (¾ pt) stock made from lamb trimmings and bones*

THE butcher will have prepared the saddle by slitting the tail and curving it over, with the two kidneys between the tail pieces and the saddle, the whole thing skewered in place with a couple of wooden cocktail sticks. One warning – for this kind of high-class butchery it is wise to go to an experienced man of mature years, and if his father was a butcher before him, so much the better.

To prepare the joint for cooking, remove the kidneys, but restore the toothpicks to their place so that the tail maintains its curves while cooking. Score the skin into a diamond pattern. Rub the fat over with salt, pepper and thyme (slivers of garlic may be stuck into the meat – this has recently become an English habit). Melt a little butter and dribble it over the joint.

Roast the saddle for 2½ hours at mark 5, 190°C (375°F), for slightly pink meat. Baste it occasionally with the port or red wine, and the pan juices. After 1¾ hours, add the kidneys to cook under the front of the joint so that they do not dry out. After 2 hours' cooking, dredge the lamb lightly and evenly with flour and a little more melted butter. Leave it to brown – raising the heat if it seems a good idea, but make sure that the tail is protected by foil from burning if you do this.

Meanwhile prepare the gravy. Melt 30 g (1 oz) of butter in a pan, and cook until it turns golden brown. Stir in 1 heaped tablespoon of flour, and then the stock to make a sauce. Leave this to simmer down gently as the saddle finishes cooking.

Place the cooked joint on a hot serving dish. Spear the kidneys back in place and keep warm while the gravy is finished. (All roast meat should rest 15-30 minutes before being carved.) Pour off the fat from the pan juices, and set the pan over a good heat. Stir in the sauce, and scrape up all the delicious brown bits which may have stuck to the pan. Taste and adjust the seasoning. Many people like a thick gravy with lamb, others prefer it to be a slightly more runny affair, so adjust the mixture in the pan by adding a little more wine or stock, or by boiling the gravy hard for a few moments to thicken it further. Pour through a strainer into a hot gravy boat.

### THINGS TO GO WITH ROAST LAMB

*Mint sauce (summer, page 350)*
*Redcurrant or medlar jelly (winter, page 363-5)*
*Laverbread, heated with orange and lemon juice (all seasons, page 60)*
*Young peas and young potatoes, cooked with mint*
*Asparagus*
*French beans*
*Spinach*
*Cauliflower*
*Purple sprouting broccoli*
*Chestnuts and Brussels sprouts*
*Chestnut purée*
*Onion sauce*
*Roast potatoes*

### TO CARVE A SADDLE

Cut slices parallel to the backbone, or else cut down into choplike slices at a sloping angle to follow the rib bones. Remove the kidneys and cut them up as fairly as you can.

## LEG OF LAMB STUFFED WITH CRAB

DO NOT BE NERVOUS OF THE STRANGE-SOUNDING COMBINATION of lamb with crab: it is delicious, as the crab gives a nutty-tasting piquancy to the meat, and is not in the least fishy. Remember that in the past meat was often 'piqued' with anchovies, or stuffed with oysters, and even cockles, and that anchovy essence still goes into our Melton Mowbray pork pies.

I will tell you how this recipe was invented. It's the habit of foreigners in a strange country to jeer at the food. An English traveller in Italy once complained of the lack of pease pudding and bubble-and-squeak. I have often heard the French laugh at our habit of eating redcurrant jelly with lamb, quite forgetting their own similar combinations of pork with prunes or duck with orange. I suppose it is a sign of insecurity, of the closed mind. This being so, it is not surprising that when our friend Guy Mouilleron then at the Café Royal found himself one evening with a group of French chefs working in

London, the conversation turned to the odd food habits of the English. Fancy, one of them said, they even eat lamb with crab! General laughter: but Guy Mouilleron thought, lamb with crab? Why not? So without further suggestions he produced this delicious combination of braised lamb with a crab stuffing. I did not have the heart to tell him that many English people would be as shocked as his French friends were at the idea, and that the combination was left behind in the early nineteenth century, as far as national dishes are concerned. ('Fill the cavity with a forcemeat containing the meat of a crab or lobster, shred and pounded, a little grated lemon peel, and nutmeg: sew it up; roast, and serve, with lobster or crab sauce under it.' 1811 edition, John Farley, *The London Art of Cookery.*)

*1 large leg of lamb*
*Salt, pepper*
*Carrots, diced*
*Onions, chopped*
*1 large stick celery, sliced*
*300 ml (½ pt) dry white wine*
*300 ml (½ pt) lamb stock*
*150 ml (¼ pt) double cream*
*1 teaspoon curry powder*

STUFFING
*1 boiled crab, about 750 g (1½ lb) weight*
*½ teaspoon curry powder*
*1 tablespoon fresh chopped mint*
*3 egg yolks*
*Salt, pepper*

TUNNEL-BONE the leg of lamb to make a good cavity (or persuade the butcher to do it for you). Use the bones and any trimmings to make the lamb stock. Season the leg inside and out.

To make the stuffing, remove the crab meat from the crab – with patience and application you will get something between 250 g and 300 g (8 and 10 oz). This is a fiddly job, I know, but frozen crab meat will not be nearly so good. Mix with the remainder of the stuffing ingredients, fill the lamb cavity and sew it up.

Chop enough carrots and onions, in roughly equal quantity, to make a good layer in the bottom of a self-basting roaster or similar type of dish. Add the celery and season everything well. Place the lamb on top. Cover with a lid, or a piece of double foil, and leave in a moderate oven, mark 4, 180°C (350°F), for 2 hours, or until the lamb is cooked. Transfer it to a roasting pan and put it back into the oven to brown, while you make the sauce. To do this pour the wine and stock on to the bed of vegetables in the braising pan. Set it over a good heat, and bring to the boil, stirring well to scrape up all the meaty bits. Simmer for 5 minutes, then strain into a saucepan. Skim off any surplus fat, add the teaspoon of curry powder and finally the cream. Correct the seasoning and heat through thoroughly before pouring into a hot sauceboat. Serve with hot buttered noodles.

## Lamb (or Mutton) to Eat like Venison

*1 leg of lamb (or mutton)*

Marinade
*150 g (5 oz) chopped onion*
*150 g (5 oz) chopped carrot*
*60 g (2 oz) chopped celery*
*3 cloves garlic, chopped*
*2 tablespoons oil*
*1 bay leaf*
*2 sprigs thyme*
*4 sprigs parsley*
*2 sprigs rosemary*
*8 juniper berries, crushed*
*8 coriander seeds, crushed*
*10 peppercorns, crushed*
*3 teaspoons salt*
*600 ml (1 pt) red wine, or dry white wine, or dry cider*
*150 ml (¼ pt) red or white wine vinegar*

First make the marinade – brown vegetables and garlic in the oil. Add the remaining marinade ingredients and bring to the boil. Set aside to cool. Remove the outer skin of the leg of lamb, if the butcher has not done so already. Score the fat into a diamond pattern, and place the meat in a deep dish. Pour over it the cold marinade. Leave the whole thing in a cool place for four days, turning the joint over twice a day. Cover the dish between whiles with foil.

To cook the lamb, you will also need

*2 onions, sliced*
*2 carrots, diced*
*2 stalks celery, chopped*
*2 leeks, sliced*
*250 g (8 oz) unsmoked streaky bacon, cut in pieces*
*60 g (2 oz) butter*
*Veal stock*

Into a deep pan put the vegetables and bacon which should first have been lightly browned in the butter. Lay the leg of lamb on top. Strain the marinade over it, and add enough veal stock to come about two-thirds of the way up. Bring slowly to the boil, cover the pot and leave to simmer for 2 hours until the lamb is almost cooked – this can be done either on top of the stove or in the oven. Turn the joint over after 1 hour. Shortly before the 2 hours is up, remove a generous litre (2 pts) of the cooking liquor and boil it down to 1 pint of strongly flavoured stock. Put the meat on to a roasting dish and give it 20 minutes in a hot oven to glaze, mark 7, 220°C (425°F), basting it frequently with the reduced stock.

Serve it with green beans, redcurrant jelly and either the pan juices, or gravy made from them, together with some of the remaining cooking stock.

A leg of pork can be treated in the same way, to taste like wild boar. When one can get it, a leg of mutton is better than lamb: it will need longer braising time, before being glazed in the oven.

## RAGOÛT OF LAMB

A BEAUTIFUL DISH OF MICHAEL SMITH'S from his *Fine English Cookery*, a book I enjoy using very much. Look out in the shops for the large uneven Marmande tomatoes: they are superior in flavour and firmness to the pallid blobs that most non-gardeners have to endure most of the time. Good tomatoes make all the difference to the flavour of the sauce.

*1 kilo (2 lb) boned leg of lamb*
*2 heaped tablespoons seasoned flour*
*Cooking oil*
*½ teaspoon Cayenne*
*2 large cloves garlic, crushed*
*1 sprig rosemary*
*Grated rind one small lemon*
*2 carrots, diced*
*½ large head celery, diced*
*750 ml (1¼ pts) chicken stock*
*18 large spring onions or pickling onions*
*30 g (1¼ oz) butter*
*1½ teaspoons caster sugar*
*5 large firm tomatoes (approximately 750 kg (1½ lb))*
*1 heaped tablespoon basil or parsley*

CUT meat into 2 cm (1") cubes. Shake them in a bag with half the seasoned flour, until coated. Brown them in oil, and transfer to a casserole. Sprinkle over them the remaining flour, plus any left in the bag. Add Cayenne, garlic, rosemary and lemon rind. Brown carrots and celery lightly in the meat pan, then add to the casserole with the lamb. Pour on the stock, cover and stew for 1½ hours or until tender (not overcooked) either on top of the stove, or in the oven at mark 5, 190°C (375°F).

Prepare the onions, leaving 2-3 cm (1") of green on the spring onions, or removing the skin from the small pickling onions. Turn them in half the butter melted in a small frying pan, and sprinkle them with the sugar. Cook until they are lightly caramelized, shaking them about to colour evenly from time to time. Add to the ragoût about 45 minutes before the end of the cooking.

Skin the tomatoes, cut them across and scoop out the seeds. Dice roughly. When the ragoût is done, skim off the fat, check the seasoning and put the whole thing into a wide serving dish. Heat the tomato dice through in the remaining butter, pour off any surplus juice and put the tomato in a cushion over the ragoût. Scatter with basil or parsley. Serve with bread or baked potatoes, and follow with a salad.

THE PERFECT late summer dish for a gardening family, when basil and tomatoes are full of the flavour of the sun.

## Boiled Leg of Mutton (or Lamb) with Caper Sauce

*1 trimmed leg of mutton or lamb*
*3 carrots, quartered*
*3 onions, unpeeled*
*2 parsnips, peeled, quartered*
*1 turnip, peeled, quartered*
*Salt, pepper*

Vegetables
*1½ kilos (3 lb) young turnips, peeled, sliced*
*1 level tablespoon flour*
*30 g (1 oz) butter*
*150 ml (¼ pt) double cream*
*Nutmeg, pepper, salt*
*Caper sauce (page 350)*

Put the meat into a large pan, with the vegetables and seasoning. Cover it with tepid water. Bring it to the boil, skim well and cover. Leave it for 2½ hours – the liquid should bubble occasionally with a slight burp, it should not be allowed to boil properly. Remove the leg to a large serving dish and cut a paper ruffle to put round the shank bone – see page 179.

Meanwhile prepare the turnips. They should be cooked in salted water; drain them well, sieve, and whisk in the butter. Stir the cream into the flour and make sure that there are no lumps, and add that to the turnip. Put back over the heat and cook until the purée thickens up nicely. Season with nutmeg, pepper and salt.

When the lamb or mutton is on its dish, take spoonfuls of the turnip and put them round it, flat side down. Cut the carrot from the cooking stock into even-sized batons, and put them between the mounds of turnip.

Serve the caper sauce separately.

Boiled leg of mutton is even more delicious if it is allowed to cool in the cooking liquor until next day. Then serve it cold with a plain salad and a bottle of claret.

## Spiced Welsh Mutton 'Ham'

*3 kilos (6 lb) leg Welsh mutton or lamb*

Spiced Salt
*125 g (4 oz) dark brown sugar*
*250 g (8 oz) sea salt*
*15 g (½ oz) saltpetre*
*30 g (1 oz) black peppercorns*
*30 g (1 oz) allspice berries*
*1 heaped teaspoon coriander seeds*

Crush the spices and mix them with the sugar, salt and saltpetre. Rub the meat over with this mixture, being particularly careful to push it down between the meat and bone. Leave in a deep dish in a cool place for 12-14 days, rubbing the meat each day with the spiced salt mixture and its juices, and turning it over.

To cook the 'ham', rinse off the bits of spice and place it in a large pot or ham kettle. Cover with tepid water, bring to the boil and simmer gently for 3½ hours. Leave to cool down in the cooking liquor for 2 hours, then remove and drain and finish the cooling process under a weight.

IN THE old days, the cured but uncooked 'ham' would be squeezed free of as much moisture as possible and left under a weight for 24 hours. It would then be smoked over smouldering oak chips for 5-15 days. If you have a small friendly bacon factory near you, which will smoke your ham, this is something I can recommend – it is a great luxury. Eat like Parma ham, uncooked in thin slices.

## LAMB WITH PLUMS

A SWEET AND SOUR DISH for early autumn, when there are plenty of dark red English plums about.

*1 joint roasting lamb for 6 people (loin or leg)*
*Butter*
*2 glasses dry white wine*
*10 large red plums*
*1 clove garlic, chopped*
*1 medium onion, chopped*
*¼ teaspoon each cinnamon and allspice or nutmeg*
*1 teaspoon sugar or more*

CHOOSE a joint that is not too fatty, or else cut away much of the fat. Brown it all over in butter. Put into a deep ovenproof cooking pot with the wine, plums, garlic, onion and spices. Cover and cook in a moderate oven if it is a large joint, or in an oven at mark 6, 200°C (400°F), if you are using a smaller rack of lamb from the best end of neck. Alternatively cook the lamb in a flameproof pot on top of the stove, turning it over from time to time.

When the lamb is cooked, remove it to a serving dish and keep warm. Skim fat from the pan juices, and then sieve them. Reheat and taste – add extra spices and sugar to taste but do not make the sauce too sweet. Pour a little sauce over the meat, and serve the rest separately in a bowl. Potatoes are the only vegetable to serve with lamb cooked in this way.

NOTE: if the sauce is too thick for your liking, add a little light stock or even water to dilute it. Remember to adjust the seasoning.

## SHOULDER OF LAMB WITH RICE AND APRICOT STUFFING

SINCE THE ARRIVAL OF FROZEN, CHEAP LAMB from New Zealand, this type of recipe has increased in common use in England, to compensate for the coarser flavour of the meat. The idea of cooking lamb with dried fruits, originally from the Middle East, has been adapted to our tastes, as curry was earlier on. If I held to the theory of folk-memory, I could say that this and similar recipes fall into the niche once occupied by sweet lamb pies; they were favourite dishes from the Middle Ages until the end of the eighteenth century. A version lingers on in southern France at Pézenas. French cookery writers assert that when Clive of India stayed for some time in the town, his chef gave the recipe to a French pâtissier: they are still made there and at Béziers, and include mutton, not very much sugar, and lemon peel. Other versions are found in locally produced cookery books from Wales and the north-west of England. I suspect that they are more honoured in the breach than in the modern kitchens of those parts. (The sweet pie recipe on page 230 came from our landlady when we were evacuated during the war to Casterton in Westmorland: her ingredients resulted in a sweet mince pie (the Pézenas pies are eaten as first course), and very good it is.

*1 boned shoulder of lamb, unrolled*
*Salt, pepper*
*Melted butter*

STUFFING
*250 g (8 oz) rice, long grain*
*150 g (4 oz) dried apricots, soaked, chopped*
*2 tablespoons seedless raisins*
*2 tablespoons blanched, split almonds*
*½ teaspoon cinnamon*
*½ teaspocn coriander*
*½ teaspoon ground ginger*
*Salt, black pepper*

SPREAD out the shoulder of lamb, which should have been boned so that a pocket is formed inside the meat. Season it inside and out.

Boil the rice in plenty of boiling, salted water. Drain it well and mix with the remaining ingredients. Use some of the mixture to stuff the lamb, and sew up the pocket with needle and button thread. Brush the lamb over with melted butter and roast it in the usual way – 1 hr per kilo (30 minutes per pound) stuffed weight, plus 20 minutes, at mark 5, 190°C (375°F). When it is done, remove it to a serving dish. Pour the fat from the pan juices, and then mix in the remaining rice mixture to reheat; add a little butter if necessary. Arrange this round the lamb, cut away its thread, and serve.

## PRIMITIVE LAMB WITH BLUEBERRY SAUCE

SINCE I FIRST WROTE *English Food*, two of the best additions to our diet have been primitive lamb and blueberries. Happily they go well together. There may be other farmers rearing these interesting breeds of sheep in other parts of the country, but I always go to Anne Petch whose product is impeccable and whose delivery system works (Heal Farm, Kings Nympton, Umberleigh, Devon EX37 9TB, telephone: 07695-2077). It is worth buying several gigots at a time, or for that matter any other joint, as they survive the freezer with hardly any loss of quality. One might also say the same about blueberries.

For 6-8

*2 gigots, 2½-3 kg (5-6 lb) in all*
*Pepper, coarse sea salt*
*Sprig rosemary (optional) or garlic*

SAUCE
*250 g (8 oz) blueberries*
*150 ml (¼ pt) dry white wine*
*150 ml (¼ pt) lamb stock*
*A little sugar*
*6 tablespoons white wine vinegar*
*2 sprigs mint, chopped, or a few leaves of rosemary*
*Meat juices from roasting the gigots (see method)*
*60 g (2 oz) unsalted butter*
*Lemon juice, salt, pepper*

PEPPER the gigot all over and roll in coarse salt (this gives a crunchy finish). Place on a rack in an ovenproof dish with a sprig of rosemary, if used, on top. Alternatively stick the joint with slivers of garlic, but not too many, one clove is enough per gigot. Leave for at least 30 minutes.

Meanwhile, preheat the oven to mark 8, 230°C (450°F), and make a start on the sauce. Cook the blueberries with wine, stock and 1 tablespoon sugar. Set aside a heaped tablespoon of the best berries for the final garnish and liquidize or process the rest, then push it through a sieve to get rid of the seeds.

Bring the vinegar to the boil in a very small pan with 2 teaspoons sugar and cook until syrupy. Add to the sieved blueberries, with the mint or rosemary and alcohol. Set aside and return to the lamb.

Put it into the oven. After 15 minutes turn the heat down to mark 4, 180°C (350°F) and leave for a further 20 minutes. Test with a skewer – push it into the fattest part, leave 30 seconds then tap it on the back of your hand. If it is cold (unlikely) the meat is not cooked, if it is warm it is pleasantly pink, if it is hot – ouch! – it is cooked through (and, to my taste anyway, overdone). Remove the joints to a warm serving dish and leave in a warm place – e.g. the plate-warming oven – for at least 15 minutes.

To finish the sauce, skim any fat from the meat juices, then pour them into the blueberry sauce. Reheat gently, correcting the seasoning and adding a little lemon juice to sharpen and enhance the mildness of the blueberries. Only add more sugar if absolutely necessary – the sauce should not be too sweet. Either serve the sauce in a bowl with the whole blueberries you set aside and garnished with mint leaves, or pour a little of it around the meat, scatter on the blueberries and tuck in a sprig or two of mint.

I would not serve a lot of vegetables with such a rare treat of a dish, just a few potatoes, or bread and a side salad.

NOTE: laverbread goes well and appropriately with primitive lamb. See recipe following for the general idea. If you do cook a best end joint of such small creatures, remember Anne Petch's warning that in the hot oven of an Aga, it takes as little as 12 minutes.

### PLAIN ROAST PRIMITIVE LAMB WITH GRAVY

ROAST as above. While lamb is resting, make the gravy by skimming off the fat from the juices, then pouring 300 ml (½ pt) lamb or light chicken stock into the pan. Set over a moderately high heat and deglaze, scraping in all the little brown crusty bits. Pour in a glass of wine and cook down to reduce for a good concentrated flavour. Season with salt and pepper and strain into a sauceboat. Peppered redcurrant jelly (see page 363) makes a good accompaniment, plus the usual runner beans or mange tout peas in summer; carrots, scorzonera or salsify, and parsnips in winter, with potatoes.

## ROAST RACK OF LAMB WITH LAVERBREAD

*1 whole best-end of neck of lamb, preferably Welsh*
*1 clove garlic*
*Salt, pepper*
*1 large tomato*
*1 carrot*
*600ml (1 pt) beef stock*
*1 glass dry white wine or vermouth*
*1 tablespoon cornflour*

LAVERBREAD
*500 g (1 lb) laverbread*
*90 g (3 oz) butter*
*Juice of 1 lemon*
*Juice of 2 oranges*
*1 orange thinly sliced*
*Salt, pepper*

ASK the butcher to split the neck into two joints right down the centre, then to remove the boniest part of the spine. Do not let him remove the meat from the long bones or chop them short.

At home, remove a long strip about 4 cm (1½") deep from the thin ends; scrape the bones free of meat. Stick slivers of garlic into the joints and season them. All this can be done the day before the lamb is to be cooked. It is also a good idea to make the gravy stock in advance, too; the fat has time to solidify, and can easily be removed before making the sauce. To make the stock, put *all* the meat trimmings, plus the backbone removed by the butcher, into a pan, together with salt and pepper, tomato, carrot and beef stock. Simmer for at least 2 hours. Strain and leave to cool. When cold, take off the fat, add the wine to the stock and reduce to a good strong flavour. Finally thicken with cornflour in the usual way.

To return to the joints, stand them upright in a roasting pan with the exposed bones interlacing, like the roof ridge of a Danish farmhouse. Cover with a piece of foil to prevent them charring. Cook for 45 minutes at mark 7, 220°C (425°F), if you like lamb pink; for 60 minutes if you like it well done. When cooked, strain off the fat, and add meat juices to the sauce.

About quarter of an hour before the lamb is ready, prepare the laver. Melt the butter in a saucepan, stir in the laverbread and add the fruit juices to taste. Season if necessary with salt, and pepper.

Spread the laverbread on either side of the joints of lamb on a hot serving dish. Arrange the slices of orange at the edge. Some new potatoes go well with this dish, or old potatoes cut into neat rounds. Pour the sauce into a sauce-boat, and serve everything very hot.

IF YOUR fishmonger doesn't stock laverbread, and you do not live in the right part of England, you can buy laverbread by post. It travels well, and is already prepared and cooked – it only needs the kind of reheating described above. Laverbread with orange and lemon also goes well with salt pork or boiled bacon. (There is more about laverbread on page 60.)

## GUARD OF HONOUR

For 7-8

*1 best end of neck*
*Salt, pepper, thyme or rosemary*
*Butter*
*Herb stuffing (page 348)*

ASK the butcher to cut the best end of neck into two, straight down the backbone, and to chine it for easy carving. Be careful he does not trim off the long bones. There will be 7-8 chops in each piece.

At home, turn the joints skin side up, and remove about 4 cm (1½") only of skin and fat at the thin end of the joints. This will expose the ends of the bones: scrape them free of meat as well as you can. Score the skin in stripes or diamonds. Rub in salt, pepper and thyme or crushed rosemary. Now stand the joints up on their thick end, skin side out, and push them together so that the exposed bones cross each other alternately. The joints will bristle like a military row of crossed stakes. Very attractive on this scale. Skewer the meat together at the base, and push some stuffing into the cavity. Protect the exposed bones from burning with a piece of foil pressed into place over them. Roast at mark 5, 190°C (375°F), for 1½ hours. To carve, cut down between the cutlets, allowing two per person.

GUARD OF Honour can be served with all the usual things for lamb (see page 152), but the best thing is stuffed tomatoes (page 63), which should be placed round the joint on its serving dish.

## CROWN ROAST OF LAMB

A CROWN ROAST LOOKS MOST IMPRESSIVE in grand butchers' shops. It can be expensive, too, on top of the price of the meat, so you will find it well worth while to tackle the construction yourself.

The thing to watch out for is the butcher bringing his cleaver down on the long bones – this may happen at any moment during the preparation. You need the long bones intact.

Ask the butcher for a whole best end of neck – this means about 14 cutlets, enough for 6-7 people – and then ask him:

*(a) to divide it in two down the backbone, so that you have two symmetrical pieces,*

*(b) to chine it,*

*(c) to make small cuts between the cutlet bones.*

THEN rapidly take the meat home, before he chops off the long thin part automatically in spite of all your careful instructions.

The first thing is to remove the skin and fatty part from the thin end, as for Guard of Honour. Then scrape the exposed bones entirely free of meat and skin.

Place the two pieces together, skin sides touching. Thread a trussing needle with fine string, or a bodkin with button thread, and sew the ends together with a couple of stitches. Knot string or thread firmly.

Now stand the whole thing up and gently push your closed fist into the centre, so that the two pieces open into the familiar crown shape. The small cuts between the bones make the pieces of meat flexible enough to do this without strain. Cover the thin bone ends with foil.

Place the joint on a piece of foil on a rack in a roasting pan. Fill the centre with stuffing (the apricot stuffing on page 157 does well, so do the stuffings at the end of the book). Cook for about 1¼ hours at mark 5, 190°C (375°F).

Remove the crown roast to a hot serving dish with the aid of the foil. Tear away as much of it as you can. Replace the foil on the bone ends with cutlet frills. Surround with vegetables and serve.

## LANCASHIRE HOT-POT

THE ENGLISH COUSIN OF IRISH STEW, and very good when made with lamb or mutton of quality. If you want to make economies, buy scrag end of English lamb, rather than best end of New Zealand lamb: the flavour will be better. In the old days, mutton was the meat used. Now it is almost impossible to buy, but if you do succeed, allow a longer cooking time.

For 6

*12 best end of neck chops*
*6 lambs' kidneys (optional)*
*500 g (1 lb) onions, sliced thinly*
*1 kilo (2 lb) potatoes, peeled and sliced thinly*
*Salt, pepper*
*Water*
*Butter*

USING a deep casserole – the traditional kind is glazed dark brown and made in a flower-pot shape, with a rim and lid – put the meat and vegetables into it in layers, seasoning each layer with salt and freshly ground black pepper. Finish off with a nicely arranged layer of overlapping potato slices. Pour in enough water to come about halfway up the pot, and brush the top layer of potatoes over with melted butter. Cover and put into a hot oven, mark 6-8, 200°-240°C (400°-450°F), for about half an hour, then reduce the heat to mark 1, 140°C (275°F), and leave for 2½ hours. Take off the lid after 2 hours so that the potatoes can brown.

SEE ALSO *Cawl* from Wales, page 20, *Leek and Mutton Broth*, page 21, *Sweet Lamb Pie*, page 230.

## LAMB'S HEAD AND BARLEY, WITH BRAIN SAUCE

I REMEMBER THIS DISH from my childhood with great enjoyment. Do not make the southern-English mistake of thinking it ungenteel food, or even savage food (the title has overtones of those Iron Age chieftains in Ireland who used to pound the brains of their victims with lime, and roll them into balls, to keep as trophies of war). We over-indulge ourselves in attitudes of this kind, and are the losers. Mrs Beeton, for instance, regarded lamb's head as an obscure Scottish dish – 'We are not aware whether the custom of eating sheep's heads at Dudingston is still kept up by the good folks of Edinburgh.' Francatelli, at one time chef to Queen Victoria included an excellent sheep's head broth in his *Plain Cookery Book for the Working Classes*. Which puts it firmly in its place. A century earlier people had more sense. More eighteenth-century cookery books give one or two recipes for different ways of cooking sheeps' – or rather lambs' – heads. The combination of different textures in this dish is what makes it so good – the different textures of meat, the smooth pearl barley with a slight chewiness, the delicate smoothness of the sauce, and the crispness and sharpness provided by the bacon and lemon. Today you will find it difficult to buy lambs' heads, and I would only trust an organic butcher or meat supplier in view of scrapie scares.

| | |
|---|---|
| *1 lamb's head* | *1 small turnip* |
| *Water* | *1 leek* |
| *Salt, pepper* | *250 g (8 oz) pearl barley* |
| *Bouquet garni, including winter savory* | *30 g (1 oz) butter* |
| *Onion, stuck with 3 cloves* | *30 g (1 oz) flour* |
| *2 carrots, halved* | *150 ml (¼ pt) milk* |
| *1 parsnip, halved* | *Rolls of bacon, grilled* |
| | *Lemon quarters* |

ASK the butcher to clean and split the head, being careful to remove the brain before it is damaged. At home, soak the head in cold salted water for an hour. Rinse it, and put it into a cooking pot with enough water to cover it. Bring slowly to the boil and skim it. Now add seasonings, herbs, vegetables and pearl barley. Cook for about 1½ hours at a steady simmer, until the meat comes easily away from the bones.

Meanwhile soak the brain in cold salted water for 30 minutes, remove the membrane that nets it and place it in a little square of cloth. Tie it up and place it in the lamb's head pot for 10 minutes to cook. Alternatively, remove a large ladleful of stock from the lamb's head and cook the brain in it. Drain and chop it. Now make a sauce by melting the butter, stirring in the flour and moistening this roux with the milk, and enough lamb stock to produce a thick but not pasty sauce. Stir in the chopped brains, the parsley and correct the seasoning. Add a squeeze of lemon juice if you like.

Extract the lamb's head from the pot. Discard the bones and cut up the meat into nice pieces. Arrange them on a serving dish with the bacon rolls and lemon quarters. Put the sauce into a sauceboat. With a perforated spoon remove some of the pearl barley and put it round the meat. Serve everything very hot.

THE LIQUID in the pan, and remaining pearl barley make a marvellous soup (discard the vegetables and bouquet), which can be eaten before the meat in French peasant style, or at another meal. Personally, I think the latter arrangement is preferable. Lamb soup, then lamb's head, is a bit too much of a good thing.

## KIDNEYS IN THEIR FAT

ALMOST THE FIRST DISH I learnt to cook on arriving in Wiltshire was this delicious way of doing lamb's kidneys. It was a particular favourite of my husband's.

ASK the butcher, well in advance, to leave the lamb's kidneys still enclosed in their fat. when you get them home you can trim off any obvious excess fat, but each one should be enclosed in roughly 1½ cm (nearly ¾") of it. Allow two or three per person, according to the rest of the meal.

Preheat the oven to mark 8, 230°C (450°F). Put in the kidneys on a rack in a roasting pan and roast them for 30 minutes, or until the fat is brown outside and translucent. The first time you make the dish, it is prudent to dig into one of the kidneys with a careful knife and fork to see if it is done. If red, rather than pink, give them all a little longer.

Drain the kidneys well and put them on to a very hot dish. People can then excavate their own, or you can excavate them as you serve them out. Inside they should be beautifully pink and tender, just ready to eat with wholemeal or oatmeal bread, and mustard. The kidneys will also need to be seasoned just before eating with salt and coarsely ground black pepper.

# PORK

## ROAST PORK WITH CRACKLING AND BAKED APPLES

THE REV. WILLIAM COLLIER, of Cambridge, led a most dissolute life; he was also a notorious *gourmand*.

*'An anecdote I had from his own mouth will prove his title to the latter character. "When I was last in town," said he, "I was going to dine with a friend, and passed through a small court, just as a lad was hanging up a board, on which was this tempting inscription:*
*'A roast pig this instant set upon the table!'*
*The invitation was irresistible – I ordered a quarter; it was very delicate and very delicious. I despatched a second and a third portion, but was constrained to leave one quarter behind, as my dinner hour was approaching, and my friend was remarkably punctual." '*

FROM REMINISCENCES OF CAMBRIDGE,
*by Henry Gunning, 1854, 1855.*

For 6

*1 shoulder, loin or leg of pork*
*Salt, pepper*
*Pork bones*
*1 onion stuck with 3 cloves*
*1 carrot, sliced*
*Bouquet garni*
*Oil*
*30 g (1 oz) butter*
*1 tablespoon flour*
*6 large Cox's orange pippins*

BUY the pork a good 24 hours before you intend to cook it. Ask the butcher to score the rind every half inch, or do it yourself with a very sharp knife of the razor-blade variety. Ask the butcher, too, to bone the joint, but not to tie it.

When you get home, season the meat all over and in particular on the boned side. Leave in the refrigerator until it is required for cooking. This pre-seasoning benefits almost all meat for roasting: if you have a brine crock, put the joint into that for 8 hours – but the crackling will not crisp, after roasting.

Put the bones into a pot with the onion, carrot and herbs. Cover generously with water, and leave to simmer for 3 or 4 hours. Strain off the liquid and boil it down to ¾ pint. Season it.

Before putting the joint into the oven, rub the crackling over with oil, and sprinkle it with salt. Calculate the cooking time at 1¼ hours to the kilo (35 minutes to the pound). Put it into the oven set at mark 7, 220°C (425°F), then after 20 minutes lower the heat to mark 3, 160°C (325°F). An hour before the end of cooking time, score the skin of the apples in a circle an inch below the top (this prevents them bursting), and place them round the pork. To make the gravy, cook the butter in a small pan until it turns golden brown, stir in the flour, and moisten with the stock. Leave to simmer gently for at least 20 minutes.

When the meat is cooked, check the crackling. If it is not crisp enough, put the oven up again to mark 7, 220°C (425°F), and give the joint another 10 or 15 minutes (without the apples).

Put the meat on a serving dish, surround it with the apples, and keep warm. Skim the fat from the roasting juices, then pour them into the gravy. Correct the seasoning and serve very hot with the meat.

INSTEAD OF baked apples, many people serve apple sauce – recipe on pages 357-9.

If you do not care for crackling, ask the butcher to remove the rind (take it home, though, and cut it in squares and use to enrich a beef stew of the kind described on pages 128-30). Half an hour before the joint is cooked, mix up a glaze of:

*1 tablespoon French mustard*
*1 tablespoon melted redcurrant jelly*
*½ tablespoon soft brown sugar*
*½ tablespoon cream*

SPREAD this over the joint, and put back into the oven to turn a beautiful and appetizing brown.

## STUFFED PORK TENDERLOIN

THE TENDERLOIN IS THE UNDERCUT OF BACON PIGS, in other words the fillet of extra-large pigs. Usually it weighs in the region of half a kilo (a pound); it seems expensive, but is well worth the price as it is always tender and there is no waste, apart from a few bits of fatty skin. The countries for tenderloin are England, Denmark and America, in other words the main bacon countries. There are few recipes in French cookery for this cut, and I have only seen it on sale there twice.

The tenderloin is versatile; it can be cut across into small steaks, cooked in the frying pan, and served with a cream and apple pan sauce; you might try cutting it in thin thin slices – chill it first – on the bias to make escalopes; or thread it on to skewers with bacon and breadcrumbs (though this is an Italian idea). But perhaps the best way is to stuff and roast or braise it:

For 6

*2 tenderloins*
*2 large slices cooked ham*
*90 g (3 oz) Lancashire cheese*
*8 sage leaves, or thyme*
*4 rashers streaky bacon*
*2 large onions, chopped*
*150 ml (¼ pt) brown sherry, Madeira or port*

SLIT each tenderloin lengthways almost but not quite through. Open them out and beat them until they are much wider and flatter. Cut the ham and cheese into strips and lay them along the cut side of the tenderloins. Blanch the sage leaves in boiling water for 1 minute, cut them in halves and lay on top of the ham and cheese; alternatively sprinkle on the thyme. Roll up the tenderloins and tie them firmly with thin string. Brown them lightly in butter.

**Either** place them on a bed of onion in a shallow ovenproof dish, lay the bacon on top and pour over the wine, then roast them for 45 minutes at mark 5, 190°C (375°F);

**or** arrange them in the same way in a heavy saucepan and cook them on top of the stove for half an hour, turning them occasionally.

Sieve the juices to make a sauce, checking the seasoning before you reheat it. The meat will cut pink, on account of the curing of ham and bacon.

## CUMBERLAND SAUSAGE

**D**O YOU AGREE WITH ME that most national brands of sausage are a bland, pink disgrace? If so, it is worth looking out for Cumberland sausage even if you do not live in Cumberland. Ignore the packages of small sausages, and go for the great coil that lies on the counter fresh and speckled and glistening. Buy it according to the length you think you are going to need, rather than by weight. Fry it still in the piece – but you may find it difficult to turn over safely; for this reason Cumberland Sausage is better baked (see below). Present it on a dish of boiled, buttered potatoes, and apple rings which have been lightly fried in butter and sprinkled with pepper and nutmeg. Or use a spiced apple sauce, page 359, instead of the rings. Many people like it with red cabbage and apple cooked together in the German style.

Discard the skin and you have the perfect unstodgy basis for pâtés and pies and stuffings.

If you want to buy the real thing, in its most superior form, you will have to visit Keswick or Carlisle. I bought some in the triangular central square of Carlisle, from a butcher tucked away under an arched snicket. He told me that it contained ninety-eight per cent pork (including plenty of fat, which sausages should have), coarsely chopped, seasoned with salt and pepper only. Nothing else, no secret. But once minced, the meat and seasoning are mixed together by hand. It seems that only butchers in the north-west have the right *tour de main*. Perhaps they know their pigs better than many large sausage-makers seem to.

However, if you would like to try your hand at making this sausage – and possess a sausage-making attachment for your electric mincer – here are the ingredients used at the Rothay Manor Hotel, at Ambleside:

*500 g (1 lb) boned, skinned shoulder of pork*
*175 g (6 oz) hard back pork fat*
*½ rasher smoked bacon*
*¼ teaspoon each nutmeg and mace*
*30g (1 oz) white breadcrumbs*
*Salt, pepper*

CUT the pork, fat and bacon into strips and put first through the coarse blade of the mincing machine, then through the medium blade. Add spices, and then the breadcrumbs which have been soaked in 8 tablespoons of hot water. Mix well together with your hands, add salt and plenty of pepper. Set aside, covered.

Now rinse the salt from the sausage skins (from Catermasters Ltd, 2 Orphanage Road, Birmingham B24 9HS). Ease one end of a piece of skin on to the cold tap. Run cold water gently through the skin, to make sure there are no splits or large holes. Turn off the tap, remove the skin and ease it on to the long spout of the sausage-making attachment. Screw the whole thing on to the mincing machine with a coarse blade in position.

Feed the pork sausagemeat through the mincer again, and as it comes through, slide the skin gently off the attachment and coil it on to a large plate. Cumberland sausage is not divided into links. Leave in the fridge until next day, then bake the whole coil – enough for four on its own, or six as part of a mixed plateful – for 30-45 minutes at mark 4, 180°C (350°F). Prick the coil before putting it into the oven.

At Rothay Manor, Cumberland sausage is served with bacon, tomato, fried egg on fried bread, apple, black pudding and mushrooms. Sustaining before a long fell walk. In Carlisle hotels, fried slices of haggis are included in this kind of mixed breakfast dish, as well as the sausage.

## TOAD-IN-THE-HOLE

For 4

*Yorkshire pudding batter (page 139)*
*30 g (1 oz) lard or pork fat*
*500 g (1 lb) pork sausages*

MAKE the batter in the usual way. Separate the pork sausages and cook them for 5 minutes quickly in the lard or pork fat in a frying pan. Strain off the fat into a large roasting pan, pour in a thin layer of batter and bake in the oven for 5 minutes at mark 7, 220°C (425°F), so that it sets. Place the sausages on top and pour over the rest of the batter. Bake for a further 30-35 minutes until the batter has puffed up and browned. Serve straightaway.

ORIGINALLY Toad-in-the-Hole was made with pieces of meat, rather than sausages. They could be freshly browned chops or steak, but were more often the left-overs of an earlier meal which gave Toad-in-the-Hole a bad name as one of the meaner English dishes – like shepherd's pie. In fact if you are able to buy really first-class sausages, Toad-in-the-Hole makes an excellent family dish which no one has any call to feel ashamed of.

## WHITE PUDDINGS

PORK BUTCHERS IN THE MIDLANDS AND WILTSHIRE AND OXFORDSHIRE often sell large white sausages tied together in a horseshoe shape at the ends. They are filled with minced lean and fat pork, chopped parsley and a cereal filler. They make a good family lunch dish, particularly when they are fried with plenty of streaky bacon. Such things are not at all to be despised. When the puddings burst, and the sausage part browns in the bacon fat, they taste even better. They can also be cut in half across, and grilled.

## BLACK PUDDINGS

BLACK PUDDINGS have to be chosen carefully unless you are lucky enough to live in Bury, Lancashire, where the best ones are made. Many manufacturers put far too much barley and oatmeal with the blood and pork fat, which makes them stodgy by comparison, say, with the delicious black puddings of

France. To my way of thinking, the inside should remain soft and spicy when cooked; it should never be dry or hard.

The usual way is to slice black puddings and fry or grill them with bacon. I think they taste better when cut into lengths, and fried with chopped bacon and chopped apple. Serve with mashed potato and mustard. Then they are really delicious.

## FAGGOTS AND PEAS

FAGGOTS ARE A GOOD-TEMPERED DISH. They can be reheated. They can be cooked at an even lower temperature, if this suits your convenience. Should they not be nicely browned, a few minutes under the grill, very hot, will do the trick.

Faggots were popular in the past as a way of using up odd bits and pieces left over after a pig was killed. They often included the lights, heart and melt – and indeed many butchers who sell their own faggots use these parts still, rather than the belly of pork in this recipe, as well as the liver. Recipes vary in different parts of the country, just as pâté recipes do in France. Welsh faggots, for instance, may include a chopped cooking apple, and omit the egg. The rich savoury pleasure of faggots – one name given to them is savoury ducks – is very largely due to the enclosing grace of caul fat which keeps the dark lean meat well basted. For this you will need to go to a small family butcher, preferably an older man, who really understands meat.

The word faggot means a bundle, like a faggot of kindling for a fire, so do not be afraid to vary the recipe with additions and alterations of flavouring.

For 6

*500 g (1 lb) pig's liver, minced*
*300 g (10 oz) belly of pork, minced*
*2 large onions, chopped*
*1 clove garlic, chopped*
*4 sage leaves, chopped, or 1 teaspoon dried sage*
*½ teaspoon mace*
*2 medium eggs*
*Up to 125 g (4 oz) breadcrumbs*
*Salt, pepper*
*Piece of caul fat*
*150 ml (¼ pt) beef or veal or pork stock*

PUT liver, pork, onion, garlic and sage into a frying pan, and cook gently for 30 minutes without allowing the mixture to be brown. Stir occasionally.

Strain off the juices and set aside. Mix the meat, etc., with the mace, eggs and enough breadcrumbs to make a firm, easy-to-handle mixture. Taste and season. Soften the caul fat in a bowl of tepid water and cut it into roughly 12 cm (5″) squares. Divide the meat into 60 g (2 oz) knobs, and wrap each one in a square of caul fat. Place side by side close together in an ovenproof dish, which is not too deep: the faggots should stick up slightly above the rim. Pour in the stock. Bake for 40-60 minutes in a moderate oven, mark 3-4, 160-180°C (325-350°F), until the tops are nicely browned. About 20 minutes after the start of cooking time, strain off the juices into the liquor that was left from the first cooking. Stand the bowl in a bowl of ice-cubes, so that the fat rises quickly to the surface and can be skimmed off. Pour the stock over the faggots about 5 minutes before the end of cooking time. Serve with garden peas in the summer time, or with a purée of dried peas (page 56) in the winter.

## BRAWN OR HEAD CHEESE

*½ pig's head, including the tongue but not the brains*
*2 pig's trotters*
*500 g (1 lb) shin of beef*
*Piece of shin bone*
*2 cloves garlic, chopped*
*Large bouquet garni*
*10 black peppercorns*
*2 tablespoons wine vinegar*
*Salt to taste*

AROMATICS
*2 onions each stuck with 2 cloves*
*2 carrots, quartered*
*2 leeks, split*

TO FINISH
*Hard-boiled eggs*
*Toasted breadcrumbs*
*Chopped parsley, chives, chervil*

ASK the butcher to chop the head into two or three convenient pieces. Try and buy good long trotters, ending in a meaty piece of hock: they should be chopped in two. Submerge the pork in brine for 24 hours, if you can (see page 174). This isn't essential but it does improve the flavour. Ask the butcher if he can let you have the shin of beef on the bone, allowing extra weight (make sure that he reduces the price per pound accordingly). He may at first be startled, but even in a supermarket meat does have bones. Don't salt the shin.

Put all the meat into a large pan. Cover it with water and add the aromatics. Bring to the boil, skim, and then cover the pot closely, using foil to wedge the lid so that as little steam as possible escapes. Incidentally, don't add salt until the pot has come to the boil, then use sparingly.

Leave the pot to simmer for 2 hours and then try the smaller pieces of meat. If they are ready, they should part easily and cleanly from their bones. Remove them as they are cooked, and start the business of picking off the meat and chopping it. The bones can go back into the pot, or be thrown away.

As you chop the meat, pull away the few odd hairs and look out for tiny bits of bone. Neither improves the finished brawn. And whatever you do, *don't mince the meat*. If you are in a hurry, put the whole thing into the refrigerator until you can spare the time to finish the brawn properly. Mincing is the ruin of dishes like this. It reduces meat to a mush.

Having dealt with the meat, put it all into a commodious basin and set it aside. Strain off the stock into a clean pan (discard vegetables, herbs, spices, etc.) and boil it down to a concentrated flavour. This will partly depend on how much salt you added at the beginning: if you were sensible, you didn't add too much because the stock is greatly improved by reduction.

The next decision is how much of the reduced stock to add to the chopped meat. You do not want the brawn to look thin and mean. On the other hand, if the meat is too solidly packed, the brawn becomes too heavy to be enjoyable. This is something that can easily be judged by eye, and from the experience of brawn bought in shops.

When meat and stock have been mixed, put them in a pan and simmer for 20 minutes. Taste and adjust the seasonings – sometimes a little lemon juice is a great improver; and continue to taste as the brawn cools.

To finish, pour a layer of meat and stock into a loaf tin. Leave it to set in the coldest part of the fridge. Sprinkle with chopped herbs, lay hardboiled eggs along the centre, and cover with more meat and stock. Leave to set. Turn out of the tin and press the brawn into warm, toasted breadcrumbs. Eat cold with salad, mustard and potatoes – mashed potatoes, for instance. Or else with wholemeal or rye bread and butter.

ALTHOUGH SHIN of beef is not an essential ingredient of brawn, it does make a big improvement in flavour and texture. And the gelatine in the meat and bone helps to make an even better jelly.

The idea of cooking two meats together may seem odd at first. True, we eat veal and ham pies, chicken or turkey and ham pies, but there the partnership is so obviously complementary that we never question it, or even think about it.

Boiling two kinds of meat together of less pronounced harmony is another matter. The Scots do it when they make a proper cockie-leekie, which consists of an old boiling fowl and a piece of boiling beef cooked together with leeks, and finished with prunes. So do the Italians, who produce a splendid *bollito misto* in Piedmont, a 'mixed boiling' of beef or veal, chicken, and a gelatinous item such as calf's or pig's head and trotters to improve the smoothness of the dish.

Such dishes as these are the surviving elegancies of iron-pot cooking over the fire. I am sure they often lacked the contrived balance of a modern 'bollito misto'. It was a case of cooking what you happened to have, with as little firing as possible – meats, vegetables, a suet pudding or dumplings all in together.

See also *Meat Pies and Puddings*, pages 225-44, for more pork recipes.

# CURED PORK, BEEF ETC.

## BRADENHAM HAM

THE FINEST OF ALL ENGLISH-CURED HAMS, with its black skin and dryish, old-fashioned flavour, a whole civilization away from the pink sweetcures of today. You can order a Bradenham from your grocer. The original recipe is said to have been brought to Wiltshire by the butler from Bradenham Park in Buckinghamshire. This was at one time the home of Disraeli but whether he was accustomed to Bradenham ham or whether his Jewish origins prevented him enjoying it, we do not know. The fine pink colour of the ham comes from true cochineal.

Each ham comes with a leaflet telling you how to cook it, but I find that the soaking time they give is not nearly long enough. The instructions I follow come from William Tullberg, who runs the Wiltshire Tracklement Company at Calne (his mustards, with the Urchfont label, go well with all English hams).

Soak the ham for four days, changing the water twice. A little longer will not hurt, say four and a half days. Put into a ham kettle (or, thick end down, into a huge upright pan, or into an electric copper) and cover generously with water. Add a jar of molasses – 500 g (1 lb) size – and a handful of pickling spices. Bring slowly to simmering point and skim. Leave 3 hours for a 13 lb ham, half an hour longer up to 18 lb. The water should never come to a full boil, but give the occasional gulp and bubble. Leave the ham to cool in the liquor.

Remove it to a dish. Cut round the knuckle end to leave a very noticeable black collar of skin (the true sign of the Bradenham is its black skin). Strip off the rest. Cover with about 300 g (10 oz) breadcrumbs toasted to an even brown in the oven at mark 2, 150°C (300°F). Leave in a cool place for 24 hours. Serve with mustard and Cumberland sauce. If you store it in the fridge between meals, wrap it closely in plastic film to prevent it drying out.

## HOW TO CURE MEAT IN BRINE

BASIC
*3 litres (5 pts) water*
*375 g (12 oz) sea salt*
*375 g (12 oz) brown sugar (granulated will do)*
*30 g (1 oz) saltpetre*

AROMATICS
*1 level teaspoon juniper berries*
*Small piece of ungrated nutmeg*
*1 bay leaf*
*3 sprigs thyme*
*1 level teaspoon black peppercorns*
*4 cloves*

THE basic ingredients are the essentials – saltpetre gives pickled meat an appetizing rosy colour (without it the meat would taste all right, but it would have a greyish appearance). Sugar counteracts the hardening effect of saltpetre and gives an extra flavour. Sea salt should be used, and it should be unadulterated; again, it's a matter of flavour. Pure rock salt is all right, but it lacks character.

The aromatics are variable, or they can be left out altogether.

Put all these ingredients into a pan, bring them to boiling point, skim and remove from the heat. Leave to cool down.

Meanwhile prepare the brine crock or plastic bucket. Clean it out with soda and boiling water. Rinse it well, and leave it upside down to drain. This is more hygienic than drying it with a cloth. At the same time, clean a plate or flat stone in the same way: this you will need to rest on top of the meat so that it remains submerged in the brine. The crock or bucket will also need a scrupulously clean lid.

When the brine is cool, strain it into the bucket or crock. Put in the meat, weight it down and put the lid in place. Always remove the meat from the brine with tongs, not fingers. And have a separate crock for each type of meat – one for pork, another for beef and so on. A certain amount of sediment falls into the brine from the meat, which is why you do not want to mix the different kinds.

On account of this, brine needs to be cleaned, reboiled and fortified every so often. The alternative is to chuck it out the moment little spots of white mould appear on the surface, and start again (the meat underneath will be all right). Naturally the crock or bucket must be washed and cleaned again with a soda solution. In pork factories, like the old Harris's factory at Calne, the brine was years old in the huge white-tiled baths; the strength was carefully measured and reinforced each time one of the baths is drained. In the uncertain hygiene of most private houses, I would recommend throwing the brine away and starting again. However, if you want to add a corrective dose, bring 1 litre (1¾ pt) of water to the boil with 200 g (7 oz) of salt and 200 g (7 oz) of sugar and a heaped dessertspoon of juniper berries; leave it to cool after skimming, amalgamate with the old brine which has been poured off through a muslin-lined strainer into a newly cleaned crock, then replace the meat. Remember that each time you remove a piece of meat from the brine, you are also removing salt – with small pieces not much, but with legs of pork quite a quantity.

The times for salting meat vary, as you might expect, with the thickness of the piece; and also with the purpose of the salting – for instance, a 2½ kilo (5 lb) joint of pork for roasting is much improved by an overnight sojourn in the brine tub. Next day it will be agreeably seasoned, without being too salty for roasting. Pigs' heads and trotters for making brawn (page 171) are also improved by 24 hours in brine. Small pigs' tongues, which weigh about 250 g (8 oz), can be cured in 36-48 hours, whereas large tongues such as ox tongues can do with five days. If you want to turn a shoulder or leg of pork into a ham, allow ten days. Never worry about over-salting. You can soak the meat in water overnight before cooking it. Alternatively, you can put it into a pan of cold water, plenty of cold water, and bring it slowly to the boil. After 5 minutes simmering, taste the liquid and if it is on the salty side, throw it away and start again. This is why one should never add vegetables and so on to the water until it has been boiling for 5 minutes – by which time you will know whether it is all right to continue, or whether you have to throw it away.

You will soon find out how long or how short a time different parts and kinds of meat take. This is also a matter of individual preference. Some people like a very light cure, others a stronger, saltier cure. Here, though, is a guide to salting times which I find useful:

*Trotters, heads of pork halved: 24 hours*
*Duck (giblets removed): 36-48 hours*
*Pork loin, leg, shoulder: 3-10 days*
*Beef silverside, brisket: 7-10 days*
*Lamb or mutton shoulder, leg, loin: 7-10 days*

THESE times are for meat that is going to be boiled. For roasting joints, 6-8 hours is about right.

THE interesting thing about old methods of preservation, like salting, is that they alter the character of the original substance – i.e. a loin of pork and a salted loin of pork are two quite different things from the eater's point of view. The trouble with freezing is that it doesn't transform the original substance (in many cases it diminishes its flavour and goodness). On the other hand, it is able to preserve food in reasonable condition for much longer periods of time. One has only to think of the ever-increasing hardness of dried haricot beans, or split peas. Or the extremes of salt in the old-fashioned hard cures needed for keeping bacon from one pig-killing to the next.

An interesting but difficult situation used to arise on farms at harvest-time. There were many extra people to feed, and they had to eat well with such hard work. The ham and bacon from last autumn's pig was uneatable by that time – and it had probably been attacked by blow-flies. Yet if one killed a pig in the early summer, curing was made difficult and uncertain by the vagaries of the weather, which is often humid at that time and hot one day, cold the next. There would be cheese and bread, and plum pudding to finish with, but that was not enough. There might be a few early apples, and plums for tarts, but meat was the thing. In the eighteenth century particularly, before the introduction of commercial refrigeration, farmers' wives expected to feed their families and workers from the resources of the farm itself, buying in the very minimum. A situation which we are quite unfamiliar with today, but one that still pertains in parts of France – and no doubt in a good deal of Europe.

When the time for grape-picking arrives, at the end of September and the beginning of October, the Touraine *vigneron*'s wife makes a review of her resources. From the hutches, she will pick out a couple of rabbits for a pâté for lunch around the wine-press. The hens will be especially well fed for the sake of their eggs. The chickens will be fattened, and eaten at the final party when all the grapes are in. There will be jars of potted pork, from the pig that was killed at Easter. And at that time of year, fruit is no problem. Neither is the wine. And when a farmer's wife does acquire a deep-freeze, she does not fill it from the bulk-suppliers, but from her own yard and sties and garden.

## TO COOK SALT PORK AND HAMS

WEIGH the joint, after rinsing it rapidly under the cold tap. Calculate the cooking times, which become progressively less as the ham becomes larger. For instance:

> Salt pork and small hams up to 2 kilos (4 lb): 1 hour to the kilo (30 minutes to the lb) plus 30 minutes – but this is not always necessary, it depends on the thickness of the piece. From 2½ to 5 kilos (5-10 lb) 40 minutes per kilo (20 minutes per lb) plus 20 minutes.

Over 5 kilos (10 lb), use the graph opposite from Bulletin 127 of the Ministry of Agriculture and Fisheries, *Home Curing of Bacon and Hams* – for instance, a 6 kilo (12 lb) ham needs 3½ hours.

Put the joint into a ham kettle – or if it is very large, suspend it with string from the lid of an electric washing copper – cover it with water and bring

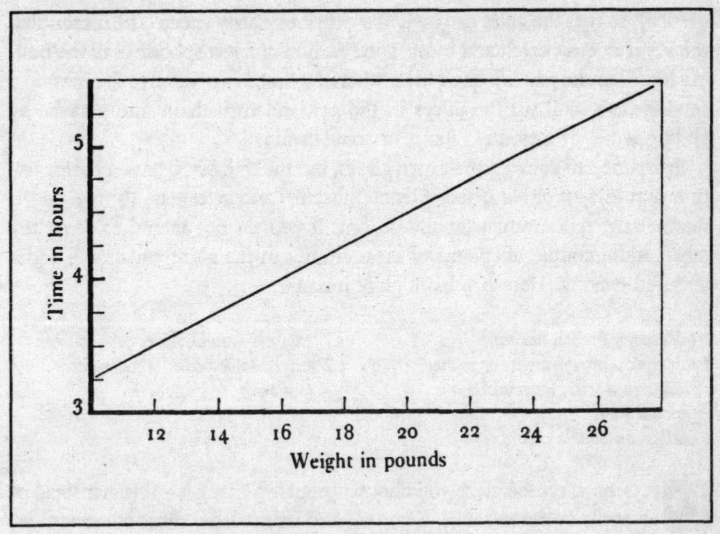


slowly to the boil. After 5 minutes' simmering taste the water, as I mention on page 183. If it tastes salty, throw it away and start again. Add vegetables and aromatics after the first 5 minutes, and count your cooking time from then. A bouquet garni, onions, carrots, leeks and turnips will all help to improve the flavour of the ham – and of the stock, which can be used for soup (particularly pea soup, page 9) later on.

## To Eat Hot

THERE are two traditional ways of doing this, or rather, three.

First, remove and skin the ham while hot, and serve it as it is, with a Madeira sauce, or with an apple sauce or onion sauce, or surrounded by appropriate vegetables – broad beans, for instance, in which case you would supply a parsley sauce.

The second way is to remove the salt pork or ham half an hour before the cooking time is up. Peel off the skin, score it with a diamond pattern, being careful not to go completely through the fat to the meat, and rub it over with a sweet, piquant glaze. The intersections of the lattice pattern can be studded with cloves. The pork or ham then goes into the oven at mark 5, 190°C

(375°F), so that the glaze can melt to a delicious crusty sheen – be careful that the sugar doesn't catch and burn. The addition of a few spoonfuls of the boiling liquor to the pan is a good idea: when the time is up, remove the meat to a serving dish, boil up the juices in the pan and turn them into a sauce by adding wine, or a fortified wine, or some cream.

Everyone can concoct their own glazes, but the thing is to have a basic mixture of mustard (either dry or French mustard) and sweetness (brown sugar, marmalade, redcurrant jelly and so on). If you do not intend to score the meat, add a couple of spoons of breadcrumbs to the glaze which will add a textured coating. Here is a basic glaze mixture:

*1 tablespoon French mustard*
*1 tablespoon brown sugar, or melted redcurrant jelly, marmalade, or apricot jam*
*1 tablespoon double cream*
*1 teaspoon ground cloves or cinnamon*
*2 heaped tablespoons breadcrumbs (optional)*

DEPENDING on the glaze you choose, prepare a garnish – this is instead of an apple or onion sauce. If you've used marmalade, slices of oranges reheated in the pan sauce would be a good idea. With apricot jam, a pilaff of rice with almonds, and dried apricots. With redcurrant jelly, or brown sugar, a few potatoes plus some glazed onions and carrots, or just potatoes with a green salad to follow. Spinach is another good vegetable for ham cooked in this way, particularly when fortified wines have been used in the pan sauce. Broad beans are not for baked ham, keep them for the plainly boiled kind.

The third way, rather a grand-looking way, is to encase the ham or pork in pastry. This is much simpler than you might suppose. Calculate the cooking time of the meat, then boil it gently for three-quarters of the time. Leave it to cool down for an hour in the cooking liquid. Meanwhile make the pastry, a shortcrust. For a 6 kilo (12 lb) ham you will need pastry made with 1½ kilos flour, and appropriate weights of butter and lard, and a little iced water for mixing. Roll it out on a large table. Take the ham from its pot, drain it well and peel off the skin. Lay it plump side down on the pastry and mould the coating round it, cutting off the surplus. Naturally the pastry should not have been too thinly rolled out. Turn the ham over on to the rack of a roasting pan, so that the 'seam' is concealed underneath. Decorate with leaves, flowers, and so on, or with abstract shapes: make a small hole for the steam to escape from, at the top of the crust. Brush over with a beaten egg mixed with a saltspoon of salt. Bake for an hour at mark 5, 190°C (375°F). Take out of the oven, pour a small glass of Madeira or other fortified wine in through the steam-escape hole, and serve – spinach and potatoes and Madeira sauce, are good accompanying items.

## To Eat Cold

WHEN the time is up, remove the pan from the heat and leave it for a couple of hours. Then remove the joint of pork or ham to a dish: the best kind to use is a large meat plate with a strainer tray fitted into it. If you do not have the benefit of an old dinner service, look in second-hand shops. They are often to be bought quite cheaply. On other occasions, the strainer tray can be removed and the dish used for a large mixed salad, or for a hot joint surrounded by vegetables.

Remove the skin as soon as it is cool enough to handle. It should peel off easily. Toast plenty of white breadcrumbs to a pale brown and roll the meat in it while it's still tepid. Do not use those appalling bright yellow crumbs sold in some grocer's shops and supermarkets.

If you decided to bone the ham before cooking it, remember to remove the string, and to cool it under a weight so that it keeps its firmness. The crumb coating will have to come last of all – as the joint will be cold, see that the crumbs are still warm and press the pork well down into them.

In my opinion, a boned loin of pork makes the best flavoured and easiest kind of home-cured ham. But many people prefer to stick to the traditional leg, complete with bones. Certainly it looks more splendid for a party, and one can decorate the knuckle end with a ham frill.

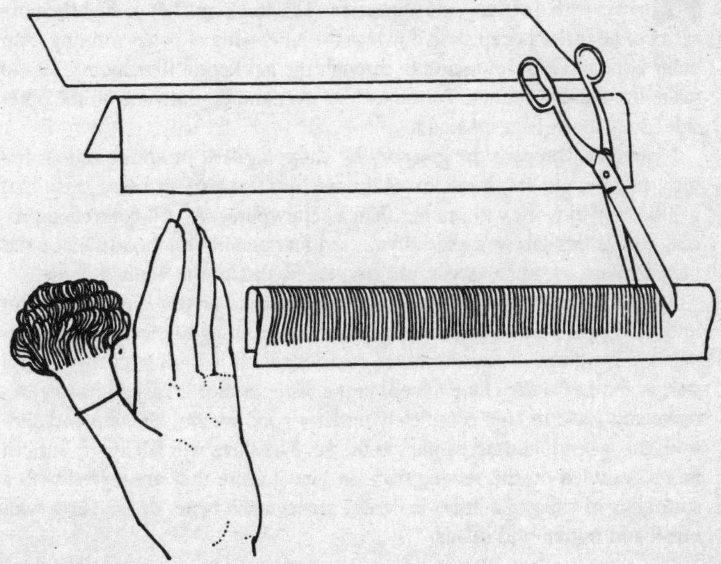

## LINCOLNSHIRE CHINE

DEREK COOPER OF THE FOOD PROGRAMME first told me about Lincolnshire chine, a magnificent dish that makes a splendid appearance on a cold table. You need a butcher, though, capable of cutting the right square block of pork and then curing it. It should weigh about 3 kilos (6 lb), with the length of its sides about 15 cm (6″). It is cut across the back of the neck, across the backbone, a section of which is included. The piece is bounded on one side by pork back fat, on the other by the backbone. Between them you see what looks like a solid piece of lean meat. In fact, through the centre, unseen, a wing of flat bones runs from the vertebrae to make an inner layer.

You make slashes at regular intervals in the lean meat, and stuff them with chopped green herbs, which gives a striking look to the piece.

The great supplier of Lincolnshire chine, uncooked and cooked, is W. Curtis and Sons, Long Leys Road, Lincoln (telephone: 0522-27212). Other branches in Scunthorpe and Newark. Available from May to December.

*Cured chine, weighing 3 kg (6 lb)*
*2 leeks or 2 bunches spring onions and a lettuce*
*2 bunches parsley, about 125 g (4 oz) in all*
*Good handful young raspberry leaves (optional)*
*Thyme, marjoram, mace, pepper*

SLASH the chine before soaking it. Place it fat side towards you, bone side away, with one lean side uppermost. Leaving 1 cm (½″) or slightly more at one side, make a deep slash down to the inner wing of bones running from outer bone to fat but not cutting through the fat. Repeat four more times to make five parallel slashes. Turn the chine over and do the same on the other side. Soak for at least 24 hours.

Meanwhile, prepare the greenery by chopping leek or spring onion, lettuce, parsley and raspberry leaves if used. Aim for a moist pasty mash that will be easy to work with, rather than a soupy purée. A well-controlled processor does this job well. Add thyme and marjoram, with ground mace and pepper. Push as much as you can into the slashes of the drained chine.

Tie the chine into shape, wrap in a cloth and tie or sew it up firmly. Put into a large pan and cover generously with water. Bring to the boil, then simmer for 3-4 hours. Taste the water occasionally. If it is salty, change it and start again. Leave the chine to cool in the water until it is easy to handle, remove and leave to cool completely under a good weight. Unwrap and slice from the fat end, cutting parallel to the fat. The slices will fall apart, but can be reassembled on the serving dish. In Lincolnshire they are served with a sprinkling of vinegar: a little vinaigrette seems much better to me. Serve with bread and butter, and salads.

## SMOKING MEAT

THIS IS SOMETHING THAT FEW PEOPLE CARE TO UNDERTAKE NOW, firstly because they don't have the right kind of chimneys and open hearths in their modern houses and flats, and secondly because they are afraid of losing an expensive piece of meat if something goes wrong. Particularly for this second reason, I would advise against smoking meat unless you have an experienced friend to guide your early steps. It is easier in one way nowadays, because smoke has been reduced to a cosmetic from its original status of preserving agent. We eat smoked food because we like the taste; we don't regard it as an essential part of winter stores. If you want to have your own smoked ham, cure it in brine yourself for a fortnight – then take it along to the bacon factory and see if you can persuade someone to complete the cure for you. Small concerns are more likely to be sympathetic to such requests. And of course it is sensible to make enquiries first.

'*When there were plenty of farm-houses, there were plenty of places to smoke bacon in; since farmers have lived in gentlemen's houses, and the main part of farm-houses have been knocked down, these places are not so plenty.*' This is William Cobbett, writing in 1821, about the cottager's life in Jane Austen's England; he might be talking about the Martin family in *Emma*, who were so genteel though not quite gentlefolk. '*However, there is scarcely any neighbourhood without a chimney left to hang bacon up in. Two precautions are necessary: first, to hang the flitches where no rain comes down upon them: second, not to let them be so near the fire as to melt.*' This is very important, the fat must not cook at all, the smoke must be cool, the fire well damped down with sawdust. And, of course, it must be a wood fire, not turf, peat or coal. '*Stubble or litter might do: but the trouble would be great. Fir, or deal, smoke is not fit for the purpose. I take it, that the absence of wood, as fuel, in the dairy countries, and in the North, has led to the making of pork and dried bacon*' – by which he means salt pork, the kind that is eaten with pease pudding in the North, and green bacon which has been salted, then dried in a good draught, and not smoked.

'*As to the time that it requires to smoke a flitch, it must depend a good deal upon whether there be a constant fire beneath, and whether the fire be large or small. A month may do, if the fire be pretty constant, and such as a farmhouse fire usually is. But over-smoking or, rather, too long hanging in the air, makes the bacon rust . . . The flitch ought not to be dried up to the hardness of a board, and yet it ought to be perfectly dry.*'

He then goes on to say that it is important to keep the bacon '*sweet and good, and free from nasty things that they call hoppers; that is to say, a sort of skip-*

*ping maggots, engendered by a fly which has a great relish for bacon'*. It's a good idea to adopt the American habit of sewing a ham into a coarse linen bag, then lime-washing it. The alternative is to store the ham, embedded in ashes, in a box or chest or in sand, which will keep out the air and the flies. You can see from this description why I do not recommend the home-smoking of bacon.

I do recommend, though, William Cobbett's *Cottage Economy*, which he finished in 1821. It's a book written with passionate concern and an earthy sense of reality, which seem to us these days very sympathetic. He has prejudices against potatoes (even for pigs) and tea. He wants to convert everyone to the virtues of maize, which he had seen growing so successfully as a main crop in America. He understood, too, how flashiness and falsity were beginning to overwhelm the country outside London, encouraging farm and cottage families to a 'niceness in food and finery in dress', that reduced many of them to a 'quarter of a bellyful and rags'.

In *Cottage Economy*, one senses the beginning of Victorian London, the desire for niceness and finery that was to send farmers' and craftsmen's children crowding up to London, the Galsworthys and Hardys, all in search of a fortune and the good life. Some of them, many of them I suppose, succeeded, if not always as solidly as the Forsytes. Others, like my own great-grandfather, came to disaster: he drank his profits and time away, and over-looked debts with an amiability he could not afford (he was a naval tailor – his clients had the disconcerting habit of disappearing with the tide). He couldn't shake off his country habits of thought. He was incapable of realizing that people in big cities were not as reliable in their ways as the slower inhabitants of Old Bewick, Morpeth and Rochester at home in Northumberland.

*Cottage Economy* describes a whole way of life, the sub-structure on which the gentry and nobility floated in such elegant style, and which was ignored by contemporary novelists apart from a few picturesque details. It makes subsequent 'shilling' cookeries for the poor look thin and patronizing. No wonder, as such things were written by grand chefs in London who had come a long way from their simple origins, who had 'risen above' such a life and found fame in the kitchens of royalty and fine London clubs. Incidentally, I wonder what Cobbett would think of today's school cookery teachers, who instruct their pupils to make cottage or Shepherd's Pie from a tin of minced steak and a packet of instant potato. Or of women in supermarkets saying, to television interviewers, that they never eat meat nowadays as chops and steak are so expensive. 'A quarter of a bellyful and rags.' Cobbett could congratulate himself on his prescience and prophetic powers, but, being the kind of generous man he was, he would be sad at such miserable ignorance. I can imagine his rage at the way such ignorance is encouraged by advertisers, and perpetuated by many of the home economists let loose in our schools.

## Boiled Salt Beef and Dumplings

*1½ kilos (3 lb) salted silverside or brisket*
*2 large onions, unpeeled*
*8 cloves*
*2 blades of mace*
*Small piece of nutmeg*
*Plenty of black pepper*

To salt your own beef, see pages 174-6. Alternatively, buy a joint of salted beef from a reputable butcher. It should not need soaking, but it is always a good idea to ask.

Put the beef into a deep, fairly close-fitting pot. Add the onions, into which you have stuck cloves – the onion peel is not removed because it improves the colour of the stock. Add enough tepid water to cover the meat by 1 cm (¼"), and put in the remaining spices. Don't stint the pepper. Bring to simmering point, and leave to cook for 3½ hours (to calculate cooking times for different-sized joints, turn to page 176). Remove the scum as it rises and taste the cooking liquor after about 10 minutes: if it tastes very salty, drain it off and add fresh water and start again. During the cooking time, the water should never boil. A few bubbles should hiccough to the surface in a desultory kind of way. When you are satisfied that the pot is over a correct heat, cover it tightly.

Many recipes suggest adding various vegetables to salt beef, but it has so much flavour already that, carrots apart, they can do little for it; and they end up sodden and uneatable, whatever the peasant school of cookery maintains. It is far better to cook them separately. Glazed carrots are a good accompaniment, as are lightly cooked leeks, and some people cannot entertain the thought of salt beef or salt pork without pease pudding (page 55). I sympathize with this, but suggest too that dumplings should not be overlooked.

### Dumplings

*125 g (4 oz) plain flour*
*1 teaspoon baking powder*
*Good pinch salt*
*60 g (2 oz) shredded suet*
*Water*
Either: *1 tablespoon chopped parsley and chives*
Or: *creamed or grated horseradish*
Or: *12 cubes of bread fried in butter*

Sieve the flour, baking powder and salt together. Mix in the suet, herbs if used, and then enough water to form a slightly sticky dough. Flour your hands and roll the dough into little balls – remember that they will swell a good deal as they cook.

Into the centre of each ball, put a little horseradish or a cube of fried bread, and fasten the dough firmly over. Remove the meat from the cooking liquor when it is ready, and keep it warm: this will leave space to poach the dumplings for 10-20 minutes. Keep the pan covered.

Just before putting the dumplings into the beef stock, it is a good idea to remove about 425 ml (¾ pt) of it and boil it down in a separate pan to concentrate the flavour. This can be served in a separate sauceboat.

SWEET-SOUR pickled cucumbers are an excellent, if not very English, addition to boiled salt beef, which makes wonderful sandwiches with rye bread and some *Moutarde de Meaux* or German mustard, particularly if it is still slightly warm. As a general principle, the larger the joint of salt meat, the better the flavour.

## BOILED SILVERSIDE OF BEEF

COOK in the same way as the salt beef in the previous recipe, but in this case it is worth adding a parsnip, carrot and a small piece of turnip to the broth. Serve with horseradish sauce, carrots, potatoes. As in the previous rècipe, the stock will make beautiful soup.

## PRESSED BEEF

SALT or fresh beef cooked in the usual way (see page 176). Leave to cool in its broth for 2 hours, then put it into a tongue-press, or wrap it up in foil and place a board with some really heavy weights on top. Serve with horseradish sauce, and an avocado and potato salad dressed with an olive oil vinaigrette (page 355), or with pickled vegetables (onions, cucumbers, etc.) and wholemeal or rye bread and butter.

## SPICED SALT BEEF

SPICED BEEF WAS A FAVOURITE of English tables of the past, especially at Christmas time, and it is still to be found regularly on sale in Ireland. Here Elizabeth David revived it in 1958, working out the spice mixture carefully, and gave the recipe to Mr Ducat, the master-butcher at Harrods. Beef spiced to Mrs David's recipe is sold by the ton every year in December and January. It is also easy to spice it yourself, but take the precaution of buying a piece of well-hung, top-quality beef. The following recipe is substantially Mrs David's. I use a little more allspice and a little less saltpetre.

For 8-10

*3 kilos (6 lb) joint silverside or round of beef, cut and tied for salting*

SPICED SALT
*90 g (3 oz) dark brown sugar*
*1 heaped teaspoon saltpetre*
*125 g (4 oz) sea salt*
*30 g (1 oz) black peppercorns*
*30 g (1 oz) allspice berries*
*30 g (1 oz) juniper berries*

RUB the beef over with the sugar. Leave it for 2 days in a cool place in a deep, straight-sided pot, turning it over once or twice. Crush the remaining ingredients together and rub this mixture into the beef. Return it to its pot, and leave for a further nine days, turning it over every day and rubbing the salty mixture into it (the salt will become very moist as time goes on with the juices from the meat, but go on rubbing it in just the same).

To cook the beef, dab off all the bits of spice, or rinse it very quickly under the tap. Place it in a close-fitting pot with 250-300 ml (8-10 oz) water. Put a layer of shredded suet over the top of the meat (this helps to keep in the moisture during cooking). Cover the pot tightly, with two layers of foil jammed in place with the lid, so that no steam can escape. Bake in the oven at mark 1, 140°C (275°F), for 1½ hours per kilo (45 minutes per lb) (if you are spicing a small joint, allow 1¾ hours per kilo (50 minutes per lb)). Take out of the oven and leave undisturbed to cool down for 3 hours. Take off the lid and foil, drain the meat and place it on a board. Cover with greaseproof and put a 1½ kilo (3 lb) weight on top. Leave for 24 hours at least before carving into thin slices. The best accompanying dishes are avocado and potato salad, and horseradish sauce (page 351).

WRAP THE beef up in greaseproof paper in between servings. It will keep in the refrigerator for three weeks. Useful for Christmas.

## BOILED OX TONGUE

For 6-10

*1½-2½ kilos (2½-5 lb) ox tongue, pickled*
*Water or light stock*
*Bouquet garni*
*Onion stuck with 2 cloves*
*1 sliced carrot*
*Stalk celery*
*12 peppercorns, slightly crushed*

SOAK the tongue for 6 hours, or as the butcher suggests. Put it into a deep pan and cover it with water or stock and bring to the boil. Remove the scum which will rise to the surface in a greyish foam. Add the vegetables, bouquet and pepper. Cover with a lid, and simmer for 3-4 hours until a larding needle or skewer goes in easily. Do not allow the liquid to boil, an occasional bubble is the best thing. It is prudent to taste the cooking liquid after half an hour: if it is unpleasantly salty, throw it away and start again, knocking half an hour off the cooking time.

When the tongue is cooked, remove it to a board and peel off the skin. See if there are any tiny bones and gristly bits at the throat end, and cut them away if there are.

### To Serve Cold

PLACE a 12-15 cm (5″-6″) cake tin – with the removable base removed – on to a baking sheet. Push the tongue into it, curling it as you go. Put the base on top and weight it down with heavy tins. Leave it to cool. Serve cut in thin slices across, with a simple salad or two and some horseradish sauce (page 351). The Victorians used to press the tongue into a slipper shape, and then decorate it with aspic jelly and bits and pieces. I think we have lost sympathy with over-presented food of this kind: it always arouses my suspicions – I wonder what the caterer is trying to conceal.

### To Serve Hot

SLICE the tongue whilst still hot and arrange it decoratively on a large shallow serving dish. Cover with a suitable sauce, boiling hot; place in the oven to heat through for about 10 minutes. Do not allow the sauce to drown the tongue – serve any extra in a sauceboat. Madeira sauce is a favourite English choice, but the black cherry sauce on page 360 is more unusual.

## POTTED TONGUE

USING an electric blender or chopper, reduce 250 g (8 oz) of cooked tongue to a paste with 125-150 g (4-5 oz) of clarified, unsalted butter. Season with salt, pepper and mace. Pack firmly into a pot. When chilled to firmness, the meat should be covered with a 1 cm (scant ¼″) layer of clarified butter, then with foil: if you intend to use the potted meat in a day or two, a thinner layer of butter – for appearance rather than preservation – will be enough. Serve with thin toast or baked bread. Beef, salt beef, venison, game may all be potted in the same way – sometimes a couple of anchovy fillets may be substituted for the mace.

To make a grander dish, cooked chicken can also be reduced to a paste as well. The two mixtures can then be layered into a pot, or placed together in uneven lumps for a marbled effect, before being pressed down and covered with clarified butter. When cut, the potted meat will have a most attractive appearance, and the milder flavour of the chicken will temper the strong-tasting cured tongue.

## To Pot Ham with Chicken

LIKE THE RECIPE ABOVE and the one following, this comes from the eighteenth century. It was in most cookery books, but the version I prefer is Mrs Raffald's in her *Experienced English Housekeeper*. An excellent way to use up the end of a ham.

*'"Take as much lean of a boiled ham as you please." Reduce it to a paste in an electric chopper, with half its weight in ham fat. Add as much clarified butter as ham fat. Season with mace and pepper – salt, too, if the ham was particularly mild. Reduce a roughly equal weight of cooked chicken (or turkey), with a slightly smaller weight of clarified butter – 'equal weight' means equal to the total weight of lean and fat ham. Barely season the chicken at all, as its blandness is "to qualify the ham".'*

LAYER the two meats into a pot. Run clarified butter over the whole thing, and leave to set. When firm cover the surface of the butter with plastic film, pressing it down, and up the sides of the pot and over the top, so that the whole thing is sealed. As an extra precaution, cover with foil and an elastic band to keep it in place. Now store in the refrigerator for at least two days – or for much longer if the clarified butter was enough to make a good seal, and your coverings are tight enough.

'When you send it to table cut out a thin slice in the form of half a diamond and lay it round the edge of your pot.' Serve with toast or bread.

## A Fine Way to Pot a Tongue

*2½-3½ kilos (5-7 lb) dressed weight roasting chicken*
*1¼ kilos (2½ lb) tongue, boiled, skinned*
*1 teaspoon each ground mace, ground cloves, black pepper*
*¼ nutmeg, grated*
*A level dessertspoon sea salt*
*About 1 kilo (2 lb) butter*

BONE the chicken (or ask the butcher to do it for you). Lay it out on a board, skin side down. Trim the tongue into a block to fit inside the chicken, cutting away the tip, and any tiny bones or gristle. Mix the spices with the salt, and rub the inside of the chicken with two-thirds of the mixture. Place the tongue on top, and wrap the chicken round it. Put the chicken cut side down, breast side up into as tightly fitting a deep casserole as possible (the better the fit, the less butter will be required). Scatter the remaining spices on the top. Melt just enough butter to cover. Put the lid on the pot. Bake at mark 6, 200°C (400°F), until you can hear the butter bubbling hard when you open the oven door – reduce the heat to mark 4, 180°C (350°F). After an hour's total cooking time, test the chicken with a larding needle to see if it is done. If the juices look a little pink, leave the bird for another 15 minutes.

When it is cooked, remove the chicken on to a rack to cool. Pour off the butter and juices into a basin. When the chicken is cold, replace it in the cleaned casserole. Bring butter, entirely freed of meat juices, to the boil and pour over the chicken. If you wish to keep it for longer than three days, add more clarified butter to cover the chicken by 1 cm (¼″). It should not be eaten until 36 hours later in any case, so that all the flavours have time to develop.

To serve, leave the chicken in the pot and cut it down into slices like a pâté. Eat with wholemeal bread and some of the butter.

## TONGUE AND MUSHROOM CRUMBLE

For 6

*1½ kilos (3 lb) pickled, uncooked tongue (pig's, calf's, or ox tongue)*
*1 medium carrot*
*2 medium onions*
*Bouquet garni*
*300 ml (½ pt) dry cider*
*Water*
*125 g (4 oz) butter*
*125 g (4 oz) mushrooms*
*1 rounded dessertspoon flour*
*6 tablespoons (3 oz) dry white wine*
*50 g (1½ oz) fresh white breadcrumbs*
*Salt, pepper*

EITHER buy the tongue(s) ready pickled, or leave in the brine on page 174 for a couple of days. Always be prepared to soak tongue overnight, if it comes from the butcher's brine tub.

To cook the tongue, put it into a large pan with the carrot, chopped, and one of the onions coarsely chopped. Add bouquet, cider and enough water to cover by 1 cm (¼″). Bring slowly to the boil, skim and cover. Leave to simmer until tongues are cooked – from 1 to 3 hours depending on individual size or sizes. Remove to a dish, peel off the skin and cut out any tiny bones. Leave to cool. Strain stock into a jug.

To assemble the dish, slice tongue and place in the bottom of a shallow, butter-greased ovenproof dish. Cook sliced mushrooms in 30 g (1 oz) of the butter, season them and distribute evenly over the tongue slices. Cook the second onion, finely chopped, in 60 g (2 oz) of butter in a small heavy pan; cover it and see that the onion doesn't brown. Stir in the flour, cook for 2 minutes, then add wine and enough stock from the jug to make a thin sauce. Leave to cook down to a well-flavoured moderately thick sauce, then tip over the tongue slices, which should be well moistened, but not swimming about. Melt the last of the butter, mix in the crumbs and spread on top of the dish. Bake at mark 5-6, 190°-200°C (375°-400°F), until everything is well heated through and bubbling, and the top nicely browned. All the preparations can be done in advance, with only the reheating to be carried out before the meal.

## ISLE OF MAN SALT DUCK

BY TRADITION ON THE ISLE OF MAN, boiled salted duck is served with onion sauce, and a mash of cabbage and potato. The method of pickling used is the dry salt cure, rather than the brine suggested on page 174.

PLACE the duck on a layer of coarse sea salt crystals on a large plate. Put a handful of salt inside it, rubbing it round the cavity, then put a layer of salt over the top. Leave for 24 hours. Rinse off any salt that you cannot brush away from the duck, and simmer it in water barely to cover for an hour or longer, depending on the weight.

Meanwhile cook equal quantities of cabbage (or kale) and potato. Drain them well, then chop and mash them well together with plenty of butter and seasoning.

Also make the following onion sauce:

*4 large onions, chopped*
*2 level tablespoons cornflour*
*300 ml (½ pt) milk*
*15 g (½ oz) butter*
*Grated rind of a lemon*
*Salt, pepper*

COVER onions on a pan with water, add seasoning and simmer until cooked (about 15 minutes). Drain them, saving the liquor. Mix the cornflour with a little of the milk. Put the remaining milk into the onion pan, with 300 ml (½ pt) of onion liquor or a little less and the butter. Bring to the boil, then mix in the cornflour and return to the heat. Stir continuously until the sauce is cooked and thickened. If it is too thick, add more milk or onion liquor. Add lemon rind, seasoning and drained onions, and heat through.

This recipe comes from *My Grandmother's Cookery Book, 50 Manx Recipes*, by Suzanne Woolley, published in 1975 by the Shearwater Press.

SEE ALSO page 175, for *Curing a Duck in Brine*.

# POULTRY

## BOILED CAPON WITH SUGAR PEAS

**A** RECIPE FROM ROBERT MAY'S *The Accomplisht Cook* of 1660, which startled me. Not on account of its simplicity, but because I had thought that sugar peas were an introduction of the early nineteenth century. It seems that they were in fact popular in the time of Elizabeth and James I. As this recipe confirms.

Robert May was born in 1588 at Wynge in Buckinghamshire, where his father was chef to Lady Dormer. When he was ten years old she sent him to Paris, then to London to learn the business. He returned to Wynge, working first under his father, then – when Lady Dormer died – for a succession of not very distinguished employers. He seems to have died a year or two after his book came out. It is an extraordinary compilation, a kind of bridge between the old-style grandeur left from the Middle Ages, which he must have learnt from his father, and the new fashionable French cookery. As well there are plenty of straightforward dishes that seem now to be entirely English, though this may not be so: it is easy to regard, say, duck and green peas as an inalienably English dish – yet it was an import from France in the seventeenth century.

SIMMER a capon in water barely to cover with a bouquet of thyme, rosemary, parsley, fennel, 2-3 blades of mace, and seasoning. When tender, thicken some of the broth with 2 whole onions, boiled and sieved, and breadcrumbs. Add a seasoning of oyster liquor and verjuice (lemon juice or cider vinegar can be used as a substitute). Serve the jointed bird on sippets, with sugar peas cooked in the following way:

'When the cods [pods] be but young, string them and pick off the husks. Take 2 or 3 handfuls and put with ½ lb sweet butter, ¼ pt water, gross pepper, salt, mace and oil.' Stew until cooked, then thicken the juices with 3 or 4 egg yolks beaten with 6 spoonfuls of sack – use dry sherry. Garnish with orange peel.

The 'bread' sauce should be served in a separate bowl, or the whole thing will look muddled.

## SALMAGUNDI FOR A MIDDLE DISH AT SUPPER

'IN THE TOP PLATE IN THE MIDDLE, *which should stand higher than the rest, take a fine pickled herring, bone it, take off the head, and mince the rest fine. In the other plates round, put the following things: in one, pare a cucumber and cut it very thin; in another, apples pared and cut small; in another, an onion peeled and cut small;*

*in another, two hard eggs chopped small, the whites in one, and the yolks in another; pickled gherkins in another cut small; in another, celery cut small; in another, pickled red cabbage chopped fine; take some watercresses clean washed and picked, stick them all about and between every plate or saucer, and throw nasturtium flowers about the cresses. You must have oil and vinegar, and lemon to eat with it. If it is prettily set out, it will make a pretty figure in the centre of the table, or you may lay them in heaps in a dish. If you have not all these ingredients, set out your plates or sauces with just what you fancy, and in the room of a pickled herring you may mince anchovies.'*

Hannah Glasse probably made use of those sets of glass or china, with a raised central bowl, surrounded by small ones at table level; but, as she says, you can lay it out in heaps on a large dish. This arrangement is more appealing than the more usual method of arranging the ingredients in layers, in a sugar-loaf shape, topped with the pickled herring.

Here are some of the other ingredients she suggests in the three other recipes she gives:

*Veal*
*Chicken (one of the most popular salmagundi ingredients)*
*Pork*
*Duck*
*Pigeon*
*Lettuce, cut in strips*
*Sorrel, cut in strips*
*Spinach, cut in strips*
*Shallots, chopped*
*Lemons, chopped small*
*Pickles*

Other garnishes suggested are peeled grapes, blanched French beans, grated horseradish, barberries, lemon slices or a whole lemon or orange set on top at the apex of the sugar-loaf.

The tastes of salmagundi are built up of piquancy such as salt herrings, anchovy and pickled vegetables, set off by bland and crisp things such as chicken, eggs, celery and fresh salad vegetables. Made with care, it becomes a splendid hors d'oeuvre, for a cold table if you like (the Danes still eat a salmagundi, with everything chopped up together, herring, chicken, apple, beetroot, onion and so on, called *sildsalat*, herring salad). It can be elegant. Disaster, though, is inherent, and may be sensed from Hannah Glasse's remark that 'you may always make Salamongundi of such things as you have, according to your fancy'.

The fancy of frugal housewives has not always been successful in this country, one must admit. Salmagundi made a perfect excuse for clearing out the larder, which probably accounts for its gradual fall from grace towards the end of the nineteenth century. 'Such things as you have' is the knell for many

English dishes. The staples of our larder do not include wine, cream, mushrooms, shallots, garlic, olive oil, and a number of green herbs, so perhaps we should be forgiven.

## LISANNE'S CHICKEN WITH MUSSELS

THIS EXCELLENT DISH WAS INVENTED BY A FRIEND when she was staying in a remote hamlet in southern France. Suddenly she had to produce a special birthday dinner. All she had in the house – apart from basic supplies – was some mussels bought that morning for the family supper. Luckily a neighbour with a poultry yard always had a chicken, but that was all she could find. This recipe is close to much older dishes of chicken with oysters, once very popular in England, which is why I include it in this book.

For 6

*2-2½ kilos (4-5 lb) (dressed weight) roasting chicken*
*1 large onion, chopped*
*1 large carrot, chopped*
*2-3 tablespoons olive oil*
*Bouquet garni*
*300 ml (½ pt) dry white wine*
*2 kilos (4 lb) mussels, scrubbed and scraped*
*Salt, pepper, parsley*

BROWN the chicken and vegetables in the oil. Transfer them to a deep, flameproof pot. Add the bouquet and half the wine. Season, cover and cook gently but steadily for 45 minutes.

Meanwhile open two-thirds of the mussels in a large pan, over a high heat, with the remaining wine. Discard the shells (and any mussels that remain firmly shut) and put the mussels into the cavity of the chicken which, after its 45 minutes' cooking, should be half-cooked. Strain the liquor into the pot and tuck the remaining mussels all round. Replace the lid on the pot, and finish cooking the bird – this will take from 30 to 45 minutes longer. Place the chicken on a serving dish and put the mussels in their shells or on the half-shell all round it. Sprinkle with parsley and keep warm. Skim any fat from the chicken cooking juices, correct the seasoning and bring back to the boil. Strain into a hot sauceboat. Serve with plenty of good bread to mop up the sauce. No vegetables, but a green salad afterwards.

## HINDLE WAKES

THIS RECIPE – as far as I have been able to find out – was first given, in a simple form, by Florence White in *Good Things in England*, published in 1932 by Jonathan Cape. She had the recipe from Mrs Kate A. Earp of Brighton, who wrote that 'We as a family in Lancashire called these fowls Hindle Wakes – why I do not know, unless it was because old hens were sold at the "wakes" [fairs].' Her recipe was for an old hen, which was stuffed with prunes soaked in water and lemon juice, and then steamed for six or more hours until it was tender: the bird was finally wrapped in bacon and roasted for an hour.

In 1954, Dorothy Hartley described a far more elaborate dish in *Food in England*. The stuffing was embellished with suet, breadcrumbs and vinegar. The fowl was then boiled in vinegar and water, and coated when cold with lemon sauce. Prunes and slices of lemon were used to decorate a rather more magnificent dish than Mrs Earp's. Moreover, it was eaten cold.

Miss Hartley says that her recipe was collected from a Lancashire family in 1900, but that it was centuries old and brought over by Flemish weavers who came to Lancashire in the fourteenth century, and settled at Bolton-le-Moor in 1337. However, the only things that they are recorded as having brought with them are wooden shoes – perhaps the origin of Lancashire clogs? – and jannock (oatmeal bread). I should have thought that it seems unnecessary to look any further than the medieval tradition of English cookery, which was influenced by France and the trade in spices and dried fruit from the Middle East.

What troubles me is the name. Miss Hartley says that it means Hen de la Wake, and Mrs Earp hints at a similar explanation. No etymologist would support a folk explanation of this kind (*hend* normally refers to hind, i.e. a young deer, as in Hindley, near Wigan, where the *ley* means place, so place of young deer).

It would seem that the name could have been taken from *Hindle Wakes*, a play written in 1912 by Stanley Houghton. It had much success, and is about the goings-on in an imaginary Lancashire town called Hindle during the annual holiday or 'wakes'. Wakes, the plural for a singular noun, came from the habit of keeping watch on the eve of the patronal festival of a parish church, a time that was celebrated as a holiday for everyone. The word continued in Lancashire when other parts of the country had given up, and came to mean the annual closure of the factories in a town.

For 10

*2½-3 kilos (5-6 lb) roasting chicken or capon, or a really good boiling fowl*
*500 g (1 lb) large prunes*
*250 g (8 oz) breadcrumbs, made from slightly stale bread*
*125 g (4 oz) chopped beef suet*
*½ teaspoon each sage, parsley, marjoram and thyme*
*Salt, pepper*
*1-2 tablespoons malt vinegar*
*1 tablespoon soft brown sugar*

STOCK
*2 level tablespoons salt*
*1 stick celery*
*1 large onion, unpeeled, stuck with 3 cloves*
*1 bay leaf*
*4 sprigs parsley*
*4 sprigs thyme*
*About 3½ litres (6 pts) water*
*6 tablespoons malt vinegar*
*1 tablespoon soft brown sugar*

SAUCE
*150 ml (¼ pt) double cream*
*Juice of 1 lemon*
*Grated rind of 1 lemon*
*White pepper*
*15 g (½ oz) butter*
*1 tablespoon flour*
*125 ml (¼ pt) milk*

PLUS
*1 lemon*
*Good bunch of parsley*
*250 g (8 oz) thinly cut slices of ham*
*Chive stalks*

REMOVE the giblets from the bird. (Apart from the liver, which can be used for another dish, they will be needed for the stock.) Soak the prunes for several hours or overnight, then simmer them for 5 to 10 minutes in the soaking water, so that they can be easily and neatly stoned. Set aside the neatest prunes for the final decoration, and chop the rest – just over half the total amount – for the stuffing. Crack the prune stones and remove the kernels.

To make the stuffing, mix the chopped prunes and kernels with the breadcrumbs, suet, herbs and seasoning. Add vinegar to taste, then the sugar. At this stage the flavour may seem odd, on account of the malt vinegar, but everything works out well in the end. Put this mixture into the cavity and crop of the chicken, and retruss or sew it up. (Some people find this stuffing heavy when cold; you may prefer – I do – just to put prunes, kernels and herbs into the cavity.)

Put the chicken into a deep pot, which fits it fairly closely. Add the giblets and all the stock ingredients, scaling the amount of vinegar down a little if less than 3½ litres (6 pts) of water is needed. Be particularly sure to cover a boiling fowl by about an inch. The roasting birds should barely be covered. One wants to get as much flavour into the stock as possible, without the chicken becoming dry.

Bring the pot slowly to the boil, and simmer gently – a bubble or two should gurgle to the surface every few seconds – until the bird is cooked. This will take from 1½ to 3½ hours, according to its antiquity. When the bird is done, remove the whole thing to a cool place. I cannot claim that the stock at this stage is particularly delicious, it takes getting used to (like the stuffing), but when it's cooked with the lemon and cream of the sauce it does have a delicious result. And as a cold dish, this is one of the best-flavoured I know.

Make the sauce while the bird is cooking, and almost ready. Bring the cream, lemon juice and rind with a little pepper very slowly to simmering point: let it simmer for 4 or 5 minutes, while you make a roux with the butter and flour. Pour 300 ml (½ pt) of the stock from the chicken on to the roux, then the milk. Simmer for 20 minutes until the sauce is really thick. Finally strain in the lemon-flavoured cream, and cook for a little while longer so that everything is well blended. Correct the seasoning and allow it to cool.

When the bird is really cold, place it on a wire rack over some greaseproof paper. Reheat the sauce slightly – it will be solid when cold – so that you can spread it right over the chicken smoothly and evenly. Use a palette knife, and dip it in hot water, if need be, to enable it to run smoothly over the sauce. Scrape up the drips from the greaseproof and use them to patch up the odd corners. Slice the lemon thinly, nick out the peel to form a zigzag edging to each slice, and cut them all in half. Cut the prunes in half too, the ones you kept aside when making the stuffing. Divide the ham into a number of scallop-edged pieces and use them to make an edging on the serving dish. Put the chicken on top carefully. With the lemon slices, prunes, tufts of parsley and chive stalks, make a fairly exuberant design on the bird: a bunch of parsley makes a good backing if stuck in at the neck end. Use the remaining prunes and lemon slices to tuck round the base of the chicken, on top of the ham.

When you carve and eat the bird, you will be surprised to see how deliciously the malt vinegar has melted into the general flavours, and how good a mixture such a collection of ingredients can make. A superb buffet dish.

## COCKIE-LEEKIE

LIKE HAGGIS, COCKIE-LEEKIE IS NOW FIRMLY TIED TO SCOTLAND in most people's minds. However, in 1867, Lady Llanover gave an identical recipe in her *Good Cookery*, which has to do with Welsh food. And if one compares the basic ingredients with the recipe for Hindle Wakes (previous recipe) it becomes obvious that these are very old dishes, European dishes if you like, which have survived from many centuries back in those parts of the country which have not been too buffeted by new fashions.

*500 g (1 lb) prunes*
*1 kilo (2 lb) piece of stewing beef*
*Boiling fowl, capon or chicken*
*1½ kilos (3 lb) leeks, trimmed*
*Salt, pepper*

SOAK the prunes overnight. Three to four hours before the meal, put the beef into a pot large enough to hold the chicken as well at a later stage.

Cover it with plenty of water, and bring it slowly to the boil. Skim off the grey foamy bubbles as they rise. Simmer for one hour, then add seasoning, and the bird if it is a boiling fowl. In any case, add half the leeks which should be tied together in a bundle. If the bird is a capon or roasting chicken, add it 1½ hours before the end of the cooking time or a little less according to size. The prunes should go in 20 minutes before the cockie-leekie is ready. Meanwhile cut the remaining leeks into slices; they should be added for the last 5 minutes of cooking time, so that they keep a little of their crispness. The big bundle of leeks should be discarded, as all the flavour will have gone into the stock.

The correct way of serving cockie-leekie is to put a slice of beef, a bit of chicken, some prunes, leeks and soup into each bowl. The convenient way is to drink the soup first, then to eat the other items as a main course afterwards.

## SMOKED CHICKEN WITH THREE-MELON SALAD

CHICKEN WHICH HAS BEEN HOT-SMOKED is on sale quite widely these days; the idea came in from France, I think. It is often coarsely flavoured and flabby to eat, an unpleasant combination. My own preference is for cold-smoked chicken, but that is more difficult to find. My source is Mr Millhouse, the famous butcher of Clifton in Bristol. Should you ever drive that way at the end of the week – they smoke the birds on Thursday – ring up and order a couple, one for you and one to present to your local smoke-house with the suggestion that they might try to copy it. At the same time I recommend you buy some of his bacon which is beautifully smoked with beech sawdust from the local coffin-maker. In the baker's opposite on Saturday I used to get the most wonderful garlic bread. Perhaps they still sell it.

The point of cold-smoked chicken is that you cook it. Certain flavours go with it particularly well, and certain textures. Dry sherry is better than wine for basting, and the textures of melon, cucumber and other squashes (see recipe following), the bitterness of bitter gourd and coriander, balance well with the light smokiness of the chicken.

For 6

*1 large smoked chicken*
*Salt, pepper*
*6 tablespoons dry sherry*

SALAD
*3 different melons, e.g. Galia, cantaloupe and pineapple watermelon*
*3 tablespoons hazelnut oil and 5 tablespoons sunflower oil, or 8 tablespoons olive oil*
*Cider vinegar or lemon juice*
*A small bunch of coriander*
*Salt, coarsely ground pepper*

Rub the chicken over with salt and pepper, roast in the manner you prefer, basting with the sherry. Remove the bird and allow to cool. Skim as much fat as possible from the juices, pour the rest into a glass and leave to cool.

Halve, de-seed and slice the melons, arranging them on a large shallow dish, with the sliced chicken. Inspect the glass of juices, remove the fat from the top and reduce the liquid to a strong flavour. Cool it down to tepid, add the oil(s), plus vinegar or lemon juice to taste, and seasoning. Chop the coriander, leaving a few perfect leaves. Spoon the dressing over melon and chicken, but avoid setting them awash in liquid. Scatter with coriander and coarsely ground pepper, and deploy the unchopped leaves as a final decoration. Serve cool rather than chilled.

## THREE-GOURD GARNISH

A GOOD ACCOMPANIMENT TO SMOKED CHICKEN, roast duck or lamb, on account of its clear and savoury flavour, and the contrasting harmony of the three gourds. It also goes well with fish, salmon for instance, and firm white fish. The Portuguese apart, Europeans are not skilful with bitterness in food though we take it well enough in drink. This surprises me with regard to the British, who have been cooking Indian dishes of a kind since the eighteenth century: even in mid-nineteenth-century cookery books, there is no mention of karela, the bitter gourd, or kantola, the spiny bitter gourd (*Momordica charantia* and *M. cochinchinensis*). All we have is Kipling's image of doom in Mowgli's song:

*I will let loose against you the fleet-footed vines –*
*I will call in the Jungle to stamp out your lines!*
*The roofs shall fade before it,*
*The house-beams shall fall;*
*And the Karela, the bitter Karela,*
*Shall cover it all!*

Now we can buy them so easily in Indian greengrocery shops, there is no reason why we shouldn't take to them as much as we have taken to green coriander. The thing is to choose them small and young and bright. Scrape off the coarsest, bumpiest part of the skin. Then slice or halve according to the recipe and remove the seeds and the pith around them. They should then be salted for 3 hours, and blanched in boiled water for 3 minutes.

For 6

*4 small to medium bitter gourds, scraped*
*Salt*
*8-12 very small courgettes, halved lengthways*
*Lightly salted butter*
*1-2 cloves garlic, finely chopped*
*Black pepper*
*½ a cucumber*
*3 tablespoons mixed parsley, coriander and chives, chopped*

HALVE the gourds, remove the pulp and extract the seeds, then slice the gourds thinly. Salt for at least an hour, then blanch for 3 minutes. Drain.

Cook courgettes gently in a little butter with a pinch each of garlic and of black pepper in a closed pan. Peel and slice cucumber in long thin strips, fry briefly to heat through and soften slightly. Finish the bitter gourd pieces in a little butter with a pinch of garlic and pepper.

Arrange to one side of a serving dish, beside poultry, lamb or fish. Keep warm while you toss remaining garlic and gourd seeds in a knob of butter to heat through. Add herbs and pour over the dish.

## DEVILLED CHICKEN LIVERS

CHICKEN LIVERS ARE AN INEXPENSIVE LUXURY that is far more common than it used to be. It is about the only advantage that I can see from the modern chicken industry. Usually the livers are sold in 250g (8 oz) frozen cartons, which means they are a useful standby. Be careful to thaw them completely before separating them out, otherwise they will be damaged and messy. To hurry up the process, stand the carton in some tepid water. These frozen livers have been freed of their dark green gall sacs as a rule, but it is wise to check them; certainly if you use fresh chicken livers, you will need to remove them first, carefully, or your dish will be spoilt by their bitterness.

Another point – never overcook chicken livers. They should be pink in the middle. The best fat for frying them is clarified butter: this means you can heat the butter without fear of burning it, to a temperature at which the livers will brown quickly so that the inside is not overdone. One carton is enough for four people in this recipe:

*250 g (8 oz) chicken livers*
*1 medium onion, chopped*
*50-60 g (1½ – 2 oz) clarified butter*
*2 teaspoons Worcester sauce*
*2 teaspoons Dijon or Urchfont mustard*
*Cayenne, salt, pepper*
*3 tablespoons white breadcrumbs*
*150 ml (¼ pt) whipping cream*
*Extra breadcrumbs and melted butter*

CHOP coarsely the chicken livers. Fry the onion in the butter gently until soft – do not brown it – then raise the heat, add the livers and stir for 2-3 minutes. Off the heat mix in the Worcester sauce and mustard, the seasonings, crumbs and cream. Taste, and add extra Worcester sauce, mustard and Cayenne if you like a spicier devil. Divide between four ovenproof ramekins, sprinkle the tops with crumbs and melted butter. Bake at mark 5, 190°C (375°F) for 15 minutes. Serve with toast.

## COARSE CHICKEN LIVER PÂTÉ

NO ONE COULD CLAIM THAT PÂTÉ IS AN ENGLISH DISH BY ORIGIN, but it seems to have taken us over in the last fifteen years to the extent that even the worst restaurants sell their anglicized versions in large quantity. Whether this is a compliment to the French, I would not like to say. Often these jumped-up meat loaves are absolutely disgusting in a manner that is shamefully English. Here, though, is a respectable version which depends for its success on using a high quality sausagemeat. In Wiltshire I can sometimes buy a superior sausage made by J.B. of Newbury. People in Cornwall and Cumberland will do even better with their local sausages.

For 8

*250 g (8 oz) chicken livers*
*1 small onion*
*2 rashers streaky bacon*
*1 small clove garlic*
*250-375 g (8-12 oz) skinned sausages or sausagemeat*
*Pinch thyme*
*Pinch oregano*
*Cayenne, salt, pepper*
*1-2 tablespoons each sherry and brandy*
*1 level tablespoon drained green peppercorns (optional)*
*3 or 4 strips thinly cut pork back fat*

SET aside the best pieces of chicken liver, leaving about half to be minced with the onion, bacon and garlic. Add this mince to the sausagemeat and season with herbs, salt, and peppers. Add the alcohol slowly to taste, and the green peppercorns if used. Layer into an ovenproof pot in three layers, with two layers of chicken liver pieces in between. Lay the strips of pork fat across the top. Stand in a pan of very hot water, and put into the oven at mark 4, 180°C (350°F). Check after 30 minutes, but be prepared to give the pâté 45. It is done when it pulls away from the sides of the pot – the time taken will depend on the depth of the mixture. When the pâté is half-cooled, put foil over the top and a light weight, and leave overnight. Pâtés are best after two days' storing. Serve with toast, or with good bread and gherkins in the French manner.

NOTE: if you do not care to taste the sausagement mixture for seasoning, make a little cake and fry it. Cool and eat it, and then adjust the seasoning.

## ROAST TURKEY WITH PARSLEY AND LEMON STUFFING

For 8-10

*6-7 kilos (12-14 lb) turkey, drawn weight*
*175 g (6 oz) lightly salted butter*
*Salt, pepper*
*Parsley and lemon stuffing (page 348)*
*150 ml (¼ pt) dry white wine, or dry white vermouth*

REMOVE the giblets from the turkey, and use to make stock – see below. Soften the butter and add a teaspoonful of salt and plenty of black pepper, mashing it together. Make the stuffing and put it in the central cavity of the bird, then weigh the bird. Remove the bird's neck close to the breast to make the neck pudding described on page 201. Put the bird on its side on a rack in a roasting pan. Smear it all over with the seasoned butter. Put a double layer of foil over the top, fastening it tightly round the edges of the roasting pan to seal the turkey in.

Calculate the cooking time – up to 7 kilos (15 lb) the turkey will need 30 minutes per kilo. Over 7 kilos (15 lb) allow an extra 20 minutes per kilo. So a 7 kilo (15 lb) bird will take 3½ hours: and a 9 kilo (20 lb) bird, 4½ hours. Preheat the oven to mark 5, 190°C (375°F). At just under half time, turn the bird on to its other side. For the last 20-30 minutes, put the bird breast up and remove the foil; sprinkle the breast with salt and pepper.

Transfer the cooked bird to a warm serving dish. Boil up the pan juices and add the wine or vermouth. This can be served as a separate thin gravy, or it can be added to the thickened gravy made with the giblet stock.

At home in the north we always used to have a piece of boiled salt pork served with the turkey. I think this is better than bacon rolls – the delicate flavour of the pork, and its fatness, set off turkey meat better than anything else. Instead of cranberry sauce, we usually have a tart, rich jelly made from the Cornell cherry bush in our garden. Roast potatoes are essential, at least for the younger members of the family, and everyone likes sprouts and chestnuts.

### GIBLET GRAVY

*1 set turkey giblets, minus liver, or 2 sets chicken giblets, minus liver*
*2 carrots, quartered*
*1 onion, halved*
*90 ml dry white vermouth, or 150 ml (¼ pt) dry white wine*
*Bouquet garni*
*250g (8 oz) stewing veal, cut in pieces*
*2 tomatoes, halved and grilled*
*Salt, pepper*
*50 g (1½ oz) butter*
*1 level tablespoon flour*

PUT the giblets, carrots, onion, wine, herbs, and veal into a large pan over a high heat. Stir everything about and when it begins to change colour, add the tomatoes and enough water to cover by about an inch. Season with pepper and a little salt. Cover tightly and leave to simmer for 2 hours. Strain carefully.

In a small saucepan melt the butter and continue to cook it until it turns a golden *noisette* brown (it will also smell delicious). Stir in the flour, and when it is well mixed in, moisten with the hot stock. Allow to cook gently for about half an hour, so that the flavour is thoroughly mellow, then correct the seasoning.

If the sauce is to be served with chicken, add the rich brown juices from the roasting pan. In the case of turkey, the juices are likely to be more abundant, so pour off the fat and add a glass of port or Madeira to them and boil up together. Serve separately from the thickened gravy.

## CAPON, GOOSE OR TURKEY NECK PUDDING
## PODDYNG OF CAPOUN NECKE (1430)

I HAD THIS RECIPE ORIGINALLY FROM A FRENCH FRIEND, a superb cook who never wastes a thing. She was spending Christmas with us, and showed me how to stuff the turkey neck skin to make a dish for Christmas Eve supper. She simmered the neck for 20 minutes in the giblet stock that we were making for the gravy next day, but I think the flavour is better when it is baked. Every year since then the turkey, and any other large bird, comes complete with head. It amuses our supplier, but I feel cross about the waste of all those other necks.

Apart from the exquisite flavour, I have always admired this dish as an example of the French skill in turning every scrap to good account. The recipe is most popular in the foie gras districts of south-west France, where the left-over carcase of the fattened goose is salted and cooked gently in its own fat, and potted – again in its own fat.

Then I came across *Poddyng of Capoun necke*, and realized that fifteenth-century court cooks in England had done exactly the same thing as farmer's wives in Périgord. In fact their recipe, using the giblets of the bird as stuffing, is closer to the modern French recipe than mine. I like to keep the gizzard, heart and neck inside the skin for the gravy stock, so substitute good sausage-meat for the giblets.

*'Take Percely, gysour – the gizzard – and the lever of the hearte, and perboye in fayre water; then choppe hem smal, and put raw yokys of Eyroun ii or iii ther-to, and choppe for-with. Take Maces and Clowes, and put ther-to, and Safroun, and a lytil pouder Pepir, and Salt; and fille hym yppe and sew hym, and lay him a-long on the capon Bakke, and prycke hym ther-on, and roste hym and serve forth.'*

For 4

*1 capon, goose or turkey neck (see recipe)*
*250 g (8 oz) high-quality sausage*
*1 heaped tablespoon parsley*
*2 egg yolks*
*Mace, cloves and pepper to taste*
*Pinch of saffron (optional)*
*Salt*
*The liver of the bird*

I ALWAYS buy poultry with the head still on in order to make this delicious pudding. As the giblets are needed for the stock for the gravy, sausagemeat provides the main filling.

With a pair of scissors, cut the skin of the neck as close to the breast of the bird as possible, right round. Then do the same as close to the beak as you can manage. Cut the skin straight up the middle, so that it can now be removed from the neck in an irregularly shaped oblong piece. Lay it out on a chopping board, skin side down.

Mix the sausagement (discard the skins) with the parsley, egg, and spices. Steep the saffron in a very little hot water, and strain the liquid into the mixture when it is a good yellow. Season with salt. Spread this mixture out on the skin of the neck. Trim gristly or greenish bits from the liver, cut it into two or three large pieces and lay them down the centre of the sausage stuffing. Moisten your hands and bring the sausage up round the liver to enclose it completely. Fold the skin over and tuck the whole thing, cut side down, into a small loaf tin – I use one made of foil about 15 cm (6″) long. Bake in the oven when roasting the bird, or if more convenient bake with other things at a temperature of mark 4, 180°C (350°F), for 45 minutes. The top will brown lightly. If possible, leave for a couple of days in a cool place for the flavours to mature. Serve cut down in slices like any other pâté.

## PULLED AND DEVILLED TURKEY, CHICKEN OR PHEASANT

ONE OF THE MOST DELICIOUS DISHES OF EIGHTEENTH-CENTURY COOKING, indeed one of the best of all English dishes. There is no better way of using up the Christmas turkey with the glory it deserves. It is also an ideal dish for a dinner party, as the bird or birds can be cooked in advance, the day before. Spread the leg and thigh meat with the devil sauce several hours before grilling them, if you can; the flavours will then penetrate the meat even more thoroughly. Adjust the quantities of mustard and Cayenne pepper to suit your taste.

For 6

Either: *About 500 g (1 lb) cooked turkey breast*
*1 leg and thigh of the turkey, preferably undercooked and pink*
Or: *1 boiled or roasted chicken, with the brown meat a little underdone*
Or: *A brace of stewed or roasted pheasants*

DEVIL SAUCE
*1 rounded tablespoon Dijon mustard*
*1 rounded tablespoon mango or peach chutney*
*1 tablespoon Worcester sauce, or ½ tablespoon anchovy essence*
*¼ teaspoon Cayenne pepper*
*Salt*
*2 tablespoons corn oil*

PULLED SAUCE
*200 g (7 oz) butter*
*300 ml (½ pt) double cream*
*Lemon juice*
*Salt, pepper*
*Chopped parsley*

FIRST pull the breast meat apart with your fingers into pieces about 4 cm (1½″) long and the 'thickness of a large quill'. Follow the grain of the meat, so that you end up with somewhat thready looking pieces. Take the brown meat off the bones, and divide it into rather larger pieces than the breast meat. Slash each one two or three times.

Mix the devil sauce ingredients together, chopping up any large pieces of fruit in the chutney. Dip the pieces of brown meat into it, and spoon the devil into the slashes as best you can. Arrange in a single layer on the rack of a foil-lined grill pan, and grill under a high heat until the pieces develop an appetizing brown crust. Keep them warm.

For the pulled sauce, melt the butter in a wide frying pan, and stir in the cream. Let it boil for a couple of minutes, and keep stirring so that you end up with thick rich sauce. Put in the pulled breast, with any odd scraps of jelly, and stir about until the pieces are very hot indeed. Season with lemon, salt and pepper. Put in the centre of a serving dish, and surround it with the devilled bits. Serve with good bread or toast. Not a dish to be eaten with two vegetables. Keep them for afterwards, or simply serve a salad.

## BOILED TURKEY AND CELERY SAUCE

**A** FAVOURITE DISH OF THE VICTORIANS and quite rightly so, because it is delicious – mild without insipidity.

For 8-10

*7 kilos (15 lb) turkey, approximate weight*

STOCK
*4 medium carrots, sliced*
*1 turnip, peeled, sliced*
*1 stick celery, sliced*
*3 onions, unpeeled, stuck with 3 cloves each*
*15 black peppercorns, slightly crushed*
*1 heaped tablespoon salt*
*2 bay leaves*
*4 sprigs thyme*
*Bunch of parsley stalks*

SAUCE
*Head of celery*
*90 g (3 oz) butter*
*500 ml (¾ pt) béchamel sauce*
*150 ml (¼ pt) double cream*
*Salt, pepper*

PUT the turkey breast down into a ham kettle or equally large pan (a kettle is best, because it has a strainer tray which helps you to lift out the cooked bird and drain it). Add the stock ingredients, and enough cold water barely to cover the legs; with smaller, 4-5 kilo turkeys, you can confidently use less water than this, as they are young enough to steam to softness. More salt may be needed. Bring to the boil and simmer for 2 hours, or until the turkey is cooked – the simplest way of judging this is to pull the bone end of the drumstick. If the leg parts easily – begins to part, that is, from the body – the bird is done. Keep the stock for soup. Place the bird on its dish.

Meanwhile make the sauce – wash, trim and string the celery. Cut into strips and blanch them in boiling salted water for 10-15 minutes. The celery should be almost but not quite cooked. Drain it well, and return to the pan with the butter and simmer for a further 5-10 minutes, until it is cooked but not mushy. Add the béchamel sauce, stir it all well together and bring to boiling point. Liquidize and sieve it if you like a smooth sauce. Stir in the cream, adjust the seasoning and pour into a sauceboat.

## DUCK STEWED WITH GREEN PEAS

For 4-5

*2-2½ kilos (4-5 lb) duck*
*Bouquet garni (bay leaf, parsley, thyme, rosemary)*
*300 ml (½ pt) giblet stock*
*1 large lettuce, shredded*
*500 g (1 lb) shelled peas*
*2 egg yolks*
*4 tablespoons double cream*
*Salt, pepper, lemon juice*

USE the duck giblets to make the stock in advance. Boil it down to 300 ml (½ pt) or a little more.

Prick the duck all over with a fork, and tuck the bouquet garni into the cavity. Brown it all over in a little oil – do this slowly so that the fat has a chance to run out. When it is a nice colour, a rich golden brown, place it in a deep pot, breast down, with the stock. Cover and simmer for 1¼ hours.

Turn the duck over. Add lettuce and peas, and some seasoning. Replace the cover and complete the cooking – another 45 minutes approximately. Take out the duck, and cut it into four pieces or carve it. Put the drained peas and lettuce on to a warm serving dish and arrange the duck on top. Keep it warm while the sauce is finished. Taste the cooking liquid. If necessary skin off fat and boil hard to concentrate the flavour. Mix yolks and cream in a basin, pour on about half the stock, whisking it in well. Return this mixture to the cooking pot and stir the sauce together over a low heat without allowing it to boil. Finish with lemon juice, and correct the seasoning. Pour over the duck and peas and serve at once.

The sauce can also be thickened with beurre manié, but the yolks and cream are best. The dish has a remarkably fresh flavour, agreeably sweet but light and sharp at the same time. An ideal summer dish.

## DUCK WITH MINT

SAUCE PALOISE MEANS SAUCE FROM PAU, which is the capital of the Béarn district of France. It is really a *sauce béarnaise* flavoured with mint instead of tarragon, a fact that the French often forget when they sneer at our habit of serving mint sauce with lamb. This recipe, which is a marriage of English and Béarnaise sympathies, was invented by Guy Mouilleron. Coming from the Béarn, with its *sauce paloise*, he experimented a great deal with mint, carrying its use further than most English cooks would have thought possible. See his other recipes on page 97 and page 152.

*1 large duck*
*1 large bunch of mint*
*1 large carrot, quartered*
*1 large onion, stuck with 3 cloves*
*1 stick celery*
*Salt, pepper*

SAUCE PALOISE
*1 tablespoon chopped shallot*
*2 tablespoons chopped mint*
*1 tablespoon chopped chervil*
*1 sprig thyme*
*¼ bay leaf*
*4 tablespoons white wine vinegar*
*4 tablespoons dry white wine*
*Salt, pepper*
*3 large egg yolks*
*175 g (6 oz) butter, cut in pieces*
*Lemon juice*
*Extra chopped mint*

SEASON the duck inside and put into it the bunch of mint. Secure the opening, and wrap the duck in a large white napkin, tying it at each end like a Christmas cracker. Half-fill a large pan with tepid water, put in the carrot, onion, celery and seasoning and bring to the boil. Place the duck in this liquid, which should just cover it, and leave to simmer, covered, for 2½ hours.

Meanwhile make the sauce, about an hour before the end of cooking time. Place the shallot, herbs, vinegar and wine in a small pan. Add a pinch of salt and a good grinding of pepper. Bring to the boil and reduce the liquid by two-thirds or a little more. Allow it to cool, then whisk in the egg yolks and set over a low heat (or over another pan of simmering water, if you are not used to making egg-yolk sauces). Whisk in the butter bit by bit, never allowing the sauce to boil. When it is thick, season the sauce with lemon juice, and more salt and pepper. Strain it into a warm sauceboat, and stir in extra chopped mint. If the sauce has to wait, suspend the sauceboat over a pan of warmed water.

To serve the duck, remove it from the napkin and drain it well. Put it on a serving dish, and surround it, if you like, with sprigs of fresh mint. Serve the sauce with it, also a purée of young turnips or broad beans.

## ROAST GUINEAFOWL

THE FIRST TIME I SAW GUINEAFOWL, they were humped along the roof ridge of a French farmhouse, like a row of black and white chequered tea-cosies. Occasionally one of them would get up and carefully pick its way along the row, or squawk down into the farmyard. They look so decorative, and – which is more important – taste so good, that I do not understand why they have become so much less common than they once were. It's true that the flesh can be a little dry, but larding or a jacket of bacon or pork fat easily counteracts this slight disadvantage. Even when frozen, they taste far better than frozen chicken or turkey, having a slightly gamey flavour. (A friend suggested to me recently that such birds, turkey in particular, are best when allowed to thaw out to *warm room temperature* before being cooked: this is true, though nothing can ever take the place of proper hanging in the matter of flavour.)

In some parts of this country, guineafowl are called gleenies, a corruption and abbreviation of the Latin '*Gallina africana*', the African hen. Certainly the Romans were the first to appreciate their delicious gamey flavour. They even appear as symbols of the soul in bliss, along with the more usual peacock, on a mosaic pavement in Justinian's church at Sabratha in Libya. 'The effect is that of a couple of dazzling check sport-suits,' wrote J.M.C. Toynbee in *Animals in Roman Life and Art*.

For 6-8

*2 fine guineafowl, 750g-1 kilo (1½-2 lb) each*
*6 rashers unsmoked streaky bacon, or 6 strips of pork back fat*
*Seasoned flour*
*1 glass port*
*300 ml (½ pt) stock made from the giblets, or from chicken giblets*
*1 bunch watercress*

STUFFING
*125 g (4 oz) good sausages*
*1 heaped tablespoon breadcrumbs*
*1 tablespoon brandy*
*1 tablespoon port*
*1 heaped tablespoon chopped parsley*
*1 clove garlic, crushed*
*Salt, pepper to taste*

FIRST make the stuffing. Remove the skins from the sausages and discard them (it is important to use a high-quality, meaty sausage, for instance, genuine Cumberland sausages, see page 167). Mix with the remaining stuffing ingredients and divide between the two birds – if the birds are sold complete with their livers, chop them up and add them to the mixture, but be sure to remove any bitter greenish parts first.

Put the bacon or pork fat across the breasts of the birds – or, better still, lard them with fat strips of pork and protect them with butter papers. Place them on the rack of a roasting pan and put them into a hot oven, at mark 7, 220°C (425°F). After 15 minutes, lower the heat to mark 6, 200°C (400°F), and leave them for 30 minutes. Take the guineafowl from the oven, remove bacon or paper and sprinkle them with seasoned flour. Return to the oven for 10-15 minutes until cooked and browned. Place the birds on a serving dish and keep them warm. Pour the port into the roasting pan juices, boil them up for a couple of minutes, scraping in all the nice brown bits that have stuck to the pan. Add the stock and boil down until you have a small amount of strongly flavoured gravy. Pour round the birds, and garnish the dish with watercress. Serve with bread sauce, and with celeriac, or celery, or the chestnut and apple mixture on page 75.

## GUINEAFOWL BRAISED WITH MUSHROOMS

For 3-4

*1 fat guineafowl*
*125 g (4 oz) butter*
*1 medium onion, chopped finely*
*375 g (12 oz) mushrooms, sliced*
*Salt, pepper, lemon juice*

BROWN the guineafowl all over in half the butter. Place it breast down in a deep, closely fitting pot and dab it all over with the remaining butter. Add the onion and some salt and pepper. Cover the pot with kitchen foil to seal it in tightly. Place in the oven at mark 5, 190°C (375°F), for 30 minutes.

Meanwhile season the mushrooms with salt, pepper and lemon juice. When the 30 minutes comes to an end, remove the bird in its pot from the oven and take off the lid. Turn it breast-side up and tuck the mushrooms in all round it. Season the breast and replace the foil. Return to the oven for a further half an hour. Discard the foil lid and leave the bird for another 10 minutes or so until it is cooked and lightly browned on top.

Carve the bird into eight – four slices of breast, two drumsticks and two thigh pieces. Arrange them on a hot dish with the mushrooms, which should be removed from the cooking pot with a perforated spoon. Taste the gravy and correct the seasoning, before pouring it over the bird. Serve immediately with good bread, or a few boiled potatoes to mop up the delicious juices.

THIS RECIPE is also good for pheasant. Indeed pheasant and guineafowl recipes are interchangeable.

## GAME

GAME, WOODPIGEONS APART, NEEDS HANGING (unless you eat it soon after it is shot), or it will be tough and thin of flavour. The general principle is to hang it until the tail feathers may easily be pulled out. In practice, this works out at 2-3 days for wild duck, mallard, teal, widgeon, etc., and about 7 days for pheasant, though in cold weather it may need 10. Venison, hare, wild rabbit should also be hung: from 3 to 10 days. A whole deer needs 2-3 weeks.

Game of all kinds is hung without being plucked, or skinned, and complete with innards. Birds are suspended by their necks; deer, hare and rabbit by the hind legs – this is particularly important when the blood of a hare or rabbit is needed for thickening the sauce.

The thing to watch when hanging game is the humidity of the weather. A warm muggy day, the kind that makes the stone floor of the cellar or back kitchen sweat with moisture, will increase the rate at which game matures in flavour. On the other hand, really cold weather will slow it down, acting like a refrigerator. One thing – always hang game before freezing it.

Plucking game birds is simple, if laborious. Hold the bird inside the mouth of a plastic sack (the plastic kind remain fairly rigid and stay open so that you can see what you are doing). Pull the feathers into the sack. Have a bowl of water to hand, so that you can rinse off the feathers that stick to the fingers. Pull the feathers the way they lie, so that the skin does not tear. Cut off the wing feathers, feet and other tricky bits. Some birds, the snipe for instance, should be skinned and not plucked: to do this chop off the wings and head, and ease off the skin and feathers. Snipe and woodcock should not be drawn as their entrails – usually referred to as the trail – are a delicacy.

Larger birds need to be drawn in the same way as poultry. This is not in the least unpleasant, and can be done quite neatly. Put the plucked bird on a large sheet of newspaper on the table; have a bowl of water handy, or do it by the sink. Make a small hole by the vent, and run your finger round the breast bone, easing the insides which are held together by membranes. Gradually they will come out, as you feel your way around and hook them out towards you. When they are on the table, rinse the bird and set it aside. Remove the liver, heart and gizzard from the guts, as they can be used to make stock in some instances when a little gravy is required: the liver should have the greenish part removed, as this will taste bitter from the gall sac which stained it; the gizzard should be slit from top to bottom, to display the inside which is usually full of grain or greens – this can be removed by peeling away the wrinkled tough skin which lies next to the grain.

## COOKING GAME

WITH THE GAME BIRDS, roast only the young ones. The older creatures, or any you are doubtful about, should be braised or casseroled.

The test for youth varies slightly with different animals, but in general the feet will be soft and pliable, the ears in the case of rabbits and hares soft and easily torn. With rabbits and hares, creatures that one is used to, size will help you to form an opinion, and the young look of the skinned carcase.

The temperature for roasting these birds should be high, mark 5-8, 190-230°C (375-450°F): the lower temperature for the larger pheasant, grouse and blackgame, the higher for snipe and woodcock. It is wise to tie a jacket of pork fat round all but snipe and woodcock, which only need to be spread with softened butter. Another way of counteracting the dryness is to put a variety of things into the carcase to provide moisture: this ranges from seasoned butter to fruit. One of the nicest ways of all of serving game is to cut a piece of bread the size of each bird before it goes into the oven. As the bird roasts, fry the bread lightly in butter, then slip it under the bird about 5-10 minutes before the end of cooking time. This will soak up the delicious juices. The bird is put on to the serving dish, on top of the bread, and needs little more than watercress to go with it, though many other delicious things are often put on the table as well to prolong the pleasure and enhance the glory of the bird.

With venison, hare and wild rabbit, roasting is more of a problem. First set the oven to a lower temperature, mark 4, 180°C (350°F). It is a good idea

*Larding poultry and game*

both to lard the game, and then to tie a jacket of fat pork round it, which can be removed for the last 15 minutes of cooking time. Allow 60 minutes per kilo (30 per pound). With a wild rabbit, it is wiser to braise it or cook it in a casserole – the usual flavourings are onion and thyme. Saddle of hare can be stuffed and roasted successfully – it is a good idea to baste it with butter, bacon fat, red wine or milk, even if it is already larded and covered with a piece of fat. Venison, unless it is really young, should be soaked in a marinade, and braised, ideally in a slow electric crockpot.

### PHEASANT

(October 1 – February 1)

*roast*: ¾-1 hour, mark 5, 190°C (375°F)
*inside*: butter with seasoning and herbs; fillet steak; mushrooms, chopped and cooked first in butter
*serve with*: bread sauce, etc. (see page 356), celery sauce (page 203), or celery salad; chestnuts; game chips, or roast, mashed or boiled potatoes

## Partridge

(September 1 – February 1)

*roast*: 30 minutes, mark 7, 220°C (425°F)
*inside*: chopped liver, chopped onion and butter; mushrooms chopped and stewed in butter
*serve with*: bread sauce, etc., as for pheasant
*braised*: with chestnuts and cabbage and white wine (page 216)

## Grouse

(August 12 – December 10)

*roast*: 35-45 minutes, covered with vine leaf if possible, then bacon or pork fat in a sheet, mark 5, 190°C (375°F)
*inside*: bananas; wild raspberries, cranberries; peeled and seeded grapes
*serve with*: bread sauce, etc., as for pheasant, rowanberry jelly (page 364)

## Ptarmigan

(August 12 – December 10, Scotland only)

*braise or stew, rather than roast*
*inside*: as grouse
*serve with*: as grouse

## Woodcock

(October 2 – January 31; in Scotland September 1-January 31)

*roast*: 18 minutes (rare), mark 8, 230°C (450°F)
*inside*: leave the trail
*serve with*: finish cooking on fried bread; when done, spread trail on the toast – or else draw birds, before roasting, and cook trail with butter and marjoram and spread on fried bread just before serving

## Snipe

(August 12 – January 31)

*roast*: 15 minutes, mark 8, 230°C (450°F)
*inside*: as woodcock
*serve with*: fried bread soaked in cooking juices, spread with trail as woodcock. Plus redcurrant jelly, orange salad, game chips; or simply with lemon quarters and watercress

## MALLARD

(below high tide, September 1 – February 20; elsewhere to January 31)

*roast*: 30 minutes (rare)
*inside*: butter with salt, pepper and herbs
*serve with*: orange sauce, page 361; orange salad; with pan sauce made from stirring a glass of port wine into the cooking juices, skimmed of fat, and a tablespoon of bitter marmalade.

## WIDGEON AND TEAL

(see Mallard)

*roast*: 10-25 minutes, mark 7, 220°C (425°F)
*inside*: liver mashed with butter, parsley and lemon
*serve with*: as wild duck. On fried bread put under bird at the end of roasting

## QUAIL

It is now illegal to kill wild quail. Japanese quail are bred for the table; they can be browned in butter and braised with a little stock, port wine and orange peel

## WOOD PIGEONS

(all the year round)

Only domestic pigeons or squabs are suitable for roasting. Wild pigeons should be cooked in a casserole – see stewed venison; or stewed with white wine, chestnuts and cabbage (see page 216)

## VENISON

(variable seasons, according to species and place)

*roast*: 60 minutes per kilo (30 minutes per lb), after marinading (page 220). Lard, and tie on a jacket of fat
*serve with*: french beans, well buttered; celery; Cumberland sauce (page 359); orange sauce (page 361); venison sauce (page 360); mushrooms, particularly wild mushrooms; redcurrant jelly or rowan jelly; orange salad; roast or boiled potatoes
*stewed*: see page 223

## HARE

(no season, but may not be sold from March to July inclusive)

*roast* (young hare only): lard, jacket of pork fat, 40 minutes per kilo (20 minutes per pound), mark 6, 200°C (400°F)

*serve with*: forcemeat balls, redcurrant jelly, port wine sauces, e.g. venison sauce; bacon rolls.
*jugged or stewed* (older hare): pages 208, 209

### WILD RABBIT

(all the year round)

*roast*: 1 hour, mark 6, 200°C (400°F)
*inside*: herb stuffing (page 348)
*serve with*: see hare
*stewed*: page 223

## ROAST PHEASANT

A BRACE OF PHEASANTS MAKES A FINE DISH for winter celebration. Round about Christmas they are in top condition, falling to the guns in plump splendour.

> *See! from the brake the whirring pheasant springs,*
> *And mounts exulting on triumphant wings:*
> *Short is his joy. . . .*

And it is still this pheasant, Pope's pheasant in Windsor Forest, that you see in the main, hanging outside the game shop, a firebird among the sober ranks of hare and partridge.

Unlike our other game birds, partridge, grouse, woodcock, wild duck, the pheasant is by origin a most un-English creature of wild legend and magic. Its story goes back to the Argonauts who are said to have brought it back to Europe from Medea's Colchis (now part of Georgia), on their return from the quest of the Golden Fleece. The pheasant strutted about in troops on the banks of the River Phasis, at home in a land of glamour and exotic princesses.

It's no legend, though, that the Romans bred pheasant for the table, even at the grey end of the world on Hadrian's Wall (fossilized bones of the bird from Colchis were found in excavations at Corbridge – a long journey to have made, from Phasis to the Tyne). Sadly, it disappeared with the Romans.

The next unassailable pheasant record dates from the eleventh century; presumably the birds had come from France, preceding William the Bastard by a few years. And the French had the pheasant from the Romans. So it's back to Italy, the intermediary for so many things coming from the East to the West.

I had always thought that the pheasant belonged to the eighteenth and nineteenth centuries. And in spite of the Argonauts my impression was not so false after all, because it was then that many new varieties were introduced into this country – Lady Amherst's pheasant, the golden pheasant and so on. They came mainly from the Far East, China in particular, where they had been hunted by falconers since the third century B.C.

Unhung pheasant, like many other game birds, and game, isn't fit to eat. There's no need to wait until the back end turns green (thought I knew of one parson's wife who thought pheasant wasn't ready for the table until maggots dropped on to the marble slab below), but they must be hung for several days. The exact number depends on temperature and humidity – and personal taste. On the whole it's a matter best left to an expert, in other words a good game butcher. Fix him with a determined eye, and make sure that the bird he presents you with has had a chance to develop the right unmistakable flavour before being plucked. Otherwise your money will be wasted.

Don't be put off by the price – there's a high proportion of meat to carcase. Quite the opposite of duck. A pheasant will go round four people nicely when the dressed weight is in the region of 1¼ kilos (2½ lb). Older birds can be casseroled in the usual way, but it is best to go for a young roasting bird whatever method you intend to use. The young cock bird has short, rounded spurs; the hen – to be preferred for fatness and fine flavour – has soft feet. Older pheasants have long and pointed spurs, and hard feet.

For 8

*Brace of pheasants*
*125 g (4 oz) fillet steak or 125 g (4 oz) butter*
*2 thin sheets of back pork fat, large enough to cover the pheasant breast and top of the legs*
*Salt, pepper*
*Seasoned flour*
*1 glass port*
*Watercress*

GIBLET STOCK
*Pheasant giblets, excluding liver*
*Light beef stock*

*1 carrot, sliced*
*1 onion, sliced*
*Bouquet garni*

BROWNED CRUMBS
*90 g (3 oz) white breadcrumbs*
*50 g (1½ oz) butter*

BREAD SAUCE
*see page 356*

POTATOES
*750 g (1½ lb) firm potatoes*
*Deep fat for frying*

FIRST prepare the pheasants for roasting – cut the fillet steak into strips and put half into each cavity, with salt and pepper; alternatively divide the butter between them. These measures are to add extra moisture; pheasant can be dry. Put the livers into the pheasants, too, having first made sure that any greenish-yellow bits have been cut away. Season the birds and tie the sheets of pork fat in place. It is a good idea to lard the birds too, which means that the fat is introduced right into the lean meat of the breast and legs. Use strips cut from the sheets of fat. Set the pheasants aside until required.

To make the giblet stock, put all the ingredients into a pan and cover them generously with water. Simmer for 2 hours, strain the stock and boil it down to half a pint. Season it.

To roast each bird, allow 40 minutes to the kilo (20 per pound), plus 10 minutes at mark 5, 190°C (375°F): this usually means 45-65 minutes. For the last 10 minutes, remove the jackets of pork fat, dredge the breasts lightly with seasoned flour and return to the oven to brown.

When the pheasants are cooked, put them on a serving dish and keep them warm. Skim the fat from the pan juices, pour in the giblet stock and boil hard for a few minutes. Scrape in any of the nice bits and pieces that may have stuck to the bottom of the roasting pan. Add the wine and bring to boiling point again. Season to taste if necessary and strain into a sauceboat.

While the birds are cooking, prepare the other items. The breadcrumbs should be fried in the butter until they are golden brown. This means regularly stirring. Tradition enjoins that they should be served on a doily in a small dish. The doily also absorbs any extra fat, so it is not an idle or pretentious refinement.

The bread sauce can be prepared in advance, and reheated over a pan of boiling water.

The potatoes should be peeled and then sliced very thinly on a mandolin into a bowl of water. If you like, use the ridge blade to produce *gaufrette* slices: for the lattice effect, run the potato one way on to the ridge blade and discard the first slice – then turn the potato and run it at right angles on to the blade to give you the lattice slices. Dry the potato well, and put it in batches into a chip basket. Cook in the deep fat at 200°C (395°F) until they're brown and crisp. Drain on crumpled kitchen paper and sprinkle with salt before serving. They too can be prepared in advance and reheated.

Brussels sprouts, mushrooms or celery can all be served with pheasant.

Don't forget to arrange the watercress round the birds before serving them.

## PHEASANT BRAISED WITH CELERY

*1 pheasant*
*90 g (3 oz) butter*
*1 onion, chopped*
*3 thin rashers unsmoked bacon, cut in strips*
*Salt, pepper*
*1 head celery, cleaned, sliced*
*1 large egg yolk*
*150 ml (¼ pt) single cream*
*150 ml (¼ pt) double cream*
*Lemon juice*
*Chopped parsley*
*150 ml (¼ pt) port*
*300 ml (½ pt) giblet stock (page 214)*

BROWN the pheasant in the butter with the onion. Put it into a deep ovenproof pot, breast side down. Add the port, stock and bacon to the frying pan, bring everything to the boil, then pour it over the pheasant. Cover the pot with a double lid of foil, and put into the oven for half an hour at mark 4, 180°C (350°F). Remove the pot from the oven, turn the bird right side up, and pack it round with the sliced celery – slip some underneath as well, and into the cavity. Season well. Replace the lid and return the pot to the oven for another half-hour or a little longer, until the pheasant is cooked.

Put the pheasant on a serving dish, surrounded by the celery. Beat the egg yolk and creams together, then add the hot liquor from cooking the bird. Pour it into a pan and heat gently, stirring all the time, until the sauce thickens. Taste it for seasoning, and sharpen with a little lemon juice. Scatter the chopped parsley over the celery just before serving. Pour the sauce into a separate sauceboat.

## PARTRIDGE OR WOODPIGEONS WITH CHESTNUTS AND CABBAGE

For 6

*3 partridges, or 6 woodpigeons*
*250 g (8 oz) fat bacon, cut in strips*
*60 g (2 oz) butter*
*24 pickling onions, peeled*
*150 ml (¼ pt) dry white wine*
*Game or beef stock*
*Crisp cabbage of Savoy type*
*250 g (8 oz) chestnuts*

BROWN the birds and bacon strips lightly in the butter. Transfer them to a casserole, putting the birds breast down. Brown the onions in the butter and add them to the pot. Finally pour the wine and about 300 ml (½ pt) of stock into the frying juices, boil it up and scrape in all the nice brown bits and pour it over the birds. Woodpigeons should be almost covered, as they are a tougher proposition than partridges, so it may be necessary to add more stock – it will depend on the fit of the birds in the casserole. Cover the casserole closely and simmer it gently either on top of the stove or in the oven. Nick and boil the chestnuts for 15 minutes, then peel them. At the same time blanch the cabbage for 15 minutes in boiling salted water. When the birds are almost cooked, remove them from the casserole – put the cabbage in, open it out as best you can and place the birds on top, with the chestnuts. Replace the lid and continue cooking until done. Put the birds, cabbage, bacon and chestnuts on a dish. Skim the fat off the sauce, and if necessary boil it down hard to concentrate the flavour. Pour over the dish and serve.

## STEWED PIGEONS IN FOIL

TOWARDS THE END OF HIS LIFE, the great chef Alexis Soyer discovered that he had a son after all, the child of a girl he had known when he was young. And this child also had a son, Nicolas, who became a chef like his grandfather. He worked for wealthy families in England, and at Brooks's Club in London. In 1911 he had an extraordinary success with *Paper-Bag Cookery*. As Helen Morris points out in her biography of Alexis Soyer, Nicolas had very much the tone and enthusiasm of his grandfather – 'I do not claim for the paper-bag system of cookery that it can cook everything. It is evident that the national beverage must still be cooked in the tea-pot.' An identical note of cheeky pomposity. I imagine he would be even more excited by the range of foil, roastabags and parchments that make life so easy for cooks today.

Allow one pigeon for each person, and for each pigeon the following ingredients:

*60 g (2 oz) butter*
*Good sprig thyme*
*1 heaped teaspoon chopped onion*
*1 tablespoon brandy*
*1 tablespoon beef stock*
*1 tablespoon lemon juice*

BROWN the breast of the pigeon in a quarter of the butter. Cool it slightly, then put a third of the remaining butter inside, with the thyme, onion and some pepper. Cut the piece of foil large enough to enclose the bird loosely. Rub the remaining butter over the centre part of the foil, and place the pigeon on top. Bend up the foil slightly, and pour in the remaining ingredients. Pepper the pigeon, but add no salt. Fasten the foil tightly, making a baggy parcel. Place on a baking sheet and put into the oven at mark 2, 150°C (300°F) for 3 hours.

Meanwhile make a purée of celeriac and potato, or Jerusalem artichoke and potato, appropriate to the number of pigeons, adding plenty of butter and parsley. Spread out on a wide shallow dish. Also make some buttered crumbs (page 215).

When the birds are ready, cut away the breast parts (keep the rest for soup or stock-making). Place them skin side up on the purée. Season the pieces. Tip the juices into a small pan and taste them for seasoning. Boil them up and pour over the pigeons. Scatter the breadcrumbs over the top and serve.

## BRAISED WILD DUCK WITH APRICOT STUFFING

*2 wild duck, dressed*
*½ onion, sliced*
*3 stalks from celery heart*
*½ teaspoon thyme*
*30 g (1 oz) butter*
*1 tablespoon flour*
*1 tablespoon bitter orange marmalade (optional)*

STUFFING
*90 g (3 oz) dried apricots, preferably the wild apricots with stones from Afghanistan*
*60 g (2 oz) breadcrumbs from day-old bread*
*60 g (2 oz) butter*
*2 heaped tablespoons chopped celery*
*Salt, pepper*

FIRST make the stuffing. Soak the apricots overnight. Drain them next day, and if they are the small kind, remove the stones, crack them, and extract the kernels. Chop the apricots roughly and add the kernels. Mix with the bread. In the butter cook the celery very gently for about 10 minutes until it is almost cooked; keep the pan covered. Add to the stuffing, season and put into the cavities of the duck.

Place the duck side by side in a deep pan or roaster. Put in the onion, celery stalks, and thyme and enough boiling water to come 1½ cm (½″) up the duck. Cover and put into a slow oven, mark 3, 160°C (325°F), for 1 hour. Remove the cover, and top up with more boiling water if necessary to maintain the original level. Put back into the oven for another half-hour. Remove the duck to a serving dish and keep them warm. Taste and boil down the cooking liquor to a good flavour. Mash the butter and flour together, and use to thicken the sauce by adding it in small knobs: the sauce should be stirred continuously and kept just below boiling point. Finally correct the seasoning, and add the marmalade gradually to taste, if you decide to use it. If not, serve the duck with redcurrant jelly as well as the sauce.

## SALMI OF GAME (OR DUCK, OR FISH)

A SALMI SHOULD REALLY BE MADE WITH GAME that has been roasted rare specially for the dish. In an imperfect world, it is more likely that a salmi contains the left-overs of yesterday's feast. Seen on a restaurant menu – at a restaurant price – it looks recherché, a dish of high-class French cookery. Don't be deceived. It is exactly what would have been eaten by Chaucer, or his son, at the court of Henry IV, or by that grand-daughter of his, Alice, Duchess of Suffolk, at her manor of Ewelme (where her husband built the church, and where she lies in such a splendour of alabaster). Only they would have called it salomene or salome. English court cooks had taken both name and recipe from medieval France, perhaps even from the *Ménagier of Paris* of

1393, where the word *salemine* occurs; meaning something salted or highly seasoned (from the Latin, *sal, salis*, salt).

Rabelais a century and a half later jazzed the word up with an extra syllable into *salmagonde*, and it soon came to have an extra meaning of a wild muddle or mixture of things, like another cookery word gallimaufry. You will see why if you turn to salmagundi on page 190. It is a highly seasoned recipe, but has no other similarity to salmi. Salmagundi gradually slipped out of favour towards the end of the last century – in England at least – but both the French and ourselves have most wisely clung to salmi. So good is the dish that the recipe has remained in principle the same for five and a half centuries: the main ingredient is roasted, then cut up and reheated in a highly seasoned wine sauce. Here is the 1430 version of salmi, using fish (in the same manuscript there is another, less well explained salome for capon):

### SALOMENE

TAKE GOOD WINE, *and good powder, and bread crumpled, and sugar and boil it together; then take trout, roach, perch, or carp, or all these together, and make them clean, and after roast them on a griddle; then hew them in gobbets; when they be cooked, dry them in oil a little, then cast them in the bruet and when you dress it, take mace, cloves, cubebs, gilliflowers; and cast them on top, and serve forth.'*

POWDER MEANS GROUND SPICES, cubebs are the berries of *Piper cubeba*, one of the pepper family, with a spicy pungent flavour. Bruet means a thick sauce.

*Game birds roasted rare*
*3 shallots, chopped*
*60 g (2 oz) butter*
*1 heaped tablespoon flour*
*Bouquet garni*
*Thinly cut peel of an orange, preferably a Seville*
*Pepper, salt, lemon juice*
*150 ml (¼ pt) red or white wine*
*125 g (4 oz) mushrooms fried in butter*
*Cayenne pepper*
*Croûtons of bread fried in butter*
*Orange quarters*

REMOVE the meat in nice neat pieces from the carcase. Use the bones and trimmings to make 425 ml (¾ pt) stock. Melt the butter and cook the shallots in it until they are a rich golden colour, then stir in the flour, and moisten with the stock. Simmer steadily for at least 20 minutes, with the bouquet and orange peel, until you have a rich, concentrated sauce almost of a coating consistency. Strain into a clean pan. Season to taste and add the wine and mushrooms. Simmer for 5 minutes, then put in the game, cover and leave for 10 minutes. The sauce should never boil properly once the game is added – it should barely simmer. Finally, add a little Cayenne pepper.

Place the pieces of game with a little sauce on top of the croûtons, and serve the sauce in a separate jug. Or else put the game and sauce into a serving dish, with the croûtons tucked round the edge. Garnish with orange quarters.

## ROAST VENISON WITH NORWEGIAN GOAT'S CHEESE SAUCE

VENISON, LIKE BEEF, should be roasted pink or rare, unlike wild boar which, like pork, should be cooked until well done. It is prudent to marinade it first. For a relatively tender piece, say of farmed venison, a short period in an uncooked marinade is enough, say 24 hours. For wild venison, or for venison from a more mature animal, bathe it in a cooked marinade for a maximum of 3 days. I now use the method recommended by Anne Willan in her *Complete Guide to Cookery* (Dorling Kindersley, 1989), and find her classic marinade admirable:

For up to 2

*½ kilo (5 lb) meat*
*1 carrot, sliced*
*2 onions, sliced*
*1 stalk celery, sliced*
*125 ml (4 fl oz) olive oil*
*1 bottle red wine, respectable and decent rather than glorious*
*125 ml (4 fl oz) red wine vinegar*
*Bouquet garni*
*12 juniper berries*
*12 peppercorns, lightly crushed*

FOR an uncooked marinade, just mix all the ingredients together. The strained liquid may eventually be used for a sauce.

For a cooked marinade, stew the vegetables in half the oil until soft but not browned. Add the rest of the ingredients and bring to the boil. Simmer until the vegetables are cooked. 15-20 minutes. Then add the remaining oil and cool.

Put the meat in a deep, close-fitting bowl and pour over the marinade so that it is completely covered. Cover the bowl and refrigerate.

*To cook the venison*: drain the meat and dry it. Butter it all over like toast and place on a rack in a roasting pan. Have the oven preheated to mark 7, 220°C (425°F). Estimate the .length of cooking time, allowing 10-15 minutes per 500 g (1 lb) for rare meat, 18 minutes per 500 g (1 lb) for medium, pink meat. Put in the joint. After 15 minutes, pour 250 ml (8 fl oz) of the strained marinade and 125 ml (4 fl oz) game or beef stock into the pan. Give it another

5-10 minutes, then lower the heat to mark 4, 180°C (350°F) for the rest of the time, basting and adding extra marinade and stock if the pan beings to dry up. I also follow my Norwegian niece's instructions and smear the meat with 2 good tablespoons of soured cream when I turn the heat down.

If you have a meat thermometer, you may like to check temperatures. 51°C (125°F) for rare meat. 60°C (140°F) for pink, medium meat. When the cooking time concludes, rest the meat in a warm place for at least 20 minutes, better still 30 minutes.

FOR THE SAUCE
*250 ml ( 8 fl oz) game or beef stock*
*250 ml (8 fl oz) crème fraîche, or half double, half soured cream*
*about 30 g (1 oz) gjetost cheese, slivered*
*Rowan or peppered redcurrant jelly (see page 363)*
*Salt, pepper*

SKIM the fat from the venison roasting juices and strain them into a wide shallow pan. Add the stock and boil the whole thing down thoroughly to concentrate the flavour. You can also add extra strained marinade, if you like. It should be really strong. Pour in the cream, and stir. When amalgamated, flavour to taste with the gjetost cheese and the jelly, added in small, alternating quantities, plus salt and pepper if necessary once the sauce has arrived at a suitable consistency.

If you find this kind of sauce difficult to manage, you can always rescue the consistency with a little slaked arrowroot or cornflour.

NOTE: don't shudder at the idea of gjetost. I know that it looks like a slab of poor quality toffee and has a caramelized sweetness of taste. This makes it perfect as a flavouring for game sauces, if used with discretion.

## VENISON CHOPS AND STEAKS

WELL-HUNG venison chops and steaks may be grilled in the same way as beef steaks. Serve them with the usual venison accompaniments, a port-wine sauce or quince jelly, French beans or mushrooms or an orange or celery salad, and roast or fried potatoes or game chips.

It is, however, a good idea to wrap them first in a piece of softened caul fat (page 209), to act as a permanent basting. Season them with a little salt and plenty of black pepper first. Allow 15-20 minutes, turning them once, under a high heat.

## VENISON PASTY

*(see page 236)*

## VENISON SAUSAGES

SEVERAL YEARS AGO NOW, the game butcher in Oxford market began to make a speciality of venison sausages. I notice that they are beginning to be sold elsewhere, too. This is the way I was told to cook them:

Brown the sausages briefly and quickly in lard. Arrange them closely together in a shallow dish and pour in just enough wine to come halfway up – red wine is the best. Give them 20 minutes in a hot oven – mark 6-7, 200-220°C (400-425°F) – on the top shelf. Serve them with mashed potatoes, Brussels sprouts and chestnuts, and something sweet such as redcurrant or rowan jelly, or pickled cherries (though these are really a French accompaniment).

## JUGGED HARE (OR RABBIT)

For 6

*1 hare or large wild rabbit, jointed*
*Strips of pork or bacon fat for larding (optional)*
*Salt, pepper, mace*
*Bouquet garni*
*1 onion, stuck with 3 cloves*
*125 g (4 oz) butter*
*150 ml (¼ pt) red or white wine*
*1 anchovy, chopped*
*Pinch Cayenne pepper*
*15 g (½ oz) butter*
*1 tablespoon flour*
*Blood of hare or rabbit (optional)*
*Lemon juice (optional)*
*Triangles of fried bread*

UNLESS your hare or rabbit is especially young and tender, you will be wise to lard it. Put the pieces into a large jug (the unlipped stoneware jugs still made in France, and widely sold in England, are ideal) after rubbing them with salt, pepper and mace. Add the bouquet, onion and butter. Cover the jug tightly and securely with kitchen foil, and string to make sure it keeps in place. Stand the jug in a pan of boiling water and keep it simmering until the hare is cooked – about 3 hours, but the time depends on the age and toughness of the creature. This can be done on top of the stove (it was an obvious solution to the problems of slow cooking without an oven) or in the oven if this is more convenient.

Remove the cooked pieces to a serving dish. Strain the juices into a pan. Add the wine, anchovy and pepper to taste. Thicken either with the flour and butter mashed together, and added in little knobs, or with the blood of the creature – in the latter case, mix a little of the sauce with the blood, then return it to the pan and stir over a low heat until thick; the sauce must not boil again once the blood has been added – like eggs, it will curdle. Sharpen with a little lemon juice if you like.

THIS RECIPE was the obvious way of cooking game slowly in the days when ovens were not common, and most cooking was done over the hearth fire. Modern 'jugged' hare is really stewed, as in the following recipe.

## STEWED HARE, RABBIT, WOODPIGEONS OR VENISON, WITH FORCEMEAT BALLS

For 6

*1 hare or rabbit jointed, or 6 pigeons, or 1½ kilos (3 lb) stewing venison, cut in pieces*
*Seasoned flour*
*250 g (8 oz) streaky bacon, cut in strips*
*250 g (8 oz) chopped onion*
*90 g (3 oz) lard*
*1 heaped teaspoon thyme*
*1 heaped tablespoon chopped parsley*
*½ bay leaf*
*Game or beef stock*
*6 tablespoons port*
*Redcurrant jelly*
*Salt, pepper*

FORCEMEAT BALLS
*125 g (4 oz) fresh white breadcrumbs*
*60 g (2 oz) chopped suet*
*1 tablespoon chopped parsley*
*1 teaspoon thyme*
*Grated rind ½ lemon*
*60 g (2 oz) finely chopped bacon*
*Salt, pepper*
*1 large egg*

TURN the joints, pigeons, or pieces of venison in seasoned flour (keep the brains, liver and blood for the final thickening, in the case of hare and rabbit). With the bacon and onion, brown them in the lard. Transfer to a casserole. Put in the herbs and just enough stock to cover them. Simmer gently until the meat is tender and parts easily from the bone. Add the port, jelly and seasoning to taste. To thicken the sauce, either mix some of the liquid with a little of the remaining seasoned flour – about a tablespoon – and return it to the pot, or mash the brains, liver and blood together, pour on a little hot liquid and then return this mixture to the pot, cook without boiling for a few minutes until the sauce is thickened. The second method produces the better flavour – a good game butcher will give you the blood of a hare or wild rabbit, a tablespoon of vinegar will prevent it coagulating.

Meanwhile mix the ingredients for the forcemeat balls, and fry them in lard until brown. Make the balls about an inch in diameter. They are also good with game soups, but should be made smaller. If you do not want to make forcemeat balls, serve the stew with triangles of fried bread.

## BOILED WILD RABBIT OR DUCK WITH ONION SAUCE

PUT the trussed rabbit or duck into a pan. Cover it with cold water. Put in a bouquet of herbs, and pepper and salt. Bring to the boil and simmer until done – this will not take long, if the rabbit or duck is a young one.

After half an hour, put 1-1½ kilos (2-3 lb) large, whole, skinned onions into the pot. Remove them after 20-30 minutes, drain and chop them and put them into a pan with 125 g (4 oz) of butter. When they are cooked to a soft golden colour, stir in 4 tablespoons of double cream. Correct the seasoning, adding a litle nutmeg if you like.

Put the cooked rabbit or duck on to a serving dish, either whole or cut into serving pieces. Pour the onion over the top so that they are smothered in the rich creamy sauce. Serve with potatoes and spinach.

A FAVOURITE eighteenth-century recipe, and a good one. If you cannot get a wild rabbit, use duck instead – domestic rabbit is too insipid for this kind of treatment.

John Farley, who was principal cook at the famous London Tavern, and published a book of his recipes in 1783, went in for startling decoration in the boar's head style. 'Pull out the jaw bones, stick them in their eyes, and serve them up with a sprig of myrtle or barberries in their mouths.' Sucking pig, with an apple in its mouth and red berries in its eyes, is almost the last survivor of this tradition.

## TO DRESS RABBITS IN CASSEROLE

For 4

*1 wild rabbit, jointed*
*Seasoned flour*
*125 g (4 oz) butter*
*150 ml (¼ pt) dry white wine*
*600 ml (about 1 pt) beef stock*
*Pepper, salt*
*Bouquet garni*
*1 rounded tablespoon flour*
*Juice of 1 Seville orange*
*2 whole Seville oranges*
*Chopped parsley*

DREDGE the rabbit with seasoned flour, and brown it in half the butter. Transfer the pieces to an earthenware casserole, and add first the wine, then enough stock barely to cover the meat. Season and tuck in the herbs. Simmer in a low oven, mark ½-1, 120°-140°C (250°-275°F), until the rabbit is tender. The time will depend on the age of the rabbit, so it is a good idea to cook the dish one day, and reheat it *thoroughly* the next. If you cannot do this, allow 3 hours at least. Meanwhile mash up a tablespoon of the remaining butter with the flour to make beurre manié. Slice the two whole Seville oranges, and nick triangles of peel from the edge of each slice – save all the tiny pieces (this decorative detail can be omitted, but it adds to the final appearance of the dish).

When the rabbit is ready, arrange the pieces on a warm, shallow serving dish and keep them warm. Strain the sauce into a wide pan and reduce it to a good flavour. Lower the heat so that it barely simmers, and add the beurre manié in small knobs, stirring them in until the sauce thickens – this takes about 5 minutes. Add the orange juice, correct the seasoning, and off the heat, beat in the final ounce of butter. Pour this sauce over the rabbit, and sprinkle it with the tiny bits of orange peel and a little parsley. The orange slices go round the edge.

LARD CAN be used for frying the rabbit in this recipe from Hannah Glasse. A teaspoon of sugar may be added to the sauce as an improver of flavour: stir it in gradually, and stop before it becomes too sweet. Dessert oranges can be used, but Sevilles are the perfect balance for the slightly rank flavour of rabbit.

# MEAT PIES AND PUDDINGS

IN COOKERY BOOKS PUBLISHED IN THIS COUNTRY, it has long been the convention to indicate the weight of pastry required by giving the quantity of flour needed to make it. For example, 1 lb pastry means pastry made with 1 lb flour; if it is shortcrust, the final weight of the dough will be about 1½ lb, but if it is puff, the dough will weigh 2 lb, on account of the larger quantity of butter used. If either pastry can be used for a pie, this makes exact quantity difficult to specify without muddling the look of the ingredients list.

There are other considerations, too. Many people these days thankfully buy puff, even shortcrust pastry in frozen packages. These are always marked with the final weight of the dough, rather than the amount of flour used.

Others when making pastry prefer to make as large a quantity as their electric mixer or hand mixing bowl will comfortably accommodate, and store the surplus in their freezer. A sensible time-saving.

Then there is the question of taste and discretion. If you make a Cornish pasty for a miner to put in his pocket to take to work, the pastry has to be pretty thick, or the whole thing will spoil. If you are making mince pies for the end of a large meal, you will need to roll the pastry thinner than if they are destined to fill up hungry young carol singers. Or you may decide to make a lot of little pork pies rather than one large one, so more pastry will be required.

This is the kind of cooking accommodation that we rapidly become used to. Therefore in all the recipes for pies and tarts in this book, only the type of pastry will be indicated, not its weight.

## CORNISH PASTY

WHEN MY HUSBAND WAS A LITTLE BOY in Cornwall, in the village of Pelynt near Looe, everyone made family-sized pasties like these (except for 'foreigners' like his mother, the vicar's wife, who was given to the sort of ladylike pasties that are sold in England today). When he needed comforting and a friendly lap, he would go to see his special friend Bessie, who worked for his mother, and she would get a large pasty out of the meat-safe and cut him off a slice. On a really good day, she might bring out an apple pasty, flavoured with cloves. He would watch her cut off the end, and pour in brown sugar and clotted cream, before handing it to him. The pasty is a good shape for holding in both hands. No need to bother with a plate or cutlery.

Individual pasties, in appropriate sizes, were baked for the men who had to go out into the fields all day, or down the mines, or for children to take to school. Different members of a family might have different ideas on the seasonings, so these pasties would be marked with initials at one corner. This had the added advantage that a half-eaten pasty could be reclaimed by its rightful owner.

In hard times, the proportion of steak to vegetables would be reduced – sometimes to nothing. Potato, onion and turnip, flavoured with herbs, would have to do, or quite a different mixture of leek, bacon and hard-boiled egg. Remember that a pasty should always be firm and full, never wet or too juicy to eat comfortably in the hands, never dry. Always chop or slice meat and vegetables – never mince them.

Cornish pasties are pronounced with a long 'a'.

For 2

*Shortcrust pastry, made with lard*

GLAZE
*Beaten egg*

FILLING
*500 g (1 lb) skirt or chuck steak*
*125-150 g (4-5 oz) chopped onion*
*90 g (3 oz) chopped turnip*
*250 g (8 oz) thinly sliced potato*
*Salt, pepper*
*Pinch of thyme*

MAKE the shortcrust pastry in the usual way. Do not be tempted to use butter or any other kind of fat, because lard gives the right flavour and texture to the crust. Leave the pastry in a cool place for an hour to rest.

Meanwhile remove the lean meat from the skin, gristle, etc., and chop it with a sharp, heavy knife. There should be a generous half pound (the trimmings can be kept for stock-making). Mix the meat with the vegetables and seasoning.

Roll out the pastry and cut it into two large dinner-plate circles. Divide the steak mixture between the two, putting it down the middle. Brush the rim of the pastry with beaten egg. Fold over the pastry, to make a half-circle, or bring up the two sides of pastry to meet over the top of the filling, and pinch them together into a scalloped crest going right over the top of the pasty (some Cornish people insist on one method, others disagree). Make two holes on top, so that steam can escape. Place the pasties on a baking sheet and brush them over with beaten egg. Bake at mark 6, 200°C (400°F), for 20 minutes, then lower the heat to mark 4, 180°C (350°F), for a further 40 minutes. Serve hot or cold.

## STEAK, KIDNEY AND OYSTER PIE

For 6

*Filling ingredients (page 243), as for Steak, Kidney and Oyster Pudding*
*Puff or shortcrust pastry*
*Beaten egg to glaze*

MAKE the filling, and leave it to cool as described in the recipe on pages 243-5. Check the liquid and add the oysters, if used.

Roll out the pastry. Cut off strips wide enough to cover the rim of the pie dish and hang down a little inside it. Before putting them in place, brush the rim with water. Next put the cold filling into the dish. Brush water lightly over the pastry rim, and cover the pie over with the remaining pastry. Some people use a pie funnel, which should be set in the middle of the filling; it's a good idea though not strictly necessary.

Press the edges of the pastry firmly together, nicking the pie at intervals if you are using puff pastry, or pressing it up in a scalloped shape if you are using shortcrust. With the trimmings make a simple leaf decoration, with a rose. Make a hole in the centre through which the steam can escape, and place the decorations round it. If you make a stem to the rose, it can be placed loosely in the centre hole and will not impede the steam escaping. Brush everything over with beaten egg. Bake at mark 7-8, 220-230°C (425-450°F), and leave for another 45 minutes, or a little less if the filling was adequately cooked before the pie was assembled.

## DARTMOUTH PIE

JOYCE MOLYNEUX REVIVED THIS RECIPE and put it on the menu of the Carved Angel, after discovering it in Cassell's *Dictionary of Cooking* (1880s). It's a variation on the old mince-pie theme, with its combination of mutton, suet, currants, sugar and nutmeg. For to-day's taste, the recipe has been lightened, and made more cheerful with the addition of a spice mixture of her own. If you cannot find good mutton, substitute venison – which I like better than mutton anyway – or chuck steak.

For 4

*500 g (1 lb) well trimmed, cubed mutton*
*Salt*
*1 teaspoon each peppercorns and coriander seed*
*½ teaspoon each ground mace and allspice*
*2-3 cm (1") cinnamon stick*
*60 g (2 oz) dripping*
*250 g (8 oz) sliced onions*
*1½ teaspoons flour*
*300 ml (½ pt) beef, veal or venison stock*
*60 g (2 oz) each dried apricots, prunes and raisins*
*Rind and juice of ½ Seville orange, or sweet orange plus lemon juice*
*Shortcrust or flaky pastry made with 250 g (8 oz) flour*
*Beaten egg to glaze*

SALT the meat. Grind spices to a powder. Using a pan that can go into the oven, brown the meat in the dripping. Add spices and cook gently, stirring, for a minute or two. Put in onions, sprinkle on the flour and mix well. Pour in stock. Add fruit, rind and juice(s). Bring to simmering point, check seasoning, cover tightly and put into the oven preheated to mark 1-2, 140-150°C (275-300°F). Leave for 1½-2 hours, until tender.

Check seasoning again, tip into a pie dish or four smaller dishes and cool. Scrape off any fat. This can all be done in advance.

Cover with pastry, decorate and brush with egg. Bake in a hot oven mark 7, 220°C (425°F) for about 40 minutes, checking after 25 minutes, until pastry is nicely browned and the contents are bubbling.

## DEVONSHIRE SQUAB PIE

THE NAME OF THIS PIE has puzzled people so much that some very odd stories have been invented to account for it. The recipe goes back at least as far as the first part of the eighteenth century – in those days squabs from the dovecot were a manorial perquisite; perhaps cottages imitated the aristocratic pigeon pies with more available mutton and lamb, but kept the name of the original meat.

For 6

*Shortcrust pastry*
*1 best-end of neck of lamb, or 750g (1½ lb) lamb fillet off the bone*
*1 kilo (2 lb) Cox's orange pippins or other good dessert apple*
*2 medium onions, finely sliced*
*16 unsoaked prunes*
*½ nutmeg, grated*
*Level teaspoon each all spice, cinnamon*
*Salt, pepper*
*150 ml (¼ pt) lamb stock*
*Clotted cream*

THIS pie is made in a deep dish and is only covered with pastry, so make pastry and set aside to chill while you deal with the filling.

Slice the meat, including a small proportion of the fat, but discarding the bones which can be used to make the stock. Peel, core and slice the apples. Cut the prunes into pieces and throw away the stones.

Grease a deep pie dish. Arrange meat, apple and onion in layers, sprinkling them with spices and seasoning and chopped prunes. If the apples are on the tart side, sprinkle them with a little brown sugar: if you are using windfalls, this may well be necessary, but do not over-sweeten the pie. Pour in the stock and cover with a pastry lid in the usual way. Bake at mark 6, 200°C (400°F), for 20-30 minutes to set and colour the pastry. Protect it with some brown paper and lower the heat to mark 3, 160°C (325°F) – leave for a further 45 minutes. Eat hot with clotted cream.

## CUMBRIAN TATIE POT

MRS BURROWS, WHO SENT ME THIS RECIPE, comes from Workington. When I looked at her letter more closely, I saw that she now lived in Marlborough, my shopping town, nine miles away. I got in touch with her and suggested that she brought over the real thing one lunchtime for us to try what looked like an impossible recipe. Mrs Burrows said that what interested her was that tatie pot is one of our few dishes in which different meats are combined, something which is common in mainland Europe. The recipe in slightly different form appears in various books of Lakeland cookery and often the beef is described as 'optional' – which it most definitely is *not*. It makes the character of the dish. So resist the national tendency to leave it out.

Tatie Pot is very much a dish of communal eating, at village get-togethers, or at society beanos, rather as baked beans are a standard item on similar occasions in America. There is always a certain rivalry to see whose version is best. Mrs Burrows gained the distinct impression as a child that this version, made by her mother and grandmother, was usually supreme. Certainly it is a wonderful dish for hungry people after a long weekend walk.

For 6-8

*1 kilo (2 lb) scrag end or best end of lamb, plus extra bones*
*1 kilo (2 lb) shin of beef, plus a beef bone*
*6 level tablespoons pulses, eg mixed split peas, red lentils, pearl barley*
*Seasoned flour*
*2 large onions, chopped*
*1 black pudding, sliced 1 cm (½") thick*
*About 1½ kilos (3 lb) medium, even-sized potatoes*
*Salt, pepper*

THE day before, use the bones and any trimmings from the meat – which should be cut into convenient but large mouthfuls – to make a simple stock with the usual aromatics. Put the pulses to soak overnight.

To assemble the tatie pot, take an old-fashioned ordinary roasting pan or other metal dish that will give you a good surface area. Turn the meat in seasoned flour, shaking off the surplus, and arrange in the bottom of the pan. Scatter with onion, tuck in slices of black pudding. Drain pulses in a sieve, rinse them and spoon over the whole thing.

Peel and cut the potatoes down their length into quarters. Put all over the dish to cover it in a single layer. You may need extra potatoes – or fewer – depending on the surface area of the dish. Put them rounded sides up, and keep the arrangement informal.

Remove any fat from the stock, heat it and strain over the contents of the pan. Add hot water, if necessary, to come halfway up the potatoes. This level should be maintained with extra hot water (or stock) during the cooking, until the end – once the meat is tender, the liquid may be allowed to reduce.

Mrs Burrows bakes her tatie pot for 4 hours at mark 6, 200°C (400°F) which gives it a dark, crunchy topping and a rich flavour. However you can cook it at a lower temperature, and protect the potatoes once they have browned to the tone you like with butter papers or brown paper. You can also lower the heat towards the end.

## SWEET LAMB PIE FROM WESTMORLAND

*Shortcrust pastry*

*175 g (6 oz) lean boned lamb*
*90 g (3 oz) lamb fat, trimmed from chops etc.*
*175 g (6 oz) apples, weighed after peeling, coring and grating*
*125 g (4 oz) currants*
*125 g (4 oz) raisins*
*125 g (4 oz) sultanas*

FILLING
*60 g (2 oz) candied chopped peel*
*Juice of 1 orange*
*Juice of ½ lemon*
*60 g (2 oz) blanched chopped almonds*
*4 tablespoons rum*
*Pinch salt*
*Freshly ground black pepper*
*½ teaspoon mace*
*½ teaspoon cinnamon*
*¼ nutmeg grated*

MAKE up this pie on a pie plate, the kind that is much used in the north of England. The best ones are tin, but the enamelled kind do quite well. Roll out some of the pastry, enough to cover the plate.

Mince the meat, both fat and lean. Put it into a basin and mix in the remaining ingredients, making sure that everything is well distributed. Taste and add a little more spice if you like. Turn enough of this filling into the pastry to mound up above the level of the rim. Roll out the remaining pastry, and cover the pie, brushing the underneath pastry rim first with beaten egg or top of the milk. Press down and decorate the edge, make a central hole, and brush the lid over with egg or top of the milk. Bake for 30 minutes at mark 6, 200°C (400°F).

PUT ANY filling left over into a jam jar, cover it and use it up for small mince pies.

## CHESHIRE PORK AND APPLE PIE

SINCE I WROTE ABOUT THIS PIE some years ago, readers have occasionally queried its status as a raised pie. Unless the pastry walls are thick, the juices burst out and spoil its appearance. Should one ever add liquid to a raised pie?

So I returned to Hannah Glasse. Her instructions are vague, but it is placed among the dish pies (raised pies start six recipes later). Later in the book she gives instructions for a Cheshire pork pie to be made at sea, with salt pork, and potatoes instead of apples; and this pie is clearly a double crust pie made in a dish.

The question remains, should the pie be eaten hot or cold? By its position, I would say hot, like the chicken pie before it, and the Devonshire squab pie that follows. But it tastes so good cold. By leaving the pie for 24 hours, you will find that the flavours blend together in the most delicious way.

*Shortcrust pastry*
*1 kilo (2 lb) boned loin of pork*
*4 rashers streaky green bacon, chopped*
*250 g (8 oz) chopped onion*
*Salt, pepper, nutmeg*
*375 g (12 oz) Cox's orange pippins, or similar dessert apple*
*Brown sugar*
*Butter*
*150 ml (¼ pt) white wine, dry cider or light ale*
*Beaten egg or top of milk, to glaze*

LINE a 1¼ litre (about 2 pt) capacity pie dish with pastry. Slice and cube the pork, then put in a layer. Mix bacon, onion and seasonings and scatter some over the pork. Then peel, core and slice the apples and arrange them on the meat; scatter with a little brown sugar; the amount depends on the sweetness of the apples, but it should not be overdone. Repeat the layers until the ingredients are used up. Dot the top with butter – about 60 g (2 oz) – and pour on the alcohol. Cover with pastry in the usual way, and brush with beaten egg or top of the milk.

Bake at mark 7, 220°C (425°F), for 20-30 minutes, then lower the heat to mark 3, 160°C (325°F), and leave for a further 45 minutes, or until the pork feels tender when tested with a larding needle or skewer through the central hole in the pastry lid.

## CORNISH CHARTER PIE

WHEN I CAME ACROSS THIS RECIPE a year or two ago in Lady Sarah Lindsay's *A Few Choice Recipes*, of 1883, I thought it explained something that had puzzled me for a long time. Now I am not so sure.

The puzzling thing was a couple of references in Parson Woodforde's diary, to 'the Charter'. It occurred in the middle of a list of dishes he had had at a dinner part on July 13th, 1775, without any explanation. Obviously it was something to eat, because on another occasion the Parson helped his niece Nancy to make the Charter, this time for a party at his brother's house in Somerset. They put the Charter into the cellar to cool, the dog got into the cellar,and the dog ate the Charter. This suggests something meaty, unless it was an especially greedy dog which guzzled anything it could get hold of. And this is why I was delighted to find the recipe above. It seemed to explain everything.

Now I have to conclude that it explains nothing, that we are left with two puzzles instead of one. I checked with the big edition of the Parson's diary, and discovered that the editor interpreted the Charter as a custard, but without explanation or reference. Possibly the words 'Charter custard' occurred in an unpublished part of the manuscript. Reluctantly I suppose he must be right. Parson Woodforde never seems to have helped out in the kitchen. Gardening was his contribution. Perhaps on holiday, he might have given Nancy a hand with a custard – stirring it until it cooled down? – rather in the way in which the lady of the house in my childhood used to venture bravely into the kitchen to make a little pudding of some kind. And that still leaves the Cornish Charter pie unexplained.

For 6-8

*Rich shortcrust pastry*
*Beaten egg to glaze*

FILLING
*2 × 1½ kilos (3 lb) chickens, jointed*
*Seasoned flour*
*1 large onion, chopped*
*125 g (4 oz) butter*
*90-125 g (3-4 oz) bunch of parsley*
*1 leek, or 6 spring onions*
*150 ml (¼ pt) milk*
*150 ml (¼ pt) single cream*
*300 ml (½ pt) double cream*
*Salt, pepper*

ROLL the chicken pieces in seasoned flour. Cook the onion gently in half the butter in a frying pan, then remove it to a large shallow pie dish. Add the rest of the butter to the pan and when it is really hot, put in the chicken and brown it slightly – a golden colour is right, not a very crusty brown. Fit the chicken into the pie dish on top of the onions, in a close, single layer. Chop the parsley leaves, and the leek or spring onions, and simmer them for 2 or 3 minutes in the milk and single cream. Pour the whole thing over the chicken, and add about a third of the double cream. Season everything well.

Roll out the pastry and cover the pie in the usual way. Make a central hole large enough to accommodate a small kitchen funnel, and put a pastry rose with a 1 cm (½″) stem down through the middle. Surround it with some leaves. Brush over with beaten egg. Bake at mark 7-8, 220-230°C (425-450°F), for about 20 minutes, until the pastry is golden. Lower the heat to mark 4, 180°C (350°F), and leave until the chicken is cooked - about an hour. Just before serving ease out the rose from the centre, and pour in the remaining cream which should be at boiling point. Replace the rose, and serve hot, very hot, or cold (the juices set to a delicious jelly).

## CHICKEN AND LEEK PIE FROM WALES

For 6

*1 boiling fowl, or roasting fowl*
*1 onion, unpeeled*
*2 tablespoons chopped celery*
*Bouquet garni*
*Salt, pepper*
*125 g (4 oz) cooked, sliced tongue*
*6 fine leeks, trimmed*
*2 tablespoons chopped parsley*
*Shortcrust pastry*
*Beaten egg to glaze*

PUT the chicken into a deep pot, with the onion, celery, herbs and seasoning. Add enough water barely to cover. Simmer until the chicken is cooked. Remove the pot from the heat and leave it to cool down. Cut the chicken into convenient pieces. Skim the fat from the cooking stock.

Take a pie dish and arrange the chicken in it, with the tongue, which should also be cut into neat pieces. Slice the leeks, cook them for 2 minutes in boiling salted water. Drain them well and add them to the chicken and tongue with the parsley. Season and pour over just enough of the chicken stock barely to cover the contents of the pie. Roll out the pastry. Cut a strip from it and place round the rim of the pie dish. Brush it with beaten egg, and lay the main part of the pastry over the pie to make a lid. Press down the edges, trim off the surplus pastry and decorate the pie with a few pastry leaves. Make a central hole so that the steam can escape. Brush the whole thing over with beaten egg and put into the oven at mark 8, 230°C (450°F),for 20-25 minutes until the pastry is a nice colour – then lower the heat to mark 4-5, 180-190°C (350-375°F), and leave for another 20 minutes or so.

## RABBIT PIE

UNTIL THE INTRODUCTION OF MYXOMATOSIS, wild rabbit was the staple protein of poor country families. One friend was so hard-up when she first married that the only meat they ate for several years was the rabbit her husband shot in the fields round our village. Now a good wild rabbit is a luxury. Domestic rabbit by contrast is as insipid as a battery chicken, even nasty in texture and taste. A thing that surprises me in France is the universal passion for hutch rabbit. I am sometimes offered one there, as a great treat. It costs more than free-range chicken, and I find it difficult to refuse tactfully.

The essential thing about rabbit pie – apart, of course, from the wild rabbit – is thyme. Plenty of it. And lemon. Some old recipes include forcemeat balls, which should in this case be flavoured with rather more lemon rind than usual, plus some lemon juice. The recipe below includes soaking and blanching to diminish the sometimes over-strong rabbit flavour: this you can omit, if you like.

For 6-8

*1 jointed wild rabbit*
*Seasoned flour*
*Butter, lard, bacon fat or dripping*
*1 large onion, chopped*
*150-175g (5-6 oz) streaky bacon or salt pork*
*Grated rind of a lemon*
*1 heaped tablespoon parsley*
*4 sprigs thyme*
*About 450 ml (¾ pt) light beef or veal stock*
*Forcemeat balls (see page 223)*
*Puff pastry, or shortcrust*
*Beaten egg to glaze*

SOAK rabbit in cold, salted water for 1½ hours. Drain. Put into a pan with enough fresh water to cover. Bring to the boil and simmer for 3 or 4 minutes. Drain and dry.

Turn the pieces in seasoned flour and brown lightly in a sauté pan, along with the onion and cured pork, cut into strips. Add rind and herbs, and enough stock barely to cover. Put the lid on the pan – or foil – and simmer until rabbit is just tender. Cool, and bone if you like.

To assemble the pie, put the rabbit, bacon, onion etc. into a deep pie dish of about 1¼ litre (generous 2 pt) capacity. Put forcemeat balls round the rabbit. See that everything is mounded up in the centre, to support the pastry crust. Taste the cooking liquor, and add more herbs and seasoning if required. Pour carefully round the meat.

Cover, and decorate the pie with pastry in the usual way. Brush over with beaten egg. Bake at mark 7, 220°C (425°F), for 20-30 minutes, until the pastry is nicely coloured. Then lower the heat to mark 3, 160°C (325°F), for another 30 minutes. If the crust colours rapidly, protect it with paper.

## ENGLISH GAME PIE

*2-4 game birds, according to size (pheasant, grouse, partridge, woodpigeon)*
*Bouquet garni*
*Stock or water*
*1 large onion, chopped*
*250 g (8 oz) mushrooms, sliced*
*60 g (2 oz) butter*
*1 rounded tablespoon flour*
*6-8 rashers bacon (optional)*
*3-4 hard-boiled eggs, quartered*
*Salt, pepper, parsley*
*Puff or shortcrust pastry*
*Beaten egg for glazing*

FOR this recipe choose older birds or woodpigeons, rather than young roasting game. Put them into a pan with the bouquet and cover with stock or water plus salt and pepper. Simmer, covered, until the meat begins to part from the bone, and can be cut away from the carcase in good-sized pieces. Arrange them in a pie dish. Brown the onions and mushrooms lightly in the butter – they should be golden rather than deep brown. Stir in the flour, and enough stock to make a rich, fairly thick but not gluey sauce. Simmer while you cut the rashers into convenient-sized pieces for small rolls: these should be lightly grilled, then arranged round the meat, along with the pieces of hard-boiled egg. Season with salt, pepper and chopped parsley. Pour over the onion and mushroom sauce which should come to within half an inch of the top of the pie dish. Cover with puff or shortcrust pastry in the usual way (puff pastry is traditionally used, but many people prefer a good shortcrust with meat). Brush over with beaten egg and bake for 30 minutes at mark 7, 220°C (425°F). The heat may be lowered once the pastry has risen well (puff) and is nicely browned (puff and shortcrust).

IF THE game has been cooked in advance, and is put into the pie when cold, allow slightly longer cooking time. The filling must be thoroughly heated through at boiling point. If you are uncertain about this, use a glass pie dish so that you can see what is happening.

## VENISON (OR GAME) PIE OR PASTY

For 6

*1½ kilos (3 lb) shoulder venison, or other game cut in pieces*
*Flour seasoned with mace, pepper and salt*
*125 g (4 oz) butter*
*150 ml (¼ pt) red wine*
*Game or beef stock*
*125 g (4 oz) chopped onion*
*1 tablespoon flour*
*Puff pastry and beaten egg to glaze*

TURN the venison or other game pieces in the flour, and brown them in half the butter. Add the wine and enough stock to cover the meat. Put in the onion, cover and simmer until the meat is cooked and can be removed, in the case of other game, from the bone. Strain off the sauce. Melt the remaining butter in a small pan, stir in the flour and add the sauce to moisten it. Taste and correct the seasoning and put with the meat into a pie dish.

Roll out the pastry. Put a strip round the rim of the dish, brush it with water and put on the lid. Press the edges firmly together.Make a hole in the centre and decorate with pastry leaves and flowers (venison pasty is always on the ornate side as far as appearance goes). Brush over with beaten egg, and bake at mark 7-8, 220-230°C (425-450°F), for about 20-30 minutes, until the crust is well risen and brown, and the contents of the pie heated through and bubbling. Delicious hot or cold.

ONE OF the best of English dishes. It cannot fail to be a success, as the cooking of the contents is done separately beforehand: this means that tenderness and seasoning can be assured.

## RAISED PIES

HOT-WATER CRUST
*200 ml (⅓ pint) water*
*175 g (6 oz) lard*
*500 g (1 lb) plain flour*
*½ teaspoon salt*
*1 egg (optional)*

GLAZE
*Beaten egg*

JELLIED STOCK
*See below*

FILLING
*See below*

To make the crust, bring water and lard to the boil, then tip it quickly into the middle of the flour and salt. Mix everything rapidly together to a smooth dough with a wooden spoon or electric beater. Add the egg if you like; it gives extra colour and richness, but is not essential – some people use a scant tablespoon of icing sugar instead which increases the crispness of the pastry. Leave the dough, covered, until it can be handled without discomfort, but do not allow it to cool. Cut off a quarter for the lid, and put the rest into a hinged raised pie mould, or 18 cm (7″) cake tin with a removable base. Quickly and lightly push the pastry up the sides of the tin, being careful to leave no cracks. If the pastry collapses down into a dismal heap, it is a little too hot, so wait and try again. Alternatively, roll out pastry.

Many butchers making their own pies used wooden pie moulds and 'raised' the dough round them. Jam jars can be used instead, but they need to be well floured, or you will find it difficult to remove the jar without spoiling the raised pastry. Before putting the filling in, a band of brown paper was tied round the pies to help them keep their shape, and this remained in place during baking. Unless you are very skilful with your hands, and have plenty of time, the first method is much quicker and more successful – particularly if you invest in one of the attractively decorated hinged pie moulds.

Having raised the crust, make the jellied stock and choose a filling from the recipes below. Pack the filling into the pastry (if it mounds up above the rim, so much the better), roll out the lid and fix it in place with beaten egg. Make a central hole and decorate the pie with leaves and roses made from the trimming (sweet pies are not decorated in English cookery, but the meat ones often end up looking very decorative). Brush it over with beaten egg, and put into the oven at mark 6, 200°C (400°F), for half an hour to firm the pastry and give it a little colour. Then lower the heat to mark 3, 160°C (325°F), and leave for 1 hour (small pies) to 2 hours (large pork and chicken pies) so that the meat can cook. Keep an eye on the lid and protect it with brown paper if it colours too quickly.

Remove the pie from the oven, cool for 30 minutes and take it out of the mould (or untie brown paper). Brush sides with egg and return to the oven for 10 minutes to colour them. When they look appetizingly brown, take them out and pour in jellied stock through the central hole, using a tiny kitchen funnel or a cone of cardboard. This stock will fill the gaps left by the shrinking meat: it is important to have it nicely flavoured.

Leave pies for twenty-four hours before eating, or even longer.

The importance of using a hot-water crust is that it absorbs the meat juices inside and the rich fat, while remaining crisp outside. A short-crust pastry has too high a proportion of butter to do this as successfully.

NOTE: if the sides of the pie show signs of cracking when you remove it from the tin, put it back quickly and leave to cool without further cooking.

## JELLIED STOCK

*Bones from the meat used to make the fillings*
*2 pig's trotters, or 1 veal knuckle*
*Large carrot, sliced*
*Medium onion stuck with 3 cloves*
*Bouquet garni*
*12 peppercorns*
*About 3 litres (4-5 pts) water*

PUT all the ingredients into a pan and simmer for 3-4 hours steadily (cover the pan). Strain off the stock into a clean pan and boil down until you have about 500 ml (¾ pt) of stock. Season with salt, and add more pepper if you like. This liquid will set to a firm jelly, and is much better than the stock-plus-gelatine recommended in some pie recipes.

## FILLINGS

For 6

### PORK Pie Filling

*1 kilo (2 lb) boned shoulder of pork or spareribs, with approximately ¼ fat to ¾ lean meat*
*250 g (8 oz) thinly cut unsmoked bacon*
*1 teaspoon chopped sage*
*½ teaspoon each cinnamon, nutmeg, allspice*
*1 teaspoon anchovy essence*
*Salt, freshly ground black pepper*

THE characteristic note of pork pies from Melton Mowbray, the great pie centre of England – at least in times past – is the anchovy essence. It makes an excellent piquancy without the least fishiness, rather as oysters do in a steak and kidney pudding.

Chop some of the best bits of pork into 1 cm (¼") dice. Mince or chop the rest with 3 rashers of the bacon (the bacon cure improves the colour of the pie on account of the saltpetre: without it the filling would look rather grey when the pie is cut). Add the seasonings. Fry a small amount and taste to see if adjustments are needed. Mix in the diced meat. Line the base of the pastry with remaining bacon, and fill with the pork mixture. You will always get a better texture if the meat is finely chopped rather than minced.

### VEAL, HAM AND EGG PIE

*750 g (1½ lb) pie veal*
*375 g (12 oz) unsmoked bacon, ham or gammon in a piece (ham must be uncooked like the gammon or bacon)*
*Salt, pepper*
*Grated rind of ½ a lemon*
*1 tablespoon chopped parsley*
*1 teaspoonful dried thyme*
*3 eggs, hardboiled and shelled*

Dice veal and bacon, ham or gammon into 1 cm (¼″) pieces – do not mince them. Season with salt, pepper, lemon rind and herbs. Put half into the pastry, arrange the eggs on top and cover with remaining meat mixture.

## RAISED MUTTON PIES

*1 best end of neck, or 500 g (1 lb) fillet from the best end if sold off the bone*
*3 shallots, chopped, or 125 g (4 oz) chopped onion*
*125 g (4 oz) mushrooms, chopped*
*1 tablespoon chopped parsley*
*1 teaspoon dried thyme*
*Salt, pepper*
*Brown gravy made from the lamb bones, slightly thickened*

Make the hot-water crust into small pies. For the filling, chop the meat finely after removing the skin, and include about a quarter of the fat. Discard the rest (with fillet bought off the bone, there will be very little fat, so include it all). Mix with shallot or onion, mushrooms, herbs and seasoning. Put into a saucepan with 150 ml (¼ pt) of water, bring to the boil and simmer for 5 minutes. Cool, then fill the pastry cases. Bake the pies for 45 minutes at mark 6, 200°C (400°F). When they are ready, pour in the gravy made from the bones, instead of jellied stock. Eat very hot, or cold.

## GAME, CHICKEN OR RABBIT PIE

*250 g (8 oz) hard back pork fat*
*375 g (12 oz) lean pork*
*250 g (8 oz) lean veal*
*250 g (8 oz) thin rashers of bacon*
*3 tablespoons brandy or Madeira or 5 tablespoons dry white wine*
*Salt, pepper, nutmeg, cinnamon, cloves*
*Heaped tablespoon chopped parsley*
*500 g (1 lb) game, chicken or rabbit cut from the bone*

Mince fat and lean pork, veal and 3 rashers of bacon together, as well as any trimmings left from removing the game, chicken or rabbit from their bones. Season with wine, salt, pepper, spices and parsley. Cut the game, chicken or rabbit into nice pieces and season them. Put remaining bacon into the pastry case to form a lining, and layer in the minced meat and game.

## TO MAKE A YORKSHIRE CHRISTMAS PYE

*'First make a good standing Crust, let the Wall and Bottom be very thick; bone a Turkey, a Goose, a Fowl, a Partridge and a Pigeon. Season them all very well, take half an ounce of mace, half an ounce of nutmegs, a quarter of an ounce of cloves,*

*and half an ounce of black pepper, all beat fine together, two large spoonfuls of salt, and then mix them together. Open the fowls all down the back, and bone them; first the pigeon, then the partridge, cover them; then the fowl, then the goose, and then the turkey, which must be large; season them all well first, and lay them in the crust, so as it will look only like a whole turkey; then have a hare ready cased [skinned] and wiped with a clean cloth. Cut it to pieces; that is, jointed; season it, and lay it as close as you can on one side; on the other side woodcocks, moor game, and what sort of wild fowl you can get. Season them well, and lay them close; put at least four pounds of butter into the pye, then lay on your lid, which must be a very thick one, and let it be well baked. It must have a very hot oven, and will take at least four hours.*

*This crust will take a bushel of flour. . . . These pies are often sent to London in a box as presents; therefore the walls must be well built.'*

THIS REMARKABLE RECIPE FROM HANNAH GLASSE'S *Art of Cookery* is not so eccentric as it sounds, nor so archaic. In Burgundy, at Saulieu, one may eat a similar dish, described on the menu as the 'Oreiller de la Belle Aurore'. It is one of the great specialities of the restaurant – inside the pastry crust, there is a good mixture of game, though it is not arranged in the Russian doll style of Hannah Glasse's recipe.

Certainly in England, the habit continued for nearly another century. Yorkshire Pies were being made and sent down to friends at Christmas time in the 1840s. I imagine that the crust was not quite so thick, now that goods came down by train, but the contents were unchanged. In 1845, Hawksworth Fawkes of Farnley Hall, near Otley in Yorkshire, sent one down to his friend, the painter J.M.W. Turner. Turner wrote back to say thank-you for the kindness 'in remembrance of me by the Yorkshire Pie equal good to the Olden-time of Hannah's . . . culinary exploits'. He is referring sadly to the years between 1810 and 1823, when he visited his great patron, Walter Fawkes, Hawksworth's father, at Farnley Hall, where so many of his paintings still are.

Such presents – pies, game, puddings – arrived every year. In 1849, a goose pie turned up very punctually – 'Mother Goose came to a rehearsal before Christmas day, having arrived on Saturday for the Knife, and could not be resisted in drinking your good health in a glass of wine to all friends at Farnley Hall . . . The pie is in most excellent taste, and shall drink the same thanks on Christmas day.'

If you feel like a similar 'culinary exploit' at Christmas time, I suggest you try the goose pie rather than the Yorkshire pie:

## TO MAKE A GOOSE PYE

*'Half a peck of flour [5 lb] will make the walls of a goose-pie. . . . Raise your crust just big enough to hold a large goose; first have a pickled dried tongue boiled tender enough to peel [page 185], cut off the root, bone a goose and a large fowl; take half a quarter of an ounce of mace beat fine, a large teaspoonful of beaten pepper, three teaspoonfuls of salt; mix all together, season your fowl and goose with it, then lay the fowl in the goose, and the tongue in the fowl, and the goose in the same form as if whole. Put half a pound of butter on the top, and lay on the lid. This pie is delicious, either hot or cold, and will keep a great while. A slice of this pye cut down across makes a pretty little side-dish for supper.'*

**A SPLENDID CENTRE-PIECE FOR A PARTY.** Unless your pie has to go by train to London, like Mr Turner's, there is no need to make such a thick crust. However, it must be thick enough to keep in the juices as far as possible. I recommend a hot-water pastry made with 1½ kilos (3 lb) of flour, and a roasting pan 30cm × 22cm × 5cm (11½" × 9" × 2") deep as a mould (unless you have something of a comparable size which is deeper). It seems that the varieties of poultry in Hannah Glasse's day were not so large as they are now, because you need to increase the seasonings. My ingredients worked out like this:

For 20-25

*Hot-water crust made with 1½ kilos (3 lb) flour*
*5 kilos (10 lb) goose, boned*
*2½ kilos (5 lb) farm chicken, boned*
*1¼ kilos (2½ lb) pickled tongue, soaked, boiled, trimmed and skinned (page 185)*
*7 g (¼) oz mace*
*2 heaped teaspoons freshly ground black pepper*
*5 rounded teaspoons sea salt*
*60 g (2 oz) butter*

To bake the pie, put it into a hot oven, mark 7, 220°C (425°F), for 20 minutes. Then lower the heat to mark 4, 180°C (350°F), and cover the top with brown paper to protect it from becoming too brown too soon. Leave for 1 hour. If, by this time, the contents are bubbling vigorously, lower the heat again to mark 1-2, 140-150°C (275-300°F), and leave for a further 2 hours. If not, leave a little longer before lowering the temperature.

It is only prudent to check the pie from time to time. Towards the end of this time, push a larding needle or skewer into the pie through the top central hole; if the juices come out very red, leave the pie a little longer. On the other hand, if they come out a pale pink, that is all right – the pie continues to cook as it cools down (I took mine out of the oven at 1 a.m., and it was still not quite cold by lunchtime next day, with the juices still liquid: It should have been left until the evening, with an hour or two in the refrigerator to set it properly).

## STEAK, KIDNEY AND OYSTER PUDDING

THIS FAVOURITE ENGLISH DISH does not, it seems, go back more than 120 years. Eliza Acton, in *Modern Cookery* of 1845, calls a steak pudding John Bull's pudding, which suggests a certain national fame which had spread to other countries. Mrs Beeton's recipe in *Household Management* of 1859 is the first to add the essential kidney.

Young Mrs Beeton started by writing the cookery section of her husband's magazine for women, *The Englishwoman's Domestic Magazine*. Then with the aid of contributions from her readers, she compiled *Household Management*, which appeared in monthly parts with the magazine, beginning in 1859. It first came out in book form in 1861. As she makes particular mention of the source of this recipe, one may presume that it was a little unusual and would not be taken for granted by the majority of her readers, at any rate. It was sent to her by a reader in Sussex, a county that had been famous for its puddings of all kinds for at least a century, so it is fitting that such a well-liked national dish should have had its roots there.

Oysters or mushrooms were the extra flavouring ingredient. In those days oysters were the cheaper of the two as mushroom cultivation in Europe was a spasmodic and ill-understood business, except around Paris, until the end of the century, when two French mycologists at the Pasteur Institute established a service of sterilized mushroom spawn for growers. Even so, the great boom in mushroom production in England didn't occur until after World War Two. Up to then, they were a luxury and priced accordingly. Though by that time, of course, oysters had far outpriced them. Which would have surprised Mrs Beeton, because for her and her readers, oysters were still a commonplace, though becoming scarcer with the increase in population and the pollution of estuaries.

For 6

FILLING

*1 kilo (2 lb) rump steak*
*500 g (1 lb) veal or ox kidney*
*2 tablespoons seasoned flour*
*1 large onion, chopped*
*90 g (3 oz) butter*
*600 ml (1 pt) beef stock, or half each of stock and red wine*
*250 g (8 oz) mushrooms, sliced*
*Bouquet garni*
*18-24 oysters (optional)*

SUET CRUST

*300 g (10 oz) self-raising flour*
*1 level teaspoon baking powder*
*¼ teaspoon salt*
*Freshly ground white pepper*
*¼ teaspoon thyme*
*150 g (5 oz) chopped suet*
*Cold water*

THE traditional method of making a steak and kidney pudding is to put the meat raw into the pastry-lined pudding basin. I think that one gets a better, less sodden crust if the filling is cooked first. This reduces the steaming time to 1½ or 2 hours from 4 or 5.

To make the filling, cut the steak into neat 2 cm (1″) pieces and slice the kidney. Discard all the fat and skin from both meats. Sprinkle them with seasoned flour. Cook the onion until lightly browned in two-thirds of the butter, put it to one side and add the meat, to colour rapidly. Transfer the meat as it is browned, to an ovenproof casserole. Pour the stock, or stock and wine, into the frying pan and allow it to boil hard for a few moments, while you scrape in all the nice brown bits and pieces. Pour this over the meat. Fry the mushrooms in the remaining butter and add them with the bouquet to the casserole. Cover it with a lid and simmer in the oven at mark 1-2, 140-150°C (275-300°F), until the steak and kidney are almost cooked – about 1½ hours. Leave the casserole to cool. If the liquid part of the filling is on the copious and watery side, strain it off and boil it down. This is important if you are using oysters, as they contribute their own liquor to the sauce. Then open the oysters and add them, liquor and all. Taste and correct the seasoning.

To make the crust, mix all the dry ingredients in a large bowl, so that the suet is evenly distributed. Stir in cold water with a wooden spoon to make a firm dough. Roll out on a floured surface to a large circle, cut away a quarter and put to one side for the lid. Butter a 1½ litre (3 pt) pudding basin generously, and press the three-quarter circle of pastry into it to fit the basin, allowing 2½ cm (1″) overhanging at the rim. Put the filling into the basin: it should not come higher than 2½ cm (1″) below the rim. Roll out the remaining suet crust and cut a circle to make the lid. Press the edges together to make a firm seal. Cut some foil to make a circle 5 cm (2″) larger all round than the top of the pudding basin. Fix it in place with your fingers so that it balloons above the pudding leaving it room to rise. Tie a string handle round the rim of the basin, so that it can easily be lifted in and out of the steamer.

When the water is boiling in the lower part of the steamer, put the pudding in and leave for 1½ to 2 hours. Keep an eye on the water, and top it up if necessary with more *boiling* water, and keep everything well covered.

If you do not have a steamer, put a trivet on the base of a large saucepan and put about 10 cm (4″) of water into it. When this water is boiling steadily, lower the basin into it. The water should come about two-thirds of the way up the sides. Put the lid on the large saucepan and leave to boil for 1½ to 2 hours.

When the pudding is cooked, tie a cloth napkin round the basin and serve immediately.

# Puddings

**English puddings have had a great reputation** since the seventeenth century – perhaps earlier – and they deserve it.

One French visitor, the protestant exile François Maximilien Misson, who came to England at the end of the seventeenth century, was lyrical in his *Mémoires et Observations faites par un voyageur en Angleterre* (published 1698, translated into English by John Ozell, 1719) about the unexpectedness and variety of English puddings. 'They bake them in an oven, they boil them with meat, they make them fifty several ways: BLESSED BE HE THAT INVENTED PUDDING, for it is a manna that hits the palates of all sorts of people.' He had in mind puddings both sweet and plain, mentioning as the most common ingredients flour, milk, eggs, butter, suet, sugar, marrow and raisins. It's rather sad that 'pudding', among ourselves, inclines to become a work of abuse. It's true that an addiction to puddings hasn't been exactly in favour of English teeth and waistlines, but these wonderful things are some of the most subtle and imaginative combinations, relying on simple and natural ingredients.

Misson has described the heftier puddings including the kind eaten with gravy, or with sugar and butter. Filling, decidedly. But there's much to be said, and more than is usually said nowadays, for a national cooking that has invented Queen of Puddings, summer pudding, syllabubs, gooseberry fool, Bakewell Pudding and that sweet concoction we now insist on calling crème brulée as if it were French and not the Burnt Cream of English cooks of the eighteenth century.

A generous hand with the cream – not to mention butter and eggs – has been the making of many of the best English puddings. Equally their downfall has been stinginess with cream and the illusion that nobody notices if you use margarine or vegetable fat instead of butter or lard.

Another blow has been the commercialization of puddings, premixed in packets, with skimmed milk powder, chemical flavour, chemical colour and chemical preservatives. Custard powder made in this way has been one of our minor national tragedies, also the commercial use of cornflour as a thickening substitute for eggs. It's cornflour that has made people loathe the idea of blancmange, turning an ancient and courtly delicacy into those cold shapes derided as 'baby's bottom' ('dead man's leg', 'dead baby', according to shape, are school names I recall for some of the less appetizing suet puddings).

Puddings unquestionably were some of the first victims of mass catering and manufacture. But they survive, though in their huge number they are barely explored nowadays. For instance, how many families have sat down to Sussex Pond Pudding (sometimes called Sussex Well Pudding), for which I give the recipe? Yet it is one of the best of our suet puddings. That is a slightly complicated affair, but many of the best puddings are also the simplest. There's nothing simpler than junket flavoured with brandy, sprinkled with nutmeg and spread with clotted cream, and there's nothing simpler than adding a quince, if you can get one, to an apple pie.

People used to talk, still do talk occasionally, of the roast beef of old England, along with the revolting image in their minds of an overfed John Bull. My English family scenario would be candles on the dining-room table, clotted cream in a large triangular Coalport bowl patterned with blue and white flowers about to be added in large helpings to cold apple pie left over from Sunday lunch. The thought of it has buoyed children – and adults too, no doubt – through the tedium of Evensong.

## DEVONSHIRE JUNKET

**NOT A NURSERY PUDDING.** Junket is an English version of those curd and cream dishes that the French still make in such delicious variety (*cremets d'Angers, maingaux, coeurs à la crème*). Like their *fromage frais,* junket is produced by curdling warm milk with rennet. Then it is left to set to a smooth jelly. The curd is not broken up and drained of whey as it would be in France, and as it once was in England (junket derives from old Norman French, *jon-*

quet, a little basket made from *jonques* or rushes and used for draining cheeses until recent times).

When we had the idea of leaving the curd alone in its smoothness, I do not know. In *Food and Drink in Britain*, C. Anne Wilson quotes the earliest recipe she can find, from 1653, in which the junket was not drained, but eaten with cream and cinnamon just as in the recipe below. She suggests that it was the popularity of unrenneted creams in the eighteenth century, the syllabubs, fools, fruit creams, which sent the junket into eclipse. Like many old dishes that have survived at the fringes of the country, it has acquired the reputation of being a local speciality, in this case of Devonshire, which is really unjustified – or perhaps one should rather say misleading. The production of rennet in convenient bottled form – rennet extract was first prepared by a chemist in Denmark in the 1870s and was in production from 1878 onwards – unfortunately meant that junket could become the bane of every nursery, with an ultimate degradation of artificial colouring and flavour. From my own experience, I recall hating the texture of junket as a child. Like apricots and rice pudding, it used to end up in the aspidistra pot which stood so helpfully in the middle of the junior dining-table at school.

For 4-6

*600 ml (1 pt) Channel Island milk*
*1 dessertspoon sugar*
*2 tablespoons brandy (optional)*
*1 teaspoon rennet*
*150 g (¼ pt) clotted cream*
*Cinnamon or nutmeg*

BRING milk slowly to blood heat – if you are not used to judging this, use a thermometer; it is surprising how hot a liquid at 37°C (98.4°F) feels. Meanwhile mix the sugar and brandy in the china bowl in which you intend to serve the junket. And put it in a convenient place in the kitchen, where it can stay until required (junket sets best at room temperature). Pour the warmed milk into the bowl, then stir in the rennet gently. Do not disturb until the junket is firmly set.

If the clotted cream is stiff, mix it with a little fresh cream, so that it can be spread over the surface of the junket without disturbing it. Sprinkle the cream with ground cinnamon or nutmeg.

If the junket tastes salty, your teaspoonful of rennet was too generous.

## A Coronation Doucet or Custard Tart

A DOUCET WAS SERVED AS PART OF THE THIRD COURSE at Henry IV's coronation banquet. There was candied quince as well (page 368) and fritters, all set on the table with curlews and partridges and quails and rabbits and small birds of many kinds. Chaucer was present.

Doucet, which means something sweet, was always a kind of custard, though it might be made in many different ways. Sometimes the mixture was thick with minced pork or beef marrow, but the flavourings would include sugar just the same. Sometimes almond milk was used instead of cow's milk and cream: this was an infusion of blanched, ground almonds and syrup, or plain water, or water and wine. The mixture was brought slowly to the boil and simmered for a little while to extract as much almond juice as possible. It was then sieved to make a 'milk'. Medieval cooks used it a great deal, especially for dishes on fast days when rich dairy products were avoided. The mixture could be made thicker by increasing the cooking time. I find that whirling the mixture in the blender, before sieving it, gives a richly flavoured 'milk' – see Almond soup, on page 5.

*Shortcrust pastry*

FILLING

*375 g (12 oz) double cream*
*90 g (3 oz) Channel Island milk*
*A good pinch of saffron*
*Honey or sugar*
*6 egg yolks, or 2 eggs, plus 2 yolks, well beaten*

LINE a 22-25 cm (9-10″) tart tin with a removable base with pastry. Bake blind as in the recipe below.

Bring the cream, milk, saffron and about a tablespoon of honey or sugar slowly to the boil. Stir it to get the best colour possible from the saffron. Pour it on to the eggs, whisking the mixture together. Taste it and add more honey or sugar if you like. Strain the mixture into the pastry case and bake at mark 4, 180°C (350°F), or until the mixture has set – it will also rise, then collapse when you take it out of the oven. Best eaten warm.

## BAKED CUSTARD TART

*Shortcrust pastry*

FILLING

*450 ml (¾ pt) single cream (or Channel Island milk, or a mixture of both)*
*2 small pieces of mace*
*2½ cm (1″) stick cinnamon*
*2 large eggs*
*2 large egg yolks*
*30 g (1 oz) sugar*
*2 teaspoons orange-flower or rose water (optional)*
*Grated nutmeg*

ROLL out the pastry and line a 20-22 cm (8-9") tart tin with a removable base. Prick it all over with a fork, and bake it blind at mark 6, 200°C (400°F) for 10-15 minutes. It should colour very slightly, but no more.

Meanwhile bring the cream or milk, or both, to the boil together with the mace and cinnamon. Beat the eggs and yolks together with the sugar and pour on the contents of the pan, whisking everything thoroughly together. Taste and adjust the spices with powdered mace or cinnamon, and add the orange-flower or rose water if you want to give the tart an eighteenth-century flavour. Pour the mixture into the pastry case, sprinkle it with a little nutmeg and bake at mark 3, 160°C (325°F), for 30-40 minutes until the custard is just set – remember that it will become firmer as it cools down. I think that all custards taste best when eaten warm, rather than hot or cold. This means that you can time the cooking to end when you are ready to serve the first part of the meal, and leave the tart in its tin to keep warm in the plate-warming oven, or on the rack above the stove. Serve on its own or with cream.

THE FILLING can be baked without pastry – pour it into small pots or ramekins, stand them in a pan of hot water and put into the oven for 30 minutes, mark 3, 160°C (325°F).

## BURNT CREAM OR CRÈME BRULÉE

THIS BEST OF ALL ENGLISH PUDDINGS, the apotheosis of the custard, is usually accredited to Trinity College, Cambridge, on the strength of the first recipe below, which comes from the sister of a former librarian. Florence White quoted it in her *Good Things in England* of 1932, and repeats the story that an undergraduate offered the recipe – which came from a country house in Aberdeenshire – to the college kitchens in the 1860s. It was refused without trial, coming from such a lowly source. When the undergraduate became a fellow, it was a different matter, and the pudding rapidly became a favourite dish of the May Week celebrations. It goes particularly well with strawberries, which are in their first glory at that time of the year; indeed, it is always a good idea to serve fresh or lightly cooked fruit with it.

The story worried me, though, not on account of its exact truthfulness, but because *crème brulée* seemed such an eighteenth-century kind of pudding. And I soon found the second and third recipes, plus one in a cookery book of 1812, which was obviously taken from Mrs Raffald although the French title of *crème brulée* was used (she called it Burnt Cream). But where did Mrs Raffald get it from? One can see from the last sentence of her recipe that she enjoyed making it. Is it a French dish after all? Did she get it from the Warburton family, at Arley Hall in Cheshire, where she worked as housekeeper with such success that she remained on friendly terms with them for years afterwards (she dedicated her book to Lady Elizabeth Warburton)?

This doubt is typical of much of our cooking. The French and English strands are interwoven from at least the time of the Conquest. The French influence became strong again in the seventeenth century, in particular when Charless II and his court returned from exile in Versailles; and eventually I did find a recipe for Burnt Cream in a seventeenth-century manuscript cookery book, although there was no indication of French influence or origin. Custards made with egg and cream were a European commonplace: the bright idea – perhaps we may claim, the English idea – was the mirror layer of caramel on top.

Below are three versions going back in time. I use the first one, but increase the egg yolks to 6 and add a flavouring of orange-flower water. Miss Jenkinson's quantities do not take account of the fact that the pint of the eighteenth-century recipes was 16 oz, or just under half a litre, i.e. the same as the American pint; bear this in mind if you use the earlier recipes, and use small eggs as well.

I: 1909, from *The Ocklye Cookery Book,* by Eleanor L. Jenkinson

*600 ml (1 pt) double cream or half each double and single*
*4 large egg yolks*
*Caster sugar*

BRING cream(s) to the boil, and boil for about 30 seconds. Pour immediately on to the 4 yolks, which have been well beaten, and whisk them together. (At this point, although the recipe doesn't say so, I return the mixture to the pan, and cook it *without allowing it to boil,* until it thickens and coats the spoon.) Pour it into a shallow heat-proof gratin dish. Leave to chill overnight. Two hours before the meal, sprinkle the cream with an even layer of caster sugar, and place it under a pre-heated grill at maximum temperature. The sugar will caramelize to a sheet of brown smoothness: it may be necessary to turn the dish about to achieve an even effect.

II: 1848, from *Domestic Cookery,* by a lady (Maria Rundell)

'BOIL a pint of cream with a stick of cinnamon, and some lemon peel; take it off the fire, and pour it very slowly into the yolks of four eggs, stirring until half cold; sweeten, and take out the spice, etc.; pour it into the dish; when cold, strew white pounded sugar over, and brown it with a salamander.'

IN PROFESSIONAL kitchens in France and England, the overhead grill of the kind that most of us have, is always referred to as 'the salamander'.

III: 1769, from *The Experienced English Housekeeper*, by Elizabeth Raffald

'BOIL a pint of cream with sugar, and a little lemon peel shred fine, then beat the yolks of six and the whites of four eggs separately; when your cream is cooled, put in your eggs, with a spoonful of orange flower-water, and one of fine flour, set it over the fire, keep stirring it till it is thick, put it into a dish; when it is cold sift a quarter of a pound of sugar all over, hold a hot salamander over it till it is very brown, and looks like a glass plate put over your cream.'

THE CUSTARD here is very thick with flour as well as extra eggs. Together they make the consistency too firm. Mrs Raffald's orange-flower water gives the authentic eighteenth-century flavour to custards – good chemists often stock it; it is also used with fruit creams, and gives a deep-flavoured muskiness almost like Frontignan. Always add it gradually, because it easily becomes too dominant.

## ELIZABETH RAFFALD'S ORANGE CUSTARDS

THE MAJORITY OF THE BEST COOKERY BOOKS in this country have been written by women (or by foreigners). And of this energetic tribe, the most energetic of all was Elizabeth Raffald. Consider her career. She started work at fifteen, in 1748, ending up as housekeeper at Arley Hall in Cheshire. At thirty she married. Eighteen years later she was dead. During those eighteen years she organized:

(a) a cooked food shop selling pies, brawn, pickles, etc.;
(b) an enlarged cooked-food shop, with a confectionery department;
(c) the first domestic servants' employment agency;
(d) two important Manchester inns, or rather posting-houses;
(e) the first street and trade directory in Manchester (then a town of something over twenty thousand inhabitants);
(f) a couple of newspapers, as an *eminence rose;*
(g) an unreliable husband;
(h) fifteen (or sixteen – some conflict of evidence) daughters;
(i) her cookery book, *The Experienced English Housekeeper*, published in 1769 ( a facsimile of the 8th edition is available from E. & W. Books). Many of her recipes can be adapted to modern kitchen machinery, which she would thoroughly have approved of. She could always see the advantages of the latest thing, and added her own contribution to progress.

For 8-10

*Rind of ½ Seville orange*
*1 tablespoon brandy (or orange liqueur)*
*Juice of 1 Seville orange*
*125 g (4 oz) granulated sugar*
*6 large egg yolks, or extra large for preference*
*300 ml (½ pt) double cream*
*300 ml (½ pt) single cream*
*Candied orange peel*

THE rind can be removed from half the orange with a potato peeler: simmer it in water for 2 minutes, then drain it and place in the blender with the brandy (or liqueur) and the orange juice, sugar and egg yolks. Blend at top speed until the peel is reduced to a very slight grittiness in the liquid. Bring creams to the boil, and add gradually to the mixture in the blender. Check the seasoning, and add more sugar and orange juice if necessary.

Pour into 8 or 10 custard cups or small soufflé dishes. Stand them in a pan of hot water and put into a warm oven, mark 3, 160°C (325°F) until just set – about 30 minutes or a little longer, depending on the depth of the mixture in the pots.

Serve warm or chilled, with a decorative piece of candied orange peel in the centre of each one.

## COCONUT CREAM WITH STRAWBERRY SAUCE

THIS CREAM CAN ALSO BE SERVED WITH RASPBERRIES, and it makes a fine accompaniment to many of the tropical fruits we find in the shops these days.

For 6

CREAM
*150 ml (¼ pt) each single and soured cream*
*Vanilla pod, slit down one side*
*125 g (4 oz) desiccated coconut*
*Generous tablespoon creamed grated coconut*
*11 g (0.4 oz) gelatine*
*Sugar*
*Juice of 1 lime or lemon*
*300 ml (½ pt) whipping cream*

SAUCE
*500 g (1 lb) strawberries, rinsed, hulled*
*Icing sugar*

FOR the cream, heat single and soured creams with vanilla, dessicated coconut and 200 ml (7 fl oz) water. Cover and bring very slowly to the boil, stirring from time to time. Remove lid, simmer for about 10 minutes, then leave to cool down to tepid. Remove vanilla pod, then process or liquidize the rest. Push through a sieve into a measuring jug. You should end up with a generous 300 ml (½ pt) liquid.

Dissolve gelatine in 6 tablespoons hot water, and stir into the warm coconut liquid. Add the creamed coconut, then sugar and lime or lemon juice to taste – the citrus juice is an enhancer, it should not be identifiable.

Chill until the mixture reaches an egg white consistency. Whip the whipping cream until stiff and fold it in with a generous tablespoon of desiccated coconut from the sieve, to add a little texture. Pour into a lightly oiled decorative mould and chill until set. Then turn out on to a dish.

For the sauce, remove about a quarter of the best strawberries, and halve them. Process, then sieve the rest and sweeten to taste. Pour round the cream and dispose of the strawberry halves in a decorative manner.

## GOOSEBERRY, PEAR, APPLE OR QUINCE CREAM

For 4-6

*500 g (1 lb) fruit*
*Sugar*
*300 ml (½ pt) cream*
*3 egg yolks*
*60 g (2 oz) butter, melted*
*An appropriate spice or wine*

PREPARE and cook the fruit, starting it off with three tablespoons of water. No need to remove peel or cores, just cut it up if necessary. Sieve the fruit into a bowl. Add sugar to taste, making it on the sweet side. Beat in the cream, then the egg yolks and butter. Flavour with a spice appropriate to the fruit you choose, or, in the case of gooseberries, a little muscat wine such as Frontignan, or some orange-flower water for an especially eighteenth-century flavour.

This mixture can either be cooked over a low heat until very thick, without boiling or the eggs will curdle; or it can be turned into a pastry case, or a pyrex dish, and baked in the oven until just set – mark 5, 190°C (375°F). Eat hot, warm or cold.

A HEAD of elderflowers, tied in a piece of muslin, is always a good aromatic addition to gooseberries as they cook. Keep tasting the mixture, and remove the elderflowers before the flavour is too strong. A substitute for Frontignan. This should also be done when making gooseberry jelly, or cooking the fruit for gooseberry fool. Home-made elderflower wine used to be known in the past as 'English Frontignan'. There is a remarkable affinity between these muscat flavours and gooseberries.

## ELIZABETH DAVID'S EVERLASTING SYLLABUB

THE RECIPE COMES FROM ELIZABETH DAVID 's pamphlet *Syllabubs and Fruit Fools* (which also includes some delicious Scottish specialities). She traces the history of syllabubs back to the seventeenth century. The simplest of all was a pastoral affair, a picturesque treat for town visitors to the country; a milkmaid would direct a stream of new, warm milk into a bowl of spiced cider or ale. After a while a light curd formed on top, with a delicious whey underneath.

The more solid syllabub, the kind we eat today – the Everlasting Syllabub as opposed to the milkmaid's simple affair of milk and cider – also goes back to the seventeenth century. In grander kitchens, cream and wine were used, though Sir Kenelm Digby, in *The Closet . . . Opened*, his notebook of recipes which was published, after his death, in 1669, does remark that concentrated fruit syrups could be substituted for the wine. They should be on the tart side, 'very weak of sugar'.

For 4-6

*8 tablespoons (4 fl oz) white wine or sherry*
*2 tablespoons brandy*
*Pared rind and juice of 1 lemon*
*60 g (2 oz) sugar*
*300 ml (½ pt) double cream*
*Nutmeg*

PUT the first three ingredients into a bowl and leave overnight. Next day strain the liquid into a bowl and stir in the sugar until it has dissolved. Still stirring, pour in the cream slowly. Add finally a grating of nutmeg. Beat the syllabub with a wire whisk until it holds its shape – do not go on too long, or too vigorously, or the cream will curdle and separate into a buttery mass.

Spoon the syllabub into small glasses or custard cups – there is enough for four to six people – and keep in a cool place (if possible, not the refrigerator) for two days or more. Of course they can also be served straightaway, but it is usually more convenient to make puddings in advance and this one keeps well. 'A tiny sprig of rosemary or a little twist of lemon peel', can, as suggested by Sir Kenelm Digby, 'be stuck into each little filled glass.' Serve with almond or sponge biscuits.

## St Valentine's Syllabub

A VERSION OF THE RECIPE above, which is well worth making for a change. Unless you are an enthusiast for the strong taste of English honey, I would suggest using the lighter flavoured Hymettos from Greece. Should your only honey be the thick opaque kind, bring it to boiling point to clarify it first.

For 2

*1 heaped tablespoon clear honey*
*3 tablespoons dry white wine*
*2 teaspoons brandy*
*1 teaspoon grated lemon rind*
*Juice of ¼ lemon*
*150 ml (¼ pt) double cream*
*2 teaspoons chopped toasted hazelnuts or almonds*

MIX first five ingredients and leave in a covered basin overnight. Next day, pour in the cream and whisk until you have a soft bulky whiteness. Pile into two tulip-shaped wine glasses or small glass dishes, and scatter with the nuts. Chill, and serve with sponge fingers or sugar thins (page 343).

## GOOSEBERRY FOOL

ANY CRUSHED SOFT FRUIT can make a delicious fool. Gooseberries, though combine acid tartness and firm but melting texture which makes them the perfect choice. They are also one of the first fruits of the spring. Their early season is the time for food in the garden, within the scent of roses and dame's violet and balsam poplar, before the leaves have coarsened to their hard summer green. Gooseberries, too, are one of our few particular fruits; no other country has appreciated them as we have done, although they will grow happily up to the Arctic Circle. In France, one rarely sees a gooseberry bush in the cherished order of the kitchen garden. In our parish there we have managed to find two or three, now part of the hedgerow round an old deserted cottage. We go quietly to pick the fruit which everyone else despises, and never seems to notice (although it has a place in French cooking as the *groseille à maquereau*, that is the mackerel gooseberry, see page 88). Then we delight our friends with an English gooseberry fool.

As Bunyard says in his *Anatomy of Dessert*, 'the plebeian origin of the Gooseberry has been, I fear, a handicap to its appreciation at cultured tables'. He remarks that it was first developed, in the early nineteenth century, by Midland workers who raised new seedlings for competitions. The criterion of excellence – as now in village summer fêtes – was weight and size . . . 'the Big Gooseberry born in the smoke and moisture of Macclesfield and other great industrial towns'. 'The result of this great interest in the Gooseberry has been to increase its size and possibly its flavour, but best of all to combine these two qualities so that the big fruit of today' – he was writing in the late twenties – 'is in many cases of excellent quality and well worthy of the gourmet's attention.'

Nevertheless, the small green gooseberry of old farmhouse and cottage gardens is the best for gooseberry fool, and the other gooseberry puddings.

For 6-8

*500 g (1 lb) young green gooseberries*
*60 g (2 oz) butter*
*Sugar*

Either: *300 ml (½ pt) double or whipping cream or half each single and double cream*
Or: *300 ml (½ pt) single cream and 3 egg yolks*

Top and tail the gooseberries. Melt the butter in a large pan, add the gooseberries, cover and leave to cook gently for about 5 minutes. When the fruit looks yellow and has softened, remove the pan and crush the fruit with a wooden spoon, then a fork. Do not try to produce a smooth purée – unless you have to consider elderly people with false teeth – by sieving or liquidizing the gooseberries; they should be more of a mash. Season with sugar to taste.

**Either** whip the cream(s) until they are firm, and fold in the cooled fruit. Taste and add more sugar if necessary, but do not make the fool too sweet. A couple of tablespoons of Frontignan gives a gooseberry fool a delicious, unidentifiable fragrance, but I would not recommend the addition of any other wine. Serve lightly chilled, with almond biscuits.

**Or** instead of cream, make a thick custard by boiling the single cream, then stirring it into the egg yolks. Return it to the pan, and keep it over a low to medium heat until it thickens – stir all the time with a wooden spoon, and make sure it doesn't boil. Combine with the fruit purée when cold. Both methods go back to the earliest recipes. What is unforgiveable is the use of package custards.

## ORANGE FOOL

For 4-6

*The juice of 3 oranges*
*3 large eggs*
*300 ml (½ pt) double cream*
*60 g (2 oz) sugar*
*Cinnamon, nutmeg*
*30 g (1 oz) unsalted butter*

Mix all the ingredients except the butter in a basin, stirring them well together. Set the basin over simmering water and stir the mixture until it is very thick. Do not allow it to boil, or the eggs will curdle. Remove the basin from the pan, and when the mixture is tepid, beat in the butter. Taste and add more sugar and spices if necessary. Put into small glasses and serve well chilled. The fool can be decorated with a few pieces of candied orange peel, and a hint of orange-flower water gives a delicious fragrance to the fool.

## WILD APRICOT FOOL OR ICE CREAM

THIS IS THE BEST WINTER FOOL. Make an effort to find the small whole Afghan Hunza apricots. They have quite a different flavour from the usual kind, very spicy and delicate, yet the richness pervades the whipped cream. One of the many blessings brought to us by the immigrant Asian communities since the war. In fact they are grown in a wide stretch of land from Persia across to the Hunza valley of Kashmir. They have a flavour of long civilization.

For 4-6

*175 g (6 oz) wild dried Hunza apricots from Afghanistan (from Asian food shops and some health food shops)*
Or: *250 g (8 oz) apricots dried without sulphur dioxide (from better health food shops)*
Plus: *30 g (1 oz) blanched almonds*
*Icing sugar*
*Lemon juice*
*300 ml (½ pt) whipping cream*

SOAK the apricots, then simmer them in their soaking water for 5 minutes until just cooked, without adding any sugar. Remove the stones from the whole wild apricots, crack them and remove the kernels; crush the fruit with a fork and mix in the kernels. Otherwise, mash the ordinary dried apricots, and add the blanched almonds, cut into slivers. Boil down the juice remaining from the fruit until it is syrupy and add that to the fruit. Sweeten further with icing sugar, and add a little lemon juice to bring out the flavour.

Beat the cream and when stiff fold in the fruit. Serve chilled, or frozen as an ice cream, with almond biscuits.

## TWO TEA CREAMS

WHEN YOU BUY GREEN OR GUNPOWDER TEA, the dried but unfermented tea required for this recipe, you will understand the names. And also the earlier Hyson, which is a corruption of the Chinese name, *hsi-ch'un*, meaning 'bright spring'. 'Andrews the Smuggler' – this is a parson, Parson Woodforde of Weston Longeville in Norfolk, writing up his diary in Norfolk for March 29th, 1777 – 'brought me this night about 11 o'clock a bagg of Hyson Tea 6 Pd weight. He frightened us a little by whistling under the Parlour Window just as we were going to bed. I gave him some Geneva [gin] and paid him for the tea at 10/6 per Pd.' Nowadays green tea usually disappears into many blends, but it can be bought from tea merchants or Far Eastern stores. The curly mass of green withered leaves has the true essence of tea in its flavour.

Incidentally, the widely tolerated custom of buying smuggled tea came to an end not long afterwards in 1784, when the high customs duties were repealed. It also put an end to the habit of adulterating tea – elder buds were dried and added to green tea – which had given a profitable employment to a number of small villages. According to Gervas Huxley in *Talking of Tea*

(Thames & Hudson, 1956), one village produced twenty tons a year of 'tea' – or 'smouch' which was made 'from the leaf of ash trees, steeped or boiled in copperas and sheep's dung'.

For 4-6

*Scant 30 g (1 oz) green (gunpowder) tea*
*3 tablespoons sugar*
*300 ml (½ pt) each single and double cream*
*Packet gelatine (11 g (0.4 oz)) or 5 leaves*
*4 tablespoons very hot water*

PUT tea and sugar into a pan. Mix the creams together and pour about three-quarters into the pan (the remaining one-quarter is a safety measure, in case you inadvertently make the tea flavour too strong and sickly). Bring slowly to the boil – keep tasting, so that the pan can be removed when the infusion seems right, but remember that flavours diminish in strength as they cool. Pour through a sieve into a basin. Add remaining cream and taste, adding more sugar if required. The flavour can be strengthened by pressing gently on the tea debris to extract the last sludge-green drops. Don't overdo the sugar: this is a dish for adults.

Melt the gelatine in water and beat into the warm cream. Brush the inside of a mould with almond or tasteless oil (preferably one of those elaborate Victorian china moulds). If oil collects in the intricacies of the design, turn it upside down to drain. Pour in the cream when cold. Serve chilled, in small quantities, with not-too-sweet plain or almond biscuits, very crisp. The flavour will be subtle, with an aftertaste of tea (gunpowder tea contains the pure tea-flavour), the texture very smooth, and the colour that fawnish dove-grey that the Victorians loved.

THIS SECOND VERSION is a tea-flavoured bavarois, and it is particularly good with raspberries and amaretti biscuits:

For 8

*600 ml (1 pt) milk*
*3 tablespoons green gunpowder tea*
*6 egg yolks*
*125 g (4 oz) caster sugar*
*1 sachet (11 g (0.4 oz)) gelatine*
*250 ml (8 fl oz) double cream*
*Hazelnut, almond or sunflower oil*
*375-500 g (¾-1 lb) raspberries*
*Icing sugar*

BRING milk and tea slowly to just below boiling point. Meanwhile, whisk yolks and sugar with an electric beater until very thick. Still beating, pour on about half the milk through a strainer. Taste and add more of the milk to give the strength of flavour you like (bear in mind that the cream to be folded in later will have a softening effect). Press on the leaves in the strainer if you need an even stronger effect than the milk alone gives you. Tip the flavoured custard into a pan and stir with a wooden spoon over a gentle heat to thicken it further. The consistency is right when you run your finger across the back of the spoon and the path it makes remains clear.

Dissolve the gelatine in 6 tablespoons of hot water in a bowl and mix it into the custard, off the heat. Put the pan into a bowl of ice cubes, and stir so that it cools and thickens up evenly.

Whisk the cream and fold it into the cooled custard. Brush out a decorative mould, or moulds, with the oil. Pour in the bavarois and leave to set in the refrigerator.

Rinse the raspberries and mix them with icing sugar. Turn out the Bavarian cream(s) and put the raspberries around them. Or sieve some of them to make a sauce and stir in the whole fruit, and pour this around the cream.

## LITTLE POTS OF CHOCOLATE AND ROSEMARY CREAM

I'VE EATEN SOME OF MY BEST AND HAPPIEST MEALS at David and Patricia Wilson's Peat Inn, in the Kingdom of Fife. The last time I was there was with Paul Bailey, who had been lecturing in Dundee. We had planned a Scottish tour, and chose the Peat Inn for our first dinner. It set a hard standard to follow. The final pleasure was these little pots of chocolate cream flavoured with rosemary; the unusual combination of flavours was so successful that Paul persuaded David to part with the recipe. Note that there are no eggs in this recipe, which we both now make instead of the classic chocolate mousse.

For 8 at least

*250 g (8 oz) granulated sugar*
*250 ml (8 fl oz) dry white wine*
*Juice of ½ lemon*
*600 ml (1 pt) double cream*
*1 stem of rosemary, or 1 teaspoon dried rosemary*
*165 g (5½ oz) good plain chocolate, grated*

IN a heavy based, stainless steel pan mix the sugar, wine and lemon juice. Heat gently until dissolved, stirring occasionally. Stir in the cream and cook over a gentle heat, stirring constantly. The mixture will soon thicken up.

Now add the rosemary, then the grated chocolate. Keep stirring until chocolate has dissolved. Bring to the boil, then lower the heat so that the mixture simmers for 20 minutes, or until dark and thick.

Cool, then pour through a sieve into eight or more little pots. I use little white custard pots of 100 ml (3½ fl oz) capacity, filling them to within about 1 cm (½″) of the top, but any similar sized pot or ramekin will do: remember this is a very rich pudding, a little goes a long way.

Cover the top with clingfilm and refrigerate (they keep well for 3 or 4 days). Decorate with a tiny sprig of rosemary and some blanched, chopped almond.

## WHIM-WHAM

For each person

*1 boudoir biscuit (sponge finger biscuit)*
*1 tablespoon muscatel dessert wine or sweet sherry*
*2 large tablespoons double cream*
*½ teaspoon chopped roasted hazelnuts*
*2 small leaves cut from angelica*

BREAK the biscuit in four and place the pieces in a small custard cup. Pour over the wine and leave it to soak in. Whip the cream and pile it on top. Decorate discreetly with the nuts and angelica – candied citron or orange peel or cumin comfits can be used instead of angelica, but avoid glacé cherries which would be out of style.

A POPULAR eighteenth-century emergency recipe, which is delicious and not too heavy. Whim-Wham means something trifling, i.e. a trifle. Double the quantities if you like, but this kind of thing is more a delicious mouthful at the end of a meal, than a pudding. In *The Complete Confectioner*, *c.* 1760, Hannah Glasse gives this recipe for Naples biscuits, i.e. sponge biscuits: sieve 250 g (8 oz) sugar with 175 g (6 oz) flour, mix with 3 small eggs, 'two or three grains of Musk', and a tablespoon of rose water. Pipe 24 biscuits with a wide plain nozzle, and bake at mark 5-6, 190°-200°C (375-400°F), for 15-20 minutes.

## TRIFLE

**A** PUDDING WORTH EATING, not the mean travesty made with yellow, packaged sponge cakes, poor sherry and powdered custards.

For 8

*6 large macaroons*
*Frontignan, Malaga or Madeira wine*
*1 glass brandy*
*600 ml (1 pt) single cream*
*2 large egg yolks*
*2 large eggs*
*1 tablespoon ground rice or flour*
*Caster sugar*
*Raspberry jam*
*Everlasting syllabub (page 253), made with the wines above*
*Ratafia biscuits (Atkinsons of Windermere still make them – to be found at good confectioners and cake shops)*
*Candied peel and other decorations*

PUT the macaroons into the base of a deep glass dish, cutting them to fit if necessary. Pour 150 ml (¼ pt) of wine over them – the muscat-flavoured Frontignan is best – and the brandy. Allow it to soak in, then add more if the macaroons are still on the dry side. Next make the custard – bring the single cream to the boil, and pour it on to the egg yolks and eggs which have been beaten together with the ground rice or flour. Return this mixture to the pan and cook gently without boiling until very thick; keep stirring with a wooden spoon. Season with sugar to taste. Pour over the macaroons and leave in a cool place to set. When firm, spread with a layer of raspberry jam. Make the Everlasting Syllabub on page 253 and put it on top. Decorate with ratafia biscuits, cut peel and other decorations. Try and avoid the brassy effect of angelica and glacé cherries: many confectioners still sell the more delicate kind of cake and pudding decorations which are closer in style to the old-fashioned sweetmeats and comfits. Leave in a *cool larder* overnight if possible, rather than a refrigerator, so that the flavours have a chance to blend well together.

## MOCHA CAKE

THE FRENCH HAVE ALWAYS BEEN MORE ENTERPRISING with boudoir biscuit cakes than we have. They seem to have invented the *charlotte russe* (often attributed to the great Carême), and nowadays every packet of sponge finger biscuits has some idea for turning them into a delicious pudding. This recipe was published in the *Daily Telegraph*, I think, just after the war. It became the universal birthday pudding in our family.

For 8-10

*125 g (4 oz) lightly salted Danish butter*
*125 g (4 oz) vanilla sugar*
*Yolk of 1 large egg*
*300 ml (½ pt) milk*
*125 g (4 oz) ground almonds*
*1 teaspoon instant coffee granules*
*1 teaspoon granulated sugar*
*2 packets boudoir biscuits*
*Small glass dry sherry*
*Toasted split almonds, glacé fruit to decorate*

CREAM butter and vanilla sugar; then add the yolk and just under half the milk, alternating it with the almonds. This cream may well develop a curdled appearance, but don't worry. Dissolve the coffee and granulated sugar in a teaspoon of very hot water, and use to flavour the cream. Taste, and make a further addition of coffee if you like – I find that one generous teaspoon is strong enough, but you may not agree.

Divide the biscuits into four piles, and find an oblong shallow dish. Pour the remaining milk and the sherry into a bowl (it may curdle, too, but that is all right). Dip biscuits from the first pile into the sherry mixture, but don't saturate them. Arrange them side by side, close together on the dish. Spread over some of the cream. Repeat with the remaining biscuits, finally covering the sides as well as the top of the cake with the cream. Press chopped toasted almonds into the cake – all over if you can afford so many – and use the glacé fruit for decoration.

## JOHN EVELYN'S TART OF HERBS

IN HIS *Acetaria*, published in 1699, Evelyn gives various recipes for the vegetables he commends. One of them is an unusual sweet tart made with greenery – a mixture of chervil, spinach and beet leaves (or what other herb you please, he says). I usually stick to spinach, or to a preponderance of spinach; if you start with a kilo, you will end up with something close to 425 g (14 oz) of well-drained, cooked greenery.

For 8

*300 ml (½ pt) single cream*
*30 g (1 oz) breadcrumbs*
*1 kilo (2 lb) spinach*
*30-60 g (1-2 oz) macaroons, crushed*
*60 g (2 oz) butter*
*4 egg yolks*
*2 egg whites*
*2-3 tablespoons sugar*
*60 g (2 oz) currants or raisins*
*Milk*
*Grated nutmeg*
*250 g (8 oz) puff pastry*

BRING the cream to boiling point with the breadcrumbs, stirring over a low heat until thickened. Mix the chopped, cooked greenery into the pan, then add half the macaroon crumbs, the butter, yolks and whites, the sugar and the currants or raisins plumped in a little hot milk. Stir over a low heat until everything is well blended, taste and add extra macaroon crumbs and sugar if it seems a good idea. Finally add a grating of nutmeg.

Roll out the pastry and line a flan tin of 22-24 cm (9-10") diameter. Pour in the spinach filling. Bake at mark 7, 220°C (425°F), for 10-15 minutes, until the pastry edges start to colour, then lower the heat to mark 4, 180°C (350°F), and leave for a further 30-40 minutes until the filling is just set. Eat hot or warm with cream, as a pudding.

In a period when the storage of fruit through the winter was difficult, vegetables provided a useful filling for sweet tarts.

## CHERRY TARTS

IN THE MIDDLE AGES, the cherry fair was a great festival in England. People wandered about the orchards when the fruit was ripe; they would dance and sing and drink and make love; the cherries were picked and sold. The poignancy of colour and glory in lives that were normally brutish had by the thirteenth century turned the fair into a symbol of the passing moment (like the cherry blossom festival in Japan at an even earlier date):

*This lyfe, I see, is but a cheyre feyre:*
*All things passe and so must I algate.*

And so the cherry season is still, though to a lesser degree: it passes too soon, and one never seems – unless one has the fortune to live in Kent – to have made the most of it.

As far as cooking is concerned, the dark acid morellos and the paler amarelles are the varieties to buy. Dessert cherries can be used, so can the tinned morellos sold under the Yugoslavian brand name, Vitaminka, but fresh acid cherries give the deep-flavoured richness that one needs. Incidentally, it is the use of over-sweet canned red cherries that makes so many restaurant dishes of duck with cherries uneatable.

'Cherry' is one of those words that convey a great deal, not just the idea of summer and love and their passing, but the whole history of the fruit. It comes from the Old French *cherise*, which comes in turn from the Latin *cerasus* – and that goes back to *karsu*, the Accadian word used by Assyrians and Babylonians who first cultivated the cherry.

PASTRY
*150 g (5 oz) flour*
*90 g (3 oz) butter*
*2 tablespoons icing sugar*
*1 large egg yolk*
*1 tablespoon lemon juice*

FILLING
*750 g (1½ lb) cherries, stoned*
*150 ml (¼ pt) double cream*
*2 eggs*
*90 g (3 oz) caster sugar*

MAKE the pastry in the usual way and line 18 small tart tins. Stone the cherries with one of those useful fruit and olive stoning machines and put a closely packed single layer in each pastry case. Beat cream, eggs and sugar together and put about a tablespoon or a little less over the cherries in each tart. Bake for 15-20 minutes at mark 8, 230°C (450°F). The filling will puff up and brown slightly in the heat, but as the tarts cool it will shrink. The tarts are best eaten tepid or moderately hot.

## BALLYMALOE FRUIT TARTS

THESE TARTS, WITH THEIR UNUSUAL ALMOND CRUST, are a speciality of Myrtle Allen's at Ballymaloe House near Cork, in the Republic of Ireland. When she ran La Ferme Irlandaise in Paris, in the Place St Honoré, it was always necessary to order them at the beginning of the meal to be sure they hadn't all disappeared by the time you got to the pudding. In no way can they be called English, but they are too good to leave out and should be part of the repertoire of every family in these islands. Not only are they delicious, they are also simple.

During the first part of the year, top them with chunks of lightly cooked pink rhubarb, next come gooseberries, then the wide possibilities of the full summer, tiny strawberries, raspberries, peach slices, blueberries, currants, loganberries, mulberries above all.

*125 g (4 oz) ground almonds*
*125 g (4 oz) caster sugar*
*125 g (4 oz) lightly salted butter*

FILLING
*Whipped cream and fruit*

GARNISH
*Mint or currant leaves (optional)*

PREHEAT the oven to mark 4, 180°C (350°F). Set out 20 small tart tins. For the almond crust, mix almonds, sugar and butter to a dough in the processor or by hand. Don't be tempted into grinding your own whole almonds, the recipe works best with the kind you buy ready ground. Put a teaspoon of the mixture into each of the tins, without spreading them. Bake for about 10 minutes, until you have 20 golden saucers rimmed slightly with brown. Keep an eye on them towards the end. Cool slightly in the tins, but remove to a wire rack before they harden and stick.

Just before serving, whip the cream, adding sugar or not depending on the fruit you have chosen. Put a blob, or pipe a rosette into each tartlet: arrange the fruit and garnish on top.

NOTE: if you feel apprehensive about such an unorthodox recipe, bake an experimental tartlet first, then fill it and eat it. Then you can judge timing and the quantity of sugar to add to the cream with confidence.

## OLDBURY GOOSEBERRY PIES

EVERY YEAR A NEIGHBOUR OF OURS makes these little raised pies with her early gooseberries. She is not from Gloucestershire, but had the recipe from a farmer's wife at Sheperdine, near Oldbury on Severn, as she liked them so much when she was visiting. After the first edition of *English Food* I had a letter from a reader, Miss M. J. Squier, now of Kenley in Surrey, whose mother had come from Oldbury. Every summer she helped her make these pies. 'She always left them *overnight* so that the pastry became quite hard before cooking. I have never cooked them straightaway as I understood that the pastry would not stand up firmly. I expect you will agree that the tarts are much nicer if the pastry is rolled *very* thinly.'

She then went on to tell me about her great-aunt, Hannah Cornock, who was born in 1870, and used to live in Sheperdine; 'she used to say that the tarts were sold at fairs at a penny each when she was young'. In *Good Things in England*, Florence White remarked – this was in 1931 – that raised gooseberry pies were still being sold at Mansfield fair in Nottinghamshire.

*500 g (1 lb) plain flour*
*125 g (4 oz) butter*
*125 g (4 oz) lard*
*5 tablespoons water*
*250 g (8 oz) gooseberries, topped and tailed*
*250 g (8 oz) demerara sugar*

PUT flour into a bowl and make a well in the centre. Chop in the butter and lard in smallish pieces. Bring the water to the boil and tip on to the fats, stirring them about briskly until they dissolve. Gradually stir in the flour to make a malleable, not too stiff dough, which has a slightly waxy look.

Using the dough in batches, roll it out very thinly and cut circles with the aid of a saucer. Bring up the sides almost 2½ cm (1"), pressing and moulding the pastry to form cases. Fill with gooseberries and sugar. Cut smaller circles for the lids. Brush the pastry edges with water and fix the lids in place. Cut small central holes for the steam to escape. Leave overnight in a cool place for the pastry to harden (this can be hurried up by putting them into the fridge, until dry and very firm). Bake at mark 6-7, 200-220°C (400-425°F), for 25-30 minutes.

THIS SIMPLIFIED hot-water pastry can be used successfully with other fruit. Try it with peeled, cored and sliced pears – to make a medieval or Shakespearean Warden Pie. Mix powdered ginger and cinnamon with the sugar, and add a squeeze of lemon juice before putting on the lid, to bring out the flavour of the fruit.

## BLAEBERRY OR BLACKCURRANT PIE

AT OUR FIRST TOWN SCHOOL, we learnt a haunting song. I thought then that it was Scottish, but as you will see I now think it must have been Irish. The first verse went like this:

*I went to gather blaeberries,*
*blaeberries, blaeberries,*
*I went to gather blaeberries,*
*and left my darling baby-O.*

While the mother was away, the baby disappeared, stolen by the fairies. She went in search of him, heartbroken:

*I found the track of the swan in the mist,*
*the swan in the mist, the swan in the mist,*
*I found the track of the swan in the mist,*
*but ne'er a trace of my baby-O.*

At our second school, in the country, we climbed the Langdale Pikes, and at last discovered blaeberries. The song returned to my mind as we sat beside the tarn under Pavy Ark.

Many years later, married to a husband who knows about plant folklore, I sang him the song when he told me about Lammas Sunday in Ireland. People in hilly places, or at least everyone who could, climbed up to a particular height to picnic. There they made rush baskets to put the bilberries into. It was the great summer holiday, with games and courting. I suppose that young mother had wanted to return to the scene of last year's Blaeberry or Height Sunday, as it was often called; perhaps it was there that she had met the baby's father.

Nowadays nobody need put on their spiked shoes for blaeberries, or bilberries as they are often labelled. High-class grocers sell them in frozen packages (from Sweden, usually). Most people will agree, none the less, that the best tart is made from fruit you have picked yourself on a July or August climb. The mint flavouring included in this recipe comes from Derbyshire and Yorkshire.

*750 g-1 kilo (1½-2 lb) blaeberries (or blackcurrants)*
*175-250 g (8 oz) sugar*
*1 heaped tablespoon cornflour*
*1 level tablespoon chopped mint leaves*
*Sweet shortcrust pastry*
*1 egg white, or water*
*Caster sugar*

TASTE the fruit and weigh out the sugar according to its sweetness. Mix the sugar with the cornflour and mint. Put the fruit in layers into a pie dish, interspersed with the sugar mixture. Cover with pastry. Brush with egg white or water and sprinkle with caster sugar. Bake for 15 minutes at mark 7, 220°C (425°F), then lower the heat to mark 5, 190°C (375°F), and leave for another 20-30 minutes. Keep an eye on the crust, and protect it with a butter paper or piece of brown paper if it seems to be colouring too rapidly.

Serve with a large jug of cream.

NOTE: although this recipe can, as the title suggests, be used for blackcurrants, the flavour will be different. American blueberries can also be made into a pie in the same way – they are quite close in flavour to blaeberries.

## RASPBERRY PIE

THIS WAS THE USUAL WAY OF MAKING A FRUIT PIE in the eighteenth century, though normally puff pastry would be used. The caudle mixes with the juice in the pie and thickens it slightly, softening the acidity of the fruit. Gooseberries could be substituted, or other soft fruit in season.

PASTRY
*375 g (12 oz) plain flour*
*2 tablespoons icing sugar*
*1 pinch salt*
*250 g (8 oz) butter, or butter/lard*
*1 egg yolk*
*Ice-cold water to mix*

FILLING
*500 g (1 lb) raspberries*
*About 125 g (4 oz) sugar*
*125 ml (4 oz) single cream*
*125 ml (4 oz) double cream*
*2 large egg yolks*

GLAZE
*1 egg white*
*Caster sugar*

FIRST make the pastry in the usual way. Roll out rather more than half of it, and use to line a 3-5 cm (1½-2″) deep pie dish. Brush the pastry with egg white and sprinkle evenly with sugar: this helps to prevent the pastry becoming too soggy. Pile in the raspberries, sprinkling them with the sugar according to their natural sweetness. Roll out the remainder of the pastry and cover pie in the usual way, making a hole in the centre wide enough to take the stem of a kitchen funnel. Decorate the pie with the trimmings, brush it over with egg white and sprinkle with caster sugar. Bake at mark 7, 220°C (425°F) for 15 minutes, then at mark 5, 190°C (375°F), until the pastry is well cooked – about 40 minutes in all.

Towards the end of cooking time, warm the creams to boiling point, and pour them on to the yolks, beating vigorously. When the pie is done, pour this custard, or 'caudle' as it used to be called, through a funnel into the central hole. Do this gently and stop before the pie overflows. Return to the oven for 5 minutes. Eat warm rather than hot; any cream and egg left over can be used to thicken a soup or sauce.

NOTE: when you turn on the oven to heat up for baking a pie or tart with pastry underneath, put a metal baking tray on the centre shelf. The pie will have a less soggy underneath if you do this, because the immediate contact with the hot metal firms the pastry before the juiciness of the filling gets through it.

## APPLE PIE

'MANY OF OUR DESSERT APPLES have sufficient acid to make them good cookers, as in Cox's Orange Pippin, James Grieve and Allington Pippin . . . Two or three apples of Cox's Orange Pippin or Ellison's Orange added to the Bramley's Seedling improve the flavour of an apple pie far better than do cloves . . .'
H. V. Taylor, *The Apples of England*
– and quinces are even better.

For 6

*500 g (1 lb) cooking apples, e.g. Bramley's*
*250 g (8 oz) Cox's Orange Pippins, or Ellison's Orange*
Or: *625 g (1¼ lb) cooking apples*
*1 large quince*

Plus: *Sugar*
*300 ml (½ pt) water approximately*
*250 g (8 oz) total weight pastry*

EITHER peel, core and slice the apples, *or* peel, core and slice the apples and peel, core and grate the quince. Fill the fruit into a pie dish, so that it mounds up in the centre, sprinkling each layer of fruit with sugar as you go. Pour the water into the dish, stopping when it comes halfway up or a little less. Roll out the pastry. Cut a strip long enough to go round the edge of the pie dish, brush this edge with water and lay the strip on top, pressing it into place. Brush the strip with water. Use remaining pastry to make a lid over the pie. Cut off surplus pastry, knock up the edges and make a central hole for the steam to escape. Brush over the pastry lid with water, sprinkle it with an even layer of caster sugar and bake in a fairly hot oven, mark 7, 220°C (425°F), for 15 minutes. Lower heat to mark 5, 190°C (375°F), and cook for another 30-40 minutes until the apples are cooked. Eat hot or warm, with plenty of cream.

NOTE: fruit pies may be cooked for 30 minutes at mark 7, 220°C (425°F), but I prefer the temperature given above, unless something else in the oven demands a steady heat.

## ENGLISH APPLE AND RAISIN PIE

JOHN DAVIES OF HEREFORD DIED IN 1618 at fifty-five, a good age for those days, and he was on his third wife. He was quite a bon viveur and expert in the good things of his native countryside, judging by a lovely, funny, appetising sonnet he wrote to that 'Virtuous Gentlewoman, whom he calleth Mistress':

*If there were, oh! an Hellespont of cream*
*Between us, milk-white mistress, I would swim*
*To you, to show to both my love's extreme,*
*Leander-like, – yea! dive from brim to brim.*
*But met I with a buttered pippin-pie*
*Floating upon't, that would I make my boat*
*To waft me to you without jeopardy . . .*

Here is an old recipe for a well buttered pie which I trust he would have approved of. Serve it with an Hellespont of Jersey cream in a glass jug to show off its rich colour.

For 8

*20 Reinette or Cox's Orange Pippins (1½ kilos (3½ lb))*
*125 g (4 oz) unsalted butter*
*125 g (4 oz) caster sugar*
*Grated rind of half a lemon*
*125 g (4 oz) seedless raisins, or 2 heaped tablespoons apricot jam*
*Puff pastry*
*1 beaten egg white*
*Extra sugar*

PEEL, core and quarter the apples; then slice each quarter into six and put them into a bowl. Sprinkle over them the sugar and rind and mix together thoroughly. Melt the butter and add that to the apples, turning everything over as you do so. Finally add the raisins or the jam. Finish the pie as given in the apricot recipe following, but cook for about 45 minutes at the lower temperature, instead of only 15. Apples, being a hard fruit, take longer.

## ENGLISH APRICOT PIE

THIS AND THE RECIPE ABOVE FOR *English Apple and Raisin Pie* are two more of the English dishes so appreciated by the French chef Carême. He gives them in *Le Cuisinier Parisien*, of 1828. He describes a brown-glazed English pie dish most carefully for his French readers, like a soup plate, with its wide rim but twice as deep. He spells out the way of setting strips of pastry on the rim, and covering it over with pastry and pressing the two edges together to make a firm, attractive seal. These two recipes are very simple, but the preliminary coating of the fruit in butter and sugar produces a most delicious flavour.

For 8

*36 fine ripe apricots (750 g (1½ lb) approximately)*
*60 g (2 oz) unsalted butter*
*250 g (8 oz) caster sugar*
*Puff pastry*
*1 egg white*
*Extra sugar*

HALVE the apricots and remove their stones. Melt the butter in a large frying pan, stir in the sugar. Keep the heat low to moderate, until the mixture begins to melt, then tip in the apricots. Turn them gently so that they are completely coated in the sugary mixture. They will become warm, but should not cook or begin to exude much juice.

Roll out the pastry, and cut from it strips wide enough to put round the rim of the pie dish and extend partway down into the dish itself. Put the apricots carefully into the dish, fitting them together so that there is as little space as possible left between them. Pour over them any juices that might be left in the pan. Brush the pastry rim with egg white. Lay the remaining pastry over the top, to form a lid, and press it down round the edge in a decorative manner. Make a central hole. Brush the lid over with white of egg, sprinkle it evenly with the extra sugar. Put into a hot oven, mark 8, 230°C (450°F), for 15-20 minutes until the pastry has risen and begun to turn golden brown. Lower the heat to mark 3-4, 160°-180°C (325-370°F), and leave for another 15 minutes. Serve hot or warm with plenty of cream.

Carême also recommends this method for other fruit – plums, greengages, damsons, gooseberries and redcurrants, cherries, and pears.

## APRICOT AND ALMOND CRUMBLE

*24 fresh ripe apricots*
*60-90 g (2-3 oz) sugar*
*60 g (2 oz) blanched, split almonds*

CRUMBLE
*125 g (4 oz) flour*
*100 g (3 oz) sugar*
*125 g (4 oz) ground almonds*
*175 g (6 oz) butter, chilled*

POUR boiling water over the apricots, leave them for a few minutes and peel off the skins. Slice them and, if you have the patience, crack the stones and remove the kernels – this is well worth doing. Arrange the apricots in a shallow baking dish, scatter them with sugar and the kernels. To make the crumble, mix flour, sugar and almonds. Rub in the butter to make a crumbly effect, and spread it over the fruit evenly. Arrange the split almonds on top. Bake at mark 6, 200°C (400°F), for 20 minutes, then lower the heat and leave for another 20 minutes at mark 4, 180°C (350°F). In fact, crumble puddings are very good-tempered – they can be cooked for a longer time at a lower temperature if this suits you better. The only thing to make sure of is that the top is nicely browned, and not burned. Serve with cream.

Many other fruits can be used instead. It is a good recipe for pears, but they should first be stewed in a very little water (just enough to prevent them sticking) with the sugar in the first list of ingredients. Tinned peaches are particularly successful, so long as they are drained well and then rinsed under the cold tap before being arranged on the dish – they will not need the sugar.

## KICKSHAWS

ROLL out some puff pasty thinly – a good way of using up pastry trimmings – on a floured board. Cut out circles or squares about 8 cm (3″) across and put a teaspoonful of firm home-made jam in the middle – quince butter is ideal, or some large pieces of fruit from home-made apricot jam. Fold the pastry over, sealing the edges with a little beaten egg. Pinch the edges as decoratively as you like. Deep fry the kickshaws a few at a time until puffed up and golden brown. Serve them sprinkled with sugar.

A MOST delicious ending to a meal. Little fried pies and dumplings were a favourite part of medieval food, but this seems to be a last survivor all on its own in the eighteenth century. Kickshaws are a sweet version of Turkish *börek* and Chinese *hun t'un*. The word is a slightly scornful anglicization of 'quelque chose', some odd thing or other. Indeed, kickshaws are small delights which need skilful hands, the refined frivolities of a well-established cooking tradition.

## CHOCOLATE PIE

OF THE MANY BOOKS ON OUR OWN FOOD that have appeared in the last few years, my favourite, the one I use most, is Michael Smith's *Fine English Cookery* (Faber). He starts from the reasonable assumption that people who sat on Chippendale chairs in elegant houses were unlikely to be eating filthy food from their Wedgwood dinner services. Therefore what they ate is worth exploring.

He adapts the recipes slightly, but keeps their originality: in this exceptionally good chocolate pie, he puts together two recipes – the crackling crust from Hannah Glasse, and the chocolate cream filling from John Farley – to make a rich and unusual pudding.

For 6-8

CRUST
*175 g (6 oz) almonds, blanched, ground*
*60 g (2 oz) caster sugar*
*1 egg white*

FILLING
*300 ml (½ pt) single cream*
*250 g (8 oz) plain chocolate, preferably Valrhonce, Menier, Velma Suchard or Côte d'or*
*300 ml (½ pt) double cream*
*1 tablespoon rum*
*1 tablespoon icing sugar*
*Chocolate flakes, toasted almonds*

THIS must be eaten the day it is made: if you keep it, the crackling crust becomes tough. It is also a good idea to delay putting in the chocolate filling until a couple of hours before the meal.

Mix the crust ingredients to a stiff paste. Chill it for half an hour, and then roll it out on a lightly floured board. Fit it into a 20-23 cm (8-9″) flan tin. The crust is likely to break, unlike pastry, but don't worry – just press the pieces gently together in the tin to close the joins. Bake blind for 25-30 minutes at mark 4, 180°C (350°F). The crust should be as golden brown as possible without scorch marks.

To make the filling, stir the single cream and chocolate, broken into pieces, in a double boiler until they are melted into a smooth sauce. Cool it quickly, then whisk until the sauce froths into a foamy bulk. Pour it into the cooled crust. Decorate with the double cream, whipped with the rum and icing sugar, and with the chocolate flakes and toasted almonds.

The pie does not cut easily into tidy pieces, but it tastes so good that you need not be apologetic.

## JOHN FARLEY'S FINE CHEESECAKE

*Puff or shortcrust pastry*
*250 g (8 oz) full fat cream cheese*
*2 generous tablespoons double cream*
*1 tablespoon orange-flower water, or rose water*
*4 large egg yolks*
*60 g (2 oz) lightly salted butter, melted*
*90 g (3 oz) crushed macaroon crumbs*
*90 g (3 oz) almonds, blanched, ground*
*90 g (3 oz) caster sugar*
*Up to half a grated nutmeg*

LINE a 23 cm (9″) flan tin with the pastry – John Farley and every other cook of the eighteenth century used puff pastry, but we prefer a rich shortcrust these days, I think, on account of its crispness.

Mix the remaining ingredients in the order given, adding the nutmeg to taste. Turn the mixture into the pastry case. Bake at mark 4, 180°C (350°F), for 30-40 minutes. The top should be nicely browned all over. Eat hot or warm, with cream.

IN ENGLAND, we are too busy with a United Nations of cheesecakes – American, Polish, Israeli, Dutch – to remember that John Farley, of the London Tavern, and one of the best-known cooks of his time in the eighteenth century, gave eight quite different cheesecake recipes in his *London Art of Cookery*. Among them was the following simple mixture of cheese, eggs and raisins, which is now often called:

## YORKSHIRE CURD TART

'IN THIS PART OF YORKSHIRE, what is called "clove-pepper" and known to the southerners as "all-spice" is still largely used to flavour cheesecakes.'

*Shortcrust pastry, made with lard and sour milk*

FILLING
*125 g (4 oz) butter*
*60 g (2 oz) sugar*
*250 g (8 oz) curd cheese (not cottage or cream cheese)*
*125 g (4 oz) seedless raisins, or currants*
*1 rounded tablespoon wholemeal breadcrumbs*
*Pinch salt*
*Grated allspice or nutmeg to taste*
*2 well-beaten eggs*

LINE a 20-25 cm (8-10") tart tin with the pastry – use the kind with a removable base. Cream butter and sugar together, mix in the curds, raisins or currants and breadcrumbs. Add the salt and spice and lastly the eggs. Taste and adjust the spice, add a little more sugar if you like (I find most recipes too sweet). Pour into the pastry case and bake for 20-30 minutes at mark 7, 220°C (425°F). The pastry should be a nice brown.

## YORKSHIRE ALMOND TART

*Puff pastry*

FILLING
*2 egg yolks*
*60 g (2 oz) sugar*
*Rind and juice of half a lemon*
*30 g (1 oz) ground almonds*
*30 g (1 oz) melted butter*
*2 egg whites*
*Pinch salt*
*Extra sugar*

ROLL out the pastry and line a pie plate with it. Beat the yolks, sugar, lemon juice and rind together in a basin. When they are thick and creamy add the almonds and butter. Put the basin over a pan of simmering water and stir until the mixture thickens – about 10 minutes. Pour this mixture into the centre of the pie plate, and bake at mark 5, 190°C (375°F), for half an hour. Whisk the egg whites with the salt until stiff. Spread over the pie, sprinkle about a tablespoon of sugar on top and return to the oven to set and brown on top – about 5-10 minutes.

## SWEETMEAT CAKE

THIS DELICIOUS CAKE WITH ITS BUTTERSCOTCH FLAVOUR and semi-transparent filling is my own favourite of the eighteenth-century open tarts. Candied peel provides the 'sweetmeat': it can be augmented with angelica, and with the hazelnuts mentioned in the ingredients, but don't be tempted to add glacé cherries as they spoil the subtle flavour.

This recipe is a forerunner of the nursery favourite, treacle tart, but it has a much superior flavour. Treacle tart is filled with a mixture of 3 tablespoons golden syrup, 3 tablespoons white breadcrumbs and the grated rind of a lemon: bake it at mark 7, 220°C (425°F), for 20-30 minutes.

*Puff or shortcrust pastry*
*125 g (4 oz) chopped peel*
*60 g (2 oz) chopped roasted hazelnuts (optional)*
*2 large eggs*
*2 large egg yolks*
*175 g (6 oz) caster sugar*
*175 g (6 oz) lightly salted butter, melted*

LINE a 23 cm (9″) flan tin with the pastry. Scatter the chopped peel over it, then the hazelnuts if used. Beat the remaining ingredients thoroughly together and pour the mixture over the peel. Bake at mark 4, 180°C (350°F), for 35-40 minutes. The top should be crusted with a rich golden brown all over – so keep an eye on it after 30 minutes in the oven. At first the filling will rise with the baking, but once the cake is removed from the oven and transferred to a plate, it will sink again as these egg mixtures usually do. Do not worry if the centre part of the filling is a little liquid beneath the crust, as it makes a delicious sauce. The consistency is a matter for individual taste.

Like most sweet tarts, this one is best eaten warm. Serve cream with it.

## BAKEWELL PUDDING

ONE SHOULD NOT APPARENTLY REFER TO BAKEWELL *tart*, but to Bakewell *pudding*, according to local pastrycooks and restaurateurs. I had always understood, from *Good Things in England*, that first bible of our regional cookery, that the original Bakewell tart/pudding did not contain ground almonds at all, but was closer to the rich custard of butter and eggs still favoured in Rouen for *mirliton* tarts. Such things are a warning to the dogmatic: food changes with time to suit different tastes, and where they are an improvement we should be receptive to the differences. I must confess that I do prefer Bakewell pudding with ground almonds, but you may leave them out if you wish to be more authentic and make the kind of thing Jane Austen may have tasted when she stayed in the inn at Bakewell. Do you remember her description of Mr Darcy's estate at Pemberley in Derbyshire, where Elizabeth Bennet began to realize how much she loved him? She and her uncle and aunt had driven over from Bakewell and they came to the top of a hill, where the wood ceased: '. . . *and the eye was instantly caught by Pemberley House, situated on the opposite side of the valley, into which the road with some abruptness wound. It was a large, handsome stone building, standing well on rising ground, and backed by a ridge of high woody hills; and in front a stream of some natural importance was swelled into greater, but without any artificial appearance. Its banks were neither formal nor falsely adorned. Elizabeth was delighted. She had never seen a place for which nature had done more, or where natural beauty had been so little counteracted by an awkward taste*'.

*Rich sweet shortcrust pastry*

FILLING
*Raspberry jam*
*125 g (4 oz) butter*
*4 eggs*
*125 g (4 oz) sugar*
*125 g (4 oz) ground almonds*

ROLL out the pastry and line a 20 cm (8") tart tin, or traditional Bakewell tins which are oval with sloping sides and about 7 cm (2½") deep.

Spread jam over the base. Melt butter and leave to cool slightly while you beat eggs and sugar until they are a pale thick cream. Pour in the butter slowly, stirring. Then fold in the almonds. Turn into the pastry cases. Bake at mark 6-7, 200-220°C (400-425°F), for 20-40 minutes, according to the depth of the puddings.

## SWEETHEART CAKE

FOR ST VALENTINE'S DAY, to eat at the end of a meal rather than at teatime.

*Puff pastry*
*2-3 tablespoons raspberry jam*

FILLING
*4 egg yolks, beaten*
*125 g (4 oz) caster sugar*
*Grated rind and juice of a lemon*
*60 g (2 oz) ground almonds*
*60 g (2 oz) melted, cooled butter*
*60 g (2 oz) blanched, slivered almonds*

MERINGUE
*4 egg whites*
*Pinch salt*
*2 tablespoons caster sugar*

PUT two strips of foil across a heart-shaped tin, of about 4 cm (1½") depth, so that you will be able to ease out the finished cake without disaster. Line the tin with pastry, and spread the jam over it.

Mix the filling ingredients in the order given. Spread over the pastry case. Bake 25-30 minutes, at mark 5, 190°C (375°F), until lightly browned.

Beat whites with the salt until stiff. Fold in half the sugar, and beat for a moment or two longer until the meringue is thick and shiny. When tart is cooked, pile the meringue on top right to the pastry edge. Sprinkle remaining sugar over it. Return to the oven for 15 minutes until meringue is peaked with brown. Eat warm.

## MANCHESTER PUDDING

THIS VERSION OF MANCHESTER PUDDING is based on a recipe in *Cassell's Dictionary of Cookery*, which was published in the 1880s.

*Puff pastry*
*Greengage, strawberry or apricot jam*
*300 ml (½ pt) milk*
*Thinly peeled rind of a lemon*
*60 g (2 oz) white breadcrumbs*
*100 g (3½ oz) caster sugar*
*60 g (2 oz) butter*
*3-4 tablespoons brandy*
*2 large eggs, separated*

LINE a 22 cm (8-9") tart tin with the pastry. Spread it with jam. Put milk, lemon peel and crumbs into a pan, and bring to the boil. Simmer for 3-4 minutes. Remove from the heat, extract the peel and mix in about one-third of the sugar, the butter, brandy and egg yolks. Pour into the pastry case. Bake at mark 4, 180°C (350°F), for 30 minutes. By this time the filling will be more or less set, possibly slightly liquid in the middle but not runny. You should be able to spread the stiffly beaten whites of the eggs, mixed with the remaining sugar, over the whole thing in an even layer. Do not raise the egg white in peaks as you do with Queen of Puddings. It should be smooth.

Return to the oven for 20 minutes. The egg white will rise and be covered with a fawny brown skin, but once you take it out of the oven it will fall back to the level of the pastry and the meringue will be a thick white layer when you cut into the pudding. Eat hot or warm.

If you want to make the pudding to be eaten cold, you can omit the egg-white layer – according to *Cassell's* – and just cover the baked custard with sifted icing sugar. But I think this spoils it. The egg-white layer makes a delicious top to the pudding, whether it is served hot or cold.

## QUICK, FOOLPROOF PUFF OR FLAKY PASTRY

OLDER ENGLISH PIE RECIPES often require puff rather than shortcrust pastry – I was much relieved to come across this foolproof method devised by Nicholas Malgieri, pastry chef at Peter Krump's famous New York cookery school. It is not really suitable for vol-au-vents, which really do need all the skill rolled into the 729 layers of classic puff pastry, but it works well for pies and tarts, for 'sandwiches' *(feuilletées)* filled with various savoury or sweet mixtures, and for a modern kind of tartlet, baked in flat discs under a light weight, which is finally topped with soft fruit, or with caramelized apples and pears. For puff pastry, always buy the best butter you can find.

*250 g (8½ oz) strong white flour*
*250 g (8½ oz) unsalted French butter*
*½ teaspoon salt*
*2 teaspoons lemon juice*
*Ice-cold water*

SIFT flour into a bowl, and rub in 30 g (1 oz) of the butter. Cube the rest, then toss it into the flour with your hands so that each cube is coated and separate. Work lightly. Dissolve salt in the juice in a measuring cup and add water to make 125 ml (4 fl oz). Pour into the bowl, tilting it so that all the flour is moistened, then quickly press everything together into a rough, lumpy dough. It will look appalling, a raggy mess. Using a dough scraper, turn it out on to a well floured surface. Shape into a 10 × 20 cm (4 × 8″) rectangle.

Flour the top and roll out to a 24 × 48 cm (9 × 18″) rectangle, sprinkling with flour as necessary. Fold the short ends over to meet in the centre, then fold over again, along the central divide, to make a book shape.

Turn the spine of the book to your left. Roll out as before and fold again, using the dough scraper and extra flour as required. Repeat. If the dough becomes very soft after the second roll and fold, put it back into the refrigerator to firm up. Wrap in clingfilm and chill for at least 1 hour, or freeze. When you roll out the dough for use, always chill for at least 30 minutes before baking.

To achieve a crisp, even, brown effect, rather than a maximum height, put the pastry, cut to shape, on a parchment-lined baking sheet, and lay a second baking sheet on top.

The temperature for this pastry is mark 5, 190°C (375°F), much lower than for classic puff pastry, though of course when it is used as part of a recipe, say for a pie, other things will dictate the temperature.

## QUEEN OF PUDDINGS

A PUDDING THAT DESERVES ITS NAME for the perfect combination of flavours and textures, a most subtle and lovely way to end a meal. The earliest recipe I have so far been able to find is from Massey and Son's *Comprehensive Pudding Book* of 1865, in which it is called Queen's Pudding. It was served cold. Apricot jam was used rather than blackcurrant or raspberry jelly.

For 4-6

*150 g (5 oz) fresh brown or white breadcrumbs*
*1 heaped tablespoon vanilla sugar*
*Grated rind of 1 large lemon*
*600 ml (1 pt) milk*
*60 g (2 oz) lightly salted butter*
*4 large egg yolks*
*2 tablespoons blackcurrant jelly, or raspberry jelly*
*4 large egg whites*
*125 g (4 oz) caster sugar, plus 1 extra teaspoonful*

PUT breadcrumbs, vanilla sugar and lemon rind into a pudding basin. Bring the milk and butter to just below boiling point and stir it into the crumbs. Leave for 10 minutes, then beat in the egg yolks thoroughly. Grease a shallow dish which holds about 1½ litres (2½ pints) with a buttery paper, and pour in the breadcrumb custard. Bake at mark 4, 180°C (350°F), for 30 minutes, or a little less, until just firm – the time will depend on the depth of the dish, and remember that the custard will continue to cook a little in its own heat so that if the centre looks runny underneath the skin do not feel anxious. Warm the jelly (if you use jam, warm it and sieve it) and spread it over the custard without breaking the surface. Whisk the whites until stiff, mix in half the caster sugar, then whisk again until slightly satiny. With a metal spoon, fold in the rest of the 125 g (4 oz) of sugar. Pile on to the pudding, sprinkle with the extra teaspoonful of sugar and return to the oven for 15 minutes until the meringue is slightly browned and crisp. Serve hot with plenty of cream.

## PAYN PUR-DEW (1420)

'TAKE FAIR YOLKS OF EGGS, and separate them from the white, and drawn them through a strainer, and take salt [a pinch] and cast thereto; then take fair bread, and cut it in round slices; then take fair butter that is clarified, or else fresh grease, and put it in a pot, and make it hot; then take and wet well the slices in the yolks, and put them in the pan, and so fry them up; but be ware of them cleaving to the pan; and when it is fried, lay them on a dish, and lay plenty of sugar thereon, and then serve it forth.'

## POOR KNIGHTS OF WINDSOR (1937)

'CUT A FRENCH ROLL in slices and soak them in sherry. Then dip them in beaten yolks of eggs and fry them. Make a sauce of butter, sherry and sugar to serve with them.'

AMBROSE HEATH, Good Sweets

YOU may be surprised to observe that the medieval instructions are more precise than the modern ones. It is important, for instance, to use clarified butter as this reduces the likelihood of the bread burning. I like, too, the stress on the quality of the ingredients – they are to be fair, or fresh. Certainly the finer the bread you use the better the dish will be. If you can find brioche, for instance, you will understand how this simple pudding delighted the court of Henry V. No wonder it has lasted down the centuries, even with its mangled French title (which means *pain perdu*, lost, i.e. smothered bread), and become a family pudding in this country. I do not know when the second title was given to the dish – it certainly contains a memory of its original grandeur as well as the feeling of having come down in the world.

Hannah Glasse flavoured her *Pain perdu* with cinnamon. It can also be served with fresh fruit.

## POOR KNIGHT'S PUDDING WITH RASPBERRIES

BEFORE THE LAST WAR, when tea was an occasion for enjoyment and not for guilt, we often used to have home-made raspberry jam sandwiches at my grandmother's house. There were always too many – raspberry jam being her favourite – and next day they would appear as a pudding, having been fried in butter. I always thought, and still do think, that their latter end was more glorious than their debut. This recipe is my adaptation of her economy. It works well, too, with really ripe apricots and peaches. In winter one can use a really good jam, but I find this too sweet.

For 4

*500 g (1 lb) raspberries*
*125 g (4 oz) icing sugar*
*Cinnamon*
*8 slices white bread*
*175 g (6 oz) butter*
*175 g (6 oz) whipping cream, or half and half double and single cream*
*1 heaped tablespoon caster sugar*

SPRINKLE raspberries with the icing sugar and about half a teaspoon of cinnamon. Leave until they produce some liquid and look like a slightly runny whole-fruit jam. Taste and add more cinnamon and sugar if necessary.

Cut the crusts off the bread. Bring the butter to the boil in a small pan, then pour it, through a muslin-lined sieve, into a frying pan; fry the bread in it.

This sounds laborious, but it is quickly done, and avoids the risk of the bread browning too much – it should look golden, and be crisp.

Keep the bread warm in the oven, while you whip the creams together and sweeten them to taste with the sugar. Sandwich the bread with raspberries, and top with a generous swirl of whipped cream. You have a delicious contrast between the keen, buttery heat of the bread, and the keen cold of the raspberries, softened by the whipped cream.

## SUMMER PUDDING

For 8-10

*1 kilo (2 lb) blackcurrants, or raspberries, or a mixture of raspberries, redcurrants and blackberries*
*250 g (8 oz) caster sugar*
*Good quality white bread, one day old*

PUT the fruit and sugar into a bowl, and leave overnight. Next day tip the contents of the bowl into a pan, bring to the boil and simmer gently for 2-3 minutes to cook the fruit lightly. It should make a fair amount of juice. Taste and add more sugar if necessary.

Cut the bread into slices 1 cm (¼-½″) thick. Remove the crusts. Make a circle from one slice to fit the base of a 1½ litre (2½ pt) pudding basin or other bowl. Then cut wedges of bread to fit round the sides. There should be no gaps, so if the wedges do not quite fit together, push in small bits of bread. Pour in half the fruit and juice, put in a slice of bread, then add the rest of the fruit and juice. Cover the top with one or two layers of bread, trimming off the wedges to make a nice neat finish. Put a plate on top, with a couple of tins to weight the whole thing down, and leave overnight – or for several days if you like – in the refrigerator. (If the bread is not thoroughly impregnated with the brilliant fruit juices, boil up a few more blackcurrants or raspberries and strain the liquor over the white bits that will occur at the top of the pudding.) Run a thin knife round between the pudding and the basin, put a serving dish upside down on top, and turn the whole thing over quickly. Remove the basin and serve with a great deal of cream; cream is essential for this very strong-flavoured pudding, which because of its flavour goes a long way and should be served in small slices.

THIS PUDDING can be made successfully with frozen blackcurrants. One family I know always has it on Christmas Day, after the turkey, as a reminder that summer will come.

## FIFTEENTH-CENTURY APPLE FRITTERS
## FRETOURE OWT OF LENTE

ALTHOUGH THE SAFFRON AND PEPPER are omitted from modern recipes, this is a shame. The saffron gives the batter a delicate flavour and a beautiful colour: the pepper adds an aromatic piquancy rather in the manner of ginger but with a less assertive taste. Pepper is still used for flavouring pear tarts in the Bourbonnais and Poitou districts of France.

Bananas make good fritters, too. Steep them in sugar and rum instead of brandy.

APPLES
*6 large Cox's Orange Pippins, or other firm eating apple*
*Sugar*
*1 liqueur glass brandy*

BATTER
*125 g (4 oz) flour*
*2 medium eggs*
*1 tablespoon oil or clarified butter*
*Up to 300 ml (½ pt) milk*
*Pinch saffron*
*Freshly ground black pepper*

PEEL, core and slice apples thickly. Put them into a dish and sprinkle them with sugar, and pour on the brandy. Leave them for several hours – or overnight – turning them occasionally in the liquid. Drain them well before coating them with batter.

For the batter, mix the flour, one whole egg, the second egg yolk and the oil. Beat in about half the milk. Pour 3 tablespoons of almost boiling water over the saffron and leave to steep for a little while; when the water is a good crocus yellow, strain it into the batter. Add more milk if the batter is too thick. Grind the pepper two or three times over the basin and stir it in. Last of all whisk the second egg white until stiff, and fold it into the batter.

Dip the apple slices into the batter and fry them in oil until golden brown. Serve sprinkled with sugar.

## CARAMELIZED COX'S ORANGE PIPPINS

A SIMPLE RECIPE, but one that needs a little care, and good control of your stove.

Peel and core a Cox's Orange Pippin for each person (choose large ones). Cut it into two or three rings – keep the top and bottom for apple sauce, or eat them as you go.

Fry the rings slowly in butter, preferably clarified butter, which will give you more leeway with the heat. Once they begin to turn a light golden brown, powder them with cinnamon sugar (1 tablespoon sugar mixed with 1 teaspoon cinnamon). If not overheated the sugar and butter will make a delicious caramel glaze. Serve hot with clotted cream.

If you are a bread-maker, serve the apples on slices of white bread or brioche, toasted and buttered. Or buttered and put into the oven to crisp.

## PEARS IN SYRUP

A MEDIEVAL RECIPE which was usually made with Wardens or cooking pears. They were as hard as quinces and were first boiled until just tender, in water. This is not necessary with the pears we buy today, though the hint might be useful if you have a tree of cooking pears.

If wine is out of the question, add three sliced quinces to the pears, and substitute a vanilla pod, split, for the cinnamon stick. Cover with water, and start with 4 tablespoons of sugar. If you cook the dish slowly enough and long enough, the juice will turn a most beautiful deep red.

For 6

*6 pears*
*Red wine*
*Sugar*
*1 stick cinnamon*
*Pinch of powdered ginger*

PEEL, core and halve the pears. Place them in a pan in a single layer, and pour in enough red wine to cover them (no need to use the best claret, a wine sold by the litre will do). Add 2 tablespoons of sugar, the cinnamon and ginger. Cover and simmer until the pears are done. Remove them to a dish with a perforated spoon and keep them hot. Boil down their cooking liquor until it is slightly syrupy. Taste it from time to time, and put in more sugar if you like – the flavour should be fairly strong, and sweet, but not over-sweet. Pour, boiling, over the pears and leave to cool. Don't strain out the cinnamon stick: it adds to the appearance, as well as the flavour of the dish.

## FRUIT SALAD WITH TEA

AS A CHANGE FROM WRITING NOVELS, reviews and Daily Telegraph restaurant pieces, Paul Bailey enjoys cooking dinner and Sunday lunches for his friends. The meal often concludes in summer with this fruit salad made mainly from dark fruit set off by strawberries. Exact proportions are not important, and you could use redcurrants, blueberries, loganberries or mulberries as well, according to the market. Or your garden.

For 8-10

*500 g (1 lb) purple plums, stoned, cut up*
*500 g (1 lb) black cherries, stoned*
*250 g (½ lb) black grapes, halved, seeded*
*250 g (½ lb) strawberries, halved*
*125 g (4 oz) raspberries or blackberries*
*About 8 tablespoons caster sugar*
*Up to 6 teaspoons Earl Grey or orange pekoe tea*

DECORATION
*Mint leaves*

TO SERVE
*Thin, crisp biscuits (optional)*

IF this salad is for dinner, aim to start at midday, layering the fruit into a salad bowl, sprinkling it with sugar as you go according to its sweetness. Try to use a glass bowl for best effect, ideally one on a pedestal so that all the fruit can be seen, and arrange the strawberries regularly around the side, as their bright colour can be most effective in a dark mixture – the pallor of the cut side has a luminous effect. Cover and leave in a cool place for at least 4 hours.

Consider the quantity of juice that has accumulated and assess how much tea you will need almost to cover the fruit (allow some of it to bump up above the surface). Make a double strength brew. After 5-7 minutes, strain the tea and when cool, pour what is needed into the salad. Taste for sweetness. Cover and leave in a cool place until required, then tuck in a few mint leaves, and serve, if you like, with biscuits. Avoid cream as it muddies the flavour – unless they happen to know the recipe, none of your guests will be able to tell what flavours the delicious juice.

## COMPOTE OF BONCHRÉTIEN PEARS

FROM *The Complete Confectioner*, by Hannah Glasse, which was first published about 1760. I had long used an adaptation of the method for our rather hard pears, leaving them to sweat in sugar in the low oven of our solid-fuel cooker. If the pears are tender, they can be cooked a little faster, but on the whole a gentle heat, especially at first, works best. Sometimes I put a vanilla pod, or some curls of lemon peel, in with the sugar as well. The orange gives a delicate, unusual flavour.

Peel and slice the pears. Drop them into a pan half-full of boiling water, acidulated with the juice of a lemon (prevents discolouring). Give them 2 minutes once the water has returned to the boil. Drain them and add enough sugar to cover; stew gently until tender either on top of the stove or in a slow oven – in either case keep the lid on the pan, or cover with foil. When cooked, squeeze orange juice over the pears and leave them to cool.

## Soyer's Orange Salad

Another recipe from Soyer's *Shilling Cookery for the People*. In the 1850s oranges were not as widely eaten as they are now, especially by the poor: even in my childhood, it was a Christmas treat at Sunday school for the children to be given an orange and a small bar of chocolate.

For 6

*6 thin-skinned oranges*
*125 g (4 oz) sugar*
*150 ml (¼ pt) Madeira, rum or brandy*

Scrub and dry the oranges, then slice them thinly. Discard the thick ends and the pips. Arrange the slices on a serving dish (preferably pink for the contrast), and scatter with the sugar, then the alcohol. Cover and chill for several hours.

## Mangoes of the Sun

This makes a light dessert after some of the heavier English meat dishes, jugged hare, oxtail and so on. Passion fruit and lime rather than lemon is used to bring out the flavour of the mangoes.

For 6

*4-5 large ripe mangoes*
*5 passion fruit*
*Sugar*
*Lime divided into ⅔ and ⅓*

Slice down either side of the mango stones, then slice and peel the halves. Arrange them on a shallow dish in a single layer, with pieces cut neatly from the central slice enclosing the stone.

Halve and scoop out the passion fruit seeds into a small pan. Add 125 ml (4 fl oz) water and a tablespoon of sugar. Put over a low heat, stirring occasionally, until hot but nowhere near boiling. The point is to free the pips from their enclosing pulp without ruining the taste of the fruit. Push through a sieve, add extra sugar to taste if needed, and a squeeze of juice from ⅓ lime. Incorporate some of the black seeds from the sieve and pour over the mangoes.

Cut the larger piece of lime into slices, halve them and halve again so that you end up with lime triangles. Dot them about on the mangoes.

NOTE: you can serve this with shortbread or other thin biscuits, or with the coconut cream on page 252, if you want a more substantial dessert.

## WORCESTERSHIRE PEAR SOUFFLÉ

For 4

*2 macaroons*
*1 large ripe pear*
*Juice ½ lemon*
*1 tablespoon kirsch or William pear brandy (optional)*
*125 g (4 oz) butter*
*125 g (4 oz) vanilla sugar (page 371-2)*
*30 g (1 oz) cornflour*
*4 egg yolks*
*4 egg whites*

FIRST prepare a 1½ litre (2½ pt) soufflé dish, or Pyrex dish, or charlotte mould, by greasing it with a buttered paper, and shaking round it one crushed macaroon so that the crumbs form an even coating with the butter. Crush the other macaroon and keep it for the top of the soufflé.

Peel, core and chop the pear to a juicy mash. Mix in lemon, and alcohol if used. Put the butter in a basin, set it over a pan of almost simmering water and stir until it's melted. Sieve the sugar and cornflour together (if you are not using any alcohol, the *concentrated* vanilla is best). Tip it into the butter and stir to a thick buttery mass. Remove basin from heat and whisk in the egg yolks one by one. Then add the chopped pear and its juices. Beat the egg whites until they are stiff; mix a tablespoon of the whites vigorously into the egg and pear, then fold in the rest with a metal spoon – the best way of doing this is to scoop the whites on to the soufflé base, then to scrape up gently from the bottom of the basin, turning it with every scrape of the spoon.

Turn the final mixture into the soufflé dish. Sprinkle the top with the remaining macaroon crumbs. Bake at mark 6, 200°C (400°F), for 3 minutes, then reduce the heat to mark 5, 190°C (375°F). Allow 30 minutes in all, and do not on any account open the oven door before 20 minutes has gone by.

## MRS BEETON'S CHOCOLATE SOUFFLÉ

For 4

*4 egg yolks*
*3 heaped teaspoons caster sugar*
*1 heaped teaspoon of flour*
*90 g (3 oz) plain chocolate, grated*
*4 egg whites, stiffly whipped*
*Extra caster sugar*

BEAT the first four ingredients together well. Fold in the egg whites. Pour into a greased cake tin and bake at mark 5, 190°C (375°F), for 20 minutes. Pin a white napkin round the tin quickly, sprinkle the top of the soufflé with caster sugar and serve immediately. Cream goes well with this soufflé, which should be taken straight from oven to table before it falls.

## BAKED ALMOND PUDDING I

For 4-6

*125 g (4 oz) butter*
*250 g (8 oz) ground almonds*
*5 bitter almonds, or a few drops of bitter almond essence (from German delicatessen shop and Culpepper's)*
*2 tablespoons double cream*
*1 tablespoon brandy*
*4-5 heaped tablespoons sugar*
*2 egg yolks*
*2 eggs*

MELT the butter, pour it into a bowl, and add the remaining ingredients in the order given. Grease a shallow pie dish or Pyrex dish with a butter paper, ladle in the mixture and bake at mark 5, 190°C (375°F), for about 45 minutes. The time will depend on the depth of the mixture; allow room for it to rise a little. The surface will brown lightly and acquire that appetizing baked almond crust. Serve with sugar, butter and a sweet wine or sherry.

A FIRM, cake-like pudding with a 'sad' centre and crisp outside. If you want to make it go further, bake it in a sweet shortcrust.

## BAKED ALMOND PUDDING II

For 4-6

*125 g (4 oz) butter*
*125 g (4 oz) ground almonds*
*4 bitter almonds or almond essence (see above)*
*4 large eggs*
*Finely grated zest and juice of ½ a lemon*
*1 glass sweet sherry, or other similar wine*
*125 g (4 oz) sugar*
*600 ml (1 pt) single cream or half cream/half milk, plus 30 g (1 oz) breadcrumbs*

MELT the butter, and add other ingredients. Bake as above. This pudding, being of the custard type, is best when the centre part stays rather liquid to provide its own sauce. Aim to have the mixture 4 cm (at least 1½") deep. A marvellous pudding.

## BAKED RICE PUDDING

I AM A RECENT CONVERT TO RICE PUDDING. All our childhood, my sister and I were carefully shielded from the horrors that my mother had had to eat at the same age. This meant that rice, sago and tapioca pudding hit us with full institutional force when we were sent to boarding school in wartime (shielding children from the realities of life often ends disastrously). For twenty-five years the thought of milk puddings made me queasy. Then a while ago, an American friend made us eat 'quick' tapioca – it was delicious. And not long afterwards, passing through Normandy, we saw some puddings with a rich dark skin on top, in a pastry-cook's shop in Isigny. It turned out that they were nothing more nor less than rice puddings – known locally as *terregoule*, which seems to mean 'mud in the throat'. The look and smell belied the name, and as soon as we got home, I set to work. Three conclusions – a rice pudding must be flavoured with a vanilla pod or cinnamon stick, it must be cooked long and slowly, it must be eaten with plenty of double cream. Like so many other English dishes, it has been wrecked by meanness and lack of thought.

*75 g (2½ oz) round pudding rice*
*About 1 litre (1½-2 pts) Channel Island milk*
*30 g (1 oz) butter*
*2 tablespoons sugar*
*1 vanilla pod, split, or 1 cinnamon stick*

PUT the rice with just over half the milk and the remaining ingredients into a heat-proof stoneware or glass dish. Leave in a gentle oven, mark 1, 140°C (275°F), for 3 hours. After 1 hour, stir up the pudding and add more milk to slacken the mixture. After 2 hours, do the same thing again and, if you like, add some single cream. Butter and cream are what form the delicious skin. Serve with a jug of double cream.

If you reduce the heat, say, to mark ½, 120°C (250°F), or even lower, you can leave the rice pudding in the oven for twice as long. Add more milk occasionally; you may need 1½ litres (2½ pts). Beneath the crust, the rice will caramelize slightly to an appetizing brown.

SOME PEOPLE add currants or sultanas to rice pudding, but I find this distasteful. Another way of enriching the pudding is to make it fairly liquid, and then finally to beat it up with 2 whole eggs and 2 egg yolks. Another 10 minutes in the oven, and you have quite a different pudding, a knobbly yellow custard.

## BAKED SEMOLINA PUDDING

*60 g (2 oz) semolina*
*Scant litre (1½ pts) milk*
*Pinch salt*
*2 tablespoons sugar*
*Vanilla pod*
*2 large eggs*
*Extra sugar*

MIX semolina with a little of the milk to make a smooth paste. Bring the rest to the boil with the salt, sugar and vanilla pod; do this slowly. When the milk is boiling, tip it into the semolina paste, working it in well to avoid lumps. Turn this mixture back into the pan and simmer gently for about 5 or 10 minutes until the mixture is thick. Remove it from the heat, and whisk in the egg yolks, then fold in the stiffly beaten whites. Pour it into a buttered dish and bake for 20 minutes in the oven at mark 5, 190°C (375°F), until the top is brown and the pudding set. Do not remove the vanilla pod – it can be rescued later for washing and drying.

## BAKED GOOSEBERRY PUDDING

A GOOD HOMELY PUDDING to make when the gooseberries first come in.

*60 g (2 oz) butter*
*4 tablespoons pale soft brown sugar*
*Gooseberries*
*Pound cake mixture (page 314)*
*Granulated sugar*

MELT butter and sugar together in the bottom of a soufflé or Pyrex dish (or use a crockpot type of electric cooker). Put in a tight-fitting layer of topped and tailed gooseberries. Over this spread the pound cake mixture. Bake for about an hour at mark 4, 180°C (350°F), or a little longer, until the top is nicely browned. Towards the end of cooking time remove the pudding, sprinkle it with granulated sugar, and return to the oven for 5 minutes or until cooked. Serve with plenty of cream, and put a bowl of sugar on the table in case the gooseberries were especially tart.

## STICKY TOFFEE PUDDING

THIS PUDDING IS SO POPULAR, and is now on so many menus, that I am afraid its originator may be forgotten. It was Francis Coulson who in 1948 opened his establishment at Sharrow Bay on Ullswater. In those grey post-war days, the rich luxury of the cooking was a revelation of pleasure and gourmandise, as was the whole style of the place. I would think it correct to say that he opened the first country house hotel, naming the category far ahead of any other hotelier and chef. I think, too, that he was the first to put hairdriers in every room, to the delight of his female clients.

If you had grown up, as I had, among people who thought it was a sin and a wicked waste to use butter and cream in cookery, his dishes shouted rebellion. With George Perry-Smith at the Hole in the Wall, and Kenneth Bell at the Elizabethan (in Oxford), he was a true revolutionary. His fortieth anniversary was celebrated with joy in 1988 by many friends and with good wishes from all over the world. This pudding is very much within the English tradition, but it is very specially in Mr Coulson's style as well.

*175 g (6 oz) dates, stoned, chopped*
*1 level teaspoon bicarbonate of soda*
*60 g (2 oz) butter*
*175 g (6 oz) caster sugar*
*2 eggs*
*175 g (6 oz) self-raising flour*
*½ teaspoon pure vanilla essence*

SAUCE
*200 g (7 oz) soft brown sugar*
*6 tablespoons double cream*
*140 g (4½ oz) butter*
*½ teaspoon pure vanilla essence*

GREASE an 18 cm (7") loose-bottomed square cake tin with butter. Switch on the oven to mark 4, 180°C (350°F).

Put dates into a pan, pour on 300 ml (½ pt) boiling water and bring to the boil. Remove from stove, stir in bicarbonate of soda and leave to stand.

Cream butter and sugar, add eggs bit by bit. Fold in the flour, then the dates and their juice, plus the essence. Pour into the tin and bake for 30-40 minutes.

Meanwhile, make the sauce by mixing the ingredients and bringing them to the boil, then simmering 3 minutes. Pour some of the sauce over the cooked pudding, put it back into the oven for the sauce to be absorbed and bubble to a nice golden brown. Serve cut in squares, with the rest of the sauce in a separate jug.

## SUSSEX POND PUDDING

THE BEST OF ALL ENGLISH BOILED SUET PUDDINGS. In the middle the butter and sugar melt to a rich sauce, which is sharpened with the juice from the lemon. The genius of the pudding is the lemon. Its citrus bitter flavour is a subtlety which raises the pudding to the highest class. When you serve it, make sure that everyone has a piece of the lemon, which will be much softened by the cooking, but still vigorous.

Once when I had no lemons, I used a couple of small limes, which were equally successful.

The name of the pudding refers to the sauce, which runs out of it, when it is turned on to a serving dish, and provides it with a moat of buttery brown liquid.

For 4-6

*250 g (8 oz) self-raising flour*
*125 g (4 oz) chopped fresh beef suet*
*Milk and water*
*Slightly salted butter*
*Soft light brown or caster sugar*
*1 large lemon, or 2 limes*

MIX the flour and suet together in a bowl. Make into a dough with milk and water, half and half; about 150 ml (¼ pt). The dough should be soft, but not too soft to roll out into a large circle. Cut a quarter out of this circle, to be used later as the lid of the pudding. Butter a pudding basin lavishly. It should hold about 1½ litres (2½ pts). Drop the three-quarter-circle of pastry into it and press the cut sides together to make a perfect join. Put about 100 g (3⅓ oz) each of butter, cut up, and sugar into the pastry. Prick the lemon (or limes) all over with a larding needle, so that the juices will be able to escape, then put it on to the butter and sugar. Fill the rest of the cavity with equal weights of sugar and butter cut in pieces – at least another 100 g, possibly more. Roll out the pastry that was set aside to make a lid. Lay it on top of the filling, and press the edges together so that the pudding is sealed in completely. Put a piece of foil right over the basin, with a pleat in the middle. Tie it in place with string, and make a string handle over the top so that the pudding can be lifted about easily. Put a large pan of water on to boil, and lower the pudding into it; the water must be boiling, and it should come halfway, or a little further, up the basin. Cover and leave to boil for 3-4 hours. If the water gets low, replenish it with *boiling* water. To serve, put a deep dish over the basin after removing the foil lid, and quickly turn the whole thing upside down: it is a good idea to ease the pudding from the sides of the basin with a knife first. Put on the table immediately.

## STEAMED GINGER PUDDING

For 4

*90 g (3 oz) butter*
*90 g (3 oz) caster sugar*
*1 large or 2 small eggs*
*125 g (4 oz) self-raising flour*
*125 g (4 oz) preserved ginger, chopped*
*1 tablespoon ginger syrup*
*¼ teaspoonful ground ginger*
*A little milk*

CREAM butter and sugar until light, add the egg(s), then the flour, ginger, syrup and ground ginger. Mix to a soft cake dough with the milk. Put into a pudding basin, leaving plenty of room for the pudding to rise. Cover and steam for 2 hours. Turn out and serve with a thin egg custard sauce, or with this wine sauce:

*2 yolks of large eggs*
*Half a tablespoon sugar*
*150 ml (¼ pt) sherry*
*150 ml (¼ pt) whipping cream*

PUT the yolks, sugar and sherry into a basin. Whisk them together, then stand the basin over a pan of just simmering water. Continue to whisk until it thickens, adding the cream gradually. It should be light and frothy. The snag with this kind of sauce is that it should be served immediately it is made – which leaves rather a gap in the meal while you attend it. On the other hand, it is a sauce worth waiting for.

HOMELIER VERSIONS of this pudding use 1 teaspoonful of ground ginger and 1 tablespoonful of golden syrup as a substitute for the preserved ginger and ginger syrup.

## Isle of Wight Pudding

A YEAR OR TWO AGO NOW, Granada's *On the Market* programme ran a competition for little-known regional recipes. A particularly good pudding came from Mrs Suzanne Whitewood of Newport, Isle of Wight. She had it from her grandmother-in-law, who used to make it with her own butter or lard, locally milled flour and blackberries from the hedgerows. I daresay the honey came from her own or her neighbour's bees. It's a lovely old-fashioned pudding that can equally well be made with blueberries, currants (red, white and black) or gooseberries.

*250 g (8 oz) unbleached plain flour*
*125 g (4 oz) butter or lard, or the two mixed*
*250 g (8 oz) blackberries or other fruit*
*125 ml (4 fl oz) runny honey*
*125 ml (4 fl oz) half cream, top of the milk or single cream*

SIFT the flour, rub in the fat and mix to a dough with a little very cold or iced water. Chill for 30 minutes or more.

Switch on the oven to mark 6, 200°C (400°F). Pick over the fruit, washing it only if necessary. Warm the honey very slightly so that it will be easy to spread, but not too liquid.

Roll out the dough into an oblong. Spread it with the honey, scatter on the fruit and roll up as for a roly-poly. Rub an oblong, ovenproof dish with a butter paper. Press the ends of the roll together and lift it into the dish. Pour the cream or top of the milk over the whole thing and bake for 45-60 minutes. A most delicious juice emerges. Serve with Jersey cream.

## Richard Boston's Guinness Christmas Pudding

WHEN RICHARD BOSTON WAS WRITING for the *Guardian*, this recipe proved so popular that he was obliged to repeat it as an annual event. Then at last he published it more permanently in his book *Beer and Skittles*, in 1976. I am not a pudding enthusiast, but I do quite like this one, and feel that the book is not complete without a recipe for such a national institution.

| | |
|---|---|
| *300 g (10 oz) fresh breadcrumbs* | *½ level teaspoon salt* |
| *250 g (8 oz) soft brown sugar* | *1 level teaspoon mixed spice* |
| *250 g (8 oz) currants* | *Grated rind of a lemon* |
| *300 g (10 oz) chopped seeded raisins* | *1 dessertspoon lemon juice* |
| *250 g (8 oz) sultanas* | *2 large eggs, beaten* |
| *60 g (2 oz) chopped mixed peel* | *150 ml (¼ pt) milk* |
| *300 g (10 oz) shredded suet* | *300 ml (½ pt) bottled Guinness* |

MIX the dry ingredients in a large bowl, then put in the liquids. It is traditional to stir such things with a wooden spoon, but I find hands are quicker and make a more efficient mixture.

Divide between one 1 litre (2 pts) and one 1¾ litre (3 pts) well-buttered pudding basins. Cover tightly with greaseproof paper and foil. Leave them overnight, then steam for 7½ hours. Cool, re-cover and store in a cool place, or freeze.

When you want to serve them, steam for a further 2-3 hours, or even longer of the puddings have come out of the freezer. Serve with rum or brandy butter.

The mixture will provide enough for 12 people, even more if the puddings come at the end of Christmas dinner.

## GINGER ICE CREAM

I THINK THAT GINGER ICE CREAM is very much a Christmas-time pudding, even a substitute for plum pudding. Those tubby porcelain and decorated jars of preserved ginger, often suspended by their rush lattice nets from the beams of old-fashioned grocery stores, are as much a sign of the season as tangerines and nuts. For those who are likely to suffer from too-much-ness, I offer a comforting thought from Dioscorides, the great Greek herbalist of the first century A.D., who still influences some odd corners of our minds: he recommends ginger, for it has 'a warming, concocting power, mollifying of the belly gently, and good for the stomach'.

Preserved ginger, which comes mainly from China, is the young rhizome, succulent, green, not yet fibrous, of *Zingiber officinale,* which is native to South-East Asia, but is now grown throughout the tropics (much of our powdered ginger comes from the West Indies; so do the 'hands' of fresh root ginger which can be bought at the best greengrocers these days, and those dry, whitish bits of 'root' ginger used in pickling and chutney-making).

There is one extraordinary fact about ginger – not its ancient use, or even its universal importance (second only to pepper), but the persistence of its name. The words *singi vera,* meaning horn stem, were borrowed into Sanskrit from the Dravidian languages which were spoken in India before the Indo-

Aryan invasions of about 1200 B.C. (and it seems that the Dravidian languages had it from South-East Asia where ginger is native). From India the name travelled west by two routes: via Greek and Latin *(Zingiber)* into Europe, and via Persian and Arabic into Africa, so that even the Swahili word is similar to ours.

For 6-8

*300 ml (½ pt) milk or single cream*
*2 egg yolks*
*1 egg*
*4 tablespoons ginger syrup*
*100 g (3-4 oz) preserved ginger, chopped*
*300 ml (½ pt) double cream, whipped*
*2 tablespoons icing or soft brown sugar*

BRING the milk or cream to the boil and pour it on to the yolks and egg very gradually, beating the whole thing together (small wire whisks are the best for this kind of operation). Return to the pan and cook slowly over a low heat until the custard thickens: it must not boil or the egg will curdle. Immediately the thickness seems right, dip the base of the pan into a bowl of very cold water. This prevents the mixture continuing to cook in its own heat. Add the ginger syrup immediately after this, to hurry further the cooling process. If I sound fussy, I apologize, but even after 20 years' experience with custards things can go wrong, and one may as well minimize the risks. Taste and add extra ginger syrup, if you like.

Place this mixture in the freezing compartment of the refrigerator, which should be set at the coldest possible temperature. When it has set solid round the edges, remove it to a bowl, stir it up well and quickly incorporate the ginger pieces and whipped cream. Taste and add sugar gradually – ices should not be too sickly-sweet, mainly on account of the flavour, but also because an oversweetened mixture freezes less well.

Return to the freezer and leave until hard. If the custard was frozen to the right amount before the ginger and cream was added, it should not be necessary to stir it at all during the second freezing process. If there was any doubt about this, stir it up gently after an hour, so that the ginger pieces do not sink to the bottom.

NOTE: jockey or other *fromage frais* can be substituted for half the double cream.

## VANILLA ICE WITH PLUM SAUCE AND LACE BISCUITS

MAKE UP A VANILLA ICE CREAM MIXTURE following the previous recipe, but omitting the ginger and ginger syrup, and including a vanilla pod when you bring the milk or cream to the boil. Leave the vanilla pod in the custard until it has thickened, then strain it out and freeze according to the instructions for whatever machine or freezer you are using. For the sauce and biscuits you will need:

SAUCE

*750 g (1½ lb) ripe plums*
*250 g (8 oz) sugar*
*A little port, Kirsch, gin or other appropriate spirit*

BISCUITS

*75 g (2½ oz) butter*
*75 g (2½ oz) rolled porridge oats*
*125 g (4 oz) caster sugar*
*1 egg*
*1 teaspoon each of flour and baking powder, mixed*

FOR the sauce, run a thin layer of water into a non-reactive pan and slice the plums into it, discarding the stones. Cook gently, stirring at first to prevent sticking. Purée in a blender for preference, or a processor, and sieve. Meanwhile in a separate pan dissolve the sugar with 4-5 tablespoons of water over a low heat. Stop stirring, raise heat and boil until you have a beautiful golden-brown caramel. Remove from the stove and gradually stir in about 6 tablespoons of water – be careful, as the caramel will spit and burn you, unless you work slowly. Once it has calmed down, put the pan back over the heat to dissolve the lumpiness. Add the plum purée, mixing thoroughly, take off the heat and cool to tepid before adding alcohol.

For the biscuits, set the oven to mark 4, 180°C (350°F). Grease two baking sheets and a rolling pin.

Melt the butter in a wide pan, until it is just liquid. Draw off the heat, and stir in the oats, sugar, flour and baking powder. Beat in the egg. Drop dessertspoons of the mixture on to the baking sheets at 5 cm (2 in) intervals. Bake, one sheet at a time, for 8-10 minutes until golden brown. Quickly lift off the sheets while still hot, and lay over the rolling pin pressing down gently to curve round the pin. After a few minutes, they will have set hard enough to transfer to a wire rack to finish cooling.

## BROWN BREAD ICE CREAM

AFTER TOO MUCH EXPERIENCE OF CREAMLESS ICE CREAMS, we were startled one day in our small village in France by the hotel-keeper's wife. She had spent a holiday in England during the thirties, as a child. 'It was marvellous,' she said. 'Your ice creams are so wonderful. We have nothing like them here. I remember at Gunter's . . .' We bowed our heads over an especially good coffee ice cream that she had made herself, and kept quiet as her memories wafted round the room. A year or two later, I managed to buy a copy of *Gunter's Modern Confectioner* of 1861. I see what she meant, and think of her every time I use it. This recipe in particular was popular in the nineteenth century, and has recently had a revival – which I imagine we owe to the excellent wholemeal bread now on sale in so many bakers' shops. The original recipe made no use of eggs or rum, it was just brown breadcrumbs, syrup and cream, but I think this version gives a lighter result and it needs no attention while freezing.

For 6-8

*175 g (6 oz) wholemeal breadcrumbs*
*300 ml (½ pt) double cream*
*300 ml (½ pt) single cream*
*125 g (4 oz) icing sugar, or pale brown sugar*
*2 egg yolks*
*1 tablespoon rum (optional)*
*2 egg whites*

SPREAD the breadcrumbs out on a baking tray and toast in a moderately hot oven. They should become crisp and slightly browned. Meanwhile beat the creams with the sugar. Mix the yolks and rum, if used, and add to the cream mixture, beating it in well. When the breadcrumbs are cool, fold them in gently and thoroughly, so that they are evenly distributed. Lastly, whip the whites of the eggs stiff and fold into the mixture. Freeze in the usual way, at the lowest temperature. There is no need to stir up this ice cream.

## SOFT FRUIT ICE CREAM

THE GRATED ORANGE PEEL and juice make all the difference to an otherwise quite ordinary soft fruit ice cream. Alcohol helps, too. If you do not have any orange liqueurs or fruit brandy, try gin. I find it a very present help in trouble. Dutch genever is even better. Whisky, brandy, Calvados are all too strong in flavour. Cherries, apricots, peaches should be stoned before weighing.

*500 g (1 lb) prepared fruit*
*1 orange*
*Icing sugar*
*300 ml (½ pt) double cream*
*150 ml (¼ pt) single cream*
*2 egg whites*
*3 tablespoons kirsch, framboise, orange liqueur or gin*

LIQUIDIZE the fruit with the thinly cut zest of the orange, its juice and 125 g (4 oz) icing sugar. Sieve out any seeds or skin that seem too intrusive. A certain graininess gives the ice character, but most people do not appreciate raspberry seeds, for instance.

Whip the creams together, with 2 tablespoons of icing sugar, until stiff, and fold in the fruit. Taste and adjust sugar. Add more orange juice, or if you like a little lemon juice, to bring out the flavour of the fruit; this is very much a matter of your own judgement, as the flavour of fruit varies so much according to variety and season. Freeze at the lowest possible temperature, or in an ice cream machine.

When it is almost completely frozen, but still slightly liquid in the centre, whisk the egg whites with an electric beater until stiff, then add in table-spoons of ice cream to make a foamy bulk. Be careful not to over-whip, so that the ice cream melts too much. Flavour with the alcohol. Put to freeze again.

## MELON WATER ICE

THE ENGLISH BECAME ADVENTUROUS GARDENERS in the sixteenth century, and many tried, without great success, to grow melons. Few of them attained perfection, as John Parkinson observed (he was apothecary to King James I, and dedicated his famous gardening book, *Paradisi in sole,* to Queen Henrietta Maria – the wife of Charles I – the title is a pun on his name). Melons were eaten then with pepper and salt, and with plenty of wine because everyone was nervous of their effect on the stomach. Catherine de'Medici, Queen-mother of France from 1559 to 1588, once complained of feeling unwell to the Queen of Navarre, and received the sharp retort that it was no wonder, seeing how many melons she ate.

In spite of the climate and nervous digestions, the English persisted and now there are a number of hardy varieties which can be raised under glass in this country. We still eat them with pepper sometimes, or ginger, or with port, though we have forgotten why, and do so because such seasonings bring out the flavour and emphasize the melon's coolness.

*125 g (4 oz) sugar*
*300 ml (½ pt) water*
*300 ml (½ pt) liquidized melon pulp*
*Lemon juice*
*1 large egg white*

SIMMER sugar and water for 4 minutes to make a syrup. Cool, then add gradually to the melon until the mixture tastes sweet enough – this will depend on the variety of melon used, and on its ripeness. If the mixture tastes too sweet, it can be diluted with a little water.

Add lemon juice to bring out the flavour. Freeze at the lowest possible temperature, in the usual way. When the mixture is just firm, whip the egg white until stiff with an electric beater and add the ice to it spoonful by spoonful. It should blow up into a foamy mass. Re-freeze. The mixture can be spooned into the emptied melon skins for serving.

THIS RECIPE can be adapted for other fruit water ices. If you wish, alcohol can be added when you whisk in the whites – a great improver.

# Teatime

CAKES HAVE COME WITH TEA, OR TEA WITH CAKES – on balance probably the first. At any rate the afternoon tea habit became universal in the upper and middle classes after the discovery of the Indian tea plant in Assam in the 1820s (Chinese varieties not having succeeded in India). Tea needs its light accompaniment – cucumber sandwiches for Lady Bracknell – but also something sweet, in spite of what Oscar Wilde's Gwendolen might have to say. And then conveniently, raising powders made their appearance.

A really effective raising powder was developed in America in the mid-1850s. So the light cake and the light scone and the light griddle or girdle cake were born, and the old yeast confections – delightful as they were, and are, if one troubles to make them – were reduced to muffins, teacakes and such regional survivals as the lardy cakes of Wiltshire and Gloucestershire and the saffron cake of West Devon and Cornwall.

Cake-making had originally come into existence as a fanciful sideline of breadmaking. The dough of flour raised with yeast was made more agreeable, a pleasure for the end of a meal perhaps, by the addition of sugar, fruit, spice and caraway seeds. Then it was made even lighter and more spongy with eggs, which have their own raising power. Paradoxically, it is now much easier to bake with yeast than when yeast cakes were going strong. Through much of the nineteenth century the most available yeast was ale barm, not modern compressed yeast which is so easy to use. The difficulty was to keep the ale barm going from week to week in sufficient quantity for the next baking. Eighteenth-century books of household management are full of lengthy advice on this matter. By the time that compressed yeast could be bought, self-raising powder had triumphed in most English kitchens, and then the self-raising flours (in France where cakes are not often made at home, they still add baking powder to ordinary flour).

In the past I think that cake very often meant seed cake, that is cake flavoured with caraway seeds. Manuscript recipe books of the early eighteenth century nearly always have their seed cake recipes. Of course they were made with yeast, but at their best I suppose they could have been as light as French brioche.

Biscuits, too, were an adjunct to the baking process, the baker making use of the last heat of the oven – the kind of brick or clay oven that was heated by lighting faggot wood inside. Early biscuits were rusks, in other words bread, yesterday's bread, baked a second time – hence the name *biscuit,* twice cooked – until they were crisp, similar in style to the modern French *biscotte.* Later, biscuits became, and have remained, some of the best of manufactured food. This has meant less temptation to make biscuits at home; a pity, in some ways. It's true that you have to stand over the baking, but biscuits are entertaining to make, they can be endlessly varied in texture and flavouring, and they store well. Water biscuits, Bath Olivers, crackers and the like are particularly English. They seem to be a refinement of ship's biscuits, which were made thick and baked as many as four times to discourage weevils with their hardness. The light flaky plain biscuits made in the last century in the Palladian kitchens of Mereworth Castle in Kent (page 345) have come a long way from hard tack. They are the lightest and sharpest of all our biscuits, too fragile to butter smoothly.

The American practice of making up rolls of biscuit dough and storing them in the refrigerator or deep freeze is very sensible. In any case, most biscuit doughs should be chilled when possible, and with a ready-prepared roll you can always slice off a few rounds and bake them as the need arises. But there's not much about biscuit-making that the Americans don't know.

## Electric Dough Hook Bread

One reads many articles these days about the joy of kneading bread, or taking out one's temper on some wholemeal dough. There is something to be said for this point of view, though it does have a pine-kitchen trendiness, but if you intend to supply your family 365 days of the year with home-made bread, I do recommend an electric dough hook of the kind that fits on to a Kenwood chef. Combined with a kitchen timer, it makes the whole business possible. One can get a lot of fun by varying the blends of flour; sometimes I use one-third rye flour, at other times half and half strong plain flour and wholemeal. The fats can be varied, too. Lard is traditional in England, but I prefer olive oil. Use 1 teaspoon of dried yeast for white flour, 2 teaspoons for mixed flours which tend to be heavier.

*2 level teaspoons dried yeast*
*1 level teaspoon sugar*
*500 ml (¾ pt) water at blood heat, i.e. no higher than 100°F*
*2-3 level teaspoons sea salt*
*4 level tablespoons fat or oil*
*750 g (1½ lb) strong plain flour, or strong plain flour mixed with other flours*
*Milk*

PUT yeast, sugar and half the water into the bowl of the mixer, whisk with a fork, and leave for 10 minutes in a warm place. Add the salt and fat to the rest of the water, and stir to dissolve.

When the yeast has turned to a creamy cushion, add the flour and salty water, and mix with the dough hook – at first it should be just switched on, then the speed can be raised to 2, and 3, until the dough has left the sides of the bowl and adheres in a muff to the hook. If it is flicking about, add a little more flour. It is best not to over-knead the dough, whatever the instruction book may say.

Disentangle the dough from the hook, smooth it into a round ball and cover the bowl over with a sheet of plastic held in place with a rubber band. Put in the warm (the rack over a solid fuel or oil-fired cooker is ideal) and leave for about an hour; white dough will double in bulk in about 45 minutes, heavier mixtures with wholemeal flour can do with 1¼ hours. If you have to leave the dough in a cooler place, say on the kitchen table, you will have to allow longer. Dough will even rise in the refrigerator if you give it long enough, so never panic. You rapidly find out how long it takes in your particular circumstances.

When the dough is puffed up, use the electric dough hook to break it down and re-form it. This takes a second or two only. You can do it with your hand if you like. I find that the first kneading is all the dough requires. Weigh out 500 g of dough, or 1 lb, and form it into a roll that will fit into a small loaf tin. Do the same with the rest, and put it into a 23 cm (9") loaf tin. Put back in a warm place to prove, covering lightly with a piece of plastic, humping it up over the tins, so that it will not get caught in the rising dough. Leave for 30-45 minutes, though again this depends on the flour used, until the dough rises more or less to the top of the tins.

Bake for 30 minutes at mark 8, 230°C (450°F). Remove and turn the loaves upside down, put back into the tins and bake for another 5 minutes to harden the underneath and side crusts.

Turn the loaves right-side up again, brush over the tops with a little milk to make them shiny. Stand across the tins to cool.

## GRANARY BREAD WITH WALNUTS

'GRANARY' IS REALLY A PROPRIETARY NAME for the malted flour produced by one miller, but people have come to use it loosely for all bread of this type, rather as the word hoover covers various makes of cleaner. It is quite a recent speciality, but the malted and moist consistency of the bread has made it a great favourite. 'Granary' flour or meal consists of a blend of wheatmeal, rye, malted wheat and whole cracked wheat grains to give what Elizabeth David calls a 'real' look. It can be bought at health food stores, if your local grocer or supermarket does not stock it. Adding walnuts makes it extra interesting to eat, and a happy vehicle for the new English and Scottish and Irish cheeses.

*500 g (1 lb) 'Granary' flour*
*125 g (4 oz) unbleached white bread flour, or strong white bread flour*
*Packet fast action dried yeast (McDougall's or Harvest Gold)*
*2 teaspoons fine sea salt*
*2 tablespoons walnut oil*
*125 g (4 oz) shelled walnuts, coarsely chopped*

MIX flours, yeast and salt in a processor, or bowl of an electric mixer. Work to a dough with about 300 ml (½ pt) warm water. When it forms a rough ball around the blade or dough hook, add the oil.

Knead briefly, adding a little extra flour if necessary to make a smooth, soft dough. Oil a deep bowl lightly, turn the ball of dough in it and leave to rise in a warm place, covered with clingfilm. Leave until doubled in bulk, at least 1 hour but be prepared for longer. Knock down, knead in the walnuts and put into an oiled tin or tins, or shape on a baking sheet. Enclose in a plastic bag, leaving room for the dough to prove – about 30 minutes.

Preheat the oven to mark 8, 230°C (450°F). Just before baking the bread, slash it across the top with a razor, leave it a couple of minutes, then bake for 30 minutes or until it sounds hollow when tapped underneath.

Brush with milk to give a shiny top, and leave to cool across the tin or on a rack in a warm place.

## CINNAMON TOAST

IT MAY SURPRISE YOU TO KNOW that the earliest recipe I have been able to find for cinnamon toast comes from *The Accomplisht Cook* by Robert May, published in 1666. It is one of winter's delights. Nice to think we have been enjoying it for at least three hundred years.

The rather brief instructions tell you to toast the bread and top it with cinnamon mixed with sugar and claret. Warm the whole thing and serve hot.

This is what I do. Toast and butter the bread. Mix sugar with cinnamon in the proportion of a tablespoon of sugar to a teaspoon of cinnamon, and add just enough claret to make it a spreadable paste. Put on to the hot toast and heat through under the grill or in the oven.

Nowadays many people just sprinkle hot buttered toast with cinnamon sugar, but the claret does add an extra goodness.

## RICE BREAD

IN HER MAGNIFICENT BOOK *English Bread and Yeast Cookery*, Elizabeth David gives her version of rice bread. Eliza Acton and Lady Llanover recommended rice bread in the middle of the nineteenth century, and it is certainly worth reviving. Lady Llanover said it was by far the best bread for sandwiches, in particular for chicken sandwiches, and it is her proportions of rice to flour that Mrs David preferred when she worked out her recipe. The metrication is the one given in Mrs David's book.

*85 g (3 oz) uncooked, long grain rice*
*15 g (½ oz) fresh yeast*
*15-20 g (½-¾ oz) salt*
*500 g (18 oz) strong plain flour*

PUT the rice into a pan, and add twice its volume of water. Bring to simmering point and leave to cook. Cream the yeast with a very little warm water. Dissolve the salt in 150 ml (¼ pt) very hot water, then add cold to make 250 ml (8 oz). Mix the hot rice (drain off any surplus water) into the flour, add yeast and salted water and mix to rather a soft dough. Cover bowl with polythene and leave 1-1½ hours until doubled in bulk and bubbly.

Break down the dough, adding a little more flour if it is too soft to handle. Knead slightly – an electric dough hook is ideal for this recipe – and transfer to a warmed well-greased sandwich loaf tin of about 1½-2 litres capacity (3-3½ pts). Cover again with polythene or a cloth, and leave until it has risen to the top of the tin, more or less. Bake at mark 8, 230°C (450°F), for 15 minutes, then reduce to mark 6, 200°C (400°F), for 15 minutes. Take loaf from tin, turn it upside down and return to oven for 5 minutes. If the crust shows signs of baking too hard, or colouring too much, cover the whole thing with a large ovenproof bowl or casserole.

## PLUM BREAD

I FIRST CAME ACROSS THIS OLD RECIPE in Theodora Fitzgibbon's *British Cooking*, published in 1965. In more recent years it has become popular, justifiably I think. Sultanas can be substituted for the plums out of season, or any other dried fruit.

*30 g (1 oz) fresh yeast*
*3 tablespoons warmed milk*
*250 g (8 oz) flour, preferably strong plain flour*
*2 tablespoons sugar*
*Grated rind of a lemon*
*Pinch of salt*
*1 large, beaten egg*
*66 g (2 oz) melted tepid butter*
*250 g (8 oz) stoned, chopped plums, weighed after preparation*

CREAM yeast and milk, then leave about 10 minutes. In a big bowl mix flour, sugar, lemon rind and salt. Make a well in the centre, and put in the egg and butter, then the yeast. Mix thoroughly, knead (an electric dough hook can be used) and leave to rise in a warm place, covered with a piece of polythene tethered with an elastic band.

Mix in the plums, this makes the dough sticky. Place in a lined, buttered loaf tin – the 22 cm (9") size – and leave to prove for 30-40 minutes. The dough will come to about the top of the tin. Bake for a good hour at mark 5, 190°C (375°F), then remove the loaf from the tin and tap its base to see if it sounds hollow and cooked. It will probably need to be put back for another 15-30 minutes. Cool before peeling off paper.

## DORIS GRANT'S LOAF

I REMEMBER THE SENSATION THIS RECIPE CAUSED when it came out towards the end of the last war. Everybody was longing for good food, and was tired of the national loaf, which was a pale fawn colour. Here was the real thing, and it took only a few minutes to make because no kneading was required. Nowadays everyone who cares about good food takes the loaf for granted – it is just 'wholemeal bread', and every member of the family can produce it successfully once they can read and measure. Doris Grant has been associated with food reform in Britain for over thirty years, but whether you share her preoccupations or not you will enjoy this superb bread. It goes particularly well with shellfish and smoked salmon.

*1½ kilos (3 lb) stone-ground wholemeal flour*
*2 teaspoons salt*
*3 tablespoons water at blood-heat (98-100°F)*
*3 level teaspoons dried yeast*
*3 rounded teaspoons Barbados sugar, honey or black molasses*
*1¼ litres (2 pts) water at blood-heat*

MIX the flour and salt. If the weather or your kitchen is very cold, warm the flour slightly in a tepid oven. Put the water into a bowl, sprinkle on the yeast and whisk it until it has dissolved. Add the sugar, honey or molasses. Leave the mixture to froth up – this takes about 15 minutes. Pour into the centre of the flour, and add the water gradually, mixing well by hand until the dough leaves the side of the mixing bowl, and feels elastic. It will be a little more slithery than a normal white flour dough, but this doesn't matter as this wholemeal dough does not require kneading. Divide it between three warmed and greased loaf tins. Cover the tins and put them in a warm place for 30 minutes, so that the dough can rise to within half an inch of the rim of the tins. Bake at mark 6, 200°C (400°F), for 40 minutes.

## Northumbrian Wholemeal Scones

*700 g (1½ lb) stone-ground wholemeal flour*
*1 teaspoon salt*
*66 g (2 oz) lard*
*1 tablespoon golden syrup*
*3 tablespoons very hot water*
*150 ml (¼ pt) milk*
*150 ml (¼ pt) boiling water*
*30 g (1 oz) yeast*

SIEVE flour and salt into a basin, and rub in the lard. Make a well in the middle. Melt the syrup in the water. Mix the milk and boiling water, and add a little of this to the syrup so that there is about a teacupful. Into the syrup and milk, fork the yeast. Leave it to work for 10 or 15 minutes. When it is creaming and frothy, tip it into the flour, plus the remaining milk and hot water – go slowly with this, as you need a fairly soft but not sloppy dough. On the other hand you may need to add extra milk and water – if you add boiling water to the milk in equal quantity, you will end up with the right blood temperature of 37°C (98.4°F).

Leave to rise until doubled in volume. This should be done in a draught-free place; temperature doesn't matter – dough will rise in a refrigerator, it merely takes longer. Roll out the risen dough on a floured board, and cut out rounds with a scone cutter. Leave to rise again, to 'prove', for another 30 minutes, then brush with milk and bake in a hot oven, mark 7, 220°C (425°F), for 20 minutes. Eat hot with plenty of butter, honey, or a savoury mixture of chopped hardboiled eggs and parsley.

## Basic Bun Dough

UNTIL YOU MAKE SPICED HOT CROSS BUNS yourself, or well-sugared Chelsea buns, it is difficult to understand why they should have become popular.

Bought, they taste so dull. Modern commerce has taken them over, and, in the interests of cheapness, reduced the delicious ingredients to a minimum – no butter, little egg, too much yellow colouring, not enough spice, too few currants and bits of peel, a stodgy texture instead of a rich, light softness. In other words, buns are now a doughy filler for children.

*500 g (1 lb) strong plain flour*
*¼ teaspoon salt*
*30 g (1 oz) fresh yeast*
*60 g (2 oz) caster sugar*
*150 ml (¼ pt) milk*
*150 ml (¼ pt) boiling water*
*90 g (3 oz) butter*
*1 egg lightly beaten*

PUT flour and salt into a large warmed mixing bowl. Crumble the yeast into a pudding basin, add 1 heaped spoonful of the sugar and 125 g (4 oz) of flour from the bowl. Pour the milk into a measuring jug, and make up the 250 ml (8 oz) of liquid with boiling water straight from the kettle. With a wooden spoon mix this hot liquid into the yeast, flour and sugar – go slowly so as to make as smooth a batter as possible: leave it in a warm place to rise and froth up – this takes about 15 minutes, or a little longer. Meanwhile mix the rest of the sugar with the flour, and rub in the butter. Form a well in the centre, put in the egg and the frothy yeast mixture. Mix to a dough with a wooden spoon. Turn it out on to a floury surface and knead for 10 minutes, adding more flour as required, until the dough is a coherent, slightly rubbery ball, with a moderately tacky, but not sticky, texture. Any dough on your fingers should rub off easily.

Wash, dry and grease the large mixing bowl with a piece of butter paper. Place the dough in it. Cover it with a damp cloth, or put the whole thing inside an oiled polythene bag. Leave to rise to double its quantity. This can take anything from 1 to 12 hours depending on the temperature.

Now the dough can be used in various ways:

## CHELSEA BUNS

*Basic bun dough (see above)*
*60 g (2 oz) melted butter*
*90 g (3 oz) dark brown sugar*
*90 g (3 oz) raisins*
*60 g (2 oz) candied peel*
*Beaten egg*
*Bun wash (page 308)*
*Extra caster sugar*

BREAK down the risen dough, and roll it out on a floured surface to a large oblong about 30 × 45 cm (12″ × 18″). Brush the butter over it. Sprinkle on the sugar evenly, then the fruit and peel. Starting with one of the long sides, roll up the dough fairly tightly. Cut it down into 18 pieces. Place these coiled pieces side by side in one or two well-greased oblong tins, 2-3 cm (1") deep, leaving 1 cm (½") between them, and between them and the sides of the tins. Brush the buns over with egg, and leave them to prove for 15-30 minutes. Bake as above. The buns should rise and come together, so that when they are eventually separated the sides have a characteristically torn white appearance, which contrasts with the sticky brown, sugared top. However, leave them to cool down in the tin before doing this.

While the buns are still hot, brush them over with bun-wash and sprinkle them with sugar.

THE BEST of all buns, on account of their buttery melting sweetness, and the fun of uncoiling them as you eat them.

## HOT CROSS BUNS

*Basic bun dough (page 304)*
*1 level teaspoon ground cinnamon*
*1 level teaspoon ground nutmeg*
*1 level teaspoon mixed spice*
*½ teaspoon ground mace*
*90 g (3 oz) raisins*
*60 g (2 oz) candied chopped peel*
*60 g (2 oz) almond paste or shortcrust pastry*
*Beaten egg*
*Bun wash (page 308)*

WHEN making the basic bun dough, mix the spices in with the flour at the beginning. Break down the risen dough, knead in the fruit and peel. Roll the dough into a long sausage shape on a floured surface, and cut it down into 18 discs. Shape them into round buns, and then place them on baking sheets lined with Bakewell paper – leave them plenty of room to rise and spread in the baking. Roll out the almond paste or shortcrust pastry and cut it into thin strips. Brush the buns with beaten egg and lay 2 strips on each bun to form a cross. Leave the buns to prove about 30 minutes; then bake them for 10-15 minutes at mark 8, 230°C (450°F). While the buns are still hot, brush them over with bun-wash.

To reheat, give the buns 10 minutes in a moderate oven – mark 3-4, 160-180°C(325-350°F).

## MRS BORTHWICK'S YORKSHIRE TEACAKES

A READER NOW LIVING NEAR Chester-le-Street sent me this recipe, with the following note, after reading the hot cross bun recipe above:

*'We always made 8, one for each evening's supper for Father, and one to give away or toast. We used to eat them cut down in vertical slices with strong Cheddar cheese. When my father was eighty, he still made himself a batch every week usually in the morning before he went to work for a full day. My parents came from*

*North Yorkshire, and my mother's family ran a home-made cake shop during the First World War. She never had a written recipe for the teacakes, so I can only assume it was passed on by word of mouth.'*

*600 g (1¼ lb) strong plain flour*
*Pinch salt*
*60 g (2 oz) sugar*
*30 g (1 oz) lard*
*30 g (1 oz) fresh yeast*
*60-100 g (2-3½ oz) mixed peel and currants*
*Nutmeg*
*300 ml (½ pt) milk*
*Extra milk for glazing*

SIEVE flour, salt and sugar into a large bowl. Rub in the lard. Add the peel and currants. In the centre hollow out a well and crumble in the yeast. Grate nutmeg over the whole thing. Have the milk at room temperature, and add 150 ml (¼ pt) boiling water to it. Pour over the yeast. Flick some of the flour over the watery mess in the centre well, cover the bowl and put in a warm place for 10-15 minutes until the yeast bubbles. Mix to a dough. Put on to a floured board and knead for a few minutes. Divide into eight equal portions (or twelve, if you are using the mixture for hot cross buns). Knead each piece and fold it inwards, then turn over and round off. Put on greased baking trays in a warm place for about 15 minutes. Bake 30 minutes in a hot oven, mark 7, 220°C(425°F). At half-time, swop the trays round. Turn the teacakes 5 minutes before the end of cooking time. Brush tops with milk when you remove them from the oven.

## WIGS

ONCE, AS LONG AGO AS THE MIDDLE AGES, buns came often in wedge-shapes, called for this reason wigs. The baker would slap down a circle of fine wheat dough, cut it across, and across again, and there were the wigs, the wedges. When breakfast became a light meal in the seventeenth century, with coffee or tea instead of ale, people realized that buttered buns or wigs were the best food to eat with the new drinks. The habit has lasted until today in Scotland, where children are sent out to the baker's before breakfast for fine white baps, hot from the oven, and in France, where croissants and brioches are ready first thing at the pastry-cooks' and bakers' shops. At one camping site near our village in Touraine, the pastry-cook even comes round the tents and caravans with his newly made croissants at eight in the morning. Hot cross buns became a speciality for Good Friday breakfast in the eighteenth century; they were made extra spicy and rich with fruit, and marked with a cross as a sign of the festival.

The recipe below comes from Elizabeth David's *English Bread and Yeast Cookery*, in which she has recreated all the breads of the past, from manchet and 'penny loaves' to wigs.

*15 g (½ oz) yeast*
*170 ml (6 oz) warmed milk*
*340 g (12 oz) plain flour*
*125 g (4 oz) softened butter*
NB *these metrications are Mrs David's.*
*125 g (4 oz) caster sugar*
*½ teaspoon each ground ginger and pudding or mixed spice*
*2-3 teaspoons caraway seeds*

DISSOLVE yeast to a cream in the milk, then mix with flour to a light dough. Beat in the butter with your hands, then the sugar and spices. Cover with polythene and leave in a warm place for 2 hours. The dough will become light and bubbly. Divide it into two equal pieces, using extra flour if it is difficult to handle. Warm and butter two 17-20 cm (7-8") sponge tins. Pat out a round of dough in each one, then make four cuts across each round of dough to form eight wedges (sixteen in all).

Prove in a warm place for about 20 minutes, covered with a humped-up piece of polythene (see recipe for Electric Dough Hook Bread, page 298). Bake about 15 minutes at mark 5-6, 190-200°C (375-400°F). Eat warm from the oven, or cool and reheat as required.

NOTE: if you wish to use dried yeast, halve the quantity, which works out at two level teaspoons.

## COBB'S BATH BUNS

THE CRUNCHY SUGAR SCATTERED OVER TODAY'S BATH BUNS is a last souvenir of the crushed caraway seed comfits which were used to flavour wigs and buns as late as the eighteenth century. Comfits were made by dipping aromatic seeds over and over again in boiling sugar, until they were thickly coated – there is a most carefully set out recipe for making them complete with a list of equipment, given in Sir Hugh Plat's *Delight for Ladies* of 1605. Sugared almonds are made on the same principle. One may still buy aniseed comfits of an exactly Tudor kind at Flavigny in Burgundy – elsewhere they seem to have disappeared. A pity, for they were much used in decorating cakes and tarts and puddings like trifle, and provided a far more discreet note and elegant flavour than glacé cherries do nowadays.

You may still eat Bath buns at Bath, in the Pump Room, and you can buy them at Cobb & Co. Ltd, 11 Westgate Street. Here is their recipe:

FERMENT
*45 g (1½ oz) fresh yeast*
*45 g (1½ oz) granulated sugar*
*300 ml (½ pt) water, at blood heat*
*450 g (15 oz) eggs, weighed in the shell, then broken into a bowl*
*150 g (5 oz) strong white bread flour*

DOUGH
*900 g (30 oz) strong white bread flour*
*375 g (12 oz) softened butter*
*90 g (3 oz) granulated sugar*
*375 g (12 oz) broken up sugar lumps*
*Pinch mixed spice*
*Pinch salt*
*Few drops lemon juice*

BUN WASH
*60 g (2 oz) sugar*
*5 tablespoons water*
*Coarsely crushed sugar lumps*

FOR the ferment, cream yeast and sugar in a large warmed mixing bowl and whisk in water. Leave in a warm place to froth up – 10 minutes – then beat in eggs and flour. Tie into a plastic carrier, or cover with clingfilm and leave in a warm place to rise for about 1 hour.

Mix in the dough ingredients, kneading well together. Cover again and leave until the dough has doubled, at least another hour, nearer two with so rich a dough. Knock back and shape the dough into pieces the size of a small Cox's orange pippin. Place them on greased baking sheets. Tie again into plastic carriers and leave to prove.

Preheat the oven to mark 7, 220°C (425°F). Bake the buns for about 20 minutes, pressing them down gently before you put them into the oven. Swop the trays around at half time for even baking.

Meanwhile, boil bun wash sugar and water together until syrupy. Brush this over the hot buns when they emerge from the oven and sprinkle them with coarsely crushed sugar lumps. Leave to cool.

## SAFFRON CAKE FROM CORNWALL

SAFFRON HAS ALWAYS BEEN EXPENSIVE, even during the Middle Ages when it was at its height of European popularity for flavouring dishes, and even more for the colour it gave them. People liked their food to look gay, so that saffron (as well as sanders from sandalwood and alkanet, which both gave reddish colours) was found in every prosperous household. Saffron can never be cheap: it consists of the bright orange-red stigmas of the saffron crocus *(Crocus sativus)*, which have to be gathered by hand and then dried. It has been estimated that it takes a quarter of a million flowers to produce one pound. Such an expensive product has always been a temptation to cheating merchants – never buy powdered saffron on this account, always go for the orange-red hairy kind sold in tiny thimbles or small packages.

The plant was introduced into England in the sixteenth century from Asia Minor (saffron goes back ultimately to the Arabic *za-farān)* and grown here at Saffron Walden in Essex and Stratton in north Cornwall – and in other places too – until the beginning of this century. In his *Gardener's Dictionary* of 1741,

Philip Miller gives a long careful account of saffron-growing in the 1720s between Saffron Walden and Cambridge. Growers had to fence their small parcels of ground with hurdles to prevent hares feeding on the leaves in winter. In July, everyone was out planting the 192,040 roots that went to the acre, noting the size of each one and placing it accordingly for maximum yield, as it cost so much. The crocus flowers were gathered early in the day, and the filaments or 'chives' picked out. Then came the tricky business of drying the saffron, which was ranged in wet 2 or 3 inch layers between sheets of white paper; the design and materials of the kiln were all worked out, but a watchful care was needed to make sure the precious filaments did not scorch. For all this labour, including free family labour, the grower might clear £5 a year. Even allowing for the difference in money values, this was a poor return. No wonder the trade died out as more profitable kinds of work became available.

Saffron cake has hung on in Cornwall and Devonshire from the days when all cakes were raised with yeast rather than eggs or baking powder. Like *bouillabaisse* or *mourtayrol* in France, and *paella* in Spain, it is a last survivor of an earlier grand passion for the flavour and colour of this elegant exotic.

*Generous pinch saffron*
*Warm water*
*30 g (1 oz) fresh yeast (not dried)*
*1 kilo (2 lb) plain flour*
*250 g (8 oz) sugar*
*½ teaspoon nutmeg*
*½ teaspoon cinnamon*
*Pinch salt*
*175 g (6 oz) lard*
*175 g (6 oz) butter*
*300 ml (½ pt) milk*
*250 g (8 oz) mixed dried fruit*
*60 g (2 oz) chopped lemon peel*

PUT the saffron into ¼ teacupful of warm water and leave it to infuse overnight. Next day, crumble the yeast into a bowl with 2 heaped tablespoons from the flour. Add 150 ml (¼ pt) of warm water mixed with 1 heaped teaspoonful from the sugar. Mix it all together thoroughly and put in a warm, draught-free corner for half an hour to rise: this is the leaven.

Put the rest of the flour into a warmed mixing bowl, add the sugar, spice and salt. Rub in the lard and butter. Make a well in the centre and pour in the risen leaven. Add, too, the milk, which has been warmed to blood heat, and the saffron liquid (some people strain out the saffron: others leave it in). Mix thoroughly to make a soft dough. Put it into a clean bowl, cover it with a cloth and leave in a warm draught-free place until it doubles its bulk.

Break down the dough, add the dried fruit and peel, and put into 2 well-greased loaf tins. Leave in a warm place for about half an hour for the dough to prove and rise in the tins. Bake at mark 7, 220°C (425°F), for 40 minutes.

## WILTSHIRE LARDY CAKE

LIKE SAFFRON CAKE, lardies are a survival of older baking habits. They are a kind of rural Chelsea bun, very good, very fattening. The more lard, sugar and fruit you can cram in, the better, so that the dough is layered with brown sweet richness. Some of our family think my quantities are on the skinny size; try it first, though, and see what you think – next time you may like to add more, or you may not. It probably will depend on how much Wiltshire mud runs through your veins.

*500 g (1 lb) bread dough, which has risen for 1 hour until doubled in bulk*
*175 g (6 oz) lard*
*175 g (6 oz) mixed dried fruit*
*60 g (2 oz) mixed peel*
*175 g (6 oz) granulated sugar*

ROLL out the dough into an oblong, spread two-thirds of it with one-third each of the lard, fruit and peel, and sugar. Fold it into three. Press the ends down together with a rolling pin, and give the dough a half turn. Repeat twice more.

Place the folded dough into a large square or oblong tin which allows enough room for it to rise. Leave in a warm, draught-free place for 20-30 minutes, then bake at mark 7, 220°C (425°F), for about 45 minutes. Take out of the oven, then put it on to a plate, upside down, the sugary, rich side uppermost. Lardy cake is best eaten warm from the oven, cut into generous sticky squares.

## FRUIT TEA LOAF

THE TEA HABIT DEVELOPED INTO A PASSION with the English in the mid-nineteenth century, when tea plantations were successfully organized in Assam and Ceylon. (The tea plant indigenous to India was discovered in 1823 in Assam; earlier attempts to introduce Chinese seeds and plants had not been successful.) It even came to have a meal to itself, rather than just a sociable hour after the main midday dinner. Elegant society drank tea between four and five o'clock; sandwiches and delicious cakes were served with it. For the working classes, 'high tea' became the full-scale evening meal after a long day's work; and it still is, though in many parts of the country it is just called 'tea' in spite of the fact that it consists of meat and two or more vegetables, followed by a substantial pudding – the tea itself will be drunk beforehand, or with the food. Yorkshire 'high tea' remains a real spread of the old-fashioned kind, in which ham, cheese, cakes, biscuits, tarts are all put on the table together as they might have been in the eighteenth century before meals were separated into savoury and sweet and cheese courses.

High tea, or a buffet meal with tea to drink, was soon recognized as a suitable event for church and chapel congregations. As Gervas Huxley remarked in *Talking of Tea*, it marched along hand in hand with the temperance movement which was so strong a part of chapel-going in the north. One of the favourite items of such occasions was fruit loaf made with tea. And the same fruit loaf was served at family gatherings, and at funeral meals, along with the inevitable ham (in Yorkshire, it is sometimes called 'slow walking bread'). It tastes all the better for keeping a few days.

*375 g (12 oz) mixed dried fruit and peel*
*125 g (4 oz) dark brown sugar*
*250 ml (½ pt) strained, cold Indian tea*
*250 g (8 oz) self-raising flour*
*1 egg*

STIR together the dried fruit, chopped peel, sugar and tea. Leave overnight, and next day beat in the flour and egg. Bake in a lined 22 cm (9″) loaf tin for 1 hour at mark 4, 180°C (350°F), then for a further 30 minutes at mark 3, 160°C (325°F). Serve thinly sliced and generously buttered. For the best flavour, keep the loaf in an airtight tin, or wrapped in foil, for two or three days.

## BANANA TEA LOAF

DESERVEDLY, this has become a popular recipe at country teas during the last ten years. The long cooking does not at all spoil the scented flavour of bananas. And their moist texture enhances the keeping qualities of this recipe. Although almonds are most generally used, I think that walnuts give a more subtle flavour.

*250 g (8 oz) self-raising flour*
*¾ level teaspoon mixed spice*
*½ level teaspoon salt*
*125 g (4 oz) caster sugar*
*125 g (4 oz) butter*
*1 tablespoon honey*
*125 g (4 oz) sultanas*
*100 g (3 oz) glacé cherries*
*60-125 g (2-4 oz) blanched almonds, chopped, or walnuts*
*500 g (1 lb) ripe bananas*
*2 eggs*
*Juice of 1 lemon*

SIFT the first four ingredients into a bowl. Chop butter into small pieces and add that, then all the remaining ingredients – remember to peel the bananas first and mash them with a fork. Mix thoroughly.

Turn the mixture into a buttered 22 cm (9″) loaf tin. Bake at mark 4, 180°C (350°F), for 1 hour, then for a further half-hour at mark 3, 160°C (325°F). Remove from the tin and cool on a rack. Serve thinly sliced and generously buttered – like most tea loaves, it tastes all the better for keeping.

## Madeira Cake

This cake was served with Madeira and other sweet wines in the nineteenth century, hence the name. Although it is now a popular cake at teatime, to enjoy it at its best serve it in the morning with Madeira in the old style.

*175 g (6 oz) butter*
*175 g (6 oz) caster sugar*
*275 g (9 oz) flour*
*½ teaspoon baking powder*
*4 large eggs*
*Grated rind of half a large lemon*
*2 strips of lemon or citron peel*

Cream the butter and sugar together until the mixture is light and fluffy. Sift the flour and baking powder together. Beat the eggs into the butter and sugar, one at a time, adding a little flour if the mixture seems to be separating. Stir in the rest of the flour and the grated lemon rind. Turn the mixture into a 20 cm (8″) cake tin which has been lined with Bakewell paper or greased and floured. Bake for 1½-2 hours at mark 4, 180°C (350°F). After 1 hour place the two pieces of peel on top, and complete the baking.

## Rice Cake

As a southerner, my mother decided it would be foolish to compete with her husband's North Country relations in the matter of baking when she asked them to tea. For these special occasions, she would visit the two best pastry-cooks in Sunderland, Mengs on the main street and Milburns. Looking back now, I remember with special affection the birthday cakes they made – thatched cottages with hollyhocks and marzipan water butts and drain-pipes, steam and fire engines, ships like the ones we saw being built on the Wear, all decorated with the most joyful realism. Their normal repertoire – mainly in the Austrian and French styles – was of a standard that seems now to be completely lost in Britain. I saw nothing like it, once war was declared, until in middle age I visited the great pastry-cooks of Paris, Le Nôtre, Fauchon and so on. Mengs and Milburns cannot have been exceptional, flaunting standards of quality in that sad, depressed north-eastern town. There must have been many other pastry-cooks in more prosperous towns as skilled as they were.

Of course such things were not cheap. My mother's happy natural extravagance was held in check by the weekly account book, so she kept her purchases within bounds and set them off with a few simple cakes of her own. I remember going, with an equal delight, from a rolled sponge cake, with its interior of cream and cherries, to this rice cake:

*125 g (4 oz) butter*
*250 g (8 oz) caster sugar*
*3 eggs*
*250 g (8 oz) ground rice*
*Grated zest 1 lemon*

CREAM butter and sugar. Beat in eggs, then add rice and zest. Bake 1¼-1½ hours at mark 4, 180°C (350°F), in an 18 cm (7″) cake tin, lined with Bakewell parchment. Test with a larding needle in the usual way.

## MRS SLEIGHTHOLME'S SEED CAKE

I HAD BEEN READING A FAMILY MANUSCRIPT RECIPE BOOK compiled between 1705 and 1730, in which there were five recipes for seed cake, when I saw this recipe in a copy of *Woman* magazine. The ingredient that set this recipe apart from the many other seed cakes of English cookery was the ground almonds. And when I made the cake it was indeed the almonds that made it moist and delicious and quite exceptional.

The recipe was given in a series of farmhouse cakes by Mrs Dorothy Sleightholme, who frequently appears on Yorkshire Television. She had had the cake from a Somerset family, but thought that it needed something extra and added the ground almonds – which make all the difference.

*175 g (6 oz) butter*
*175 g (6 oz) caster sugar*
*3 eggs*
*1 rounded dessertspoon of caraway seeds*
*1 level tablespoon ground almonds*
*250 g (8 oz) self-raising flour*
*A little milk*

CREAM the butter and sugar, and stir into it the caraway seeds – if you are not sure about the tastes of the people likely to eat the cake, use a level dessertspoonful the first time. Separate the eggs. Whisk the whites until they are stiff, but creamy rather than dry. Beat the yolks together and fold them into the whites carefully, until they are mixed together. Add to the butter and sugar. Lastly stir in the ground almonds and flour, adding a little milk if the mixture doesn't fall off the spoon when you shake it with a firm flick of the wrist.

Line a 23 cm (9″) loaf tin with Bakewell paper. Pour in the cake mixture and smooth it down with the back of a spoon. Bake it at mark 4, 180°C

(350°F), for 1 hour 5 minutes. It should spring back when pressed lightly with a finger, and if you stick a larding needle into it, it should come out clean. Allow the cake to cool in the tin for 20 minutes, before removing it to a wire rack.

A few blanched, slivered almonds can be put on top of the cake before baking.

## POUND CAKE WITH VARIATIONS

WHEN FAMILIES WERE LARGE, this cake was made with a pound of each ingredient – flour, butter, sugar and eggs. And until the mid-nineteenth century, it was laborious to make: 'beat it all well together for an hour with your hand, or a great wooden spoon,' says Hannah Glasse, writing in 1747.

Size and labour have now been beaten by modernity, as you will see, to the extent that pound cake – without loss of quality – has become the ideal cake for the non-cake-maker. I confess that it is almost the only one I produce regularly.

The first reduction comes with ingredients. Nowadays we use a pound in all (the French, who like this cake too, call it a *Quatre-quarts*).

The second reduction comes with the slave-labour. Thanks to self-raising flour and baking powder, the ingredients can be flung together in no particular order, producing a dough that will rise as it should, in seconds if you use an electric beater, or in three minutes if you have to make do with your hands or a wooden spoon. The only snag is remembering to remove the butter from the fridge in time for it to soften.

*125 g (4 oz) soft butter, lightly salted*
*125 g (4 oz) vanilla sugar*
*125 g (4 oz) self-raising flour, mixed with 1 level teaspoon baking powder*
*125 g (4 oz) eggs, approximately 2 medium size*
*1 rounded tablespoon ground almonds (optional)*

PUT all the ingredients into a bowl (minus the egg shells, of course), and mix to a smooth dough. The ground almonds improve the texture, but are not essential.

Take a 23 cm (9″) loaf tin. Cut a piece of Bakewell paper the width of the long side of the tin, and long enough to go down, across and up the other side. Fit it into place – there is no need to grease or line the shorter ends. Spoon in the mixture evenly. Bake for 1 hour 5 minutes at mark 4, 180°C (350°F). As ovens can vary, test it with a larding or knitting needle. Leave it to cool in the tin for 15 minutes, then take hold of the Bakewell paper edges and lift it on to a cake rack.

## SEED CAKE

HANNAH Glasse added caraway seeds – a generous dessertspoon is right for this amount of mixture.

## NUT CAKE

ADD 60 g (2 oz) shelled, blanched, chopped nuts to the mixture. Ice as for walnut cake (below), decorating with whole or toasted nuts, or walnut halves according to what you added to the mixture. A walnut cake can also be flavoured with a tablespoon of very strong coffee, or 2 tablespoons of rum.

## ORANGE CAKE

ADD the grated rind of a large orange to the cake mixture, and the juice of half the orange. Fill and ice with orange butter cream:

*125 g (4 oz) sugar*
*3 tablespoons orange juice*
*2 beaten egg yolks*
*125 g (4 oz) lightly salted Danish butter*

BRING sugar and juice to the soft ball stage 120°C (240°F), or a fraction higher, then tip on to the egg yolks; beat vigorously all the time an electric beater or a helper makes this operation more successful. Before the cream is cold, add the soft butter and beat again until light and creamy.

The cake can be scattered with slivered almonds, or decorated with candied orange peel, or with glacé orange and lemon slices.

An orange cake could equally well be iced with glacé icing or the walnut cake icing below, and decorated with peel.

## BUTTERSCOTCH CAKE

SUBSTITUTE soft dark brown sugar for vanilla sugar, and add 2-3 tablespoons rum. If you have a really sweet tooth, you can make a butterscotch icing by boiling together until the soft ball stage 175 g (6 oz) soft brown sugar, 2 tablespoons cream and 30 g (1 oz) butter. Beat and spread over the cake when it is tepid to cool.

## WALNUT CAKE

AN *OBSERVER* READER SENT ME this recipe from a women's magazine of 1939. It was part of a bride's course on cake-making, and it is very good. If you keep a jar of sugar with vanilla pods, you will need little vanilla essence.

*150 g (5 oz) butter*
*175 g (6 oz) caster sugar*
*2 eggs, beaten*
*250 g (8 oz) self-raising flour*
*Scant 90 g (3 oz) coarsely chopped walnuts*
*4 dessertspoons milk*
*½ teaspoon vanilla essence*

ICING
*500 g (1 lb) lump sugar*
*150 ml (¼ pt) water*
*Large pinch cream of tartar*
*2 egg whites, stiffly beaten*
*1 teaspoon vanilla essence*
*9 walnut halves*

FOR the cake, cream the butter and sugar. Mix in eggs, then flour, walnuts and milk. Add essence slowly to taste. Turn into an 18 cm (7″) cake tin, lined with Bakewell paper. Bake at mark 4, 180°C (350°F), for 1¼ hours, or until cooked – test with a larding needle. Cool on a wire rack.

For the icing, stir sugar and water over a gentle heat until dissolved. Raise heat, add cream of tartar, and boil without stirring to the soft ball stage, 120°C (235-240°F). Pour immediately on to the beaten egg whites, stirring all the time, until the icing is very thick and almost setting – it helps with this operation to use an electric beater, or an assistant who will beat while you pour. Flavour to taste with the essence and spread over the cooled cake, smoothing it off with a knife dipped in boiling water. Decorate with the walnut halves.

## SPONGE CAKE I

*3 eggs*
*90 g (3 oz) sugar*
*90 g (3 oz) plain flour, well sieved*
*Pinch salt*

WHISK eggs and sugar in a large bowl, set over a pan of warm water – not boiling – until they are creamy and frothed up into a pale-coloured bulky mass. If you use an electric beater, it is not necessary to place the bowl over the water. Mix the flour and salt and gradually fold it into the eggs and sugar with a metal spoon: do this lightly so that as little air as possible is lost from the mixture.

Grease either a 18 cm (7″) cake tin, or two 18 cm (7″) sandwich tins, and sprinkle them with flour or sugar. Pour in the mixture. If you are making one large cake, sprinkle it evenly with caster sugar and cook it for 45 minutes at mark 4, 180°C (350°F): the smaller cakes will need about 15 minutes at mark 5, 190°C (375°F), and they are usually sprinkled with sugar after baking. To cool the cake or cakes, remove from the tin and place on a wire rack.

ALTHOUGH SPONGE cakes of this kind are often used as the basis for much elaboration, they are best when served plain and unadorned with a filling of some good home-made jam, or with strawberries and cream in the summer. Then they are really a treat.

To make a chocolate sponge cake, substitute 2 heaped teaspoons of cocoa for the same quantity of flour; sandwich with chocolate butter cream (see below). You can do the same with the next recipe.

## SPONGE CAKE II (WITH MELTED BUTTER)

*3 fresh eggs*
*175 g (6 oz) caster sugar*
*60 g (2 oz) slightly salted butter*
*2 tablespoons water*
*125 g (4 oz) self-raising flour*

WHISK eggs and sugar together until they foam up to a creamy bulk. Use an electric beater if possible. Melt butter with water over the lowest heat, so that it never becomes really hot. Stir it when tepid or cool into the eggs and sugar. Fold in the flour lightly with a metal spoon – the best way to do this is to sieve a little of it on to the eggs, etc., and fold it in gently, then to repeat the process until all the flour is used up.

Pour it into two greased and floured sandwich tins – 22 cm (8″) ones are the best size, but 18 cm (7″) ones will do. Bake at mark 5, 190°C (375°F), for 20 minutes. Fill with home-made jam and whipped cream.

THIS DELICATE, foolproof cake of the genoese type is worth knowing about (the recipe came originally from *Come Cooking!* compiled by the West Sussex Women's Institutes). It makes the ideal basis for all kinds of cakes in the elegant French style, when baked in a large oblong tin and cut into squares or circles as required. In the summer time, cover the underside of each cake with whipped cream and strawberries, or raspberries, which have been sprinkled with sugar and kirsch or an orange liqueur. Try it with peaches, too.

Whatever else you do, don't fill it with that coarse mixture we have the effrontery to call 'butter cream' – a mash of salted butter, or even margarine, and far too much icing sugar. Nothing demonstrates better the English love of positively unpleasant food, except the habit of extinguishing fish with malt vinegar.

Here are two recipes for a proper butter cream – be careful to buy an unsalted or very slightly salted butter of the unblended European type, as their flavour and consistency are better for this kind of recipe:

## BUTTER CREAM I

*125 g (4 oz) caster sugar*
*1 tablespoon water*
*2 egg yolks*
*125 g (4 oz) unsalted butter*

MELT the sugar and water together over a low heat, in a small heavy pan. Then raise the heat and boil until the sugar reaches 135°C (280°F), the 'soft crack' stage. If you do not possess a thermometer, I do recommend you to save up and buy one. Until you do, the 'soft crack' stage means that some of the sugar dropped into a mug of cold water will form hard but not brittle threads. Pour this boiling mixture quickly on to the egg yolks, beating vigorously so that the whole thing is well amalgamated: the heat of the sugar cooks the egg yolks slightly and thickens them. When the mixture is tepid, add the butter in small bits, whisking it in so that it melts into the cream without oiling.

The mixture can now be flavoured in various ways – add 90-125 g (3-4 oz) of melted, cooled plain chocolate; or a tablespoon of Nescafé mixed with the least possible amount of water to form a paste, or with a liqueur to taste.

## BUTTER CREAM II (MADE WITH CUSTARD)

*150 ml (¼ pt) milk*
*3 large egg yolks*
*125 g (4 oz) sugar*
*250 g (8 oz) unsalted butter*

POUR milk into a heavy pan and bring to the boil. Beat egg yolks and sugar to a thick foam, preferably with an electric beater. Keep the beater going, while you pour in the boiling milk. Return the mixture to the pan and cook over a low heat until it is very thick and thickly coats a wooden spoon – it is important to keep stirring, and to keep the custard well below boiling point so that the eggs do not scramble to graininess and spoil the smooth texture. Strain into a clean bowl.

As the custard cools down, begin to add the butter – which should be at room temperature and soft – in small chunks, gradually. Flavour to taste.

## PARSNIP CAKE

IN RECENT YEARS, AMERICAN CARROT CAKE – sometimes, and I am not sure why, called passion cake – has become popular in Britain. A friend from San Diego sent me her recipe, and I thought it might be good made with parsnips instead of carrots. And it was, in fact it was even better. That is my excuse for including it in a book of English food.

*375 g (12 oz) peeled, grated parsnip*
*125 g (4 oz) chopped hazelnuts or walnuts*
*400 g (13 oz) golden granulated or caster sugar*
*250 g (8 oz) flour*
*2 teaspoons baking powder*
*2 teaspoons ground cinnamon*
*1 teaspoon salt*
*250 ml (8 fl oz) oil, either sunflower, or half hazelnut or walnut oil, and half sunflower*
*4 eggs*
*Inside of a vanilla pod or 1 teaspoon pure vanilla essence*

FILLING
*250 g (8 oz) full fat soft cheese*
*125-175 g (4-6 oz) softened, unsalted butter*
*About 4 tablespoons icing or caster sugar*
*1 teaspoon pure vanilla essence or lemon juice*

FOR *a moist cake*: take two 22 cm (9") straight-sided shallow cake pans, put in two wide bands of foil, criss-cross. Butter and flour the interiors, including the foil. Preheat oven to mark 4, 180°C (350°F).

*For a drier, crisper cake*: take three 20 cm (8") sandwich tins; put criss-cross bands of foil as above. Butter and flour. Preheat the oven to mark 5, 190°C (375°F).

Mix parsnips and nuts in a bowl. Process or blend or beat together electrically the next six ingredients. When smooth, add eggs one by one, then the parsnips and nuts, and vanilla gradually to taste.

Divide between the pans. Bake for 15 minutes, check and switch the pans round for even cooking. The cakes are done when they spring back lightly if touched. The two-pan cake can take up to 40 minutes. Remove from oven, leave a few minutes, then ease out on to a rack with the aid of the foil bands. Leave to cool.

For the filling, cream cheese and butter together, add sugar, then essence or juice to taste. Use to sandwich the cakes.

## CARROT AND HAZELNUT CAKE

COOKS IN ENGLAND HAVE KNOWN ABOUT USING SWEET CHEAP CARROTS as a substitute for expensive imported dried fruit for well over a hundred years. Sometimes, as in Mrs Beeton's carrot tart, it is used for itself, for its combination of sweet chewiness and glorious colour. In this cake, carrot is used for the latter reason I would say. Although it is completely different from American carrot or passion cake. I can recommend filling it with the cream cheese mixture that American cooks use for their darker, heavier version.

CAKE
*4 standard eggs, separated*
*125 g (4 oz) caster sugar*
*60 g (2 oz) lightly toasted hazelnuts*
*125 g (4 oz) grated carrot*
*125 g (4 oz) finest flour, sieved*
*Icing sugar*

FILLING
*See previous recipe, or use whipped crème fraîche, or ½ double, ½ soured cream*

BUTTER two 23 cm (9") sandwich tins, line them with Bakewell paper. Preheat the oven to mark 5, 190°C (375°F).

Whisk egg yolks and sugar until they form a pale, frothy cloud with an electric beater. Meanwhile, chop the hazelnuts in the processor (not too finely), then shred enough carrot to give you the right weight, using a fine blade – the shreds should be closer to hair than matchstick thickness. Fold both into the yolk mixture, then add the flour.

Whisk the whites until stiff and fold in carefully. Divide between the two tins and bake until nicely browned, about 25 minutes, or until the cake springs back when gently pressed in the centre. Put on a rack to cool, removing the tins first. Sandwich with the filling and sprinkle the top with icing sugar.

## GINGER CAKE

THE DARKEST, RICHEST GINGERBREAD of them all. It keeps beautifully; in fact I think it tastes better after three or four days. Serve it in slices with coffee, or with whipped cream as a pudding. The recipe comes from *Au Petit Cordon Bleu,* by Dione Lucas and Rosemary Hume.

If you do not like the idea of a strong-tasting, gooey cake, which will almost certainly sink in the middle, cut the quantity of treacle to 200 g (7 oz). 30 g (1 oz) of coarsely chopped walnuts, added with the ginger and sultanas, gives a most agreeable bite to the cake.

*125 g (4 oz) butter*
*125 g (4 oz) Barbados or Demerara sugar*
*2 eggs*
*300 g (10 oz) black treacle*
*250 g (8 oz) flour*
*1 teaspoon ground ginger*
*60 g (2 oz) sultanas*
*60 g (2 oz) preserved ginger, sliced*
*2 tablespoons milk*
*½ teaspoon bicarbonate of soda*

CREAM the butter, add the sugar and continue beating for a few moments. Mix in the eggs and treacle. Sift the flour and ginger together, stir in the sultanas and ginger pieces, then tip into the cake mixture. Warm the milk very slightly with the bicarbonate of soda and mix that in last of all.

Pour into an 18 cm (7″) cake tin, lined with Bakewell paper, or else buttered and floured. Bake at mark 3, 160°C (325°F), for 1½ hours if you like a sticky gingerbread, for 1¾ hours if you like it a little drier. The cake will come away from the side of the tin in a rounded shape, and may sink in the middle if you take it out after 1½ hours. Don't worry – it will taste delicious, all the same. Let it cool for a few moments in the tin, then turn it on to a rack.

NOTE: when weighing treacle, golden syrup or honey, place a small pan on the scales, adjust to zero or make a note of the weight, and pour it in until you have the required weight.

## WELSH CINNAMON CAKE

THE TRADITIONAL RECIPE HAS BEEN ALTERED SLIGHTLY and improved by Mrs Bobby Freeman, who used to run the Compton House Hotel at Fishguard. The sad thing is that, apart from a few enthusiasts who are not always Welsh, it is difficult to find restaurateurs in Wales who are prepared to make a speciality of the dishes of their own region.

*125 g (4 oz) butter*
*125 g (4 oz) granulated sugar*
*2 egg yolks*
*250 g (8 oz) flour*
*½ teaspoon baking powder*
*1 rounded teaspoon cinnamon*
*Apricot jam*
*3 egg whites*
*3 tablespoons caster sugar*

CREAM butter and granulated sugar, beat in the yolks. Sift flour, baking powder and cinnamon together, then mix into the butter, etc. Knead to a dough and roll out to fit into a 20 cm (8″) tart tin with a removable base. Bake at mark 6, 200°C (400°F), for 20 minutes. Cool the cake on a wire rack after removing it from the tin. Heat a good tablespoon of apricot jam with a little water, sieve it and brush thinly over the cake. Beat the egg whites until they are stiff, fold in the caster sugar and beat again until the mixture is thick and creamy. Pile on to the cake, swirling the top into decorative points. Bake at mark 4, 180°C (350°F), until the meringue is golden and set – about 15 minutes.

## MR FROST'S CHOCOLATE CAKE

MR FROST RUNS A RESTAURANT IN CIRENCESTER, at No. 1 Brewery Court, where you can buy real food and sit in an attractive glass-walled room to eat it. He gave me his recipe for uncooked chocolate cake, which my husband Geoffrey adored, and I tackled it with dubiety after many years' experience of infant cornflake cookery. If you take the trouble to use a good quality plain chocolate from the supermarket it tastes good: with fine quality dessert chocolate, even better.

WEIGH out equal quantities of chocolate, butter and digestive biscuits. Then half their total quantity in nuts – blanched almonds and hazelnuts are best (I would say that hazelnuts are essential), walnuts work well, peanuts are right out as with all confectionery and cake-making.

Toast almonds and hazelnuts in a low oven, then rub hazelnut skins away with a cloth. Chop all nuts roughly. Make piles of the biscuits and cut them downwards so that you get pieces measuring roughly 1 cm (½″), and plenty of crumbs.

Melt the butter over a low heat. Break in the chocolate and stir gently until the mixture is smooth (don't overheat). Stir in nuts, biscuit pieces and crumbs. Smooth down into a shallow Bakewell-lined tin, making a layer about a finger thick. Cool and chill. Cut into fingers and store in a closed box in a cold place or the refrigerator.

## STUFFED MONKEY

A RECIPE THAT WE MAKE OFTEN, from *Jewish Cookery*, by Florence Greenberg. It is good and unusual, and is a special success with friends in France. We usually bake two or three just before we go and take them with us, as they travel and keep well. Unfortunately there is nothing to say whether the cake is especially Jewish, or how it got its name.

*175 g (6 oz) flour*
*½ teaspoon cinnamon*
*125 g (4 oz) butter*
*125 g (4 oz) soft brown sugar*
*1 egg, separated*

FILLING
*50 g (1½ oz) butter*
*60 g (2 oz) chopped peel*
*30 g (1 oz) caster sugar*
*60 g (2 oz) ground almonds*
*1 egg yolk*

FIRST make a dough with the flour, cinnamon, butter, sugar and egg yolk only, as if you were mixing pastry. Roll it out and cut two rounds to fit into a 20 cm (8″) sandwich tin. Make the filling by melting the butter and beating the rest of the ingredients into it. Spread over the pastry. Cover with the second round of dough. Brush over with the egg white and bake for about 30 minutes at mark 5, 190°C (375°F). Cool in the tin.

## MURRUMBIDGEE CAKE

YEARS AGO, WHEN SOPHIE WAS AT OXFORD HIGH SCHOOL, I used to buy this cake at the Straw Hat bakery in Summertown. Now at last I've found a recipe, given – with its proper name – in *Edible Gifts* by Claire Clifton and Martine Nicolls (Bodley Head). The attraction of the cake, and of very similar American cakes, is the large pieces of candied fruit and nuts held together with a small amount of cake batter. It has a jewelled look, keeps well and tastes rich without the dark closeness and icings that put many people off Christmas cake.

*200 g (7 oz) Brazil nuts, whole*
*150 g (5 oz) whole walnut halves*
*250 g (8 oz) stoned, halved dates*
*100 g (3½ oz) chopped candied peel*
*175 g (6 oz) glacé cherries, several colours if possible, or the dark undyed organic glacé cherries*
*100 g (3½ oz) seedless raisins*
*Grated rind of 1 lemon*
*100 g (3½ oz) flour*
*½ teaspoon each baking powder and salt*
*150 g (5 oz) caster sugar*
*3 large eggs*
*1 teaspoon pure vanilla essence*
*Plus brandy, rum or other spirit or liqueur*

INE a loaf tin with Bakewell parchment or buttered greaseproof paper. Preheat the oven to mark 2, 150°C (300°F).

Mix nuts, peel and fruit. Sift dry ingredients together and add to the nuts etc. Beat eggs and vanilla, stir into the mixture to make a stiff batter. Put into the tin, smoothing the top down.

Bake for 1½-2 hours, protecting the top with paper if it browns too fast. Test with a skewer. When cooked, cool 10 minutes in the tin, then turn on to a clean cloth. Make several holes and pour in the alcohol of your choice. Wrap cloth round the cake, then enclose in clingfilm or foil and store in the refrigerator. Every week for 1-2 months, add more alcohol.

## CHRISTMAS CAKE

THIS IS THE RECIPE I ALWAYS USE THESE DAYS for Christmas and special birthday cakes. Even if you make it just beforehand and cannot leave it to mature, it tastes good. Unless you like seeding and chopping raisins, and washing and drying the other fruit, I suggest you buy those bags of mixed fruit and peel sold by the chain groceries. No one could tell the difference.

*750 g (1½ lb) mixed dried fruit*
*125 g (4 oz) blanched, slivered almonds*
*125 g (4 oz) chopped peel*
*125 g (4 oz) glacé cherries, well rinsed, then quartered*
*300 g (10 oz) plain flour*
*1 teaspoon cinnamon*
*1 teaspoon nutmeg*
*Grated rind of a lemon*
*1 teaspoon vanilla essence*
*250 g (8 oz) lightly salted butter*
*250 g (8 oz) soft brown sugar, light or dark*
*1 tablespoon black treacle*
*4 eggs*
*½ teaspoon bicarbonate of soda*
*1 tablespoon milk*
*Brandy*

MIX fruit, almonds, peel and cherries in a huge bowl. Turn them well and add the flour, spices and lemon rind. Cream the butter and sugar thoroughly, then add the vanilla essence and treacle. Still beating, incorporate the eggs, and stir in the fruit and flour. Finally, dissolve the bicarbonate of soda in the milk and stir in thoroughly. Add brandy by the spoonful, until you have a soft dropping consistency.

Turn into a 20 cm (8″) cake tin, lined with a double layer of brown paper, then a layer of Bakewell paper. Hollow out the top slightly. Bake at mark 1, 140°C (275°F), for 3½ hours, then test it with a larding needle or skewer. Remove the cake from the oven when it is done, and leave to cool in its tin. Next day peel off the Bakewell and brown paper. Wrap in fresh greaseproof paper, then put it into an airtight tin (or in foil). The usual thing is to keep the cake for at least a month before icing it, and to sprinkle it occasionally with more brandy.

To finish off the cake for Christmas, you will need marzipan and icing. Do not buy the marzipan ready made – your own may not look so yellow as it does in the shop, but it will taste much better. Moreover, you can reduce the sweetness by putting in less sugar:

## ALMOND PASTE OR MARZIPAN

*250 g (8 oz) icing sugar*
*500 g (1 lb) ground almonds*
*1 large egg (weighing about 75 g (2½ oz))*
*3-4 teaspoons lemon juice*

GLAZE
*1 tablespoon apricot jam*
*1 tablespoon water*

SIFT the icing sugar and mix it with the almonds. Beat the egg thoroughly, then add the lemon juice and the dry ingredients. Use a wooden spoon to beat everything to a firm paste, then knead it on a board or formica surface, which has been sprinkled with icing sugar. (Incidentally, if you do not agree with me that most almond paste is too sweet, add another half pound of sugar and use two medium eggs instead of one large one.)

Slice the top from the cake to make it even, then turn it upside down and put on a wire rack. Boil the jam and water in a small pan, sieve it into a bowl and while still hot brush it over the top of the cake (that is, over what *was* the bottom).

Set aside a third of the almond paste, and roll out the rest to a circle just a little larger than the cake – do this on a sheet of clean greaseproof paper and use the cake tin as a guide. Press the glazed side of the cake down on to the circle of almond marzipan; reverse it so that you now have the greaseproof paper on top, then the marzipan and then the cake – remove the paper and smooth the marzipan down over the sides. Measure the depth of the cake and its circumference. Roll out the remaining marzipan to these measurements, again on a sheet of greaseproof paper. Brush the cake sides with apricot glaze and roll it slowly along the strip of marzipan. Pat everything into place, closing the cracks and so on, and replace the cake on its rack. Leave for two days before icing it.

## Royal Icing

*2 small egg whites*
*2 teaspoons lemon juice*
*500 g (1 lb) icing sugar*

WHISK the eggs until they are white and foamy, but not stiff. Stir in the lemon juice, then the sugar, which should first be sieved. Do this bit by bit, using a wooden spoon. When everything is mixed together, continue to beat the mixture until it is a dazzling white. Cover the basin and leave it for an hour or two before using it.

To ice the cake, put a bowl of hot water beside it. Put about half the icing on the cake and spread it about with a palette knife which you have dipped in the water. It should be hot and wet, but not wet enough to soak the cake and ruin the icing. Cover the cake all over, then put on the remaining icing, either roughly to make a snowy effect, or in an elegant design with the aid of a forcing bag and nozzles.

## To Make Mince Pies

LINE small tart tins with shortcrust pastry. Put a spoonful of mincemeat in each one, but be careful not to put in too much, as the suet will melt and bubble out if it has no room to spare. Brush the edges of the pastry with beaten white of an egg, and add pastry lids, pinching the two edges together. Make a small cross with a knife in the centre of each pie. Brush over with white of egg, sprinkle with sugar and bake at mark 7, 220°C (425°F), for 15 to 20 minutes.

Mince pies are sometimes served with brandy or rum butter (page 369). Very good.

Puff pastry can be used instead of shortcrust, but I find this is too fatty unless the pies are eaten straight from the oven and not allowed to cool down.

## Mrs Beeton's Traditional Mincemeat

I CAN RECOMMEND THIS RECIPE FOR A REAL MINCE *meat*. It is particularly good. The steak is perfectly preserved by the sugar and brandy, and seems to give the mixture a moist texture and extra delicious flavour. I have noticed that the years when I make this mincemeat for Christmas, the mince pies disappear more quickly than usual.

*500 g (1 lb) seedless raisins*
*750 g (1½ lb) currants*
*375 g (12 oz) lean rump steak, minced*
*750 g (1½ lb) beef suet, chopped*
*500 g (1 lb) dark brown sugar*
*30 g (1 oz) candied citron peel, chopped*
*30 g (1 oz) candied lemon peel, chopped*
*30 g (1 oz) candied orange peel, chopped*
*½ small nutmeg, grated*
*750 g (1½ lb) apples, weighed after peeling and coring*
*The rind of 1 lemon*
*The juice of ½ a lemon*
*150 ml (¼ pt) brandy*

Mix all the ingredients together in the order given. Chop or mince the apples before adding them to the fruit and peel. Pour in the brandy when everything else is well mixed together. Press closely into jars, to exclude the air. Cover and leave for at least a fortnight.

## ORANGE MINCEMEAT

*250 g (8 oz) candied orange and lemon peel, chopped*
*1 kilo (2 lb) apples, peeled, cored, chopped*
*500 g (1 lb) suet, chopped*
*500 g (1 lb) raisins*
*500 g (1 lb) sultanas*
*500 g (1 lb) currants*
*500 g (1 lb) dark brown sugar*
*1 whole nutmeg, grated*
*125 g (4 oz) blanched, slivered almonds*
*The rind and juice of 2 oranges*
*4 tablespoons brandy*
*6-8 tablespoons orange liqueur*

IX the ingredients together in the order given. Pot and cover the mixture, as above.

## BROAD TOWN MINCE PIE

I MADE THIS RECIPE UP TO EKE OUT THE LAST HALF-JAR OF MINCEMEAT when unexpected visitors arrived. It was such a success that we now have it every Christmas. The proportions of almond cream to mincemeat can be varied according to your resources, but this is what I usually make, in a shallow tart tin about 20 cm (8″) in diameter. You could always make a plate tart (see page 328), with less filling and more pastry.

*Shortcrust pastry made with butter and lard*
*1 egg white*
*Sugar*

FILLING
*½ jar (250 g: 8 oz) mincemeat*
*125 g (4 oz) ground almonds*
*125 g (4 oz) caster sugar*
*30 g (1 oz) melted butter*
*2 small egg yolks*
*2 tablespoons cream*

LINE a tart tin with a removable base with just over half the pastry. Then spread over it the mincemeat in as even a layer as possible. Mix the remaining ingredients from the filling list together and spread over the mincemeat. Cover with the remaining pastry in the usual way. Brush over with egg white, sprinkle with sugar and bake at mark 7, 220°C (425°F), for 15-20 minutes, then at mark 4-5, 180-190°C (350-375°F), for half an hour.

Serve hot or warm, with cream or brandy or rum butter.

## CUMBERLAND CURRANT CAKE

GROWING AND STORING APPLES AND PEARS becomes more difficult as you go north. Perhaps this is why dried fruit pies, such as sly cake, Eccles cakes and these Cumberland squares, are not just Christmas food, as mince pies tend to be further south. In Jane Austen's time in Surrey, when you went visiting friends in February or March you would be offered baked apples to eat, the last of the winter's store. In the north-east, certainly up to the last war, we would eat this kind of thing. We loved it, and called it squashed fly cake, and giggled in a corner, while the family talked. No one realized that they were eating a cake with a history, and medieval ancestors.

PASTRY
*500 g (1 lb) flour*
*150 g (5 oz) butter*
*150 g (5 oz) lard*
*Pinch salt*
*Cold water to mix*

FILLING
*300 g (10 oz) currants or raisins*
*125 g (4 oz) mixed peel*
*175 g (6 oz) cooking apples*
*150 g (5 oz) butter*
*125 g (4 oz) pale or dark brown sugar*
*5 tablespoons rum*
*1 teaspoon allspice*
*½ teaspoon each cinnamon and mace*

MAKE the pastry in the usual way. Roll out half and line an oblong tin about 18 × 28 × 2½ cm (7″ × 11″ × 1″). Spread currants or raisins and peel on top. Peel, core and grate the apples before weighing them, and put them over the currants, etc. Melt the butter, and, off the heat, stir in the remaining ingredients – if your hand slips with the rum, it doesn't matter. Taste this mixture and add more spices if you like. Pour over the fruit. Roll out the remaining pastry and cover the filling. If you like, brush the pastry with top of the milk, or beaten egg glaze, and sprinkle with caster sugar. Put into a mark 6, 200°C (400°F), oven for 30-35 minutes. Eat hot as a pudding (with cream or rum butter or egg custard), or cold, cut into squares.

## CUMBERLAND PLATE TART

A LIGHTER VERSION OF THE CUMBERLAND CAKE ABOVE – the almonds give it a good flavour and texture – which makes a good pudding at the end of a winter lunch party. In the north a shiny tin plate is used for baking this kind of shallow double-crust pie, but a non-stick or enamel one could quite well be used instead.

To measure syrup, put a small pan on the scales, and note the weight; then pour in syrup until you have the pan weight plus the weight required by the recipe. Some scales are adjustable, so that you can put the pan on the tray and turn a knob until the needle returns to 0 – don't forget to readjust the needle afterwards.

*Shortcrust pastry made with butter and lard*
*1 egg white*
*Caster sugar*

FILLING
*100 g (3½ oz) golden syrup*
*30 g (1 oz) butter*
*150 g (5 oz) raisins or currants*
*30 g (1 oz) chopped peel*
*30 g (1 oz) ground almonds*
*¼ teaspoon each nutmeg, allspice and salt*
*2 teaspoons lemon juice*

ROLL out the pastry thinly, and line the plate leaving enough to make a lid. Next make the filling:

Put the pan of syrup on a moderate heat with the butter. Stir until they are melted together and tepid. Mix with the remaining ingredients, and spread over the pastry, leaving a clear rim.

Brush the pastry rim with egg white; roll out the remaining pastry and cover the tart, pressing down the edge. Knock up the edge, or scallop it, and make a central hole. Brush over with white of egg, sprinkle with caster sugar and bake for 15 minutes at mark 7, 220°C (425°F), then for half an hour at mark 5, 190°C (375°F). Serve hot or warm for the best flavour.

## ECCLES CAKES

*Shortcrust pastry made with lard*

FILLING
*125 g (4 oz) currants*
*30 g (1 oz) chopped candied peel*
*½ teaspoonful each allspice and nutmeg*
*60 g (2 oz) sugar*
*30 g (1 oz) butter*
*Plus*
*Egg white and extra sugar*

ROLL out the pastry and cut into circles about 10 cm (4″) round. Mix currants, peel and spices. Put the sugar and butter into a small pan. When they are melted, mix in the currants, etc., and heat through. Leave until cold, then put a spoonful into the centre of each pastry round. Draw the circles together, pinching the edges over the filling. Turn them over, then press gently with a rolling pin to flatten the cakes. Make a hole in the centre. Brush over with egg white, sprinkle with sugar, and bake at mark 7, 220°C (425°F), for 15 minutes.

## BANBURY CAKES

IN THE *English Hus-wife* of 1615, Gervase Markham gives a recipe for Banbury cakes that is quite different. The modern ones, sold at Banbury, are more like the northern Eccles and Chorley cakes in type, though the puff pastry and rum make them seem lighter.

*Puff pastry*

FILLING
*As for Eccles Cakes, plus an extra 30 g (1 oz) of butter, ¼ teaspoon cinnamon and a tablespoon of rum*

Plus: *White of egg and extra sugar*

ROLL out the pastry thinly and cut into 18 cm (7″) circles. Melt the butter, and mix in remaining ingredients without heating them. Put a spoonful of the mixture in the centre of each circle in a band of filling about 12½ cm (5″) long. Bring the pastry round it, as for Eccles cakes, but form an oval shape; cut away surplus pastry. Turn over, flatten slightly with the rolling pin and make three slashes across the top. Brush with egg white, sprinkle with sugar, and bake at mark 7-8, 220-230°C (425-450°F), for 15 minutes.

## ALMOND FINGERS

ONE SEES MANY COMMERCIAL BRANDS of almond slice. They are made with a view to profit and long shelf-life. Try this recipe instead; the difference in flavour is startling – principally because it is not mean with butter and almonds and eggs.

PASTRY
*125 g (4 oz) butter*
*3 heaped tablespoons icing sugar*
*1 egg*
*1 tablespoon lemon juice*
*250 g (8 oz) flour*

FILLING
*Apricot jam*
*150 g (5 oz) butter*
*150 g (5 oz) vanilla sugar,* *see pages 371-2*
*2 eggs*
*125 g (4 oz) ground almonds*
*1 heaped tablespoon flour*
*2 tablespoons rum*
*60 g (2 oz) blanched, slivered almonds*

To make the pastry, cream butter and sugar together. Beat in egg next, and then the lemon juice and flour. Leave to rest for one hour in the refrigerator. Roll out and line an 18 cm × 28 cm (7″ × 11″) tin.

Spread the pastry base evenly with apricot jam. Cream the butter and vanilla sugar together from the filling ingredients. Add the eggs, then the flour, ground almonds and rum. Spread evenly over the pastry. Sprinkle the top with almonds. Bake for 35-40 minutes at mark 4, 180°C (350°F). The top should be a light golden brown and the almonds slightly coloured. Leave to cool in the tin, and cut into fingers when cold.

## MAZARINES

THE NAME IS A PUZZLE. It may derive from France's Cardinal Mazarin, or from the Duchesse de Mazarin who died in Chelsea in 1699. In a dictionary of 1706, mazarines are defined either as little dishes which can be set in the middle of a larger dish, or – which is more relevant to this recipe – as 'a sort of small tarts fill'd with sweet-meats'.

PASTRY
*60 g (2 oz) butter*
*1 tablespoon caster sugar*
*1 egg yolk*
*125 g (4 oz) flour*
*30 g (1 oz) ground almonds*

FILLING
*Apricot jam*
*2 egg whites*
*125 g (4 oz) caster sugar*
*60 g (2 oz) blanched, flaked almonds*
*1 tablespoon grated plain chocolate*

To make the pastry, cream butter and sugar, then add egg yolk, and finally the flour and almonds. Roll out and cut into strips about 5 cm (2″) wide. Lay them on a baking sheet lined with Bakewell paper, and bend the edges up slightly. Spread the apricot jam down the strips. To make the rest of the filling, beat the egg whites until stiff, then fold in the sugar, almonds and chocolate. Put into a saucepan and heat to boiling point, stirring as you do so. Spoon this mixture quickly along the pastry strips. Bake at mark 4, 180°C (350°F), for about 45 minutes. Allow to cool, then cut the strips diagonally into little fingers.

A recipe from *Come Cooking!* compiled by the West Sussex Women's Institutes in 1969.

## OATCAKES

OATCAKES HAVE WITH MOST OF US THE REPUTATION OF BEING SCOTTISH. We're used to triangular tartan packages of farls or quarters, that is, quarters of a large round bannoch (from the Gaelic *bannach*, meaning cake), stacked one on top of the other. But oatcakes belong just as much to Wales, Ireland and the north of England. In the eighteenth century, sacks of oatmeal were as common a sight in Manchester market as sacks of wheat were in the south. Fine white flour was a luxury in the north until modern times.

After their cooking on the griddle, oatcakes used to be propped up to harden beside the fire against a toast-stone or oatcake rack or plain block of wood (there is a fine collection of implements for making oatcakes in the Welsh Folk Museum near Cardiff, at St Fagan's). Nowadays the hotplate of an electric or solid-fuel stove, or a medium-hot grill or oven, has to do instead very often. It doesn't matter what you use, so long as the oatcakes are really crisp. Nowadays, too, they have to be stored in an airtight tin, rather than in the meal-chest where they were kept buried in oatmeal.

*125 g (4 oz) medium oatmeal*
*125 g (4 oz) plain flour*
*60 g (2 oz) lard or dripping or poultry fat*
*1 level teaspoon salt*

GLAZE
*1 egg*
*1 tablespoon milk*
*1 teaspoon sugar*

MIX the oatmeal and flour in a basin. Rub in the fat, add the salt and mix to a soft but not a tacky dough with cold water. Roll out on an oatmeal-strewn board. Cut out circles with a scone-cutter; and, if you like your oatcakes really thin, slap them out between your oatmealy hands (this is tricky as the edges begin to crack, but it's the old Welsh method and it does produce very good oatcakes). Alternatively, cut out a dinner-plate round, and quarter it.

Cook the oatcakes on an ungreased medium-hot griddle, without turning them. The moment the first batch are in place, brush them over with the glaze – it will turn to a shiny coating as they cook. Store in an airtight box, and toast lightly before the fire before serving them.

## WEST YORKSHIRE OATCAKE OR RIDDLE BREAD

I HAD A LETTER FROM LIVERPOOL, lamenting the difficulty of buying oatmeal there. How odd that would have seemed to our ancestors. The writer lived as a child in the West Riding of Yorkshire and she remembers oatcakes that were about a '*foot long, oval, about eight inches wide across the middle; thin and soft like a piece of cloth. Certain people – some farmers – used to come around with a basketful and our mother would buy perhaps half a dozen. These were then spread on the bread-creel to dry [a creel is a wickerwork basket], and when they were crisp they were eaten, either with slabs of butter, or broken up in milk. Either way they were delicious! And I wish I knew how to make them!'*

Here is the recipe:

*1 scant teaspoon salt*
*Water at blood heat*
*500 g (1lb) fine oatmeal*
*15 g (½ oz) fresh yeast*

Put the oatmeal and salt in a bowl. Cream the yeast with a teacupful of water, and leave it to rise to a creamy froth. Mix into the oatmeal and add more water until the batter is like a thick cream. A ladleful is thrown on to the heated griddle or 'bak' stone, in a narrow strip. It immediately puffs up with steam, which makes it smooth underneath and rough on top. 'When baked it is damp and flexible and is hung on the wooden clothes rail before the fire to dry or on lines across the kitchen ceiling. It must be crisped quickly immediately before it is to be eaten.' The flavour is slightly bitter and very appetizing. 'It can be used for soups, fish, fowl, cheese, butter, or any other kind of meat in place of any other kind of bread or biscuit.'

The quotations come from Florence White's *Good Things in England*. In her day, oatcakes could be bought from an oatcake baker at Skipton, whose business was established in 1858.

## Potato Cakes

*625 g (1¼ lb) potatoes*
*30 g (1 oz) melted butter*
*½ teaspoon salt*
*1 egg (optional)*
*125 g (4 oz) flour*
*1 teaspoon baking powder*

Scrub, boil and peel the potatoes in the usual way (left-over potatoes may be used, but newly cooked ones taste better). Weigh out a pound of them and mash thoroughly, or put through the coarse blade of a vegetable mill. Mix in the other ingredients quickly, using enough flour to make a coherent and not too sticky dough. Roll out thinly and cut into saucer-sized rounds. Bake on a griddle greased with lard, beef suet or bacon fat, and eat immediately, rolling the cakes like pancakes round little sticks of salty butter.

*Or:* roll the dough out to about 1 cm (½") thickness, and cut with a scone cutter. Cook on the griddle, and eat with bacon, eggs and so on. They will need 15 minutes' cooking time.

*Or:* in the Welsh manner, add 2 tablespoons of brown sugar and 1 tablespoon granulated sugar to the mixture. Cut into 1 cm (½″) rounds with the scone-cutter – 15-20 minutes' cooking time on the griddle, greased with suet or lard.

## MUFFINS

*500 g (1 lb) strong plain flour*
*300 ml (½ pt) milk*
*15 g (½ oz) fresh yeast*
*1 egg*
*1 teaspoon salt*
*30 g (1 oz) butter*

BREAK the egg into a bowl. Warm the milk and butter together to blood heat, and beat it with the egg. Cream the yeast with 4 tablespoons of warm water.

Put the flour into a warm bowl, and make a well in the centre. Pour in the yeast, and then the egg-butter-milk liquid. Knead thoroughly, adding more flour, or more water if necessary (different kinds of flour absorb different amounts of moisture). The dough should be soft but not sticky. Cover the bowl with a damp cloth and leave in a warm place for about 1½ hours, or until the dough has doubled in size.

Roll out the dough to a 1 cm (½″) thickness on a floured board. Cut out the muffins with a large scone-cutter – about 5-6 cm (2½″) across. Knead the trimmings together, and roll and cut them out in the same way.

Immediately you have finished this, start cooking the muffins on a lightly greased griddle, turning them over when they are floury and slightly brown on the base. Alternatively, cook them in a very hot oven, with plenty of bottom heat, and turn them over after 6 or 7 minutes.

The muffins will rise and swell to look rather like a puffball fungus. They should not cook too fast, so the centre of the griddle may have to be avoided, and they should keep a floury look. Toast them by the fire, then pull them apart and put a big knob of butter in the middle; muffins are never cut, always pulled apart. Keep them warm in a muffin dish, as you toast the rest, turning them over after a few minutes so that the butter soaks into both halves.

## ELIZABETH DAVID'S CRUMPETS

*500 g (1 lb) plain flour*
*600 ml (1 pt) milk*
*2 tablespoons oil*
*1 teaspoon sugar*
*15 g (½ oz) yeast*
*1 tablespoon salt*
*Good pinch bicarbonate of soda*
*150 ml (¼ pt) warm water*

WARM the flour in a bowl in the plate-warming part of the stove, or stand it in a rack above the cooker. Heat the milk, oil and sugar to body temperature (use a thermometer if possible), then fork up the yeast with 3 tablespoons of the milk. It will soon cream and swell into frothiness. Make a well in the centre of the flour, add the salt and pour in both the yeast mixture and the warm milk. Beat for a good 5 minutes (an electric beater can be used – 3 minutes will be enough). Cover the bowl and leave the dough to rise in a warm place for 1½-2 hours. Dissolve the bicarbonate of soda in the warm water, add it to the mixture, beating it in thoroughly, then leave it to rise for another half-hour.

Grease the griddle with lard or suet, and grease the crumpet rings (Tala make them, but they are not essential). Place the rings on the griddle and heat it when the dough is ready. Pour spoonfuls of mixture to fill the rings by two-thirds, and leave to cook gently for 7-10 minutes. Turn them over when the top part loses its liquid appearance and is a mass of holes, and finish the cooking. Ease off the rings and start again with some more dough.

Eat these crumpets toasted in the usual way, with plenty of butter. They make a good base for fried eggs, or scrambled eggs with anchovies. Some people like them with syrup as well as butter.

NOTE: if the first crumpets are not holey enough, add more warm milk or water to the batter.

## SINGIN' HINNIES

PEOPLE WHO HAVE LEFT BEHIND THEM A NORTH-EASTERN CHILDHOOD should be forgiven for insisting that singin' hinnies are the best of all griddle cakes (in fact I think the Welsh *pice ar y maen* are better, but it's a close thing). The affectionate name recalls the warmth of home and community life – 'hinny' being the local pet name, a charming corruption of honey, and the equipvalent, more or less, of 'luv' and 'ducks' in other parts of the country. The singing comes from the way the cakes sizzle with richness as they cook.

This is one of the few regional dishes that can compare with, say, the regional dishes of France. Not in substance, but because they are – or were, to my knowledge, until the fifties – eaten by everyone in the area, rich, middling and poor. I remember as a child going to birthday parties at one shipyard owner's house in the thirties. The food was lavish, but we always started off with hot singin' hinnies; he could afford to put many silver sixpenny and 'thruppenny' pieces inside, their greaseproof wrapping transparent with melted butter. When we went for a large family tea-party on Sundays to our great-aunt's house, there would be great-uncle Bob in his seaman's jersey making sure we started with plenty of singin' hinnies. One way and another we were lucky in that depressed time. Other people remember singin' hinnies 'as substitutes for the birthday cake we could not afford, and the paper-enclosed coins being halfpennies, and few at that. I have known when the birthday child was carefully guided to choose the only scone containing a coin.' Moreover the singin' hinnies made less of a song for many people, as they could not afford the full complement of butter and lard.

*500 g (1 lb) flour*
*125 g (4 oz) butter*
*125 g (4 oz) lard*
*¼ teaspoon bicarbonate of soda*
*½ teaspoon cream of tartar*
*½ teaspoon salt*
*175 g (6 oz) currants, raisins or sultanas*
*Milk to mix*
*Piece of lamb or mutton fat for the griddle*

SIFT together the flour, raising powders and salt. Rub in the butter and lard, then mix in the fruit. Add enough milk to make a firm dough. Roll out, then cut into rounds of about 6 cm (2½") in diameter. Spear the mutton fat on a fork and grease the heated griddle with it thoroughly. Put on the cakes, and turn them when the underneath is a nice mottled brown. Cut in half and put a big knob of butter in the middle. Keep the singin' hinnies warm in the oven until they are all cooked. If you are making them for a children's party, or at Christmas, put coins that have been briefly boiled, then wrapped in greaseproof paper, in the middle of some of them.

## CACEN GRI (GRIDDLE CAKES)

*500 g (1 lb) flour*
*1 teaspoon baking powder*
*1 teaspoon salt*
*125 g (4 oz) butter*
*125 g (4 oz) lard*
*90 g (3 oz) dried fruit and peel*
*1 large egg*
*A little milk*

SIFT the flour, baking powder and salt together into a bowl. Rub in the butter and fat. Add the fruit and peel, then mix to a dough with the egg, adding a little milk. Roll out thinly, and cut into dinner-plate rounds. Grease the girdle or bakestone with a piece of suet or lard, and bake the rounds for about 2-3 minutes a side. Have ready a warm plate and a pat of butter. Butter each one lavishly and stack them into a pile and serve hot.

## PICE AR Y MAEN (WELSH CAKES ON THE STONE)

*500 g (1 lb) flour*
*1 teaspoon baking powder*
*Generous pinch salt*
*1 teaspoon mace*
*125 g (4 oz) butter*
*125 g (4 oz) lard*
*125 g (4 oz) currants or raisins*
*175 g (6 oz) sugar (optional)*
*2 large eggs*
*Milk to mix if necessary*
*Extra sugar*

MIX and bake as above. When cooked, do not butter them but turn them in the extra sugar. The richness of a second egg, and the delicate unmistakable flavour of mace, makes these the most delicious of all the girdle cakes.

## GLOUCESTER PANCAKES

GLOUCESTER PANCAKES HAVE A DELICIOUS, richly sandy texture inside, which comes from using suet. No other fat will achieve the same result. It is also important to fry them in lard, on account of the flavour.

For 4

*175 g (6 oz) flour*
*Pinch of salt*
*1 teaspoon baking powder*
*90 g (3 oz) chopped suet*
*1 egg, beaten*
*A little milk*
*Lard*

MIX the flour, salt and baking powder together in a bowl. Stir in the suet and mix everything well together, using the beaten egg and a little milk to make a firm dough.

Roll out the dough on a lightly floured board until it is about 1 cm (½″) thick. Cut out 9 cm (3½″) rounds with a glass or scone-cutter. Fry the little cakes in hot lard on both sides until golden brown. Serve hot with golden syrup. (These cakes can be cooked on a lard-greased griddle, but are best done in a frying pan.)

## WELSH LIGHT CAKES OR PANCAKES

LIKE THE BRETONS, who have a repertoire of pancakes still, the Welsh cling sensibly to a fine variety of griddle or bakestone cakes and pancakes. This may be a primitive style of cooking by origin, but with the subtle addition of a number of extra ingredients – extra, that is, to the basic mixture of flour/eggs/milk – the results can be elegant. This recipe would surprise the Viking housewife whose stone griddle, a true bakestone, was dug up in the excavations at Jarlshof in the Shetlands:

*6 rounded tablespoons flour*
*2 rounded tablespoons sugar*
*3 tablespoons soured cream*
*Pinch salt*
*3 eggs*
*½ teaspoon bicarbonate of soda*
*1 rounded tablespoon cream of tartar*
*4 tablespoons water*
*About 150 ml (¼ pt) buttermilk or milk*

BEAT together the first five ingredients. Mix the bicarbonate of soda and cream of tartar with the water – it will froth up rapidly – and add it to the batter. Dilute to a bubbly, not too thick consistency with the buttermilk or milk, adding it gradually. Cook the batter in small round cakes – they will spread a little, and the surface should rapidly become netted with holes. If the mixture seems too thick, add some more of the buttermilk or milk.

Apart from a preliminary greasing with a butter paper, you will not need to do more than brush the pan occasionally with a little oil or melted butter.

To turn the pancakes, ease the delicate, lacy edge from the pan with a thin, pointed knife, before pushing in the slice.

The Welsh way of eating these deliciously light pancakes is to spread them with Welsh butter and pile them up, one on the other. The butter melts in the heat and falls through the holes, so that the whole thing is rich and succulent, as well as light. To serve, cut the pile of pancakes in quarters.

IF you wish to serve them with Suzette sauce, which is not in the least English (it was invented by a French chef, Henri Charpentier, for Edward VII), here is his recipe:

*1 heaped tablespoon vanilla sugar*
*2½ cm (1") square lemon peel*
*2½ cm (1") square orange peel*
*125 g (4 oz) unsalted butter*
*1½ liqueur glasses maraschino*
*1½ liqueur glasses kirschwasser*
*2 liqueur glasses curaçao*

PUT the vanilla sugar into a small screw-top jar a day or two before you need it. Cut the peels into thin strips, and add them to the sugar. Shake the mixture about, after closing the jar tightly.

When you make the pancakes fold each one in half, then in half again to make a quarter-circle. For four people you need eight large ones. Dispose them on a plate in two circles, one on top of the other. They can, like the sugar, be prepared in advance, and stored in foil in the refrigerator.

Just before serving the dish, cut the butter into even-sized pieces. Mix the liqueurs together. Melt the butter in a pan, pour just over half the liqueur mixture into the butter, stir it about and tilt the pan towards the heat so that it catches fire. As the flames die down, put in the sugar, and then the pancakes to reheat. Turn them over so that they are bathed in the delicious sauce, but be careful not to disturb their triangular folds. Finally add the remaining liqueur, allow it to flame again and serve the pancakes. This last part is usually done at table in restaurants – a bit flashy, and you pay far too much for the spectacle. Such a simple dish is best made at home.

## PANCAKES FOR THE RICH, OR A QUIRE OF PAPER

IT IS SAD THAT THIS KIND OF RECIPE should survive as a commonplace in France, but not in England. We have let it vanish from our tables and cling masochistically to the poor man's recipe (page 339). This shows the different attitudes to food. The eighteenth-century farmer from whom this particular version of the recipe came labelled it firmly as being for the rich. In France, in Brittany, Normandy, Touraine, it would be regarded as a recipe for Sundays or other feast days; the poor man's version as an everyday family dish. Obviously the poor would eat the simpler pancakes more often than the richer, thinner kind, but they would not feel that the latter were not for them.

There is another, more sensible way of looking at these two kinds of pancake. The plain, thick batter produces a pancake that is more suitable for the strong flavours of meat and fish, for cheese and for eggs. This has nothing to do with the housekeeping money: or with frugality. You might, after all, choose to make a lobster filling. It would be quite wrong to wrap it up in the thin laciness of this recipe. For the dessert course, which should come lightly at the end of a meal, this 'rich man's' recipe is the one to choose, whether you serve it with nothing more than sugar and lemon juice, or whether you raid the brandy and liqueur bottles to make a sauce like Charpentier's in the recipe above.

*125 g (4 oz) butter*
*300 ml (½ pt) single cream*
*90 g (3 oz) flour*
*1 large egg*
*2 tablespoons brown sherry*
*1 teaspoon triple-distilled rose water or orange-flower water*
*½ grated nutmeg*

MELT butter over a low heat. Add to the cream, and with remaining ingredients make a pancake batter. If it seems a little thick, don't worry – the butter cools in contact with the other ingredients, but will melt again in the hot pan, making the mixture more liquid.

Rub an omelette pan over with a butter paper and heat it. Pour in a tablespoon or a small ladleful of the liquid (depending on the size of the pan), and tilt the pan so that it runs evenly over the base. The edges of the pancake will be thin and lacy, so ease them up with a knife before attempting to turn it. There is no need to keep greasing the pan, as the mixture is rich enough not to stick. These elegant, thin pancakes – paper-thin as the charming eighteenth-century name indicates – are like the French *crèpes dentelles*, and can be dressed up in the Suzette style (recipe on page 337). The English way was simply to sprinkle them with sugar and serve them very hot.

Rose water and orange-flower water can be bought at good chemists' shops. Channel Island milk can be substituted for half, or all, of the cream.

## HARVEST PANCAKES FOR THE POOR

| EIGHTEENTH-CENTURY INGREDIENTS | MODERN TRANSLATION |
|---|---|
| *1 pottle wheat flour* | *150 g (5 oz) flour* |
| *2 quarts new milk or mild ale* | *300 ml (½ pt) milk or mild ale* |
| *4 eggs* | *½ egg (1 is better)* |
| *Powdered ginger to taste* | *½ teaspoon powdered ginger* |
| *Lard for frying* | *Lard to grease the pan* |

MIX flour to a batter with milk or ale, and the egg. Flavour with ginger, and fry in lard in a heavy pan, a ladleful at a time. Try out a small pancake first to see if the consistency is right, add more liquid if it is too thick.

Chopped apple was sometimes added to enliven the pancakes.

A POTTLE was a measurement of bulk, equivalent to half a gallon (that is, 2½ litres, 4 pints). As far as flour was concerned, it meant just over a kilo (2½ lb) in weight. The word pottle was also used for small, conical chip baskets of strawberries or mushrooms.

This mixture – particularly when only half an egg is used – makes solid, heavy pancakes, which were ideal for the labourer's family at harvest, the busiest time of the year when everyone was needed in the fields. They were quickly cooked, which saved on firing as well as time. They were easy to carry, like a Cornish pasty or an apple turnover. They were reckoned to be an adequate substitute for both meat and bread – and they were thought of as a treat, 'a pleasant Part of a Family Subsistence'.

They make much better picnic food than a sandwich, particularly if you wrap them round a fried sausage, or a finger length of pâté, or cream cheese beaten up with chives and parsley. A Breton habit still, a habit that we once shared, of using the pancake as portable food, with embellishments when they could be afforded. Another Breton habit is to break an egg on to the pancake when it has been turned once, and leave it to cook. Delicious.

## CREMPOG LAS

THE WELSH EAT *crempog las* HOT, with butter; but when Mrs Freeman ran the Compton House Hotel in Fishguard she served them at breakfast time with sausages and bacon, and found they were a popular dish on the menu.

*125 g (4 oz) flour*
*1 large egg*
*1 dessertspoon chopped parsley*
*1 heaped teaspoon finely chopped shallot*
*Pepper, salt*
*Milk to mix*

MIX and cook in a greased pan, like a pancake, keeping the batter on the thick side.

## GRASMERE GINGERBREAD I

IN SPITE OF THE NAME, Grasmere gingerbread is a crumbly biscuit, not in the least like our usual soft dark gingerbread. You can buy it in a cottage by the churchyard at Grasmere, where William and Dorothy Wordsworth – and members of their family, and friends – are buried. In those days I suspect that fine-ground oatmeal would have been used, or a mixture of oatmeal and wheat flour, which was a luxury as it had to come from the south.

In Grasmere, the gingerbread was also known as 'rush-bearer's cake' because by the beginning of the 1820s the rush-bearers were usually children, and gingerbread was a more appropriate refreshment for them than the ale of earlier days. With only one break of thirteen years, the gingerbread has been handed out since 1819. One old lady at the end of the century remembered the 'clogger' who came to dance and organize everyone, and she described how the Wordsworths came over from Rydal Mount and never missed. They would sit in her family's little room to see the procession start. I wonder if Dorothy remembered, on these occasions, a cold Sunday night of 1803 in January . . .

*'Wm. had a fancy for some ginger bread. I put on Molly's cloak and my Spenser, and we walked towards Matthew Newton's. I went into the house. The blind man and his wife and sister were sitting by the fire, all dressed very clean in their Sunday clothes, the sister reading. They took their little stock of gingerbread out of the cupboard, and I bought 6 pennyworth. They were so grateful when I paid them for it that I could not find it in my heart to tell them we were going to make gingerbread ourselves. I had asked them if they had no thick – "No," answered Matthew, "there was none in Friday, but we'll endeavour to get some." The next day the woman came just when we were baking and we bought 2 pennyworth.'*
It was the last entry in her Journal.

One thing I do not understand. Here were the rush-bearers – and the Wordsworths – enjoying a well-established Grasmere speciality at the beginning of the nineteenth century, and yet in 1855 Mrs Sarah Nelson started selling Grasmere gingerbread in the cottage by the churchyard where you still buy it today. And she claimed to be the 'sole maker'. Moreover she patented her recipe and kept it secret. It is still kept secret today. From Dorothy Wordsworth's account, the Newton's gingerbread was thin, like the gingerbread of today. Perhaps Mrs Nelson had her own small variations on the local style, which made it special enough to warrant registration. Or was she more concerned to protect the name and the right to exclusive sale at a time when the tourist industry in the Lake District was growing fast?

If you have ever tasted the 'celebrated Grasmere gingerbread', you will see that the following recipes produce a different, better result – though they are all of a similar style, and quite different in kind from the squidgy dark cake – see page 320 – that most of us think of as gingerbread:

*250 g (8 oz) plain flour or fine oatmeal, or 125 g (4 oz) of each*
*125 g (4 oz) pale soft brown sugar*
*1 teaspoon ground ginger*
*¼ teaspoon baking powder*
*150 g (5 oz) lightly salted butter*

Mix the dry ingredients together. Melt the butter over a low heat, and when tepid use it to bind the mixture. Line a roasting pan or oblong tin with Bakewell paper. Spread the mixture over the tin in a thin layer, pressing it down lightly. Bake until golden brown, at mark 4, 180°C (350°F), for 30 to 35 minutes. Mark into oblong pieces straightaway, but leave to cool in the tin.

This is a good mixture for fruit crumbles (see page 270).

## GRASMERE GINGERBREAD II

**A** READER HAS KINDLY SENT ME A 'BROWNER' VERSION of the recipe above, which she learnt as a child when her mother was helping to manage a hotel in Grasmere.

*250 g (8 oz) wholewheat flour*
*½ teaspoon each bicarbonate of soda and cream of tartar*
*3 generous teaspoons ground ginger*
*175 g (6 oz) butter*
*150 g (5 oz) soft dark brown sugar*
*1 dessertspoonful golden syrup*

Sift flour, bicarbonate of soda and cream of tartar with the ginger, into a bowl. Rub in the butter. Add sugar and syrup and mix well. You will have a crumbly mixture. Press it into a roasting pan or oblong tin, lined with Bakewell paper. Bake for 45-50 minutes at mark 3, 160°C (325°F), until golden brown. Trim and cut into oblong biscuits.

BOTH VERSIONS of Grasmere gingerbread are delicious when served with whipped cream, sweetened with a little syrup from preserved ginger, and the ginger itself cut into slivers. Other recipes suggest a butter cream sweetened in the same way with syrup and chopped ginger, but make a good butter cream in the French style, not the nasty mixture of butter and twice as much icing sugar that so many English cookery books recommend.

## MEDIEVAL GINGERBREAD

GINGERBREAD OF THE PAST, the gingerbread of fairgrounds, the gingerbread that might lose its gilt, was not in the least like either the Grasmere recipes or the sticky gingerbread cake on page 320. For one thing, it was made of honey, not treacle, which until the sixteenth and seventeenth centuries was regarded as a medicine – particularly as an antidote for poisons – rather than a cheap sweetening substance. (Golden syrup was not made until the 1880s: even then black treacle remained popular in the north of England, where gingerbread and parkin are still among the most commonly made cakes.)

A medieval recipe, from about 1430, gives a good idea of what this early gingerbread was like. You warmed a quart of honey and skimmed it, then added breadcrumbs until the mixture was thick enough to be shaped into a square loaf without further cooking. Before the crumbs were added, the honey might be coloured yellow with saffron, or red with sanders, which was a preparation of sandalwood from India. It was also flavoured with black pepper and cinnamon, and presumably with ground ginger too, although this is not mentioned, perhaps because whoever copied the manuscript overlooked it – such slips were commonplace in those days and they are still the nightmare of modern cookery writers, who have printers and editors to help them check their manuscript.

However, since *English Food* was first published, I had a letter reminding me about the flat German spiced honeycake – *lebkuchen* – that is flavoured with cinnamon, cloves, nutmeg and cardamon, but no ginger, and used to make Hansel and Gretel 'gingerbread' houses at Christmas. I also think of the slightly rubbery French *pain d'épices* which some food writers translate as gingerbread, which is inadequate and misleading, although there is perhaps a relationship between all these cakes.

I made some gingerbread to the medieval recipe, and found that you needed about 30 g (1 oz) of breadcrumbs to one heaped dessertspoonful of honey. The size of a cake made with over a litre (2 pts) of honey must have been enormous. Some kind of colouring was needed, because the mixture would have been too pale without it: I used powdered saffron. By stirring the crumbs into the very hot honey, I made a thick paste which could easily be handled and moulded into shape, like almond paste though rather more grainy. When the cake was cool, we ate it in slices and found it a little close in texture, but the spices and the pepper in particular combined well with the honey sweetness and made it good to eat.

Medieval cooks decorated their 'gingerbread' with box leaves held in place by cloves; sometimes the cloves had gilded heads – 'the gilt off the gingerbread' – and were used in a diaper pattern.

## SHORTCAKES

SCOTTISH SHORTBREAD is only one of the many international variations on the shortcake theme. The particular blend of richness and crispness and lightness is achieved by using a blend of flour sifted with either cornflour or rice flour, in the proportion of 3:1. It is a good idea to have a jar of this handy, if you often need to make biscuits or light sponge cakes for which it is equally good.

*Shortbread biscuits:* weigh out 300 g (9 oz) of the flour-and-ground rice mixture. Sift it into a bowl. Add 200 g (6 oz) of butter, cut into cubes, and 100 g (3 oz) caster sugar. Mix to a dough. Roll out and cut with a large biscuit cutter. Bake in the oven preheated to mark 4, 180°C (350°F) until cooked but barely coloured.

You will notice that the quantities above give the proportion of 3:2:1, whether you work in imperial or metric. Very easy to remember.

*Viennese shortcake:* used to be a favourite of English teatables until commerce ruined it. Made at home properly, with butter, they are a delight. Weigh out 250 g (8 oz) flour-and-cornflour and beat it into 250 g (8 oz) of lightly salted Danish butter. Add 100 g (3 oz) sifted icing sugar and mix to a dough. With a rosette tube, pipe into paper bun cases set in tart tins, leaving a depression in the centre. Chill until really firm. Bake as above for about 20 minutes until cooked but uncoloured. When cold, dredge with icing sugar and drop a blob of raspberry jelly or jam in the centres.

This mixture can be baked as fingers and eaten plain. Or the ends can be dipped in melted chocolate.

## ELEGANT SUGAR THINS

*250 g (8 oz) butter*
*250 g (8 oz) caster sugar*
*1 egg*
*1 tablespoon double cream*
*300 g (10 oz) plain flour*
*½ teaspoon salt*
*1 teaspoon baking powder*
*Vanilla essence (or lemon juice or ground ginger)*
*Extra sugar*

CREAM the butter and sugar, then add the egg and cream and the remaining ingredients. If you like, divide the dough into three, and flavour each part differently. Form the dough into a long roll or rolls, about 5 cm (2″) in diameter, and wrap in foil. Put into the refrigerator until next day. Shave off the dough in the thinnest possible slices. Put them on a baking tray, sprinkle them with sugar and cook them for 5 minutes at mark 5, 190°C (375°F): they should remain pale in colour. There is no need to bake the dough all at once: cut off what you need and put it back in the refrigerator or the deep freeze.

This recipe and the next one can be flavoured in a variety of ways, to give you a large repertoire of biscuits.

## WALNUT BISCUITS

*220 g (7 oz) butter*
*150 g (5 oz) caster sugar*
*250 g (8 oz) self-raising flour*
*1 large egg*
*90 g (3 oz) shelled walnuts, chopped*

MIX in the same way as the Elegant Sugar Thins, but bake them for 10 minutes, as it is not possible to cut them into such fine rounds. Particularly good with coffee. A crisp, rich biscuit.

## BRANDY SNAPS

Makes 20-30

*125 g (4 oz) butter*
*125 g (4 oz) golden syrup*
*125 g (4 oz) granulated sugar*
*Pinch salt*
*125 g (4 oz) flour*
*2 teaspoons ground ginger*
*1 teaspoon lemon juice*
*2 teaspoons brandy*
*300 ml (½ pt) double cream, whipped*

MELT butter, syrup and sugar over a low heat in a medium-sized pan, stirring until you have a smooth mixture. Do not allow it to become really hot. Remove the pan from the heat, and when the mixture is barely tepid, stir in salt, flour, ginger, lemon juice and brandy.

Spread baking sheets with Bakewell paper and put teaspoons of the mixture on to it, allowing room for them to spread a great deal. About six teaspoons a sheet is right – although this will depend on whether the teaspoons were generously measured. Bake at mark 6, 200°C (400°F), for 8-10 minutes.

Press the brandy snaps round the handle of a wooden spoon into cigarette shapes while they are still hot. If they cool and become difficult, replace them in the oven to regain their suppleness. When cold store them in an airtight tin. Fill them with whipped cream, piping it in at both ends, not long before they are required.

THERE ARE many versions of these biscuits in English cookery, because they were popular as fairings – along with eel pies and gingerbread. Indeed at some fairs, like the Marlborough Mop, you can still buy them in flat, irregular, lacy rounds, much better than candy floss to sustain you on the Big Wheel or at the boxing booth. Old versions use black treacle – golden syrup, a refined product, did not come in until the 1880s.

## MEREWORTH BISCUITS

THIS RECIPE MAKES A HUGE NUMBER OF LIGHT BISCUITS, which taste delicious with butter alone, or with butter and a soft cheese. The thinner you can roll them the better. Some will puff up into a balloon; others will have two or three bubbles.

We once looked down on the perfect Greek cross of Mereworth Castle through young beech leaves, not long after we had visited the Villa Capra at Vicenza, which stands right up on a dusty hill surrounded by long grass. And here in the spring countryside of Kent was this perfect replica, with the same collected elegance, far below in a valley. I should like to see the kitchens of Mereworth, where these biscuits were made in the nineteenth century. The recipe is so simple, the results are so good – quite in keeping with the ambience. It comes from Lady Sarah Lindsay's *Choice Recipes*, published in 1883.

*250 g (8 oz) plain flour*
*30 g (1 oz) butter*
*Pinch salt*
*Hot milk*

RUB the first three ingredients together. Then mix to a dough with hot milk – it should be firm but soft. Knead it well. Roll out small bits of the dough to paper thinness: it will look and feel like a piece of cloth. Cut into approximately 5 cm (2″) rounds with a plain scone-cutter and bake at mark 7, 220°C (425°F), for about 5 minutes, until they are slightly browned and puffed up. Cool and store in an airtight box.

## CHEESE AND OAT BISCUITS

CHEESE-FLAVOURED OATMEAL BISCUITS set off a good home-made soup well – lamb and barley broth for instance, or a spinach soup. Another excellent way of eating them is to heap them with curd cheese and then to sprinkle them with finely chopped onion and Cayenne pepper.

A word about cheese. In cooking there is nothing to compare with Parmesan, bought in the piece (avoid the ready-grated kind if you can). It is not as expensive as it may seem, since you need far less of it than other hard cheeses for the same intensity of flavour. For this particular recipe I use two-thirds of mature farmhouse Cheddar that has dried out to hardness, and one-third Parmesan, but it is worth juggling with these proportions to find out what you prefer. The dough should be well salted and peppered to bring out the flavour of the cheeses.

*75 g (2-3 oz) rolled oats*
*150 g (5 oz) plain flour*
*100 g (3½ oz) salted butter*
*125 g (4 oz) grated cheese*
*2 egg yolks*
*Salt, pepper*

MIX oats and flour. Rub in the butter. Stir in cheese and season, then mix to a dough with the yolks and a very little iced water. Taste and add more seasoning if necessary. Roll out thinly on a board sprinkled with flour and rolled oats. Do this in batches – it makes life easier, especially if you are restricted with space. Cut with a scone-cutter and bake on greased trays at mark 6, 200°C (400°F), for 10 minutes, or until nicely golden. Leave to cool on wire trays.

# Stuffings, Sauces & Preserves

## Oyster Stuffing for Turkey and Other Poultry

*2-3 dozen oysters*
*300 g (10 oz) white breadcrumbs made from stale bread*
*150 g (5 oz) chopped suet*
*2 heaped tablespoons parsley*
*Grated rind of a lemon*
*2 heaped teaspoons thyme*
*¼ teaspoon each mace, nutmeg*
*A pinch Cayenne pepper*
*Salt, pepper*
*2 large eggs beaten*

OPEN the oysters. Save their liquor for the oyster sauce which is usually served at the same time. Chop the oysters in four, so that the pieces are quite large. Mix them with the remaining ingredients, adding salt and pepper to taste.

This quantity is enough for a 7 kilo (14 lb) turkey.

## Oyster Sauce

*2 dozen oysters*
*60 g (2 oz) butter*
*2 tablespoons flour*
*300 ml (½ pt) milk*
*150 ml (¼ pt) cream, preferably double cream*
*Grated nutmeg*
*Pinch Cayenne pepper*
*Lemon juice to taste*

OPEN the oysters, saving their liquor carefully. Put it with the liquor from the stuffing oysters. Chop the oysters themselves into fairly large pieces. With the butter, flour, milk and cream make a smooth béchamel sauce; add the oyster liquor and simmer for 20 minutes. Season to taste, and sharpen with a little lemon juice. Just before serving the sauce, stir in the chopped oysters – they will dilute it slightly. The sauce should be about the consistency of double cream or a little thinner.

THIS SAUCE is to go with the oyster stuffing for a turkey. For a large chicken, halve the quantities of both recipes.

If you cannot manage to buy oysters, try the recipes with mussels. It would be wise to start with a chicken, to see how you like the flavours together. See the *Chicken and Mussels* recipe on page 192.

## HERB STUFFING

**A** GOOD GENERAL STUFFING FOR VEAL, POULTRY, AND STUFFED TOMATOES. It can be used as a basis to which extra flavourings may be added to suit the occasion.

*1 medium onion, chopped*
*60 g (2 oz) butter*
*60 g (2 oz) chopped ham or bacon*
*1 tablespoon chopped parsley*
*1 teaspoonful thyme*
*125 g (4 oz) breadcrumbs*
*1 egg*
*1 egg yolk*
*Salt, pepper*

COOK the onion gently in the butter until softened, and golden, but not in the least brown. Put it into a bowl with the juices. Mix in the ham and remaining ingredients, seasoning the mixture to taste.

## PARSLEY AND LEMON STUFFING

**E**NOUGH FOR THE CENTRE CAVITY of a 6 kilo (12-13 lb) turkey. Remember that stuffing should never be packed in tightly – it must have room to swell. And to be cooked through properly.

*1 large white loaf*
*Grated peel of two lemons*
*Juice of 1 lemon*
*100 g (3½ oz) parsley*
*1 teaspoon lemon thyme (optional)*
*1 teaspoon dried marjoram*
*250 g (8 oz) lightly salted butter, creamed*
*3 eggs*
*Salt, freshly ground black pepper*

CUT the crusts from the bread, and reduce it to crumbs. Spread them out on baking sheets and dry them in the oven – they should not colour, so keep the temperature very low. Weigh out about 250 g (8 oz), and put into a basin. Mix in the lemon peel and juice. Discard the parsley stems and chop the leaves into the breadcrumbs. Add the lemon thyme if used, and the marjoram. Amalgamate thoroughly with the creamed butter and beat in the eggs. Elizabeth David's recipe.

## HAZELNUT STUFFING FOR POULTRY OR LAMB

READY-PREPARED CHOPPED TOASTED HAZELNUTS can be used for this stuffing with great success. Instead of the ginger the chopped liver of poultry and a heaped teaspoon of thyme may be added to make a more savoury mixture.

It is important to choose good hazelnuts. They need not be large, but they must have a fine flavour. The most delicious I have tasted were served with wine in Avellino, behind Vesuvius. They had been baked very slowly to a pale golden brown, and they were the same colour all through: I wish I had brought some home to make this recipe with, as they had the most delicious crispness. Avellino has been known for its hazelnuts since the Roman era (the botanical name is *Corylus avellana*), and you come to it through miles of hazel woods.

Kentish cobs are another variety (cobs, cobbles, that is, small stones): children used them, incidentally, in playing conkers, before the introduced horse-chestnut tree became common. Filberts are a different species – *Corylus maxima* – their name anglicized from French *noix de Philibert*, in other words, Saint Philibert, who was abbot of Jumièges in Normandy 1300 years ago. In much of France filberts ripen around the time of his feast day of August 22nd.

*1 large onion, chopped*
*60 g (2 oz) butter*
*125 g (4 oz) fresh white breadcrumbs*
*60 g (2 oz) hazelnuts, lightly grilled, chopped*
*4 knobs preserved ginger, chopped*
*Juice of 1 lemon*
*Grated rind ½ lemon*
*1 large egg, beaten*
*Salt, freshly ground black pepper*
*2 tablespoons chopped parsley*

COOK the onion until soft and golden in the butter. Keep the lid on the pan so that it doesn't brown. Mix with the remaining ingredients in the order in which they are given. Taste and correct the seasoning.

FOR A turkey, double or treble the amount, according to its size, remembering (see previous recipe) that stuffing should always be loosely packed. The ginger adds a chestnut-like texture and a subtle flavour which is difficult to place.

## Mint Sauce

The first point is not to be mean with the mint. The second is to use boiling water, which releases the fragrance of the mint into the sauce. The third is to avoid malt vinegar, which is harsh and can ruin any wine that is being served.

Mint with lamb and new potatoes is one of the pleasures of summer. Mint jellies which try to hold this pleasure for winter eating I find disgusting, because they are too sweet, too green.

*Mint leaves (see recipe)*
*3 tablespoons boiling water*
*3 level teaspoons sugar*
*4 tablespoons wine vinegar*

Chop enough mint leaves to fill a small jug of a size to hold 150 ml (¼ pt) comfortably. Pour on the boiling water and leave the mixture to infuse. When it is almost cold, stir in the sugar and then the vinegar. Mix well and adjust the seasonings to taste. Serve with roast lamb.

## Caper Sauce

Capers are the pickled flower-buds of the caper plant, *Capparis spinosa,* which is native to the Mediterranean region. They have been imported in barrels of vinegar since Tudor times; their first written record in English goes back to the fifteenth century.

Caper sauce is served with boiled leg of mutton or lamb, with skate and with salmon. Capers on their own go well with scrambled egg when it is being served cold, as part of an hors d'oeuvre; arrange them in a diamond pattern over the surface.

*30 g (1 oz) butter*
*1 tablespoon flour*
*500 ml (¾ pt) stock from cooking the main ingredient, e.g., mutton or lamb, or fish*
*Salt, pepper*
*1 egg yolk*
*2 tablespoons cream*
*1 heaped tablespoon capers (or more)*
*½ tablespoon chopped parsley*

Melt half the butter, stir in the flour and cook for a few moments. Moisten with the stock, which should be hot. Allow to simmer down to a smooth sauce the consistency of single cream. Season with salt and pepper. Mix in the remaining butter, then the egg yolk beaten with the cream, and keep the heat very low as you stir the sauce for a little while longer until it thickens. Add the capers and parsley at the last minute – if you know the tastes of your company, you can add more capers.

## HORSERADISH SAUCE

HORSERADISH SAUCE GOES WITH BEEF in English cookery, as everyone knows. The surprising thing is that it goes well with fish, too (Charles Cotton, Izaak Walton's friend the poet, gives a recipe for cooking trout in a stock flavoured with horseradish which works very well).

Anyone who has observed the tenacity of a colony of horseradish plants in their garden may be surprised to learn that it's a comparative newcomer to northern Europe, being a native of west and south-east Asia. This hot-climate plant was first named in England in 1597 by Gerard in his *Herball*. By then it was already well established in Germany, where people had become as fond of its pungent taste as we were of mustard. They called it *meerettich*, sea root, meaning root from over the sea. The English confused *meer*, sea, with *mähre*, mare, and arrived at horseradish.

*2 tablespoons grated horseradish root, or a good proprietary brand of creamed horseradish*
*150 ml (¼ pt) double cream*
*Sugar, salt*
*Juice of half a lemon*

WHEN grating horseradish remember that the outside of the root is the hottest part, so that a tablespoon from the outer root will have far more punch than a tablespoon grated across it.

Whip the cream, then fold in the horseradish to taste. Add salt and sugar, and, finally, lemon juice to sharpen it.

## WHITE DEVIL SAUCE

MUSTARD OF THE DIJON TYPE would be the normal thing to use for this recipe, but I like the grainy *Moutarde de Meaux* which has an especially good flavour. The recipe comes from *Food for the Greedy*, by Nancy Shaw, which was published in 1936.

*1 teaspoon French mustard*
*1 teaspoon anchovy sauce*
*1 teaspoon wine vinegar*
*1 teaspoon salt*
*1 teaspoon sugar*
*½ teaspoon Harvey Sauce*
*½ teaspoon Worcestershire Sauce*
*150 ml (¼ pt) double cream*

MIX all the ingredients together, except the cream. Whip the cream until it is fairly stiff, then add the seasoning mixture to taste.

This can be used as a sauce to be served with cold chicken, game, etc. Better still, spread the cold meat with French mustard lightly, having cut it into nice pieces. Arrange them in a small ovenproof dish, and pour over the sauce. Place in a hot oven, mark 6, 200°C (400°F), till thoroughly heated through and lightly browned.

## MELTED BUTTER

IN EARLY RECIPES YOU will often notice that fish or a vegetable are to be sent to the table with 'good melted butter'. This does not mean literally what it says – a piece of butter melted and perhaps flavoured with lemon juice – but a sauce largely composed of butter, thickened with flour rather than the egg yolks of *sauce Hollandaise*. This is the 'one sauce' of bad English cookery in the past; by adding shellfish or herbs or mustard or anchovy, its flavour and name became different. But only slightly so, as the general texture and weight of the sauce remained identical. The problem of this sauce is not of course curdling, but oiling: overheating is the cause, so that it is wise to add the second lot of butter just before the sauce is served. (A spoonful of ice-cold water will often bring an oiled sauce back to a proper consistency.)

I suspect that melted butter, or English butter sauce, is in for a come-back. With the popularity of the *nouvelle cuisine*, the light but rich texture of butter-thickened sauces has become popular again.

This particular version comes from *The Cook's Guide* by Charles Elmé Francatelli. He was chef at one time to Queen Victoria, but the filthy state of Buckingham Palace kitchens, before the Prince Consort reorganized the housekeeping, prevented him staying very long.

*275 g (9 oz) unsalted or lightly salted Danish butter*
*Pepper, nutmeg*
*30 g (1 oz) flour*
*Lemon juice, salt*
*1 tablespoon double cream (optional)*

THE first time you make this sauce, use a double boiler or bain-marie. This gives you greater control, though it does slow things down.

Melt one-third of the butter with pepper and nutmeg. Stir in the flour, then 150 ml (¼ pt) of cold water. Use a balloon whisk so that the sauce remains smooth. Heat until the sauce is at simmering point. Leave for 20 minutes, then beat in the remaining butter in small pieces, using the whisk. Any flavouring you decide to add – see below – should be put in at this point. Correct the seasoning with a little lemon juice, salt and more pepper. Add the cream if you like.

### Shrimp Sauce

SEE page 89. Note from this recipe that the water used in the recipe can be a fish stock or any other appropriately flavoured liquid.

### Lobster and Crab Sauces

ADD the chopped cooked flesh, with Cayenne pepper. Lobster sauce can be coloured by pressing the coral through a sieve into the sauce.

### Anchovy Sauce

FLAVOUR with anchovy essence.

### Herb Sauces

ADD enough chopped herbs – parsley, fennel, tarragon, or chervil, or chives – to make a good flavour. With large-leaved herbs such as sorrel and spinach and watercress, a cooked purée of the leaves colours the sauce as well as flavouring it. With fennel, a purée of the root of Florentine fennel can be added to the sauce, as well as the chopped green leaves from the top, or from garden fennel. A good sauce with fish.

## HOLLANDAISE SAUCE

*3 tablespoons white wine vinegar*
*2 tablespoons water*
*10 white peppercorns, slightly crushed*
*3 large egg yolks*
*175 g (6 oz) unsalted butter, cut into 12 pieces*
*Salt and lemon juice to taste*

### Method One

BOIL the first three ingredients together in a small pan, until there is a tablespoon of liquid only. Strain it into a pudding basin and leave it to cool. Beat in the egg yolks. Set the basin over a pan of not-quite-simmering water and beat in the butter, piece by piece, using a small wire whisk, or wooden spoon. The sauce should never be overheated, or the egg will scramble, and you will have to start again mayonnaise-style with a fresh egg yolk. At the end flavour with salt and lemon juice to taste.

### Method Two

BOIL the first three ingredients down to a tablespoon in the same way. Strain into the blender, add the eggs and switch on. Gradually add the butter, which should be melted and tepid but not hot. Finally season with salt and lemon juice. Place in a bowl to reheat over a pan of almost simmering water, stirring gently but steadily.

A FRENCH sauce, which has also become part of the English repertoire. Delicious with asparagus and other fine vegetables, or with fish.

## MAYONNAISE

MAYONNAISE, like Hollandaise Sauce, was first made in the eighteenth century. There are many legends about its origin and name: it seems to have become popular in England in the middle of the last century. Eliza Acton, who published her *Modern Cookery* in 1845, felt the need to reassure her readers about it; by 1861 Mrs Beeton took it for granted. Both writers include Hollandaise Sauce under the heading 'Dutch sauce', which, in spite of its name, it is not.

Mayonnaise and Hollandaise are the cold and hot versions of the same principle: they are the ideal partners for simply cooked food of quality.

*3 egg yolks*
*1 teaspoonful French mustard*
*Lemon juice or wine vinegar*
*300 ml (½ pt) olive or groundnut oil*
*Salt, pepper*

BEAT the egg yolks with the mustard and a dash of lemon juice or vinegar, until they begin to thicken; beat in the oil drop by drop at first until the sauce begins to emulsify – then you can go a little faster. Finally flavour with more lemon or vinegar, and salt and pepper. Be sure that eggs and oil are at warm room temperature before you start; rinse the bowl out with hot water, too, and then dry it. This way you will never have a failure. But *if* you do – one sometimes makes a careless slip with the oil – either put another egg yolk in a clean basin, or a tablespoon of mustard, and add the curdled sauce drop by drop, then the remainder of the oil. The mustard is a useful tip, if you are short of eggs, and if the food you are serving the sauce with can stand it.

Mayonnaise can be made successfully in a blender (use 1 whole egg and 2 yolks), or with an electric beater. The method is the same.

## ENGLISH SALAD SAUCE

APART FROM AN EXTRA EGG YOLK, this is Eliza Acton's recipe from *Modern Cookery* and it cannot be bettered. Anyone who remembers the unpleasant salad sauces we were reduced to making in the last war, or who had a baptism of bottled salad creams and 'mayonnaise' as a child, can feel safe with this recipe. It really is good, and lighter than mayonnaise. Nothing to be ashamed of at all. It can be used as a basis for extra flavourings appropriate to the salad, just as mayonnaise can – crushed anchovies, chopped green fresh herbs, capers, tomato concentrate and so on. It is not a sauce for plain green salads of lettuce, but for mixed salads of fish, meat, rice and so on.

*2 small hardboiled egg yolks*
*1 raw small egg yolk*
*Salt, freshly ground white pepper*
*Pinch Cayenne pepper*
*¼ teaspoon sugar*
*1 teaspoon water*
*150 ml (¼ pt) double cream*
*Chili, shallot or tarragon vinegar, or lemon juice*

SIEVE the hardboiled yolks (keep the whites to decorate the salad) into a basin. Stir in the raw yolk, the seasonings and water. Stir in the cream gradually. Finally flavour with vinegar or lemon juice.

## FRENCH DRESSING

THE IDEAL SAUCE FOR GREEN SALADS, and salads of fine vegetables which are being presented on their own. Tomatoes, cooked asparagus, purple-sprouting broccoli, new potatoes and so on. If you intend to dress a salad with mayonnaise, mix it first with a few spoonfuls of French dressing then drain off any surplus. The mayonnaise will mix in much more easily, and the result will be lighter.

We call this most useful of sauces French dressing or vinaigrette, and occasionally talk about it as if it was something Elizabeth David brought to England (like Raleigh and potatoes to Ireland) at the end of the 1940s. In fact, it has been around since the seventeenth century. In 1747 Hannah Glasse gives what might seem a very modern salad – broccoli, boiled and served cold with a dressing of oil and vinegar. 'Garnish with Stertionbuds' (Nasturtium buds were picked as a substitute for capers). She is referring to purple or green-sprouting broccoli, which does make an excellent salad.

*1 clove garlic, finely chopped*
*¼ teaspoon sugar*
*1 teaspoon French mustard (optional)*
*Freshly ground pepper*
*1 tablespoon wine vinegar*
*5 tablespoons olive oil*
*Salt*

CRUSH the garlic down in the bowl with the sugar, and mustard if used. Sprinkle with pepper and mix to a paste with the vinegar. Whisk in the

olive oil, and when everything is properly amalgamated, taste it and add salt – and more of any of the other seasonings that seem a good idea.

Fresh green herbs are a good addition to this sauce – parsley and chives are the usual ones, but tarragon, chervil, and savory can be added when they are appropriate.

## BREAD SAUCE

IN THE MIDDLE AGES many sauces were thickened with bread. This wasn't because cooks failed to realize that flour or egg yolks could do the job, but because sauces had on the whole to be coherent enough not to run off the bread trenchers which were used as plates, and not to sink into the trenchers too quickly or completely. With flour, thickening beyond a certain point turns a sauce to glue. With a lot of egg yolk, the sauce turns to custard. Bread is the thing for an agreeable un-sloppy moistness of texture, providing the crumbs are allowed to retain a certain identity, and not beaten back into a floury paste.

English bread sauce (and a mushroom soup still made in the Bresse district of France) are two survivors of this old cookery practice. Another, which older readers may remember from their childhood, is the supper dish of bread and milk, which declined into a dish for children and invalids, before it disappeared altogether under the onslaught of patent cereals. Like the sauce given above, bread and milk is delicious when bits of first-class baker's bread, and not factory flannel, are crumbled into hot creamy Jersey or Guernsey milk.

In some early recipes, stock is used instead of milk. Serve with poultry – roast chicken, turkey, guineafowl – and with game. Or with sausages. Or with sweetbreads (page 148).

*1 small onion, stuck with three cloves*
*500 ml (¾ pt) rich milk*
*90-125 g (3-4 oz) fresh breadcrumbs from a good loaf*
*Mace or nutmeg*
*Salt*
*Freshly ground white pepper*
*Pinch Cayenne pepper*
*50 g (1½ oz) butter, or 2 tablespoons double cream*

PUT the onion and milk into a basin and bring it to just below boiling point – this can be done over a pan of simmering water, or in a slow oven. The point is to infuse the milk with the flavour of onion and cloves, so the longer the milk takes to come to boiling point the better.

Remove the onion and whisk in the breadcrumbs until the sauce is thick, with all the milk taken up. Keep the basin over the boiling water until the sauce is heated through. If it seems on the thin side – bread sauce should not spread very much when put on to a plate – add more crumbs. If it seems so firm that a spoon stands up in it, add a little more milk. Season with mace or nutmeg, with salt and the peppers. Finally stir in the butter or cream and put into a sauce tureen. Scatter a small amount of Cayenne pepper on the top, and put Cayenne on the table for those who like their sauce fairly hot.

## SAWCE NOYRE FOR ROAST CAPON

CHICKEN LIVERS were used to make a favourite European sauce in the Middle Ages, and recipes still bob up in unexpected places in France and Italy. The Italians use white wine and lemon juice as a flavouring, and include dried ceps (mushrooms), a slice of Parma ham, onion and garlic, all cooked in together. I like the flavour of aniseed with poultry: it may sound odd, but the famous chickens of Le Mans are fed – or were until recent times – a proportion of aniseed to give them their delicious flavour.

In France *sauce noire* or *sauce infernale* is served with game (the game livers are included in the sauce) and spread on croûtons of fried bread placed under the birds as they are served. In Italy it comes to the table on its own, as a first course, with thin toast: or spread on slices of hot roast veal interspersed with pieces of toast also spread with the sauce. It's called *salsa di fegatini* – sauce of little livers.

*500 g (1 lb) chicken livers*
*Chicken fat*
*Aniseed, ginger and cinnamon*
*1 slice of bread*
*Cider vinegar or lemon juice*
*Salt, pepper*

FRY the livers in chicken fat for about 4 minutes, until they are brown outside but still pink inside. Add aniseed, ginger and cinnamon to taste – start with ¼ teaspoon each. Cut the crusts from the bread, and reduce it to crumbs with the liver (if you have a Moulinex chopper). Otherwise put the liver through the fine plate of the mincer and mix it with the crumbs. Sharpen the reheated sauce to taste with vinegar or lemon juice. Season with salt and pepper. This sauce is more of a spreading than a runny pouring consistency, and thicker than the bread sauce of the recipe above, as you would expect from a medieval recipe. (This one comes from a manuscript of 1439, now in the Bodleian Library at Oxford.)

## APPLE SAUCE I

MOST NORTH EUROPEANS serve apple cooked in various ways with pork, fresh or salted, and rich poultry such as duck and goose. We might well extend the use of apple with pheasant, chicken and black pudding, in the French style that is especially typical of Normandy. By using different varieties of eating apple, as well as the traditional sour cooker, apple sauce can be altered to suit different meats and different occasions.

*250 g (8 oz) Bramley's Seedlings*
*1 small or moderate quince*
*150 ml (¼ pt) water*
*1 heaped tablespoon sugar*
*1 strip orange rind*
*30 g (1 oz) butter*
*Freshly ground black pepper*

CUT the apples up roughly, and slice quince rather more finely. Do not peel or core the fruit. Put with water and sugar and orange rind into a pan, and simmer, covered, until soft. Sieve into a clean pan, and cook briskly for a few minutes until the purée is lightly coherent, not sloppy and wet. Stir in the butter, and, last of all, a little freshly ground pepper.

## APPLE SAUCE II

*375 g (12 oz) Cox's Orange Pippins or Laxtons or James Grieve apples*
*90 ml (3 oz) water*
*1 strip lemon peel*
*30 g (1 oz) butter*
*Freshly ground black pepper*

COOK in the same way as Apple Sauce I and serve with pork, salt pork, sausages, duck, goose.

## APPLE SAUCE III

*500 g (1 lb) Cox's Orange Pippins, Laxtons, or James Grieve*
*Clarified butter*
*90 ml (6 tablespoons) cider or dry white wine*
*90 ml (6 tablespoons) double cream*
*Lemon juice*

CORE and dice the apples (peel them, too, if you like, but it's not necessary). Fry them gently until they are golden and slightly softened in some clarified butter. Remove the apples to a serving dish. Deglaze the pan with cider or wine, scraping in all the apple juices and brown bits and pieces. When this liquid has reduced to a concentrated essence, stir in the cream. Heat through, sharpen with lemon juice and pour over the apples. For veal and chicken.

## SPICED APPLE SAUCE

*500 g (1 lb) Bramley Seedlings*
*30 g (1 oz) butter*
*2 tablespoons water*
*2 tablespoons white wine vinegar*
*¼ teaspoon grated nutmeg*
*¼ teaspoon cinnamon*
*¼ teaspoon freshly ground black pepper*
*About 30 g (1 oz) soft dark brown sugar*

PEEL, core and cut up the apples. Put them in a pan with the butter, water, vinegar and spices. Cover and cook until soft enough to beat to a purée. Add sugar to taste, and more spices if you like.

A GOOD recipe, with chutney-like overtones. Ideal for boiled salt pork, and duck or goose.

## CUMBERLAND SAUCE

IN *Spices, Salt and Aromatics in the English Kitchen,* Elizabeth David has a long and interesting discussion on the origins of Cumberland sauce (one thing is sure – it didn't come from Cumberland).

'What basis there is for the story that it was named after Ernest, Duke of Cumberland, that brother of George IV's who became the last independent ruler of Hanover, nobody has ever explained. Still, as legends concerning the origin of dishes go, it's as good as another, and better than some: the sauce itself being as obviously German in origin as was its supposed royal namesake of the House of Hanover.'

Then she goes on to point out that there is no recipe for it in any of the standard nineteenth-century cookery books, where one would expect to find it. Its rise to popularity occurred at the beginning of this century, when fruit sauces with game and so on became popular in England (see *Black cherry sauce,* page 360). There are earlier, similar sauces – Francatelli gives a German sauce for boar's head and brawn in an edition dating from his *Cook's Guide* of the early 1880s. The major difference is that his contains an inordinate amount of horseradish (it takes Teutonic courage, I think, to grate 'a large stick of horseradish' into half a pot of redcurrant jelly).

Some modern recipes add the unnecessary embellishment of glacé cherries, which really strike a false note. Another thing to avoid is a stiffening of cornflour or gelatine: the sauce thickens quite enough as it cools, and its flavour should not be blunted with such things.

*2 Seville oranges, or 1 sweet orange and 1 lemon*
*250 g (8 oz) redcurrant jelly*
*1 teaspoon Dijon mustard*
*5 tablespoons port*
*Freshly ground black pepper, salt*
*Ground ginger*

PEEL the oranges, or orange and lemon, thinly. Cut the peel into matchstick strips and blanch them for 5 minutes in boiling water. Drain them in a sieve.

Meanwhile heat the jelly and mustard together over a low heat, whisking them to a smooth thickness. Add the juice of the oranges, or of the orange and the lemon, and the remaining ingredients, with plenty of black pepper, and a little salt and ginger to taste. Stir in the peel, and then simmer for 5 minutes. Pour into a glass dish or a jar and serve cold with cold or hot ham and tongue, with venison and game, duck and goose.

If Cumberland sauce is stored in a covered jar in the refrigerator, it will keep for weeks quite satisfactorily.

## VENISON SAUCE

*2 tablespoons port wine*
*250 g (8 oz) redcurrant jelly*
*Small stick of cinnamon, bruised*
*Thinly pared rind of a lemon*

SIMMER all the ingredients together for about 5 minutes, stirring to break down the jelly (this may require the addition of a tablespoon or two of water, if commercially made redcurrant jelly is used). Strain into a hot sauceboat.

A SIMPLE version of the many varieties of port wine sauce for venison. It was invented by Queen Victoria's chef, Francatelli.

## CHERRY, PLUM OR DAMSON SAUCE

AN EARLY VERSION OF THIS SAUCE is given by Francatelli. It is related to other fruit sauces such as Cumberland Sauce, and the very simple venison sauce above. They are obviously German in origin, though whether we owe them to the Hanoverian kings or to Prince Albert's influence is uncertain. Their great popularity occurred in Edwardian times, although, as I have said, a few earlier recipes of the kind do appear occasionally.

*250 g (8 oz) stoned morello or amarelle cherries, plums or damsons*
*150 ml (¼ pt) red wine*
*150 ml (¼ pt) port*
*1 tablespoon sugar*
*2 cloves*
*1 piece cinnamon, 2 cm (1") long*
*2 generous tablespoons redcurrant jelly*
*Juice of 3 oranges*
*Juice of 1 lemon*
*Black pepper*
*30 g (1 oz) butter*

PUT the fruit, wine, port, sugar, cloves and cinnamon into a pan. Bring to the boil and simmer for 10 minutes until the fruit is tender. Add jelly, fruit juices and season with pepper. At this stage plum or damson sauce may be sieved and sweetened a little more: cherries are best left whole. When the sauce is well amalgamated, remove it from the heat and whisk in the butter.

Serve immediately with hot boiled tongue (page 185), venison and game.

CANNED MORELLO cherries may be used. And in any case avoid using sweet dessert cherries, as they do not have the right acidity of flavour.

## ORANGE SAUCE FOR DUCK AND GAME

AN ENGLISH VERSION of the French *sauce bigarade*, which goes back to the eighteenth century. The meat can be served with a garnish of orange slices heated in a little of the sauce: the main thing is not to make the whole dish too sweet, as it sometimes is in some restaurants.

*50 g (1½ oz) butter*
*1 rounded tablespoon flour*
*500 ml (¾ pt) hot duck, game or beef stock*
*2 Seville oranges, or 2 sweet oranges and 1 lemon*
*1 tablespoon sugar*
*Any meat juices available from cooking duck or game*
*4 tablespoons port (can be omitted for duck)*

MELT the butter in a small pan and let it turn a delicate golden brown colour. Stir in the flour, cook for 2 minutes, then moisten with the stock. Allow this sauce to simmer gently for at least 20 minutes – the longer the better. Meanwhile remove the peel thinly from the oranges, cut it into matchstick strips and simmer in water for 3 minutes. Drain and add to the simmering sauce. Add the juices of the oranges, and lemon if used, and stir in sugar to taste; start with a little and add more if necessary. Finally pour in the meat juices from roasting duck or game, which should be well skimmed of fat, and finally the port.

## PRESERVED SPICED ORANGES

*10 large thin-skinned seedless oranges, or 18 smaller ones*
*1¼ kilos (2½ lb) granulated sugar*
*600 ml (1 pt) white wine vinegar*
*1½ sticks cinnamon*
*1 heaped teaspoon cloves*
*6 blades mace*

WIPE the oranges. Cut into slices at least 1 cm (¼") thick, and remove any pips if the oranges are not as seedless as they might be. Put into a pan and cover them with water. Put a lid on the pan, and simmer gently for 40 minutes, or until the peel is soft. Be careful not to overcook the slices, or they may disintegrate.

Meanwhile dissolve the sugar in the vinegar, put in the spices and bring to the boil. Simmer for 3-4 minutes.

Drain the orange slices, but keep their cooking liquor; place them in a shallow pan and cover them with the vinegar syrup – if there is not quite enough, add some of the orange cooking liquor. Simmer with a lid on the pan another 30-40 minutes, or until the slices look clear. Again do not overcook, or allow the syrup to boil hard. Remove the pan from the heat and leave for 24 hours, slices and syrup together.

Drain the orange slices and put them into jars. Cover them with the syrup. Keep topping up with the syrup for three or four days. The jars can then be sealed, and should be left alone for six weeks. Serve the orange slices with pork, duck, ham, either hot or cold. Syrup left in the jars when the slices have gone, makes a good orange sauce for duck.

## BANANA CHUTNEY

SMALL CAVENDISH BANANAS, the best bananas of all, once came only from the Canaries. Now they are grown all over the world, though we rarely see them in our shops these days. They seem to have been swamped by the big, coarser West Indian kind. I have often thought we would never see them again but they are being re-introduced in such varieties as lady's fingers, red fig, silk fig or just fig bananas. Keep them for eating, as their fine fragrance deserves.

For this recipe the big West Indian bananas are ideal. It comes from a little booklet of recipes brought out about 1906 to publicize what was in effect a new fruit. The mass trade in bananas did not begin until 1901 when Fyffe, Elder inaugurated their fleet of refrigerated ships.

*12 West Indian bananas, peeled, sliced*
*300 ml (½ pt) white wine or cider vinegar*
*250 g (8 oz) sugar*
*2 medium onions, finely chopped*
*125 g (4 oz) sultanas, finely chopped*
*Up to 3 teaspoons salt*
*30 g (1 oz) curry powder*
*Cayenne pepper*
*½ teaspoon ground cinnamon*

SIMMER bananas in the vinegar until soft and pulpy. Add sugar while very hot, then leave to cool. Mix in onion, sultanas and salt slowly to taste, with the curry powder, a pinch of Cayenne and the cinnamon. Leave to stand

12 hours, taste again and adjust seasoning. Pot in small sterilized jars and store in the refrigerator, or a very cool, dark, dry place. Do not use metal tops which will react with the vinegar.

Good with ham and cold salt pork, and chicken.

## SPICED REDCURRANT JELLY

AN UNUSUAL RECIPE from *The Llandegai Recipe Book*, which was first published in 1958 to help raise money for the organ and bells of St Tegai's Church at Llandegai (llan means 'church of'). These local pamphlets and small books of recipes, brought out to raise money by schools, monasteries, the Women's Institutes, often contain a handful of regional recipes that have been popular for centuries, although they have never quite reached the main cookery books. Often, one hears an echo of some medieval or Tudor dish, undimmed by additions of baking powder, or the substitution of margarine and vegetable fats for butter and lard.

*1½ kilos (3 lb) redcurrants*
*Scant litre (1½ pts) water*
*3 cloves*
*1 teaspoon cinnamon*
*250 ml (8 oz) malt vinegar*
*1½ kilos (3 lb) granulated sugar*

PUT the redcurrants into a large pan as they are – do not remove stalks, leaves, etc. Add the water and spices. Bring to the boil and simmer until the redcurrants are soft. Strain through a jelly bag (or put through a sieve, if you do not mind cloudy-looking jelly). To the liquid, add the vinegar and sugar and boil until setting point is reached. Pour into sterilized jam jars; cover while still very hot.

## PEPPERED REDCURRANT JELLY

MAKE up as in the spiced recipe above, but use 250-500 ml (8-16 fl oz) red wine, and water to bring the quantity up to 1¼ litres (2¼ pts). Omit the spices. When the jelly is beginning to set, stir in plenty of coarsely ground black pepper – it is important that you can see the particles quite clearly, that they make a pleasant roughage in the smooth texture. Then pot in small jars in the usual way.

This makes a particularly good jelly with winter lamb and venison.

## CORNEL CHERRY, ROWANBERRY, BILBERRY OR CRANBERRY JELLY

WEIGH the berries, freed of stalks and leaves, and put them into a pan with an equal weight of tart apples (windfalls do very well) cut into pieces. Do not peel or core the apples. Cover them with water and simmer gently, covered, until the apples and berries are reduced to a soft pulp. Strain the juice through a muslin-lined sieve, without pressure if you want your jelly to remain clear (personally when I have a very few cornel cherries I do not want to waste a drop of the flavour, so I squeeze the pulp as hard as I can and expect everyone to overlook the opaque appearance of the jelly in the interests of flavour).

Measure the juice, put it on to boil with 500 g (1 lb) of sugar to every 600 ml (1 pt). When the jelly reaches setting point, pot in the usual way.

THESE JELLIES are not quite so tart as the ones above, but they go well with pork. Medlar jelly is good with poultry and game.

## QUINCE, MEDLAR, SORB OR CRAB APPLE JELLY

ALTHOUGH QUINCES SHOULD BE RIPE, medlars and sorbs are best used before they get to the softened, bletted stage when they are pleasant to eat as a dessert fruit. Crab apples should be used when they are just ripe.

Cut up the fruit after washing it. Cover it with water, and continue as in the recipe above. Precious quinces can be eked out with a proportion of windfall apples – in very thin years, I have used 1 part quinces to 3 parts of apples and the jelly has still been delicious.

THESE JELLIES are the ideal accompaniment to game and turkey or guineafowl, to roast lamb as well. Their tart flavour is good, too, with thin bread and butter.

## HERB JELLIES

THESE are basically apple jellies, flavoured with one or another herb, which make an agreeable accompaniment to meat. Mint for lamb, thyme for rabbit and pork, rosemary for lamb, and so on.

CUT UP and weigh windfall apples or green cookers and put them into a preserving pan. To each 1 kilo (2 lb), add 100 ml (3½ fl oz) white wine vinegar and enough water barely to cover the fruit. Tuck in three or four generous sprigs of the chosen herb and simmer until the fruit is very soft. Strain through a jelly bag, leaving overnight to drip.

## HOT RED PEPPER JELLY

A RECIPE OF MY DAUGHTER SOPHIE'S for a clear red jelly with bite. It goes with cold meats or spread on crackers or pumpernickel with cream cheese. Do not be tempted to leave out the pectin or your jelly will not set: this is something to do with the chili peppers, as the less you use the less pectin you need. Normally apple jelly sets without any trouble at all.

*1 kilo (2 lb) cooking apples*
*3 medium sweet red peppers, deseeded, roughly chopped*
*4 fresh red and/or green chili peppers, deseeded, roughly chopped*
*450 ml (15 fl oz) cider vinegar*
*Sugar*
*90-125 ml (3-4 fl oz) liquid pectin, e.g. Certo*

CORE apples, reserving core and pips. Chop flesh roughly and process with sweet and hot peppers to give a rough mash. Scrape into a large pan and add apple cores, pips, vinegar and 450 ml (¾ pt) water. Bring to the boil, then simmer for 20 minutes. Tip into a jelly bag, or a large piece of double muslin, hang up and leave to drip for 4 hours or overnight.

Measure the juice and for each 600 ml (1 pt) weigh out 500 g (1 lb) granulated sugar. Warm the sugar and place with juice in a pan, stirring over a moderate heat until sugar is dissolved. Bring to boil and boil for about 20 minutes. Skim off the scum. Remove from heat, let the bubbles subside, and stir in 90 ml (3 fl oz) pectin. Test for setting by putting a few drops on to a chilled saucer. Cool, then push gently with your fingernail. If the surface wrinkles, it is fine. If not stir in another 2 tablespoons of pectin and test again.

Pour into small hot, sterilized jars, seal (do not use metal lids which will corrode) and leave to cool. Store in a cool, dark place.

## APRICOT AND PINEAPPLE JAM

I HAVE INCLUDED THIS RECIPE for jam because it is one I have never come across outside England – most jam recipes are common to all the countries of northern Europe and America. My mother used to make it when I was a child for special occasions, but she lost the recipe during the war. Then, quite unexpectedly, someone sent me the recipe because he, too, had associated it with the splendid teas provided by his mother in the days before calorie-counting became a national passion. He recalled the puff pastry rolls filled with various savoury mixtures, the sandwiches, angel cakes with cream and jam, coconut pyramids and other small cakes, then larger cakes for filling up the gaps – and this magnificent jam.

*500 g (1 lb) dried apricots*
*1½ litres (2½ pts) cold water*
*375 g (12 oz) tin pineapple*
*1½ kilos (3 lb) sugar*
*125 g (¼ lb) blanched, sliced almonds*

WASH and then soak the apricots in the water for 24 hours. Remove any stones and crack them to get at the kernels, which should be put with the almonds. Simmer the apricots in their soaking liquid for half an hour. Meanwhile drain the pineapple – keep the juice – and chop it fairly small. Add the pineapple, the juice, the sugar, the almonds and any kernels to the apricots. Bring back to the boil and cook for about 20 minutes until the jam reaches setting point. Pot in the usual way.

## LEMON CURD

*2 large lemons*
*90 g (3 oz) unsalted or slightly salted butter, cut in bits*
*200 g (7 oz) sugar lumps*
*3 large eggs*

EITHER grate the lemon rind finely into a basin, or rub the skins all over with half a dozen sugar lumps to remove the fragrant zest and oils, and put the lumps into a basin (the first method gives a slight graininess to the lemon curd which many people prefer). Add the strained lemon juice, the butter and the sugar. Stand over a pan of simmering water and stir occasionally until the sugar is dissolved into the juice and butter. Meanwhile beat the eggs, and pour them through a strainer into the basin. Stir steadily until the mixture becomes thick. Do not allow it to boil. Pour it into clean pots and cover in the usual way.

IF YOU like a milder flavour, add an extra ounce of butter and another egg to the ingredients above.

When using lemon curd for tarts, sprinkle a layer of crushed sponge finger biscuits over the pastry before adding the lemon curd. 125 g (4 oz) of almonds, ground to a coarse powder with their skins on, are even better than sponge finger biscuits.

## PASSION FRUIT CURD

LIKE LEMON CURD, this can be eaten with bread and toast, or used as a filling for tarts and cakes. The proportions can be varied if you want to experiment with other fruit – raspberries, gooseberries, apricots, anything with an acid edge to it. This recipe has far less sugar than lemon curd: if you think the result is not going to be thick enough, chip in extra butter at the end while the mixture is still warm enough to soften it to an emulsion, but not hot enough to turn it to oil.

*4 large passion fruit, or 6 medium size*
*125 g (4 oz) sugar*
*125 g (4 oz) slightly salted Danish, or unsalted Normandy butter*
*3 large eggs or 2 large eggs and 2 egg yolks, beaten*
*About 1 tablespoon lemon or lime juice*

HALVE passion fruit and scrape the pulp into a non-stick pan. Add sugar and butter cut into cubes. Stir over a low heat until dissolved together. Bring to the boil and whisk thoroughly into the eggs. Return to the pan and stir over a low heat until the mixture reaches 80°C (170°F). Do this slowly and keep raising the pan from the heat, so that the curd has a chance to thicken. Alternatively you can use the *bain-marie* method of the recipe above.

Remove the curd from the stove and stir as it cools down from time to time. Pour through a sieve, rubbing the seeds to get through as much curd as possible. Stir in some of the passion fruit seeds. Season to taste with lemon or lime juice. Pour into two small sterilized jars, cool completely, cover and store in the usual way.

NOTE: lemon and passion fruit curd are best eaten fairly quickly and stored in the refrigerator, for up to a fortnight.

## TWO WHOLE ORANGE MARMALADES

THE SIMPLEST, quickest, best-flavoured marmalades.

*3¼ litres (6 pts) water*
*3 kilos (6 lb) sugar*
*1½ kilos (3 lb) Seville oranges, scrubbed*

SIMMER oranges in water for about 1½ hours until skin is tender and easily pierced. Remove the oranges, cool them and cut them in quarters; leave the liquor in the pan. Remove the orange pips and tie them in a muslin. Either cut the quarters into shreds of the size you like, or whizz them briefly in a liquidizer in batches, which must be done carefully or you will end up with a coarse slosh rather than shreds. Some machines have a shredder attachment, which does the job perfectly.

Put pulp and bag of pips into the orange liquor in the pan. Add the warmed sugar. Stir until the mixture boils, then leave to boil until setting point is reached. Let the marmalade stand for 10-15 minutes until potting in the usual way (if you pot it immediately, the peel will sink).

IF YOU like an even stronger Oxford style of marmalade, weigh the shredded pulp and boil it with an equal weight of sugar, plus 300 ml (½ pt) of the cooking liquor for each 500 g (1 lb) of pulp. This gives you the finest marmalade of all: it may seem expensive, but one eats less of it as it tastes stronger.

## QUINCE COMFITS

**A** RECIPE FOR THOSE WHO HAVE WISELY PLANTED A QUINCE in their garden. This best of all fruit trees has flowering globes of pink in the spring, and in autumn fruit of such golden fragrance that they scent the house when you bring them in.

An old recipe popular throughout Europe. 'Quyncys in comfyte' were served at Henry IV's coronation banquet in 1399. By the eighteenth century, this 'marmelade' of quinces was a standard household recipe. If you cook the above mixture less, or add less sugar – say 250 g (8 oz) to each 500 g (1 lb) of sieved quinces – you will end up with a softer quince 'cheese' or 'butter'.

Incidentally, the word 'marmalade' properly belonged to the quince rather than the orange. The word goes back via French, Portuguese, Latin and Greek to the Arcadian *marmahu*, the word the Assyrians and Babylonians used for quince.

QINCES are precious, to be used sparingly, but try and set aside six or seven for these delicious sweets. Wash them, and rub off any of the grey fluff which may still be clinging to their yellow skins. Cut them up roughly, put them into a pan with 2-3 cm (1″) of water. Cover and simmer until they are soft enough to sieve. Weigh this pulp, and put it with an equal weight of sugar into a clean, heavy pan. Bring to the boil and boil slowly for at least an hour, until the mixture is very thick indeed and leaves the side of the pan. Stir fairly frequently, so that the bottom doesn't catch. It will splatter from time to time with a soft explosive plop, so keep your stirring hand wrapped in a cloth.

Pour into metal baking trays or swiss roll tins, lined with Bakewell paper. Dry for 3-4 days over the solid fuel or oil cooker, or in the airing cupboard. Cut into squares with a knife dipped into hot water and dried. Put these squares into an airtight box with caster sugar and shake them about so that they are well coated. The surplus sugar will prevent them sticking together, but in fact the mixture should be so firm that this is not likely.

Try to keep them stored away for Christmastime desserts. They can be put on top of grilled pork chops, and left under the heat for a few moments, too.

## HARD SAUCE OR BRANDY BUTTER

*250 g (8 oz) unsalted butter, cut in pieces*
*125 g (4 oz) icing sugar*
*3 tablespoons brandy*
*Squeeze of lemon juice*
*Grated nutmeg*

PUT the butter in a warmed bowl and cream it, either with a wooden spoon or an electric beater. Tip the remaining ingredients, except for the nutmeg, into the bowl and mix everything together with your hands; grate in a good amount of nutmeg, mix again, taste and adjust the seasoning. The flavours combine much better in the warmth from your hands than they do with a spoon or beater.

## CUMBERLAND RUM BUTTER

IN OUR FAMILY, these butters were always made – as in this recipe, and the one above – with less than the usual quantity of sugar. They tasted all the better for it, particularly when they were being eaten with Christmas Pudding and mince pies, which are sweet. (A Frenchman visiting the court of Queen Elizabeth I was shocked to see that most people's teeth were black and rotten from eating too many sugary things – our national sweet-tooth has a long history.)

In Cumberland, rum butter and oatcakes were given to friends who called at the house to see a new baby. In turn they would leave 'a silver coin, and on the day of the christening, when the butter bowl was empty, the coins were placed in it. A sticky bowl, with plenty of coins sticking to it, meant that the child would never be wanting.' There are many people still alive today whose birth was celebrated with rum butter, oatcakes and silver sixpences, and whose heads were washed with rum soon after they were born (then the rum bottle was handed to the father and his friends, who washed the child's head in a more symbolic manner).

*250 g (8 oz) unsalted butter, cut in pieces*
*175 g (6 oz) soft brown sugar*
*3 tablespoons rum*
*Grated nutmeg*

FOLLOW the method given above. Sometimes the butter is melted rather than creamed, but the result is a little on the close, heavy side.

## GRANNY MILTON'S PEARS IN BRANDY

A BONUS FROM WRITING ABOUT FOOD is the friends one makes. Some of them become regular suppliers of information and recipes, which is particularly valuable when they live in a part of the country I don't know well. For nearly 20 years now Mimi Errington, a cookery writer herself, has been sending me bulletins from Nottinghamshire. Her subjects have ranged from the risqué folklore of the skate to local cheeses, fruit – she lives near the original Bramley apple tree in Southwell – and vegetables. This year she was given some excellent pears in brandy. She asked the giver for the recipe and passed it on to me, as it makes such good use of hard pears that are so often thrown away unappreciated.

*3 kilos (6 lb) hard windfall pears*
*3 lemons*
*8 cloves*
*2 kilos (4½ lb) granulated sugar*
*10 cm (4½") stick of cinnamon*
*6 tablespoons brandy*

PEEL, quarter and core pears. Grate rind from lemons, then squeeze their juice. Layer pears, lemon rind and juice, and sugar into a large bowl. Cover and leave overnight. Transfer pears to a large pan, covering them with their juices. Tuck in the cloves and cinnamon. Cover and cook in a low oven – mark 1, 140°C (275°F) – for 6 hours.

Leave pears to cool, stir in brandy. Remove cloves if you can find them, and the cinnamon stick. Transfer to jars, cover closely and leave in a cool, dark place for 3 months.

## QUINCE VODKA

A LONG TIME AGO I wrote somewhere that quinces made anything delicious. 'Yes,' said one reader, 'but first catch your quinces.' And he enclosed a good recipe for those who can only bag a couple.

WASH and grate two ripe yellow quinces, peel, core and all, and put into a litre (2 lb) bottling jar. Add 60 g (2 oz) sugar. Fill up the jar with vodka (you could also use gin, rum or brandy). The bottle need not be full, but the fruit must be covered. Close tightly. Leave in a dark place for two months. Taste (this is the good part). Add more sugar if you prefer a liqueur-like sweetness. Strain into a clean bottle, and close tightly.

## RICH ORANGEADE (AND LEMONADE)

A VICTORIAN RECIPE, which must have been popular at dances towards the end of the winter when Seville oranges are in season. It can be made without them, and without orange-flower water, but it will not be such a delicious drink.

Follow exactly the same principle for making lemonade. More sugar may be needed, but this is the kind of thing that can always be adjusted at the end. Omit the orange-flower water.

*6 large, sweet oranges*
*1 Seville orange*
*250 g (8 oz) sugar*
*Orange-flower water*
*Juice of 1 lemon (see recipe)*

REMOVE the peel in thin strips from all the oranges. Be careful not to include the white pith. Put the strips into a large pan with 1 litre (1¾ pts) of cold water. Bring slowly to simmering point, and keep at this temperature for 5 minutes; do not allow the water to boil or it will draw too much bitterness from the peel. Leave the pan to cool down. Bring sugar to the boil with 500 ml (¾ pt) of water, and boil for 3 minutes to make a syrup. Cool it down, too. Finally mix together the strained peel water, the syrup and the strained juice of all the oranges. Add a light flavouring of orange-flower water, and a little lemon to sharpen the flavour if this seems a good idea. Serve well chilled.

## VANILLA SUGAR

THE simplest thing is to put four vanilla pods in a large bottling jar, and keep it filled up with caster sugar. Although the pods seem expensive, they are a good investment: they can be used whole in cooking, for instance, when making a custard or stewing fruit, and afterwards they can be washed and dried, before being returned to the sugar jar. This process can be repeated for quite a long time. If you make ice creams, fruit fools and custards, it is wise to keep a second jar with icing sugar and vanilla pods; the powdery sugar dissolves instantly. On the same theme, dried orange or lemon peel can be used instead of vanilla pods; or cinnamon sticks.

On occasions when you must have vanilla essence, look closely at the label first before buying it to make sure you are getting the real thing, not a synthetic imitation.

VANILLA COMES from the Spanish word *vaina*, meaning a scabbard or sheath, and so a pod.

## CONCENTRATED VANILLA SUGAR

TIP 125 g (4 oz) of granulated sugar and 2 vanilla pods, cut into 2 cm (1″) lengths, on to the whirling blades of a liquidizer (top speed). Do this through the hole in the lid, quickly replacing the stopper because the sugar disintegrates to a cloud of white dust. After a few seconds sugar and pods will have turned to a slightly sooty-looking mixture. Don't worry about tiny black specks.

Mix the powder with 250 g (8 oz) caster sugar, and keep in a separate, tightly closed jar from the ordinary vanilla sugar. This concentrated sugar is ideal for ice creams, sweet soufflés and custards when you want vanilla to be the predominating flavour. Always add it gradually to whatever you are making, and stop when the taste is right, making up the total weight of sugar with ordinary vanilla sugar.

## CANDIED PEEL

PEEL two grapefruit, one fine large pomelo, or 4 oranges, slashing the fruit first so that the sections can be neatly removed, with their white pith. Boil the pieces in water to cover for 15 minutes, then drain. Repeat twice more – or three times if need be – until the peel is tender and the citrus bitterness reduced to a palatable level.

Drain, cool and cut into strips if you like (for instance if you intend to dip them in chocolate to serve with coffee at the end of dinner).

Dissolve 300 g (10 oz) sugar in 150 ml (¼ pt) water over a low heat, add the strips and boil steadily until the sugar is absorbed. Stir if necessary to make sure of even cooking. Drain in a strainer, then on paper until cool. It can now be stored for use in baking, or rolled in granulated sugar as a sweetmeat. Another way is to coat the pieces, half or entirely, in chocolate. Use the very best quality you can afford. Break it up into a basin and set over a pan of very hot, but not boiling, water. Stir until melted. Do not overheat or the chocolate will turn to an unworkable mud. Use the microwave to melt the chocolate, if you have one.

Remove chocolate basin from water, spear each piece of peel with a wooden cocktail stick and dip halfway, or completely into the chocolate. Stick the other end into a potato so that the chocolate can set.

# INDEX

## INDEX

## INDEX